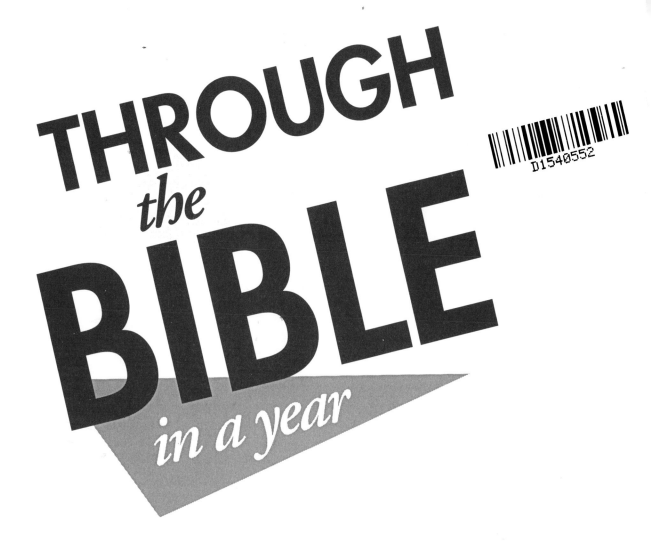

THROUGH the BIBLE in a year

by Bev Gundersen

Illustrated by

Beth Baker; Monica Boh; Bob Korth;
Setting Pace; Andy Rector; Dina Sorn; Ron Wheeler;
Sherry F. Willbrand; Sandy Wimmer

STANDARD
PUBLISHING
Cincinnati, Ohio

The Standard Publishing Company, Cincinnati, Ohio
A division of Standex International Corporation
©1993 by The Standard Publishing Company
All rights reserved
Printed in the United States of America

00 99 98 97 96 95 94 93   5 4 3 2 1

Library of Congress Catalog Number 93-83399
ISBN 0-7847-0030-3

3

CONTENTS

Introduction
Welcome to *Through the Bible in a Year!*

FIRST QUARTER:
The Book of Beginnings

SECOND QUARTER:
The Story of Ancient Israel

THIRD QUARTER:

The Life of Christ

FOURTH QUARTER:

The Church of Jesus Christ

INTRODUCTION

Welcome to *Through the Bible in a Year!*

This survey of the Bible course has been written for students, grades four through six. Through it they will learn why the Bible is different from any other book. Although it was written by about forty men over a period of fifteen hundred years, its real author is God. Students will discover that one main story runs all the way through the Bible. It tells all people everywhere how they can live in the right way in order to have fellowship with God here on earth and go to live with Him forever in Heaven when life here ends.

Your students have probably never thought of the Bible as one book with a central theme. They have only seen portraits of the more prominent people in the various individual books. These fifty-two lessons will help them get acquainted with the Bible as a great library. They will also find that the people told about in this wonderful library were real people who had to make decisions whether or not to obey God's commands. And more importantly, they will learn that they, too, have to make those same choices today.

Miracles, signs, wonders—God's Word abounds with accounts of the demonstration of His power over nature, disease, death, and evil. The book of Genesis opens with a sentence that states one of the greatest miracles, the creation of the universe: "In the beginning God created the heavens and the earth." God fashioned the universe from nothing and hung it in space. His crowning creation was man. Adam and all who followed him were promised guidance, protection, and fellowship with God, if they would trust and obey Him.

After creation, sin entered the world. God's people disobeyed His commands. At the time of Noah, wickedness dominated the world. The great flood was a miracle of destruction. God washed the earth clean and a new start was made with Noah's family. Many years later, God founded a new nation, His chosen people, with Abraham as their leader. Through many supernatural acts God helped His people conquer the land He had promised them. But in spite of the resources of God's power, sin kept the people from accomplishing all that was possible.

A series of judges and kings prepared the nation of Israel to become a kingdom. During this period, God's mighty acts extended through the people's disobedience and punishment into their repentant obedience and blessing. As you study this period, the books of history, poetry, and prophecy will become more meaningful to you and your pupils. Always, God was working to bring about redemption for all men through a Savior, His Son. He would be the perfect sacrifice for the sins of the world.

At last the time was right and God sent His Son, Jesus Christ, into the world. From His birth, through boyhood, His three-year ministry and finally His death and resurrection, Jesus moved steadily to complete God's plan of salvation. God's Son won the victory over sin, death, and the grave. The Gospels each

6

tell that "good news" in their own way. Now it was up to men to carry this story to the uttermost parts of the earth. God planned for them to do this through His church.

God's plan for the church is very simple. The church, Christ's body, is people—Christians. The book of Acts paints a vivid picture of the Holy Spirit's enabling of the first

Christians to turn the world upside down and preach the Gospel throughout their world. Everything contemporary believers need to know about the church is found in the New Testament. In the letters included is a plan for the spiritual growth of each person in that body with Jesus Christ as its head. God's Word, the Bible, is a wonderful book indeed!

Each lesson follows this active learning four-point format:

PRESESSION
(5-10 minutes)

This is a game, dialogue, or activity students can join in as they gather for class. Its purpose is to draw students into the lesson by involving them in an activity as soon as they arrive. It is a quick lead-in that gets them excited about the subject by highlighting

some need or concern with which they are familiar and which is related to the topic of the lesson. The entire class does *not* need to be present to do this activity. From this fun beginning you move into the next section of the lesson.

PERSPECTIVE
(10 minutes)

This gives a background introduction to the subject for the day and any fascinating facts that will set the subject apart from other sections or topics in the Bible. It includes people or events involved and any unique aspects that identify the subject. The segment pro-

vides information needed to clarify the situation or topic as seen from a Biblical-historical context. This sets the stage for your Juniors to discover what God's Word has to say about that particular subject.

PROBE
(20 minutes)

Here the Bible teaching is presented in creative, exciting way that brings Bible people and events to life. Each story is appropriate for Juniors' age-level. A variety of skits, puzzles, raps, newspapers, and other activities

keep your students' interest. They will discover that although this amazing book was written hundreds of years ago, it still speaks powerfully to people today.

PERSONALIZE

(20 minutes)

The last segment of each lesson allows your students to understand how it applies to their lives. It gives them an opportunity to personally respond to the lesson. They will be encouraged to move from what God says about the subject to decide, "What am I going to do about what I've learned?". Also included in this section is a brief closing entitled "Praise/Prayer." This includes a prayer suggestion or some other activity, allowing you and your students to express your thankfulness and special needs to the Lord.

Bible Investigators

is a unique term that is used for students throughout the course. It encourages your Juniors to experience the personal feelings of belonging to a featured club that specializes in discovering new and exciting things about God's Word. Members become detectives, diligently uncovering specific resources God has given in His Word for handling contemporary life. Those students who complete one quarter or more of the Bible study become Fantastic Bible Investigators or elite members of the "FBI."

Special Lesson Features include:

Suggestions for teacher's comments are in bold type. Also in bold type are discussion questions for you to ask your students. Typical answers are given in parenthesis. These responses also allow you to suggest possible replies should you need to get group discussion started.

Optional Activities are given in italics. These allow you to adapt your teaching methods to different time schedules or try diverse ones. They also suggest ways you can meet varying needs of students within your class.

God bless you as you adopt and adapt this course as desired!

MY BIBLE LIBRARY

AIM: That your students will understand the Bible is God's Word and to help them get acquainted with its books and divisions

SCRIPTURE 2 Timothy 3: 16, 17 (The Bible is God's Word)

PREPARATION:
1. Photocopy activity sheets—one for each student.
2. Create a large scroll of "old manuscript" paper as described in PRESESSION.
3. Make individual "old manuscript" papers as described in PRESESSION—one for each student.

PRESESSION (5-10 minutes)

ACTIVITIES
* Examine a variety of Bibles
* Write a verse of Scripture on a scroll

MATERIALS
* Variety of Bibles such as family, old, New Testament
* Large scroll of "old manuscript" paper
* Markers

PERSPECTIVE (10 minutes)

ACTIVITIES
* Read a fictional newspaper about finding the Dead Sea scrolls

MATERIALS
* "Judea Journal" Activity Sheet

PROBE (20 minutes)

ACTIVITIES
* Locate and identify the major divisions of the Bible
* Learn what makes the Bible different from all other books

MATERIALS
* Bibles
* "Match These" Activity Sheet

PERSONALIZE (15-20 minutes)

ACTIVITIES
* Paraphrase 2 Timothy 3:16, 17 and make a scroll of it

MATERIALS
* "Old manuscript" paper
* 10" dowels—2 for each student
* Markers
* *Optional: wooden beads for the scroll—4 for each student*

LESSON 1   **UNIT THEME: GOD'S WORD**

PRESESSION

(5-10 minutes)

Before class create a large scroll of "old manuscript" paper by using a sheet of 8 1/2" x 14" (legal size) paper. Crumple the sheet and soak it overnight in a solution of coffee or tea.

Lay the soaked page out to dry on newspapers, then iron it. This will give a yellowed, creased look that simulates ancient manuscripts. Use two 10" dowels to finish the scroll.

Also make "old manuscript" paper for the individual student scrolls using 8 1/2" x 11" paper and the above method.

Before your students arrive, set up a display of different Bibles—an old, family Bible, a New Testament, different language, tapes, a computerized version. As kids arrive, encourage them to write a Bible verse on the large scroll. If desired, you can have a list of brief verses for them to choose from.

Talk about the development of Bibles from the first handwritten scrolls to modern computerized versions.

PERSPECTIVE

(10 minutes)

How many of you have heard of the Dead Sea scrolls? Hand out copies of "Judea Journal" activity sheet. (page 6) **We don't have a copy of the newspaper that announced their discovery, but if we did it might have been something like this.** Ask several students to read the articles aloud.

Talk about the scrolls. How were the scrolls found? How old did the scholars think some of the scrolls were? What complete book of the Bible was found? Where are the scrolls displayed today?

Wouldn't it be wonderful to find an ancient scroll containing God's Word? You can make a great discovery, however, without exploring a cave or ruins near the Dead Sea! You can open your Bible and discover the great message that God has for you!

PROBE

(20 minutes)

Before class make "old manuscript" paper for the individual scrolls. Crumple sheets of 8 1/2" x 11" paper—one for each student (see directions under PRESESSION).

Probably most of you have been inside a library. What is your favorite kind of book? Allow students to share. **If you want a mystery book, where would you look?** (Mystery section) **What about a history book?** (History section)

Explain how you have to learn to find your way around the libraries in your school and town if you want to be able to get the help you need. The librarian will answer your questions and give you directions.

One special book is like a library because it contains adventure stories, poems, lessons, songs, and many other good things to read. Can you tell me what it is? (Dictionary, encyclopedia, Bible.) **The Bible is**

the most important library in the world.

You should learn to find your way around in this library too. Who are some people that can answer your questions and give you directions for the Bible library? (Sunday school teachers, ministers, youth directors.)

Have students look at the "Judea Journal" again and notice the scrolls. Each book of the Bible was first written on a scroll like this. **The word "Bible" means "books" and there are sixty-six different books between its covers.**

Have students open their Bibles and get acquainted with them. **There are two large parts of the Bible.** Open your Bible to the division between the Testaments and have students do the same. Point to the Old and New Testaments. If some kids have difficulty, ask other classmates to help them.

The Old Testament tells about things that happened before Jesus was born. It is helpful to us because we can learn of the history of the world from the very beginning. We can see how God chose certain people to be His helpers and gave them jobs to do. We can see that God blessed the ones who obeyed Him and punished those who disobeyed.

We can see how God planned from the very beginning to send a Savior to the world, and how He sent this message to His people by the prophets.

The first five books of the Old Testament are called the books of law. As you mention each book, have students find it in their Bibles.

Genesis means "beginning." It tells of the beginning of the world, of people, animals, plants—all living things.

Exodus means "going out." It tells the story of God's people as they were led out to freedom after being slaves in the land of Egypt. It also contains the laws God gave to Moses on Mount Sinai.

Leviticus is the book that tells how God chose the family of Levi to be the religious leaders of His people. This book tells of the rules He gave them to follow.

Numbers tells of the counting of the children of Israel, God's chosen people.

Deuteronomy is a word that means "second law." This book repeats the laws that God gave to Moses.

Later we will have stories from other books of the Old Testament. Besides these five books of law, there are twelve books of history, five books of poetry, and seventeen books of prophecy. These thirty-nine books make up the Old Testament in our Bibles.

The Old Testament books in Jesus' time were written on scrolls in the Hebrew language. They are the very same stories and lessons that Jesus studied nearly two thousand years ago.

The New Testament was written after Jesus came to earth and returned to Heaven. It tells about Jesus' life, His death for the sins of all people, His resurrection, and His ascension into Heaven. The New Testament, too, is filled with stories that show the great power of God, His Son, and the Holy Spirit. **These twenty-seven books were written on scrolls in the Greek language.**

Explain how long it must have taken for people to hand-write these books of the Bible on scrolls. For hundreds of years, each copy of God's Word was very precious because so few were available. Since the invention of the printing press, copies of God's Word have been printed in hundreds of languages and distributed throughout many lands.

Detectives are often called P.I.'s which stands for "Private Investigator." Today, all of you are going to have an opportunity to become a B.I. or a "Bible Investigator." Distribute copies of "Bible Investigator" activity sheets. Ask someone to read the directions at the top of the page. Students can work at this individually. Answers are: d, g, h, j, a, k, b, l, e, n, o, f, q, m, i, c, r, p, s, t.

Optional: If you prefer, this activity can be done as a class as you locate and identify the major divisions of the Bible.

PERSONALIZE

There are all kinds of storybooks, history books, poetry books, and lesson books today. What makes the Bible different? (It's older, has all those books in one, is God's Book.) **The Bible is God's Word. He told the writers what to say. This is called "inspiration."**

The Bible was written by about forty men over a period of about fifteen hundred years. They wrote truthful accounts of history.

Although the Bible was written by so many different people over a long period of time, it has one story running all the way through it—the story of God's love. **Suppose that each one of you would write a chapter of a story. Would we be able to put them all together to make one long connected story? Why or why not?** (No. They're written by different people.) **But God's Word is special because He is the real author of each and every book.**

Down through the years, wicked people have tried to destroy God's Word. But God protects His Word from enemies.

One very important difference between the Bible and any other book is that the Bible has a message for all people everywhere—including us. **The Bible tells us how to live in the right way, enjoying friendship with God, in order that we may go to Heaven when our life on this earth ends.**

Have students open their Bibles to 2 Timothy 3:16, 17 and read God's message to us about His Word. **What do these verses mean to you?** (Let kids answer.)

Ask students to work in pairs to write a paraphrase of these verses. Explain that a paraphrase is a retelling of the Bible truths in a simpler and more modern language. Have your class work on a simple version of these verses for a younger child.

For example, "All of the Bible is given by God and shows us what is wrong in our lives. It helps us stop doing wrong and teaches us how to live right. When people who serve God use the Bible, they will be ready and have everything they need to help them do what God wants all of us to do."

Hand out the "old manuscript" paper and two dowels for each person. When each team has decided on its version, have them write it on their scrolls.

PRAYER/PRAISE

Our heavenly Father gave us the Bible. He wants us to study it and discover His message in every Bible story and lesson. Close with prayer asking God to help you listen to His message and obey it.

JUDEA JOURNAL

DEAD SEA, JUDEA   MONDAY, FEBRUARY 17, 1947   25 CENTS

ANCIENT SCROLLS FOUND

Public Opinion Poll

Today's question: *"What do you think of this discovery?"*

Andrew: I wish I'd found the scroll with the whole book of Isaiah!

Hassan: They are so old they are brittle and decayed. What good are they?

Leah: This discovery proves that God's Word is like no other book. It's very precious and lasts forever.

Judea—Nearly 100 scrolls and pieces of scrolls written in the Hebrew language have been found in caves all around the Dead Sea. They are wrapped in scraps of linen cloth.

Scrolls Are Bible Parts

Scholars say these scrolls are books of the Old Testament written in the Hebrew language.

"They are priceless," said the committee chairman.

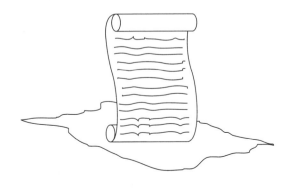

Bedouin Boy Tells His Story

"I was hunting my lost goats," said Abdullah. "I never thought I'd find something like this!"

The simple goatherd threw a rock into a cave and heard a crash. Upon entering the cave he found several broken clay jars containing leather scrolls.

"My friends and I took them to the market at Bethlehem. Then the merchants took them to the scholars."

Although experts can't determine how old they are, it is believed some of the scrolls were written one or two hundred years before the time of Jesus.

The Isaiah scroll is made of leather strips, 1 foot wide, sewn together to make a strip 24 feet long.

"The scrolls will soon be displayed in a special museum in Jerusalem," said Abdullah.

Match These

How good a B.I.
(Bible Investigator)
are you? Write the letter
that completes the sentence in
the blank in front of the number
in column one.

___ 1. The word "Bible" comes from

___ 2. The Bible is divided into two parts:

___ 3. There are thirty-nine books

___ 4. There are twenty-seven books

___ 5. There are five books

___ 6. The name of the first book, Genesis,

___ 7. The name of the second book, Exodus,

___ 8. The third book, Leviticus,

___ 9. The fourth book, Numbers,

___ 10. The fifth book, Deuteronomy,

___ 11. Also in the Old Testament there are

___ 12. The Old Testament was written

___ 13. The Old Testament was

___ 14. The New Testament was

___ 15. The New Testament was written

___ 16. For many, many years, copies

___ 17. When Jesus was a young boy

___ 18. Jesus did not have a New Testament

___ 19. In both Old and New Testaments we read

___ 20. The New Testament tells us

a. in the "books of Law."

b. means "going out."

c. of the Bible were written on scrolls.

d. a Greek word meaning "books."

e. tells of counting God's people.

f. in the Hebrew language.

g. Old Testament and New Testament.

h. in the Old Testament.

i. in the Greek language.

j. in the New Testament.

k. means "beginning."

l. is named after the tribe of Levi.

m. written after Jesus came.

n. means "second law."

o. books of history, poetry, and prophecy.

p. because it had not yet been written.

q. written before Jesus came.

r. He studied the Old Testament.

s. stories of God's great power.

t. what we must do to go to Heaven.

OUR LIVING BIBLE

AIM: That your students learn they have to make the choice whether or not to obey God's commands

SCRIPTURE: Genesis 2:7; 6:22; 12:1, 2; Exodus 3:11, 12; 2 Samuel 5:3, 4; Isaiah 9:6; Luke 2:52; Acts 18:9-11 (Stories of real people who were given commands from God and had to decide whether or not to obey them)

PREPARATION:
1. Photocopy activity sheets—one for each student.
2. Make role play cards as described in PERSONALIZE.

PRESESSION (5-10 minutes)

ACTIVITIES
* Cut apart figures for PROBE and try arranging them in order

MATERIALS
* "Choicemakers" Activity Sheet
* Scissors
* Envelopes—one for each student

PROBE (20 minutes)

ACTIVITIES
* Learn about eight real-life Bible people and their choices in obeying God

MATERIALS
* Bibles
* Bookmark figures from PRESESSION
* *Optional: Chalkboard or large sheet of paper and marker*

PERSPECTIVE (10 minutes)

ACTIVITIES
* Use an activity sheet to learn how our choices affect other people

MATERIALS
* "It's Your Choice" Activity Sheet

PERSONALIZE (15-20 minutes)

ACTIVITIES
* Role play some situations to learn how to make wise choices

MATERIALS
* Role play cards

PRESESSION

As students arrive, involve them in cutting apart the bookmarks from "Choicemakers" activity sheet.

Each of these men was a real person. Can you arrange them in the order they appear in the Bible? Encourage everyone to try but be sensitive to kids who may not have a Christian background or Bible knowledge. Hand out envelopes and have students put their names on them. Then they can put their bookmarks in the envelopes. Collect the filled envelopes for later use in PROBE.

PERSPECTIVE

All our lives we have to make choices. What is your favorite kind of candy? Talk about times when students were very little and had some money to buy whatever they wanted in the candy section of the store. Was it a hard choice?

What is another hard choice you had to make? By sharing a hard choice you had to make, you can encourage your students to share their choices too. As they grow up they will make more and more of their own choices. When they are adults they will be making all of their own decisions.

When God made us, He gave us the power to make decisions. Distribute copies of "It's Your Choice" activity sheet. Choose one of your better readers to read the story aloud while the rest of the group follow along on their sheets.

Have students make individual choices and complete the rest of the activity. Then talk about it together. Stress that every choice we make has results. They can be good or bad. Our decisions affect other people as well as ourselves. **As you grow up the choices between right and wrong become more difficult.**

Display your Bible. **The Bible is the best book in all the world. But it is not just a book, it is God's Word. Every story in God's storybook is absolutely true.** Many storybooks today tell us only good stories and good things people do, and everything usually ends happily. But the Bible tells us the bad things people did as well as the good things. Some of the stories have sad endings. We can learn lessons from the mistakes other people have made.

The Bible's stories are about real people who lived many hundreds of years ago. **Every person we'll be reading about in God's Word had to decide whether or not to obey God's Word.**

PROBE

Hand back the "Choicemakers" bookmarks from PRESESSION. Let students fill in the blanks and place each figure at the proper Bible chapter as you proceed through the lesson.

In the first book of the Bible, Genesis, we read about the first man created by God.

His name was Adam. Have group turn to Genesis 2:7 and ask someone to read it aloud.

Adam was given a loving wife, Eve, and a beautiful home, the Garden of Eden. Adam and Eve were told by God that they could eat anything they wanted in the beautiful garden except the

fruit from one tree. **Their story doesn't have the happy ending it could have had, because they disobeyed God.** They had to leave the beautiful garden after they gave in to the temptation of Satan. Fill in the blanks on the bookmark of Adam. (Adam disobeyed God.)

There were other people who lived after Adam, and almost all of them began to disobey God's Word. Finally they got so bad that God made a hard decision. **God said, "I will destroy man from the face of the earth." There was one man, however, who still obeyed God. He was Noah.** Noah and his family were the only good people left. **God told Noah that He would send a great flood to destroy the earth. Noah would be saved if he would build a huge boat for himself, his family, and the animals God wanted to spare.**

Have students turn to Genesis 6;22 and ask someone to read it aloud. **Noah would have to follow God's directions.** Fill in the blanks on the Noah bookmark. (Noah followed God's directions.)

The world started all over again with Noah's family, and after many years there were thousands of people living on the earth. **God wanted to have a special family of people to serve Him. He chose a man named Abram to be the head of this family.**

Students can turn to Genesis 12:1, 2. Have someone read it aloud. God told Abram to take his family and leave his homeland. He was to travel to a new land that God would show him. **Abram obeyed God without asking any questions, and God took care of him and made Abram the father of a great nation.** Later his name was changed to Abraham. The blanks should read "Abram obeyed God without asking any questions."

Many years later God chose another leader, Moses. **God wanted Moses to lead the people of Israel out of the land of Egypt.** The king of Egypt had made slaves out of God's people. God wanted to set them free and give them a land of their own. Ask students to turn to Exodus 3:11, 12 and have someone read it aloud. **Moses did as God commanded.** The blanks on this bookmark should read "Moses did as God commanded."

God's people were brought to the promised land, Canaan. The nation grew and finally the people wanted to have a king. The first king chosen was Saul. When he disobeyed God, another king was chosen.

Students can turn to 2 Samuel 5:3, 4. Ask someone to read these verses. **King David ruled God's people well, and he was faithful to God.** (David was faithful to God.) But most of the other kings who followed him did not obey God, and the people were taken captive by other countries.

God sent His prophets with messages for the people. One of these prophets was Isaiah. Have group turn to Isaiah 9:6 and ask someone to read it aloud. **Isaiah gave the message that God was sending a Savior to the world.** (Isaiah announced that God was sending a Savior.) He would be the King of kings and Lord of lords. Jesus was born as promised! He lived on earth to show us how to live.

Students can turn to Luke 2:52. Have someone read it aloud. **Jesus came to earth to give His life for us. He took the punishment for our sins, so that we might have salvation and eternal life in Heaven.** (Jesus took the punishment for our sins.) **He gave His followers the "Great Commission"—to go and tell others about the Savior of the world.** One of the men was the apostle Paul who became a great missionary.

Ask students to turn to Acts 18:9-11 and have someone read it aloud. **Paul traveled all around preaching, teaching, and winning people to the Lord.** Fill in the bookmark of Paul. (Paul preached, taught, and won people to the Lord.)

Optional: If you have a longer class time, review the lesson briefly by having students help you name the eight Bible people. Write the names on a chalkboard or large sheet of paper. Beside each name, write how that person obeyed or disobeyed.

All of these Bible people had a part in God's great plan.

PERSONALIZE

Before class prepare role play cards. On a 3" x 5" index card write the following situation:

Zach worked hard on the program committee for Wednesday night Kid's Club at church. In fact, he spent so much time on it that he didn't study his vocabulary list. His best friend, Danny, always got good grades on vocabulary. He offered to help Zach. "I'll fix it so you can see my paper easily. Then you can copy the answers."

Zach knew God said cheating was wrong, but after all, he had been helping with God's work on the committee, hadn't he? Zach said, ". . .

Make two copies of this beginning conversation for the role play.

We are God's people too. Have the group turn to Psalm 100:3 and read it aloud. God made each one of us and He has given each of us a heart, a mind, and a soul. **If God commanded you not to do certain things, would you obey His commands?** (Try to obey Him; depends on the situation.)

Ask for volunteers to take part in a role play. Encourage them to do this and constantly affirm them. If they are hesitant, offer to take one part to show them how it might be done. Involve the group by having them take the role of observers.

They will be responsible for adding to the discussion that follows the role play.

Have students role play the conversation that might have taken place between Zach and Danny. Then discuss the action.

End the role play when you feel that students have reached a standstill or the group has watched enough to go on to helpful discussion.

When you played Zach, how did you feel about God's command? What reason did he have for feeling it might be all right to cheat on this test? Do you think he obeyed or disobeyed God? How do you think God felt about his choice? Why do you think we often act like this character? How did you feel as Danny? Why do you think he offered to help Zach? Students, why do you think we find it so hard to obey God?

Optional: If time permits, let different people take the roles and replay the scene again.

God wants us to obey His commands and receive His blessings. He will not make us obey Him. That's a choice we have to make.

PRAYER/PRAISE

Close by singing a chorus: "The B-I-B-L-E" or "I Have Decided to Follow Jesus."

CHOICEMAKERS

ADAM
Genesis 2:7; 3:6, 17

ADAM

d ——————— d

GOD

PAUL
Acts 18:9-11

PAUL

p ——————— d

t ——————— t

and w ——— n

p ——— e

to the LORD.

MOSES
Exodus 3:11, 12

MOSES

d ——— d

as GOD

c ——————— d.

ISAIAH
Isaiah 9:6

ISAIAH

a ——————— d

that GOD was

s ——————— g

a s ——————— r.

DAVID
2 Samuel 5:3, 4

DAVID was

f ——————— l

to GOD.

NOAH
Genesis 6:22

NOAH

f ——— d

GOD'S

d ——————— s.

JESUS
Luke 2:52

JESUS

t ——— k the

p ——————— t

for our

s ——— s.

ABRAM
Genesis 12:1, 2

ABRAM

o ——————— d

GOD without

a ——————— g a —— y

q ——————— s.

2A

It's Your Choice

Mother was tired. Scott could tell by the way she sighed and pushed back her hair from her forehead. There was a knock at the door and Scott ran to answer it. It was Jason and Mark.

"Hey, Scott! How'd you like to go to the mall with us?" Mark asked.

"Sure, if Mom says it's okay," Scott answered.

Just as he went back inside to ask, the telephone rang. His mother answered.

"I'd love to go with you to the missionary meeting, Mrs. Norris, but I can't. The house is a mess and I just got the baby to sleep. She'll probably sleep for a couple of hours so I simply must stay home."

"If I would baby-sit for Mom," Scott thought, "perhaps she would go to the meeting! I could clean up the house while the baby slept." But that would mean he could not go to the mall with his friends.

What do you think Scott should do?

Choice #1: Forget about Mom and go with his friends to the mall.

Choice #2: If he quickly cleaned up the house, he could invite his friends to stay and play games while he baby-sat.

Choice #3: Offer to baby-sit and clean up the house. Tell his friends he would go with them some other time.

Why? _____

_____

What do you think will happen because of that choice? _____

_____

_____

THE CREATION OF THE WORLD

AIM: That your students will recognize God as the creator of earth and be encouraged to be thankful for this beautiful world and help care for and protect it

SCRIPTURE: Genesis 1:1-31; 2:1-7 (God creates the earth as man's home)

PREPARATION:
1. Photocopy activity sheets—one for each student.

PRESESSION (5-10 minutes)

ACTIVITIES
* Find pictures of things that had their beginnings in Genesis 1

MATERIALS
* Bibles
* Magazines or calendars with pictures from nature
* Scissors

PERSPECTIVE (10 minutes)

ACTIVITIES
* Use an activity sheet to discuss scientific discoveries about the world's creation

MATERIALS
* "In The Beginning" Activity Sheet
* Paper and pencils

PROBE (20 minutes)

ACTIVITIES
* Make a mobile showing some of the things God made

MATERIALS
* "Nature Mobile" Activity Sheet
* Nature pictures from PRESESSION
* Scissors, paper punch, thread or monofilament

PERSONALIZE (15-20 minutes)

ACTIVITIES
* Work in small groups to discover ways to help care for and protect the wonderful world God has given us

MATERIALS
* Paper and pencils
* Chalkboard or large sheet of paper

PRESESSION

(5-10 minutes)

Lay out the magazines or calendars so students can reach them easily. As they arrive, have them look up Genesis chapter one. They can then cut out *small* pictures of things that are mentioned as being created in the beginning in that chapter such as plants, stars, fish, animals, etc.

As they work on this, talk about the many beautiful and wonderful things in nature. Lay aside these pictures for later use in PROBE.

How do you think life in our world began? (Some answers might be: it just happened; came from particles of space dust; God gave life to us and all living things when He created the world and our universe.) **Let's take a closer look at our home planet as a scientist might see it.**

PERSPECTIVE

(10 minutes)

Hand out copies of "In The Beginning" activity sheet. You can do this as a play by having two people read the parts of Don (or Dawn) Philahue and Dr. "Si" N. Tist.

Optional: You can add to the feeling of this being a real radio or TV interview by having the actors sit together and talk into a disconnected microphone or using a prop such as a large serving spoon.

In the skit, the interviewer said, "Somebody must have the right answer as to how life on our world began." One group of people who lived on earth thousands of years ago, knew from the earliest times the true story of how the world and life on it began. That group was God's chosen people, the Israelites. **In the very beginning, God spoke directly to His people. Later He guided Moses and others in writing down the history of the beginning.** The five books of Moses are also called the books of law. **Today we are going to read from the first and second chapters of the first book, Genesis. Let's see how good you B. I.'s (Bible Investigators) are at finding the answers to these two questions: (1) Where did the world come from? (2) Where did man come from?**

PROBE

(20 minutes)

Ask students to work with a partner and turn to these chapters. They are to look for the answers to the questions and write down the answers on a piece of paper. **Where did the world come from?** (Genesis 1:1, God made it.) When we make something, we have to have some materials with which to work. **God made the world from nothing!** He has such great power that He can speak words and things appear.

How many things can you name that God created in the beginning? (The following should be included: heaven, earth, light, sky, water, land, grass, seed-bearing plants, trees, sun, moon, stars, birds [winged birds], fish and whales [sea creatures], cattle and horses [livestock], insects [creatures moving on ground], lions and bears [wild beasts], man and woman.

Optional: If your class schedule permits, you could also look up these Scriptures that tell of the marvelous works of nature all around us.

Jeremiah 31:35—sun, moon, stars, sea; Psalm 104:5-8—earth, waters, mountains and valleys; Genesis 8:8—dove; Mark 14:72—rooster; Matthew 17:27—fish; Genesis 47:17—horses, sheep, goats, cattle, and donkeys.

Why do you think God made these things? (Because He was lonely, don't know, wanted to express His love.) God didn't need to create them, but did so because He is love and love expresses itself to others.

The Bible is not a science book, but it is a true record of what happened. There are many men who have studied both God's Word and science very carefully. They have learned that facts of science agree with God's Word. **Check out Genesis 1:31. How did God feel after He finished His wonderful work of creating the world.** (It was very good.) **What does this tell you about how God feels about you?** (He made me the way He wanted to, and is glad He did.)

Do you read news stories in the daily paper? Often a reporter sums up his whole story in the headlines to let you know what happened. Then he tells the story again adding more information. The first chapter of Genesis gives us a picture of creation. The second chapter tells us a little more about what happened. Ask someone to read Genesis 2:1-7 aloud.

What was God's greatest creation? (Man.) Stress that this means both men and women. **What do you think it means when the Bible says man was made in God's image?** (Man looked like God, thought and had feelings like God, reflected God's glory.) Man was given a mind and power to use it. The Bible tells us that God gave man power over every living thing that moves on the face of the earth! God gave man

the plants and the trees for food. He also made a companion for Adam. She was called Eve.

To those who know God's Word, the two biggest mysteries are explained in these two passages. We don't know *how* it was done, but we know *who* did it. God has all power. He can do things that people cannot do.

The universe is filled with secrets that men would like to know. Little by little God is allowing scientists and others to uncover clues to these mysteries. **What are some of these discoveries?** (Let students share some of the current scientific discoveries such as the space probes.) **The most important thing to know is that God created the world and everything that is in it—including you!**

Distribute copies of Nature Mobile activity sheet. Cut out the spiral, discarding the shaded center section. Punch out the dots. Punch holes in the top of the pictures from PRESESSION and add parts to the mobile by tying the pictures on with short threads. Complete the mobile by punching a hole at the X and attaching a long thread to hang the mobile.

This wonderful world is a place that God has prepared for His people. In it He has put all the beautiful things to see and all the good things to eat. He has given us more than we can ever imagine or understand. **We should be thankful to Him for these blessings and never forget that God's greatest creation is people.** Lay aside the mobiles for take-homes.

Optional: If you have a longer class period, you could have the group list what God made or did on each of the seven days in the very beginning of the world. A variation of this would be to have them make a mural where they could draw the items on different panels.

PERSONALIZE

(15-20 minutes)

Have someone read Genesis 2:15. **What were Adam and Eve to do?** (Take care of the beautiful Garden of Eden.) Work was given as a gift to Adam and Eve before their fall into sin. It was not meant to be a punishment but an opportunity to share in God's creativity.

We are God's people; He made us and He loves us. How can we show Him how thankful we are for our earthly home? (Thank Him in prayer and song, invite others to come and share God's blessings, read God's Word, the Bible, and find new ways to say "thank You" to God, enjoy our world, take care of it.) **One of the best ways we can show our thanks to God for His beautiful world is to help care for it.**

Have the group work in pairs or small groups to brainstorm ways they can (I) enjoy our world and (2) take care of it. The object of brainstorming is to suggest as many things as possible. Right now you are interested in quantity. Don't worry about the quality. You can always refine that later. Allow about 10 minutes on this, then have the group help you list their ideas on the chalkboard or a large sheet of paper.

Some suggestions for enjoyment could be: take a walk or hike, bicycle tour, have a picnic, go on a camera "safari" for wild birds and animals, plant a vegetable or flower garden and share the harvest. Ideas for taking care of our earth could be: not using Styrofoam; recycling glass, paper, aluminum, plastic; not wasting water when you shower or brush your teeth; keeping drinking water in the refrigerator instead of running it from the faucet until its cold; planting trees to replace those cut down; helping clean up roadways.

PRAYER/PRAISE

Have the students work in the same pairs or small groups they were in for PERSONALIZE. They can offer pantomime prayers of thanksgiving to God for His wonderful creations. Each group chooses one or more creations from nature. They repeat aloud, "Thank you, God, for . . ." and then pantomime the creations chosen. If desired they can reveal their choices. Close by having the entire group repeat the phrase, "We will do our best to care for and protect this wonderful world You have given us."

Be sure to send the nature mobiles home with the students.

DON or DAWN PHILAHUE: Hello, fans. Today we are talking to the world famous Dr. Silas "Si" N. Tist about our wonderful world. Welcome to our program, Dr. Tist.

DR. TIST: You can call me "Si."

DON: There are many mysteries about our universe. How is information about it obtained?

"SI": Astronomers today study the sun, moon, stars, planets and all other things in space. They are constantly searching the heavens with high-powered telescopic cameras for clues. When astronauts are sent on missions, their space capsules carry special instruments for gathering new information to study.

DON: What about life on this earth? How do scientists try to solve the mystery of how life began here?

"SI": Some of them travel around looking for fossil remains of animal and plant life. Those are the bones or hardened tracks of animals that lived long ago. They left their prints on the floors of oceans and on rocks.

DON: I see, sort of like kids leaving footprints on their mom's clean floors.

"SI": Right, only now the scientists have to find out what kinds of animals and plants lived that long ago. It's like a detective story where they find clues the robber left behind and have to find out who he was. They use gigantic pieces of machinery, deep-sea diving equipment, and delicate tools to help them.

DON: It's really interesting to read about the discoveries that are being made every day. People have always wondered about how the world began and where life came from. Thousands of years ago, people in different lands made up stories about how the world began. The wise men of India taught that the earth was held up by elephants who were standing on turtles. The turtles were swimming in water.

"SI": Who knows what was beneath the water? The Greeks believed that a god named Atlas carried the world on his back.

DON: What was Atlas standing on?

"SI": That's a good question! I have no idea! There are many very strange ideas about the world's beginning and life on earth.

DON: Some scientists say it all began with a big bang and that men came from monkeys. What do you think about that?

"SI": Sounds like someone made a monkey out of someone all right!

DON: The Bible says that God made the world out of nothing. He just spoke and living things were created. What do you think about that?

"SI": That's very interesting. That would make our job a lot easier. It's really hard trying to find answers to all our questions, you know.

DON: Wouldn't it take a lot of faith to believe God created all life?

"SI": Are you kidding? It takes a lot more faith to try and make up answers that would answer all our questions. Where did you say it tells us about God?

DON: In the Bible. I think it's in the first and second chapters of Genesis.

"SI": If you'll excuse me, I think I'll go read it for myself. God as the creator of everything. Wonderful!

DON: Well, somebody must have the right answer, "Si." Thank you for being our guest today.

In the Beginning

NATURE MOBILE

Punch holes at the dots and hang mobile parts.
Punch a hole at the X and attach thread for hanging.

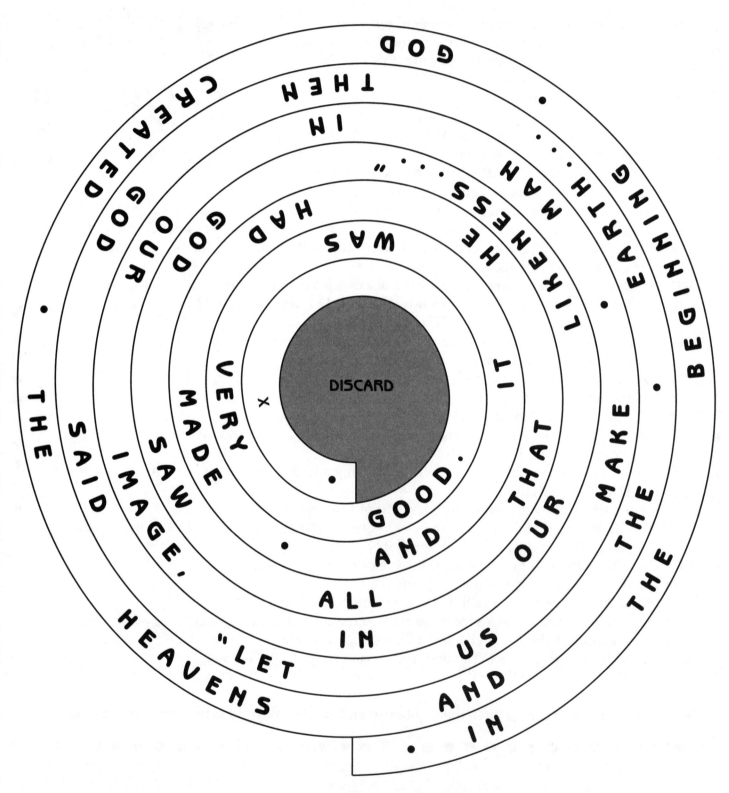

SIN ENTERS THE WORLD

AIM: To teach the unhappy results of disobedience to God and to encourage students to listen to the voice of God rather than the voice of Satan

SCRIPTURE: Genesis 2:8-15; 3:2-4, 6, 8 (Adam and Eve disobey God)

PREPARATION:
1. Photocopy activity sheets—one for each student.
2. Prepare beans for use in PERSPECTIVE by soaking them in water overnight.

PRESESSION (5-10 minutes)

ACTIVITIES
* Design a perfect robot

MATERIALS
* Paper
* Pencils

PERSPECTIVE (10 minutes)

ACTIVITIES
* Plant seeds for a garden

MATERIALS
* Dried beans or packet of seeds
* Water
* Paper towels
* Shallow saucer—one for each student
* Typing paper—a piece big enough to cover about 3/4 of the saucer—one for each student

PROBE (20 minutes)

ACTIVITIES
* Complete a skit about Adam and Eve
* Participate in an object lesson

MATERIALS
* Bibles
* "Who's to Blame?" Activity Sheet
* Water, shallow bowl, small stone

PERSONALIZE (15-20 minutes)

ACTIVITIES
* Determine right responses that show obedience to God

MATERIALS
* "Dear Gabby" Activity Sheet
* Slips of paper
* Pencils

PRESESSION

As the group gathers, give each person a piece of paper from which to design a perfect robot. **You have been selected to design a perfect robot. This robot will always do what you want it to and never disobeys. Tear the paper into the shape of your robot. Then write on it a description of what it is like.**

While students do this, guide the conversation with comments like these: God designed a perfect world and wanted everything in it to be perfect. Did He create the first man and woman to be perfect? Are there any perfect people? If so, what makes them perfect? If not, why not?

God made man with a mind and power to make choices. He didn't want Adam and Eve to be mere robots who had no choice but to obey. Instead He wanted them to lovingly obey Him.

PERSPECTIVE

How many of you have ever planted something? (Let group share their experiences.) **Today we're going to have an opportunity to grow something.** Give each person a shallow saucer and several sheets of paper towels. Have students spread several layers of paper towels on the bottom of the saucer. Soak these with water. Arrange several beans in a single layer on top of the paper towels. Be sure to give them enough room so they don't touch each other. Lay the piece of typing paper over the top of the saucer. Don't let it touch the wet paper towels or it will get soggy. Place these dish gardens aside to be taken home at the end of class.

What do you think the Garden of Eden was like? (Don't know, beautiful, peaceful.) We can only imagine what this perfect garden was like. Even the most beautiful outdoor area you have enjoyed would be only a fraction of the Garden of Eden. When God made this wonderful place everything was perfect. The flowers, trees, and grass were watered by several rivers. Singing birds flew through the trees. Bright butterflies danced on the edges of fragrant flowers. Animals of all kinds roamed together or rested in the shade of the trees.

Into this perfect place, God placed a man and woman. They were to enjoy and care for this garden and the animals. What a joy it must have been to grow plants and never have to weed them! **Every evening they walked and talked with God. Nothing could ruin this perfect world. Or could it? Let's drop in and listen to an imaginary conversation between Adam and Eve.**

PROBE

Distribute copies of the activity sheet "Who's to Blame?" Have students open their Bibles to Genesis chapter three. They can complete this skit by finding the answers to fill in the blanks.

References are given to provide clues.
Answers are: garden, tree, serpent, serpent's, surely die, eyes, opened, God, good, evil, food, pleasing, eye, wisdom, took, ate, ate, not, eat, fig

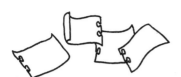

leaves, hide, ground, thorns, thistles, cherubim (angel), flaming sword, life.

Optional: If you have a longer class period, let your students read this skit of Adam and Eve. Choose two readers who can portray the sad and angry feelings involved. Remind them that both Adam and Eve tried to blame someone else for their own disobedience.

The first thing Satan did was to get Eve to doubt God's goodness. (verses.1-3) Often we forget all the good things God gives us and focus on what we *don't* have. Satan twisted God's words to make them just the opposite. **Eve believed Satan's voice rather than the voice of God. How does this tempter come to us?** (In the voice of a friend or evil pictures or thoughts.)

Satan also made Eve feel that *doing* evil was the best way to know the difference between good and evil. That's as foolish as saying we have to walk in front of a train to know it's a dangerous thing!

Eve had a wonderful desire—to be more like God. The problem was that the serpent convinced her that it was all right to do wrong in order to reach that goal. Eve decided she could make the best choice. How amazing that she did not think the One who created her would not know what was best for His creation! She rebelled against God and looked at the fruit. This strengthened the temptation and put her at real risk for yielding to it.

Pour some water into a shallow bowl. Gather the group around this and let someone drop the stone into the center of the water. **What happened when the stone fell?** (Ripples spread out from it.) **That is a picture of what happens when we disobey God. We not only hurt ourselves, but also involve others.** First Adam tried to blame Eve. In doing so he even blamed God (the woman You gave me.) Then Eve tried to blame the serpent. Worse yet, they discovered

that all nature suffered because of their sin. The ground was cursed, weeds sprang up, and animals preyed on each other. Death entered the plant and animal worlds.

Sin made Adam and Eve want to hide from God. Their disobedience broke their relationship with Him. **Is it possible to hide from God? Why or why not?** (No. He is all-knowing and all-seeing.)

God came seeking Adam and Eve, but they hid. **When we are disobedient we try to hide our sins from God. What are some ways we do that?** (By not confessing them, blaming someone else, lying, staying away from church or Sunday school.)

How do you think God felt about the disobedience of Adam and Eve? (Angry, sad, upset.) **God had given Adam and Eve so many wonderful things.** He had given them a living soul and a mind with which to think and make choices. He created them in His image. He loved them and wanted to be with them.

Why do you think God prevented Adam and Eve from gaining access to the tree of life? (As a punishment for their sin, don't know.) When God created Adam and Eve, He intended them to be immortal, to live forever. In a state of sinless obedience this would be an eternal delight. But after they had sinned, such an immortal life of disobedience would have meant hiding from God eternally. God did not want this "living hell" to happen to the creatures He loved so dearly. Even in this punishment, God demonstrated His unconditional love for us! Only a life of trust and loving obedience through Christ restores that eternal delight to mankind.

How do we know what is right and wrong? (What God tells us is right, read the Bible to know.) **Now you're going to have a chance to help some people make the right choices, ones that will honor God.**

PERSONALIZE

Distribute copies of "Dear Gabby" activity sheet. This activity is a number of problems submitted to a fictional advice columnist. It can be done individually.

Optional: If you have a shorter time period, form small groups and let each team work on just one problem.

Have the group share their answers. Some things to consider are questions like the following. **Why is it wrong to fake a note from your parents?** (God wants us to be truthful.) **What good could come from lovingly telling your friend you didn't want the good luck medal?** (You could share why and how you trust in God alone.) **Why should you be faithful in attending Sunday school and church?** (Because you want to maintain a relationship with God, want to keep the Lord's Day holy.) **What do you think Jesus would do with the girl who had no friends?** (Reach out to her in love and friendship.)

Satan's ways are tempting and appeal to our selfishness. Although learning to distinguish God's voice from Satan's is difficult, we find that the more time we spend with God in prayer and reading His Word, the easier it becomes. God's commands reach out to others, while Satan's are always directed back to ourselves in self-satisfaction.

Have you ever made a wrong choice? What was it? Share a personal one with your students. When they realize that you make mistakes too, they will be more open to sharing their problems. Sharing in this manner with your kids will help them to identify with you and establish a better rapport as well. **God wants us to obey Him because we love Him, not because we have to. He wants what is best for us.**

PRAYER/PRAISE

Give out slips of paper to your students. They can write one area in which they especially need help in listening to God's voice and obeying it. Assure them this is completely between them and God alone. Have them fold these slips in two and place them in a pile on the table. Each person prays silently for help in the area written. **God has promised to help us hear and obey Him. No matter how weak we are, He loves and helps us.** Then all shout "Amen!"

Each person takes his or her dish gardens home. Remind them to put them where they can get indirect sunlight. They can water them at home and report on the seeds' progress. They will be surprised at the strength of the plants as they grow strong enough to throw off the paper covers and reach out to the light.

who's ◆to◆ Blame?

EVE: I can't believe it! Evicted from our beautiful home in the _____. (v. 3) It's all your fault, Adam!

ADAM: My fault? What about you? Who's the one that offered me the fruit from the _____ in the middle of the garden?(v. 2) I should never have listened to you.

EVE: Well, it wasn't all my fault either. If that _____ (v. 2) hadn't tempted me to try it, I would never have done it. It's all the _____ fault. (v. 2)

ADAM: You didn't have to listen to him, you know. You could have just walked away. But no, you not only listened, you let him convince you to do it.

EVE: I didn't listen at first. But what he said seemed so, so, I don't know, right I guess. He said that we would not _____. (v. 4)

ADAM: You mean you really believed that eating it would be all right? How could you fall for that line—"God knows that when you eat of it your _____ will be _____ and you will be like _____, knowing _____ and _____." (v. 4)

EVE: I thought how wonderful God is and that it would be great to be like Him. I hoped it would make our relationship with Him even better. Besides, the fruit was good for _____, _____ to the _____ and desirable for gaining _____. (v. 6)

ADAM: So you _____ it and _____ it! (v. 6)

EVE: I wasn't the only one, you know. You _____ it too! (v. 6)

ADAM: Just because you gave it to me! How was I to know it was the tree God told us _____ to _____ from? (v. 11) And another thing, trying to cover ourselves with _____ wasn't very smart. (v. 7) It didn't hide our disobedience.

EVE: Look who's talking. Your plan to _____ from God wasn't so great either! (v. 8) You should have realized He knew the truth.

ADAM: Now even the _____ is cursed. (v. 17) I'm going to have to pull _____ and _____ to get food for us.(v. 18)

EVE: Do you think we could just go back and tell God we're sorry?

ADAM: It's too late. You saw the _____ with its _____ flashing back and forth to guard the way to the tree of _____ (v. 24) We have broken our loving fellowship with God!

EVE: You're right. God has forgiven us, but we have to bear the punishment for our disobedience. If only we had listened to God, not Satan! There's no one to blame but ourselves.

DEAR GABBY

Dear Gabby,

I want to be part of the "in crowd" at school. To get in I have to fake a note from my parents. What should I do?

Want-to-be-in

Dear Want-to-be-in,

_____
_____
_____
_____
_____

Dear Gabby,

My uncle is good in all kinds of sports. I think he's really great! Usually he goes boating, golfing, or racing on Sundays. I have been going to Sunday school and church for several months, but my uncle has been trying to get me to skip the Sunday services and go on trips with him. I want to be with him, but also want to obey God. What should I do?

Torn-between

Dear Torn-between,

_____
_____
_____
_____
_____
_____

Dear Gabby,

One of the girls in my class has no friends at all. I feel sorry for her and would like to help her. I mentioned it to my friends, but they said if I hung around with her I could forget about them. They don't want her in their group and don't want me if I am friends with her. I think I should help this girl, but I don't want to lose my friends. What do you think?

Confused

Dear Confused,

_____
_____
_____
_____
_____
_____

Dear Gabby,

My friend gave me a "religious medal" to bring me good luck. I don't want to lose my friend, but I don't want to keep the medal either. I don't believe in luck or trusting in charms. What should I do?

Trusting God

Dear Trusting God,

_____
_____
_____
_____
_____

THE WORLD IS DESTROYED

AIM: That your students will understand that they need to be obedient to God's commands

SCRIPTURE: Genesis 3:22-24; 4:1-8; 6:13-16, 22; 7:1; 9:13, 15 (Noah unquestioningly obeys God's commands and is saved from the punishment God gave to the wicked)

PREPARATION:
1. Photocopy activity sheets—one for each student.
2. Make Join-in cards as described in PROBE.

PRESESSION (5-10 minutes)

ACTIVITIES
* Use an activity sheet to list facts about the ark

MATERIALS
* Bibles
* "Don't Miss The Boat!" Activity Sheet

PERSPECTIVE (10 minutes)

ACTIVITIES
* Complete a puzzle about how God destroyed the world

MATERIALS
* "Pyramid Puzzle" Activity Sheet (same sheet as above)

PROBE (20 minutes)

ACTIVITIES
* Take part in a Join-in Bible story

MATERIALS
* Join-in cards

PERSONALIZE (15-20 minutes)

ACTIVITIES
* Use finger puppets to role play situations about obeying God
* Make a "Feetograph" to show willingness to live in obedience to God

MATERIALS
* Bibles
* "Join the Crowd?" Activity Sheet
* Pencils and large sheets of paper—one for each student

PRESESSION

(5-10 minutes)

Hand out copies of "Don't Miss The Boat!" activity sheet. Students will look up the Scripture in their Bibles and do only the top part of the sheet. Answers are: cypress, 450 feet, 75 feet, 45 feet, one, three, 18 inches from the roof, pitch

(black tar which oozed from the ground).

The boat you described was one that God asked Noah to build. God's command was a very strange request. Let's see why.

PERSPECTIVE

(10 minutes)

It was a big project and took many years to build. Bible scholars believe Noah worked on the ark 120 years. Help your students to better visualize the ark. It was the length of one and a half football fields and as high as a four-story building. It was six times longer than it was high. Modern shipbuilders still use this ratio.

The ark wasn't meant to sail, but merely to float. Instead of having sloping sides, a rudder, and a mast, it was more like a big barn or box. About half of its height was under water making it almost impossible to capsize. It also increased its carrying capacity by one-third.

Its gross tonnage was about the same as large, metal, ocean-going vessels of today. This gave it the carrying capacity of about 522 railroad stock cars. Many Bible scholars estimate that between 35,000 and 45,000 animals could have been carried in it.

God's command to Noah to build the ark
was not only strange because of the size of the task, but also because of the circumstances in the world at that time. The ark was probably built many miles from any water. It was the first boat ever built and likely a great curiosity to everyone! As unusual as it was, it was God's plan for preserving the lives of an obedient man who loved God, his family, and at least one pair of every kind of air-breathing animals.

God wanted Noah to build the ark for a very important reason. To find the answer, complete the pyramid on the bottom of the activity sheet. Answers are: F, FL, FLO, FOOL, FLOOD.

How many of you have been in or seen pictures of a flood? (Let students share any experiences they may have.) **Today we're going to learn about the greatest flood the world has ever known. It was so big that God used it to destroy the world.**

PROBE

(20 minutes)

Before class, prepare join-in cards for students. Make the cards large enough to be easily seen. Read the story aloud holding up the join-in card at designated places in the story where the whole group says the phrase aloud. Phrases are: WATCH OUT; OH NO!; YEAH, NOAH!; BUILD A BOAT,

NOAH; ANIMALS, ANIMALS, TWO BY TWO. ANIMALS, ANIMALS, WHAT A ZOO!; GLUB, GLUB, GLUB; OH, JOY!; OOH, AAH. Before you begin the story, have the group practice by saying the phrases several times.

God had given Adam and Eve the beautiful

Garden of Eden as their home. He told them they could eat the fruit from every tree in the garden except one. (WATCH OUT!) Eve listened to Satan as he told her the fruit would help her. She gave in to his temptation, ate the fruit, and then brought some for Adam to eat. (OH NO!)

God had given Adam and Eve the ability to choose either good or evil. They chose evil and disobeyed Him. They were made to leave the beautiful garden, told that one day they would die because of their sin, and could not live forever. (OH, NO!)

Two sons born to these first parents were Cain and Abel. Cain, a farmer, brought his offering of grain to the Lord. Abel, a shepherd, brought one of his lambs. Cain's offering was not acceptable to God because he did not have the right attitude in his heart. Abel's offering was accepted. Cain's jealousy of Abel caused him to do a terrible thing. He killed Abel. (OH, NO!)

Many hundreds of years had passed since God created the world. The population had multiplied. Now the people did only evil all the time. (OH, NO!) God found that only one man and his family really wanted to lovingly obey Him. (YEAH, NOAH!)

God spoke to Noah and told him that He was going to destroy every living thing on the earth because of man's wickedness. Then God said, (BUILD A BOAT, NOAH.)

Noah listened carefully to the directions. The boat was to be big enough to hold Noah and all his family, one pair of every kind of air-breathing animal and seven pairs of every kind of animal that could be used for sacrifices and eating. (ANIMALS, ANIMALS, TWO BY TWO. ANIMALS, ANIMALS, WHAT A ZOO!)

Noah and his sons, Ham, Shem, and Japheth, worked hard and long. While they worked, the animals gathered around them. When the boat was ready, God told Noah to load the animals onto the boat. Then Noah, and his family went in and God shut the door. They waited for seven days. Then on the eighth day the rain began. It continued raining for forty days and nights. The water covered the highest mountains. There was nothing left alive except the people and animals in the ark. (GLUB, GLUB, GLUB)

Finally, after many months, the waters began to go down. First Noah saw the tops of the mountains. Then he could see the ground. Finally God told Noah to leave the ark and take his family and all the living creatures with him. They walked out on dry land. (OH, JOY!)

The first thing Noah did was to build an altar and make an offering to God. God was pleased with this and Noah's prayers of thanksgiving. He promised Noah that He would never again send a flood to destroy the earth. A beautiful rainbow arched across the sky as a sign of His promise. (OOH, AAH.)

Every time we look at the rainbow we can remember God's promise to Noah, the man who loved and obeyed God.

PERSONALIZE

(15-20 minutes)

How do you think people acted toward Noah? (Made fun of him, called him crazy, ignored him.) **How do you think Noah felt about it?** (Knew he was doing the right thing, sad, angry, disappointed.)

How sad it is to think that people became so wicked that God had to make this decision. Have someone read Genesis 6:7 aloud. **God was heartbroken. He was sorry to see what His perfect creation had done to themselves.** He was sad that they had chosen sin and death instead of a loving relationship with Him. **Sin could not be allowed to continue. It must be stopped.**

However, God was pleased to find that Noah and his family were living examples to all the people of what it was like to have a loving, joyful relationship with God. God saved them and used them to care for the animals so that the earth could be replenished.

It must have been hard for Noah and his family to do right when everyone else was doing wrong. Many times it is just as hard for you to do right and follow God when your friends or classmates do wrong. It is true that people are either an influence on others or are being influenced by them.

Hand out copies of "Join the Crowd?" activity sheet. Ask someone to read the instructions aloud. Have students work in pairs on this activity. That way each person can be one of the characters in the stories. The stories are true-to-life situations kids may find themselves in someday. When they have had an opportunity to make their decisions for the endings, ask several volunteer teams to share with the group. Your students may come up with some very different and innovative choices.

Optional: If you have a longer time schedule, have partners in each pair reverse roles to have an opportunity to see the circumstances from different viewpoints.

Try to keep this activity as upbeat as possible. Encourage the students to be good witnesses and influence their friends as well as doing what is right and obeying God. Noah was a faithful witness to his wicked neighbors as he built the ark. He may have even hired several of them to help him and his sons complete the project.

In Matthew's gospel, Jesus tells how the people of Noah's time went on with their daily activities right up to the day that Noah entered the ark. They paid no attention—unless perhaps to laugh at Noah—and then suddenly the flood came and took them all away!

Jesus said that the end of the world will also come suddenly. Those who have paid no attention to Christ or His followers and disobeyed God's commands will not be saved from the terrible punishment that God has prepared for Satan and his followers.

Those who love God, trust in and obey Him will be saved, just as Noah and his family were saved from the flood. Maybe there are times when you feel you are alone in wanting to do right. Remember that when you are on God's side, it doesn't matter how many are on Satan's side!

PRAYER/PRAISE

Distribute large sheets of paper and have the group make "Feetographs." People draw around their feet on paper and sign their names. **Never forget that our great and powerful God, who made the whole universe, cares about you.** You are special to Him. He wants you to love and follow Him, no matter what others do. Then He will bless you.

If you want to walk in obedience to God, then march in place on your feetograph and repeat an affirmation statement, "I will do what God says is right even if everyone else does wrong."

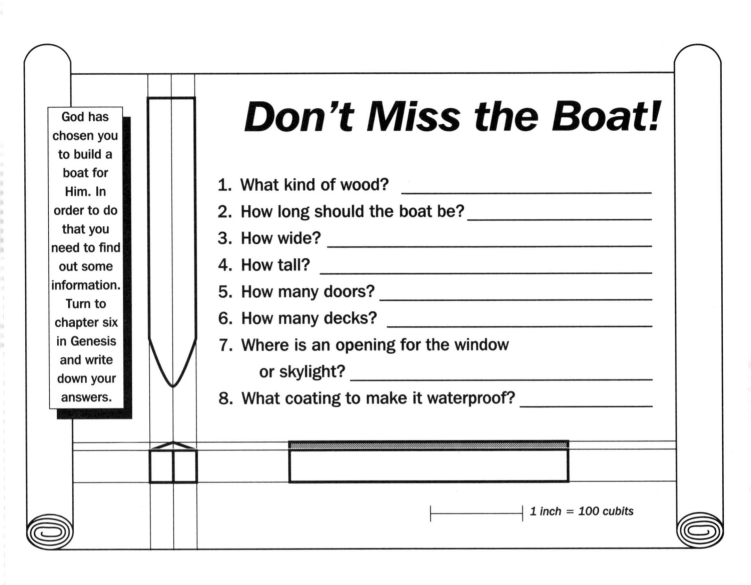

Don't Miss the Boat!

God has chosen you to build a boat for Him. In order to do that you need to find out some information. Turn to chapter six in Genesis and write down your answers.

1. What kind of wood? _____
2. How long should the boat be? _____
3. How wide? _____
4. How tall? _____
5. How many doors? _____
6. How many decks? _____
7. Where is an opening for the window
   or skylight? _____
8. What coating to make it waterproof? _____

1 inch = 100 cubits

Pyramid Puzzle

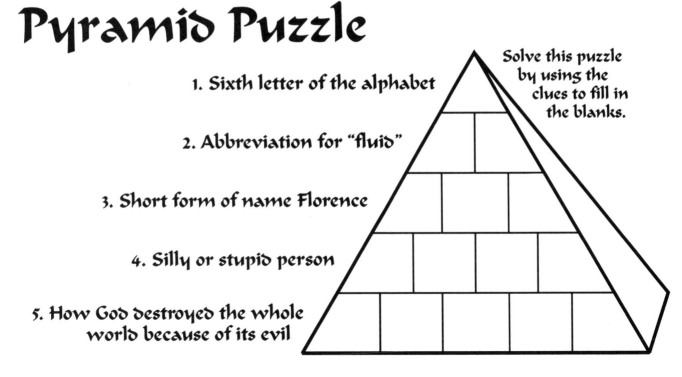

1. Sixth letter of the alphabet

2. Abbreviation for "fluid"

3. Short form of name Florence

4. Silly or stupid person

5. How God destroyed the whole world because of its evil

Solve this puzzle by using the clues to fill in the blanks.

JOIN THE CROWD

Read each story below and think about what the person should do to stand up for God. Cut out the finger puppets and tape the ends of the bands together, then use the puppets to act out the stories and possible endings.

On the way home from school, Dave offers Jordan some pills. "They'll make you feel good," he tells Jordan. "All the popular kids take them. C'mon. Don't be a jerk." Jordan remembers that just last week his Sunday school lesson was about his body being God's temple. He tells Dave ". . ."

"You've just got to come to the party on Saturday. All the really important kids will be there." Angela knew that she had promised to help the kid's club at church with a car wash that day. The proceeds were to go to an orphanage in India. Angela remembered the sad faces of the children in the picture her youth leader had shown them. She swallowed the lump in her throat and said ". . ."

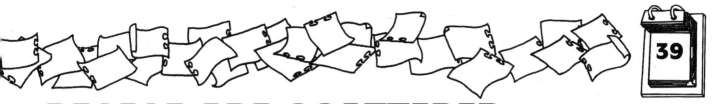

PEOPLE ARE SCATTERED

AIM: That your students will realize that the Lord is pleased when we praise Him, not ourselves

SCRIPTURE: Genesis 11:1-9 (God miraculously separates the people who are building a tower to bring glory to themselves)

PREPARATION:
1. Photocopy activity sheets —one for each student.
2. Prepare an object lesson about different languages as described in PRESESSION.

PRESESSION (5-10 minutes)

ACTIVITIES
* Become aware of materials in different languages
* Play a game to point out our basic self-centeredness

MATERIALS
* Books or tapes in several different languages
* Jelly beans—5 for each student

PERSPECTIVE (10 minutes)

ACTIVITIES
* Build a tower with different materials

MATERIALS
* Game cards, building blocks, toothpicks

PROBE (20 minutes)

ACTIVITIES
* Participate in a skit about the tower of Babel

MATERIALS
* Bibles
* "I Witness News" Activity Sheet

PERSONALIZE (15-20 minutes)

ACTIVITIES
* Survey the areas in which we honor and obey God

MATERIALS
* "My Life House" Activity Sheet

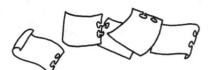  
PRESESSION

Before class, write these words to the chorus of "Jesus Loves Me" in the Telegu language of India on the chalkboard or a large sheet of paper:

Yesu preminchun
Nanu preminchun
Ounu preminchun
Bible lo nerchithin

Lay the foreign language books where they can be examined. To help students think about how self-centered we are, play a game throughout this and the PERSPECTIVE section. Give each person five jelly beans. Every time they say "I" they must give up one jelly bean. Be sure to keep check on this game throughout these lesson sections.

Discuss different languages. Can you guess the language and familiar song on the board? How many languages do you think there are in the world? (More than 7000 languages and dialects) How many of you know some words in a different language? Why do you think there are so many? How do you think they began? **Believe it or not they all began because of a building.**

PERSPECTIVE

Let's see how good you are at building things. Divide group into small teams of two or three people. Give each team a different building material. (Game cards, toothpicks, building blocks) **The object of this activity is to see which team can build the highest tower.**

Continue playing the "I" game while you talk about big constructions. **Nearly everyone who visits New York City wants to go to the Empire State Building.** There are 102 stories above street level and two stories below. **But what about trying to build before there were earth-moving machines, building equipment, or ready-made materials?**

The temple of Ramses II is in Egypt at Abu Simbel. It was built 3,200 years ago to honor the sun god. It was made so that the sun's rays touched the inner sanctuary of the temple, 200 feet back into the mountain cliff, on the Pharaoh's birthday!

In 1964, the temple had to be moved 200 feet higher to save it from the backed-up water of Lake Nasser when the Aswan Dam was built on the Nile River. Modern engineers from 48 nations worked for five years to restore the temple to its original plan. But despite all the technology available, they were one day off! **This amazing construction was built when everything was done by hand.**

Stop the tower building activity and talk about it. How did your building go? Were you able to work together? Did the team members have different ideas of how to build the tower? How do you feel about your creation? Are you proud of it?

Also stop the "I" game and have people lay aside any jelly beans they have left. **(It's hard to talk about ourselves and not use the word "I," isn't it?)** Why do you think it is so hard? (Normal to refer to self, seems natural to call attention to ourselves.)

Our story today is about a building that was started thousands of years ago by a group of people in the land of Shinar. Like some of us, these people found it difficult not to talk about themselves and what they had done.

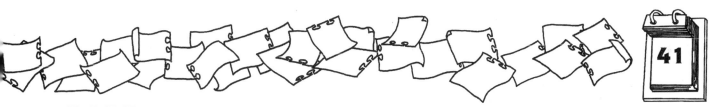

PROBE

Write on the chalkboard or a piece of paper these four words meaning "work." Help students learn how to pronounce the words.

1. TRABAJO (trah-BAH-ho)—Spanish
2. ARBEIT (ARE-BITE)—German
3. TRAVAIL (tra-VAIL)—French
4. SHIGATO (she-GOT-oh)—Japanese

Divide the group into four teams. Assign one word to each group. When you come to the word **"WORK"** in the skit, have all four teams say their word at the same time to demonstrate how it must have sounded when God confused their language.

Distribute copies of "I Witness News" activity sheet. You will need people to read the parts of the announcer, Eber, Obal, and Joktan in this simulated news report. Have these characters read through the skit while the rest of the class follow on their activity sheets. Finish reading the skit.

What happened after Noah and the flood? Have someone check out Genesis 10:32—11: 2 and read it aloud. (Number of people increased, had one language, moved eastward to plain in Shinar and lived there.) Shinar was an early name for Babylon.

Ask someone to read aloud verses 3 and 4. **What did the people do?** (Made bricks, used tar to hold them together.) The bricks were made of mud and baked at high temperatures to strengthen them.

What did the people want to build? (City, tower that reached heaven.) This tower was probably a ziggurat. It looked like a pyramid with steps or ramps leading up the sides. Each story was slightly smaller than the one below it, making it look steplike. The tower was one of the largest ziggurats measuring about 300 feet on each side. It was probably about 300 feet high. Each of the seven levels may have been painted a different color so the building looked like a huge rainbow.

Why did they want to build this great tower? (To call attention to themselves and their accomplishments.) These people were not working hard to honor God. The were honoring themselves with this monument. They felt they didn't need God. The tower was a symbol of human pride and ambition.

How do you think God felt about their attitude? (Sad, upset, angry.) God wanted people to want to spend time with Him and talk with Him. Ask someone to read verses 5-7. **What did He do about their plan?** (Gave them different languages.) God could not allow the people to continue in such open defiance and rebellion. **What happened then?** Choose someone to read verses 8 and 9. (Stopped building the tower, were confused, scattered over the earth.) People probably hunted for others they could understand. They formed small groups or tribes and moved away from those they couldn't understand.

This construction is commonly called the tower of Babel. In Babylon's native language "Babel" meant "the gate of God." A similar word in Hebrew means "to mix or confuse."

How do people today try to call attention to themselves? (Wear fancy clothes, have big houses, expensive cars, powerful jobs.) **What do you think your life shows about who is number one in your life?**

PERSONALIZE

(15-20 minutes)

Ask someone to look up I Corinthians 6:19 and read it aloud. **When we trust Jesus to be our Savior, who lives in us?** (Holy Spirit.) Distribute copies of "My Life House" activity sheet. Have someone read aloud the directions.

Imagine that your life is like a house. It has different areas or rooms. Aid your students to see the correlation between this house floor plan and their own lives. Each room in the plan corresponds to one area of their lives.

The kitchen is the area where people eat. It corresponds to your eating habits. Do we eat junk food or wholesome food to make our bodies healthy? The recreation room has to do with what you do in free time. The study portrays the area of school and homework. The bedroom area is that of proper rest for healthy bodies and also time for daily devotions, the time spent with God in prayer and Bible reading. The bathroom is the realm of outward appearances. It also covers the area of harmful substances such as drugs. The family-living room has to do with our relationships with other family members.

Encourage students to be honest in their survey. Also reassure them that this information will be strictly between them and God. It is only to help them see areas of their lives where they need to deal with personal pride and ask God for help to praise Him instead.

Optional: To help reassure them that this activity is strictly personal, let people move around the room so they have enough private work space.

How do kids try to call attention to themselves? (Buy lots of expensive clothes, go out for sports, get good grades, join clubs.) None of these things is essentially wrong, but when they are done for the wrong purposes, to impress others or leave God out of their lives, they are harmful.

Did you find some areas where you honor yourself instead of God? (This is only a thought question and doesn't need to be answered aloud.) **Probably all of us have at least one room that is a problem. What are some ways that we can praise God?** (Thank Him for His gifts—good brain, healthy body, etc. and take care of them, love and help others, study and learn how to serve Him, spend time with Him in prayer and reading our Bibles.)

Whenever people are proud and call attention to themselves, God is displeased. He wants His followers to work hard for the right reasons. We should be thankful for all of God's blessings and give Him honor and praise.

PRAYER/PRAISE

Close by singing a praise chorus such as "Praise Him, Praise Him" or "Let's Just Praise the Lord."

Send home five jelly beans with each person as a reminder of today's lesson.

Witness news

ANNOUNCER: Good evening and welcome to the six o'clock news. Tonight we have a special in-depth report from our "I" team about that construction marvel, the tower in Shinar. For a background check we call upon our historical reporter, Eber.

EBER: The leaders of the people decided to build this tower so they can keep all the people from scattering. They want it to reach up to heaven so everyone can see it and know how great they are. It's really a monument to themselves.

ANNOUNCER: Thank you, Eber. Now we go to our correspondent, Obal, at the brickworks.

OBAL: Things are humming here. Some of the people are making bricks. Others are baking them in ovens so they will be very hard. Still others are filling containers with the tar-like pitch that oozes from the ground nearby. This pitch will be used to hold the bricks together. There's no end to the number of people and bricks needed to complete the project.

ANNOUNCER: Thank you, Obal. Since you brought up the topic of completion, let's hear next from our reporter at the building site. Joktan, you've been on location all day at the tower. What is the feeling of the workers there?

JOKTAN: Everything is moving rapidly. The feeling is that of strength and pride. When it is finished this tower will be over 300 feet tall. Everyone will be able to see it. The workers want to call attention to how wonderful they are so they can become famous. You can probably hear them calling directions to each other in the background. It's a good thing they all speak the same language. Wait a minute. Something seems to be changing here. What's that? I can't quite understand what they're saying. Oh no! This can't be happening!

ANNOUNCER: What's going on, Joktan? Can you be more specific?

JOKTAN: Suddenly, people are speaking different languages. It's terrible. It's as if some superhuman being unexpectedly made the people speak in different languages. Things are so confusing right now that it's hard to make any sense out of it all. They won't be able to continue to build if they can't understand the orders. I'll have to go and find someone I can understand. Maybe then I can give you more specific information. I'll work . . .

ANNOUNCER: Are you all right, Joktan? Can you hear me?

JOKTAN: Que ? (keh)

ANNOUNCER: We seem to have a bad connection there. Perhaps our engineer can straighten things out for us later. But for now, I'm afraid that's the end of our "I" Team Report for tonight. This is your Channel 7 news anchor saying goodnight. What's that? What do you mean, "Sayonara?" (sigh-oh-NAR-ah)

6A

MY LIFE-HOUSE

Directions: Think about each area of your life as a room in your life-house. Which of your life-rooms are occupied by God? Write **GOD** in those rooms. If you are occupying some rooms, write **SELF** in them. Then write down some ways you could praise GOD instead of yourself.

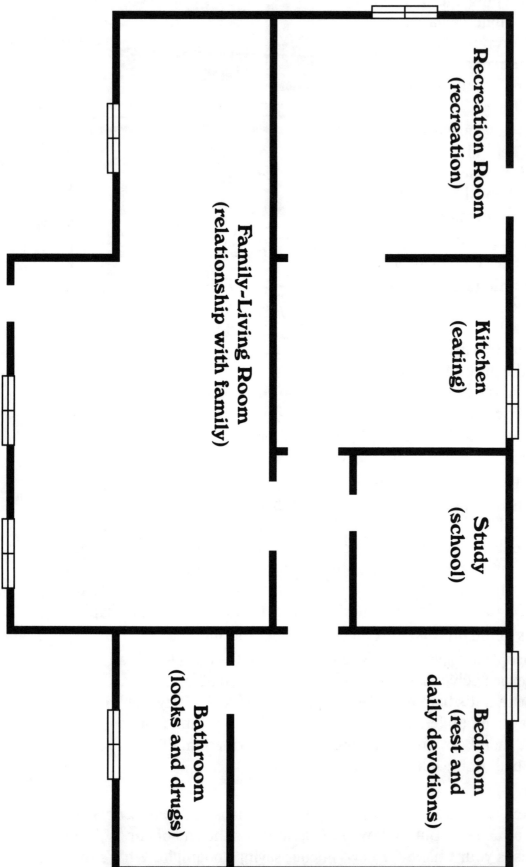

Recreation Room
(recreation)

Kitchen
(eating)

Study
(school)

Family-Living Room
(relationship with family)

Bathroom
(looks and drugs)

Bedroom
(rest and daily devotions)

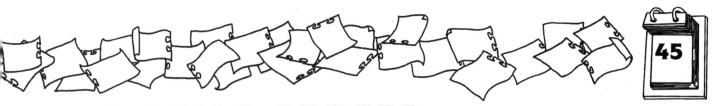

GOD CALLS ABRAM

AIM: That your students will understand that they should trust and obey God

SCRIPTURE: Genesis 11:31; 12:1-3, 7, 8 (Abram obeyed God without question, even though he did not know just what was before him)

PREPARATION:
1. Photocopy activity sheets—one for each student.

PRESESSION (5-10 minutes)

ACTIVITIES
* Play a game to illustrate trust in someone

PERSPECTIVE (10 minutes)

ACTIVITIES
* Talk about trust
* Learn about the Pilgrims' search for religious freedom
* *Optional: Make a mural of transportation in Bible times and today*

MATERIALS
* *Optional: Long piece of shelf paper, scissors, glue, reference books showing Bible times transportation methods*

PROBE (20 minutes)

ACTIVITIES
* Complete a simulated diary of Abram

MATERIALS
* Bibles
* Road map from your own state
* "Abram's Diary" Activity Sheet
* *Optional: Map of Bible lands*

PERSONALIZE (15-20 minutes)

ACTIVITIES
* Discover ways to trust and obey God

MATERIALS
* "Reach Out to God" Activity Sheet

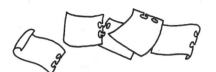  
PRESESSION

To help students start thinking about trust, play this game. As people arrive have them form pairs. One person is a camel, the other is a driver. Camels hold their hands extended and keep their eyes closed. Drivers steer their camels by placing hands on shoulders.

One pair is "IT" and a game of tag ensues with drivers steering camels around each other. When the "IT" camel tags another, then that camel and driver become "IT." Stop game and have people regroup.

PERSPECTIVE

Before class write this mystery word on a chalkboard or large sheet of paper. P LGR M.

Discuss the previous game using questions similar to these: How did it feel to be a camel and play with your eyes closed? (Scary, fun, hesitant to move.) What relationship did the camels need to have with their drivers? (Needed to trust them.) How should this have made the drivers think about their camels? (Want to see that they didn't get hurt.) What did the camels have to do when drivers steered? (Obey.)

It took a lot of faith to play this game. Not being able to see where you are going means moving out into the unknown. Those kinds of experiences can be scary. In order to do it safely, you need to be able to depend upon someone who is trustworthy to help you.

See if anyone can guess the secret word. **What does pilgrim mean?** (A wanderer or traveler; one who goes to a holy place as part of a religious act.)

Several hundred years ago, a group of people in England were very unhappy because they could not worship freely as they pleased. King James I declared that only he and the bishop of the church could tell people how to worship God. **These people decided to go to Holland. They stayed for ten years. Then a few of them suggested going to America.** Some argued that there were many great dangers in the new world. Others said that they should put their trust in God and ask for His protection.

Three years later, in 1620, nearly one hundred people boarded the Mayflower. Those who were seeking religious freedom became known as the Pilgrims. It took much faith for them to make this voyage. **Our "Pilgrim Fathers" endured countless hardships in their search for freedom to worship God.**

The man who is called the father of the Hebrew nation also had to have great faith. He was a pilgrim who made a journey into a strange land.

Optional: If you have a longer time schedule, make a mural of various means of transportation. Divide the class in two groups. Draw a highway on a piece of shelf paper. Have one group cut pictures of cars, buses, bikes, planes, etc. from old magazines and newspapers. They can glue these on one side of the road.

The second group can cut pictures from recycled Sunday school materials or draw their own pictures of methods of travel in Bible times. If possible have encyclopedias or other materials available for reference.

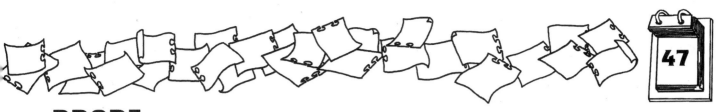

PROBE

(20 minutes)

Hold up your state road map with the city or area where you live marked clearly. **Here is a map of our state. We live right here. If we wanted to take a trip to _____, we would first look at the map and decide which roads to take. How else might we find out the best road to get there?** (Ask someone who had been there before, ask a travel service such as AAA.)

Suppose someone came to you and said "Pack up everything you own, put it in the car and start traveling." What are some things you would want to know? (Where am I going? Why should I take this trip? How long will it take? When will I be back?) **Something like that happened to a man named Abram.**

Abram lived in Ur of the Chaldees many years after the great flood. At the time Abram was born, the city is estimated to already have been 1000 years old! It was on a main trading route. The surrounding countryside was lush with fig and date palm trees and broad fields of grain watered by a grid of irrigation ditches. The Euphrates River was full of ships exporting surplus commodities.

Optional: If you have one, use a map of Bible lands to show the city of Ur.

Ur had a well advanced culture and religion. Mathematicians figured sum formulae for the extraction of square and cube roots. Astronomers studied the stars. Doctors practiced medicine and wrote textbooks. Political leaders established well-written laws to protect both citizens and travelers. Writers recorded history-making events. It was a good place in which to prepare Abram for his trip by giving him wide knowledge of the geography of the inhabited world.

A huge ziggurat made as a three-step pyramid honored a moon god, Nanna, with a one-room shrine at the very top, overlooking the entire city and surrounding area. But contrary to his surroundings and culture, Abram worshiped the true and living God.

Abram and his wife Sarai lived happily in Ur.

Abram was wealthy and owned large numbers of cattle, camels, donkeys, and sheep. All his servants and helpers were considered part of Abram's household.

Their home was probably quite luxurious with up to thirteen or fourteen rooms on two levels, stone staircases, inside lavatories, beautiful mosaics, and exquisite jugs.

As many as twelve different kinds of clothing were available and costumes were decorated with precious stones, gold, silver, and intricate beadwork.

Abram and Sarai probably planned to spend their lives in that city. But one day God spoke to Abram. Have someone read aloud Genesis 11:31. **How do you think Abram and Sarai felt about this?** (Puzzled, afraid, hesitant, eager to go.) Abram had no idea where God wanted him to go! However, Abram had already learned to love and trust God. Instead of asking questions, he gathered together his possessions and got his large household ready to travel.

God first led Abram and his family to a place called Haran. Show Haran on the map. They stopped here for a long time. Haran was another city where the citizens worshiped the moon god. While they were here, Abram's father, Terah, died.

Hand out copies of "Abram's Diary" activity sheet. Ask someone to read the directions. Depending on your time period, you can complete this activity together, pausing to write entries in the diary, or have students finish it on their own.

What was the promise God gave to Abram? (He would make him a great nation, bless him, make his name great, God would bless those Abram blessed and curse those Abram cursed, make him a blessing to all the people on earth.) **There was a condition Abram had to fulfil before God would do this. What was it?** (Had to obey God.)

Why do you think God led Abram and his family into the wilderness? Couldn't He bless

Abram in Ur or Haran just as well? The sinful, pagan civilizations of the world were hindrances to Abram. The wilderness was a clean, quiet place where a God-centered new nation could be established.

What new promise did God give Abram when he arrived in Canaan? (He would give the land to Abram's offspring.) **What did Abram do next?** (Built an altar and worshiped God.)

What did Abram do when he lived between Ai and Bethel? (Built another altar to worship God.) The altars Abram built were a symbol of his communion with God. They were constructed for prayer and worship and to remind Abram of God's promises to him. They were a visual reminder that God was to be the center of his life. All through his wanderings, Abram continued building altars to worship God in this manner.

PERSONALIZE

(15-20 minutes)

Abram put action into his worship by trusting and obeying the Lord. Hand out copies of "Reach Out to God" activity sheet. Have students work on this individually. The first half of the activity is a review listing specific ways Abram trusted and obeyed God. The second half gives references of specific ways people today can trust and obey God.

God seldom shows us His way all at once. Abram traveled as far as Haran, on to Canaan, then built altars as he slowly traveled across the promised land. As Abram was obedient in each step, his trust grew and he was enabled to obey and take the next step. **As we obey God a step at a time, our trust grows and we are able to take another step.**

PRAYER/PRAISE

Close with a circle prayer asking God for His help to trust Him more so we can obey Him better. Allow a time of silence where people can add their own individual requests about specific matters.

ABRAM'S DIARY

Abram was a man who both trusted and obeyed God. He left his country, home, and friends to go to an unknown place. You can read about it in Genesis 11:31 and 12:1-8. Use the diary page to make brief entries that Abram might have written as he traveled. References are given to help you.

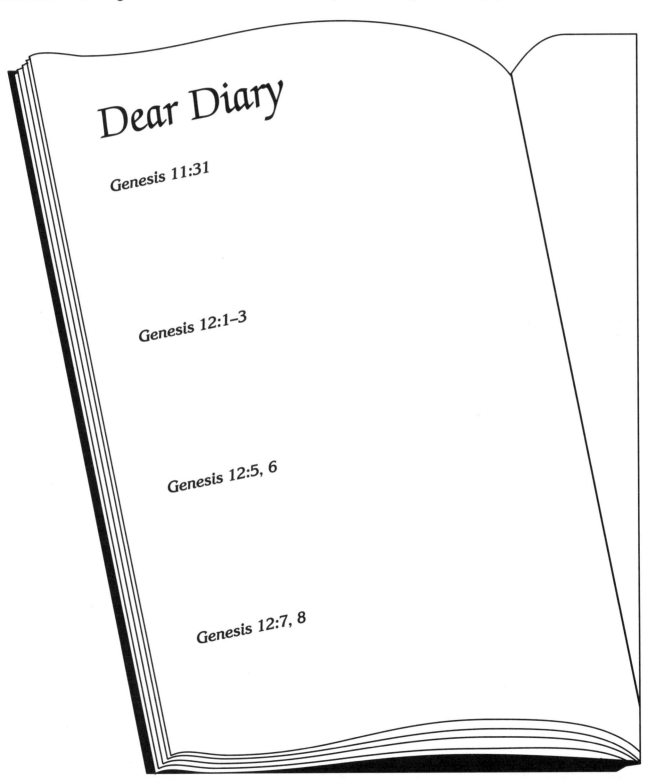

Dear Diary

Genesis 11:31

Genesis 12:1–3

Genesis 12:5, 6

Genesis 12:7, 8

Reach Out to God

Look up the passages to help you complete this activity.

Abraham reached out to God in trust and obedience. Write some examples in this box.

_____

_____

_____

_____

_____

_____

_____

_____

What are some ways you can reach out to trust and obey God? Write them in this box.

Psalm 37:3 _____

_____

John 14:1 _____

_____

Ephesians 6:1 _____

_____

Hebrews 13:7 _____

_____

1 Timothy 6:18 _____

_____

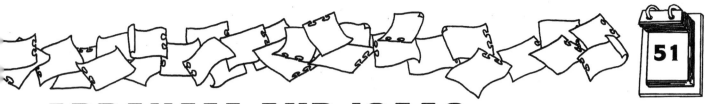

ABRAHAM AND ISAAC

AIM: That your students will understand what "sacrifice" means and that faithful obedience and loving service to God are the highest forms of sacrifice

SCRIPTURE: Genesis 22:1, 2, 6-13 (Abram obeys God and is willing to sacrifice Isaac)

PREPARATION:
1. Photocopy activity sheets—one for each student.
2. Make case study prompt cards as described in PERSPECTIVE.

PRESESSION (5-10 minutes)

ACTIVITIES
* Cut or tear out pictures of items people treasure
* *Optional: Make a montage of treasures*

MATERIALS
* Old newspapers, catalogs, or magazines
* Scissors
* *Optional: large sheet of paper, glue*

PERSPECTIVE (10 minutes)

ACTIVITIES
* Use a case study to discuss situations where someone must choose to give his best to God

MATERIALS
* Index cards

PROBE (20 minutes)

ACTIVITIES
* Play a game to see how Abraham might have responded to God's command about Isaac
* Discover how Abraham really did react to God's will

MATERIALS
* Bibles
* "What If?" Activity Sheet

PERSONALIZE (15-20 minutes)

ACTIVITIES
* Make an acrostic about sacrifice

MATERIALS
* "The Key to Excellence" Activity Sheet
* *Optional: dictionary or thesaurus for reference*

PRESESSION

As students arrive have them use the old magazines or papers to cut or tear out pictures of things they feel are treasures. Guide the conversation by using questions like these: What if someone wanted you to give them your greatest treasure. How would you feel? What if the person was your best friend? An enemy? A stranger? What if the person was a parent or someone you love and trust very much?

It makes a great deal of difference in our obedience if we love and really trust someone. When we feel that way it helps us to trust them with our dearest treasures.

Optional: If time permits you can make a montage of these treasure pictures by gluing or taping them on a background sheet.

PERSPECTIVE

To help your students understand sacrifice, use a case study. By telling this study, instead of reading it, you'll get better attention from your students and see how they are responding. If necessary, jot down a few important notes on index cards. You can glance at these to be sure no important points have been left out.

Case studies don't give final answers. They only set up a real-life situation which students can discuss. But as people hear the opinions of others, they become aware of different possibilities and opinions. This enables them to take the Scriptural principles to everyday life.

"The sacrifice"

David blinked and swallowed hard. He couldn't believe what his kid's club leader had said. "There's room for only one more person to go to Bible camp."

Last year David had gotten to go to camp with his church group, Kids, INC. (In Christ). He'd had a wonderful time swimming in the lake, playing games with the other kids, eating great cookouts, and looking through the tent flaps to see the stars. He'd learned about God's love and how Jesus had died for him. Best of all had been the final service around the campfire when kids gave their testimonies. David told how he had accepted Jesus as his Savior. Then he had thrown a piece of firewood on the blazing bonfire as everyone prayed for him.

From then on, he planned to go back to camp. He saved money from his paper route to pay his way. That fall he got to be friends with Juan Sanchez. Juan's family were migrant workers who moved further north with the field work, then stayed on. They were very poor and David knew Juan sometimes didn't even have enough to eat.

He really liked Juan and had been praying for an opportunity to share Jesus with him. He thought taking him along to camp would be the perfect time to do it. The church always gave money to help needy kids go to camp. But this year there wasn't as much money as usual.

"You should have said something earlier, David. Now even if we had the money to pay for Juan, I haven't room for both of you," the club leader said.

David thought about how hard he had worked to save the money to go. He knew how happy Juan had been when he'd invited him to go with him. He had been so sure everything would work out. After all, he had prayed about it and God always answered prayer, didn't He?

"Well, David, what do you want to do?"

DISCUSS:
* What would you do if you were David?
* What do you think the club leader could suggest to David?
* What do you think will happen to Juan?
* Based on what you know, what do you think God would want David to do?

Last week we learned how Abram trusted and obeyed God by leaving his home and traveling to a place he knew nothing about. God promised Abram that he would become the father of a great nation. He changed Abram's name to Abraham which meant "father of many." God also changed Sarai's name to Sarah, meaning "princess." This meant that she would be the mother of nations and kings who would serve the Lord. **Now let's see how God fulfilled that promise.**

PROBE

(20 minutes)

Time passed and Sarah and Abraham were getting very old. Although he believed God's promises and patiently waited for a son to be born to him, Abraham wondered how he could be head of a large nation when he didn't have even one son. Then a miracle happened. A son was born to Abraham and Sarah. They were so delighted that they named him Isaac, which means "laughter."

As Isaac grew, Abraham taught him to worship and obey God. He probably told him that he was the fulfillment of God's promise and that a great blessing for all people would one day come from their family. As the years passed, father and son grew to love each other dearly.

God knew Abraham still worshiped Him, but perhaps the love-gift child, Isaac, now had first place in Abraham's heart instead of God. He decided to test Abraham.

One day God spoke to Abraham and asked him to do the most difficult thing any father was ever asked to do. Have someone read Genesis 22:1, 2 aloud. **What a hard choice Abraham had to make! What should he do?**

Distribute copies of "What If?" activity sheet. Have students cut out and tape together the cubes. Divide the group into pairs. Each partner will take turns throwing the cube and telling what they think might have happened to Abraham, Isaac, and God, if Abraham had chosen to handle the crisis in this way. Allow several minutes for playing this game, then have the group turn to Genesis 22:6-13. They can take turns reading this passage aloud.

How do you think Abraham felt when he heard what God wanted him to do? (Sad, fearful, trusted God.) **How might he have felt after he saw how God provided an offering for the sacrifice?** (Relieved, happy, thankful that he didn't have to kill Isaac, knew that Isaac too trusted and was obedient to God.)

How do you think Isaac felt about his father's willingness to make him the offering? Scholars think that Isaac might have been a young man, in his mid to late teens, when this event took place. It would have been easy for him to overpower Abraham and to avoid the expected outcome. But Isaac had learned well from his father. He loved Abraham dearly, and, like him, put God first in his life. This made it possible for Isaac to trust and obey God even when death appeared imminent.

After this event, how do you think Isaac felt about God? (Trusted and obeyed Him more, realized he was precious to God.) **What do you think this teaches us about God?** (God keeps His promises, we can trust Him, He never disappoints those who trust in Him, each of us is special to Him.)

Abraham and Isaac were willing to prove their love and obedience to God. They had put their faith in God and found they could count on His faithfulness. Together they had passed His test.

PERSONALIZE

What is a sacrifice? (Giving something valuable to someone.) In Old Testament times, sacrifices were made to thank God for what He had done, to show obedience to Him, or to show sorrow for sin. **Abraham put his faith in God and was willing to sacrifice his greatest treasure, Isaac.**

Sometimes we put our faith in things. You might get into the family car and discover that it won't run so you can't take a trip that day. **Faith in things often brings disappointment.**

Sometimes we put our faith in people. A trusted friend may be a liar. Someone else we think is very honest is seen cheating. **People can also disappoint us.**

Faith in God is never disappointing! But what about us? Can God put His faith in us? We are quick to say "I love God" or "I trust God." We must prove our love and trust by obeying Him. **How can God know that we really love and trust Him?**

Hand out copies of "The Key To Excellence" activity sheet. Ask someone to read the verse and directions at the top of the page. **Today, God desires us to live as He wants us to.**

Students can make individual acrostics. Dictionaries or a thesaurus can help students find words beginning with those letters. An example is:

Sing songs of praise
Act in love towards others
Create peace wherever possible
Refuse to doubt God's promises
Increase my prayer time
Faithfully tells others about Jesus
Identify sin in my life and ask God to forgive it
Choose to put God first
Expect God to keep His promises

Allow several minutes to complete the acrostic. Have the group share as time permits.

PRAYER/PRAISE

We can't just tell God we love Him. We need to show it by our actions. Close by having the group sing "Trust and Obey" or "I Have Decided to Follow Jesus." Encourage those who want to give their best to God, to serve and follow Him every day. They can show their willingness by "presenting" their outstretched hands.

WHAT IF?

Cut on solid lines only. Fold on dotted lines to form a block and tape together so that printing is on the outside.

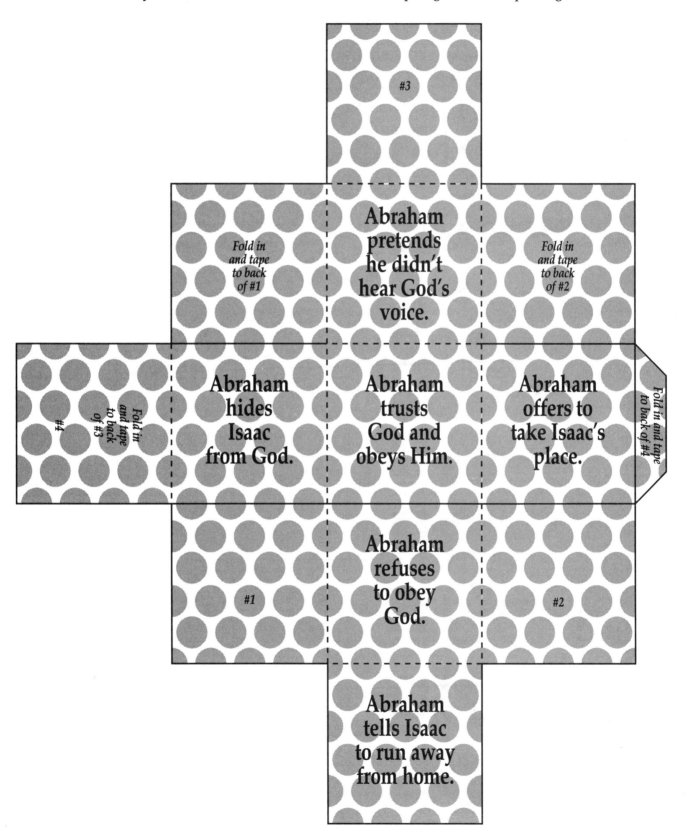

THE KEY TO EXCELLENCE

" . . . Offer your bodies as living sacrifices, holy and pleasing to God—this is your spiritual act of worship."

Romans 12:1

This verse is the key to how you can give God the highest form of sacrifice. On each line below, write ways you will try to faithfully obey God with loving service. Start each way with the letter shown. The first one is done to help you.

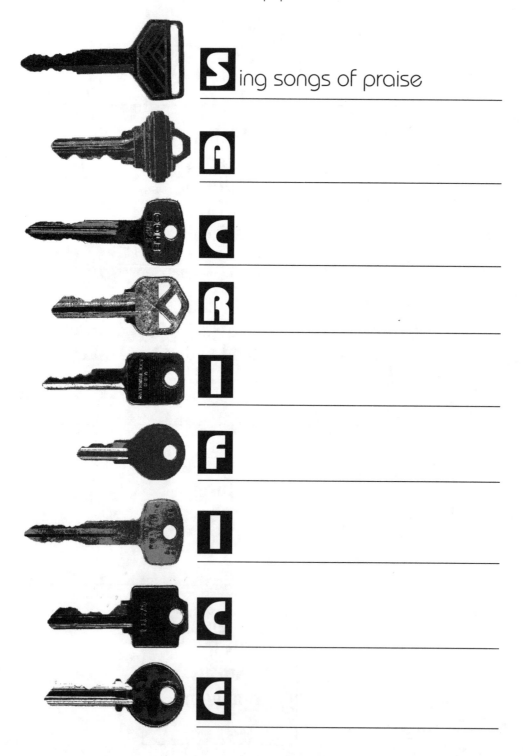

Sing songs of praise

A

C

R

I

F

I

C

E

JACOB AND ESAU

AIM: That your students will learn to give the things concerning eternal life first place in their lives

SCRIPTURE: Genesis 25:27-34 (Esau considers immediate needs more important than long-range benefits while Jacob looks to the future and has a sense of eternal values)

PREPARATION:
1. Photocopy activity sheets—one for each student.

PRESESSION (5-10 minutes)

ACTIVITIES
* Play a game which requires players to work to achieve goals
* Share a food treat

MATERIALS
* Old newspapers
* Treat such as slices of fruit or pizza, individual packets of raisins, cookies

PERSPECTIVE (10 minutes)

ACTIVITIES
* Take part in a chain-reaction story about choices

MATERIALS
* Paper, pencils

PROBE (20 minutes)

ACTIVITIES
* Take part in a skit to learn about choices involving short-term versus long-term results

MATERIALS
* Bibles
* "The Mystery of the Mixed-Up Motive" Activity Sheet

PERSONALIZE (15-20 minutes)

ACTIVITIES
* Complete a creative writing story about life priorities

MATERIALS
* "First Place" Activity Sheet

PRESESSION

As students arrive get them involved in a newspaper relay which illustrates the value of working at a long-time goal. Fold several sheets of newspapers into fourths, making a piece big enough on which to place a foot. You will need two of these pads. Have half of the group stand on one side of the room and half on the other, facing them.

The first player on one side must put down the newspaper and step on it, then put down the other pad and step on it. Players must continue this way until they have reached the opposite side of the room. The first player then touches the next player and that person crosses in the same manner.

Stress that no one is <u>required</u> to play the game. But for those who finish this task, there will be a reward. *Keep the treats a surprise!* Wait until everyone who chooses to play has finished.

As the group regathers to enjoy their treat, guide the conversation with questions like these: How did you feel about having to work for an unknown reward? Did it seem fair to ask you to do the task in order to gain this treat? Would it have made a difference if you knew beforehand what the reward was?

PERSPECTIVE

Suppose you had a friend who needed to make a choice about what was most important in his life—things right now or future unknown rewards. Let's see what kind of advice you can give him. Today we're going to write a chain-reaction story about a boy named Kevin.

Distribute paper and pencils. Read the background information aloud. Then read each sentence and have students fill in the blanks. After they've written an ending, have them fold their answers down, so no one can read them, and pass them to the person on their left. That person will finish the next sentence, fold the paper back, and pass it to the next person on the left. Continue in this manner until you have finished all the sentences.

Kevin knows that a lot of kids take steroids as a shortcut to getting big muscles so they can be better in sports. If you don't use them, you have to spend extra hours in physical training. He also knows that steroids can cause damage to the body and also the mind by making a person more aggressive. Kevin really wants to be a big hero in sports. If you were Kevin you would _____.

April wants to play in the school band. Her parents bought her a flute so she could take lessons. But April would rather play outdoors than practice. If you were April you would _____.

Tim wants to go on a trip with the Kid's Club. His parents have told him that he may if he gets better grades. If you were Tim you would _____.

Ask students to pass the stories around once more. Now have them unfold the answers and share them as you discuss the stories. What did people feel was the most important thing? Why do you think they decided that way? What will probably happen as a result? **Often the best things are those we have to work at or wait for a long time. It's much easier to receive things right away. There is a story in the Bible about a young man who didn't think very much about what might happen because of the choice he made. His name was Esau.**

PROBE

(20 minutes)

Jacob and Esau were twins, but they didn't look very much alike. They didn't act alike either. Have students take turns reading Genesis 25:27-34.

Isaac and Rebekah's twins were the grandsons of Abraham and Sarah. Jacob was a quiet, thoughtful man who liked to stay around home. He probably helped his mother and soon became her favorite. Esau, the oldest son, was an outdoors person who enjoyed wilderness hunting. Because Isaac also liked outdoor activities and appreciated the wild game Esau shared, Esau became his father's favorite.

In Bible times it was the custom for the oldest son to receive a birthright. This privilege meant that he would take his father's place as head of the tribe. The father's property was divided equally among his sons, except that the oldest son received twice as much.

This double portion was needed because the oldest son also had to manage the family property and provide for any remaining parent as well as any unmarried sisters. The birthright was his to keep, to give, or sell. However, once he gave it up, it could never be taken back.

Pass out copies of "The Mystery of the Mixed-up Motive" activity sheet. Read the directions aloud. People can take turns reading the story while the rest follow along on the activity sheet.

How did Esau feel about the birthright? (It wasn't very important, was too long to have to wait for it, wouldn't do him any good if he died from hunger right then.)

Why did Esau give up his birthright? (He wanted food more than he wanted God's blessings, didn't want to have to take on responsibilities.) All Esau could think of was how hungry he was. He felt that satisfying that immediate need was far more important than waiting for the privileges the birthright held for him at his father's death.

Esau acted on impulse. Then he exaggerated the problem of hunger to justify his choice. He lost his perspective and despised the eternal spiritual blessings that he could have had if he had kept the birthright.

Do you think Esau felt differently later? Why or why not? Esau later regretted his hasty decision and wept because it was gone forever.

How did Jacob feel about the birthright? (Realized how important it would be later on, knew that it was a blessing from God as well as his father.)

Jacob and Esau got what each of them wanted. Esau got food which was gone in a few minutes. Jacob got the birthright which would bring him riches, honor and eternal value. When Esau begged for some type of blessing from Isaac, he was told he would live by his sword. His family would serve Jacob's family for awhile, but later they would not serve Jacob. Some of these things were prophecies that happened later to the descendants of these two men.

How do you think Esau felt about Jacob after he lost his birthright? (Angry, bitter, didn't want to have anything to do with him.) Esau quickly forgot that he had willingly sold his birthright. He probably felt his bargain with Jacob could be cancelled and he could regain it. Later, he felt very sorry that he had done such a foolish thing.

There are more stories in the Bible about these two brothers, but this very first story, when Esau sold his birthright, decided what would happen to them the rest of their lives. **Esau only thought first of what he wanted for the moment while Jacob wisely looked ahead to the future and the things of God which never change or pass away.**

How do you think God felt about Esau and his low opinion of God's blessings? (Sad, upset, angry.) **How do you think He felt about Jacob choosing the eternal things and being willing to wait for them?** (Happy, wanted to bless him.)

Like his father, Isaac, and his grandfather,

Abraham, Jacob was greatly blessed by God. His name was changed to Israel, meaning "he struggles with God." His descendants became known as Israelites. From Israel's family came the twelve tribes that later made up the nation of Israel. From one of these tribes, Judah, would come the Messiah, the One who would bring a blessing to the whole world.

PERSONALIZE

(15-20 minutes)

Sometimes it is hard to decide just what is most important in life. The attitude of most people is instant gratification of all their needs or desires. It can be stated: "I want what I want, when I want it and I want it now!" In this age of throwaways and rewards that quickly pass, people are not willing to wait or work for things that have lasting value.

Distribute copies of "First Place" activity sheet. Read the directions aloud. Allow about half the time period to let students complete this activity. Encourage them to share their answers with the group.

How do you decide what is most important in life? Every decision we make has a result. These consequences should be considered before the final choice is made. Questions to ask yourself are: Will my choice affect me in a harmful or helpful way? Hurt or help others? Will I still be happy with my choice next week, next year, ten years from now? How does it affect my relationship with God? **Only things that help us to love and honor God and encourage others to follow Him are important and have lasting values. They are the things that truly satisfy us.**

PRAYER/PRAISE

Close with prayer something like this: God, thank You for things that have eternal value. Give us wisdom to think through our choices before we make them. Help us choose things that will really satisfy us, both now and in the future. Amen.

THE MYSTERY OF THE MIXED-UP MOTIVE

What happens when people consider the satisfaction of their immediate needs more important than looking to the future and developing a sense of lasting values? Read through the story and look for clues as the famous detectives Sheerluck Holmes and Dodger Watson solve this mystery.

Dodger Watson shook his head as he moved several of the files making up the mountainous mass before him. "I don't know, Holmes, we've solved myriads of mixed-up matters, but this mystery is driving me mad. My mind gets more muddled up the longer we meditate on it."

"Make no mistake, my modest friend. No matter how misleading the information may appear, we shall, as always, make its meaning clear. Now, first of all, make a mental note of the facts. The melancholy male hunter states that he was mistreated by his younger brother. He maintains that it was all a mistake and he never meant to mess up and turn over his privileges as the more mature son."

"But Holmes," Watson remarked, "if my memory is correct, this mourner willingly made such a move."

"Right you are. The mighty hunter returned from a miserable hunting trip in a foul mood. That's when he met his minor brother in the middle of making a mixture of vegetable soup. The marvelous smell moved him to ask for some of this memorable food. It was then that his brother . . ."

"Made his move and managed to make the birthright of the oldest son his instead."

"Correct, Watson. The younger boy marveled that his brother placed so little merit on the myriad spiritual blessings God wanted to give him. Instead, that mournful hunter made light of important things. He dismissed the long-range benefits and made the massive mistake of thinking the meeting of his immediate needs was more important."

"But how do you know it wasn't his brother who is to blame for this monstrous mishap?"

"Elementary, my dear Watson. This was no mere mischievous prank by a young boy nor a minor mistake by a muttering madman. The older brother had the right to give or sell his birthright. He was a moral misfit, despising the things of God. The main motive of his entire life was to simply satisfy his immediate desires. In this particular instance he was hungry and decided that "munch" was the most important thing in his life. He gave in to the temptation of the moment."

"Then what is the right method to master the pressure of momentary temptations?" Watson questioned.

"Meditate over the consequences of your choices before you make them, my friend. Remember that short time results are minor. They disappear quickly. Future benefits are major and well worth working and waiting for."

Your Sunday school teacher has asked you to teach this Sunday. The aim of the lesson is to encourage people to give first place in their lives to the things having eternal value. What will you tell the group?

FIRST PLACE

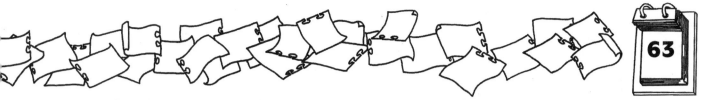

JOSEPH AND HIS BROTHERS

AIM: That your students will recognize that God will be with those who continue to trust in Him through troubled times

SCRIPTURE: Genesis 37:5-36; 40:9-45:11 (Joseph forgives his brothers)

PREPARATION:
1. Photocopy activity sheets—one for each student.
2. Prepare a playing area as described in PRESESSION.

PRESESSION (5-10 minutes)

ACTIVITIES
* Play a game to learn how we trust others

MATERIALS
* Boxes, chairs, books, wastebaskets

PERSPECTIVE (10 minutes)

ACTIVITIES
* Talk about people's troubled times and how God can help us through them

MATERIALS
* Old newspapers

PROBE (20 minutes)

ACTIVITIES
* Take part in a game about Joseph

MATERIALS
* Bibles
* "Troubled Times" Activity Sheet

PERSONALIZE (20 minutes)

ACTIVITIES
* Use a worksheet to find how Jesus can help us in times of trouble

MATERIALS
* "Trust Me!" Activity Sheet
* Old newspapers, a trash bag

PRESESSION

Before class, prepare an obstacle course by choosing an area in the room about six feet wide. Place obstacles such as books, chairs, boxes, and wastebaskets in this area. Don't use anything that might hurt a player.

As students arrive, group them into pairs. One pair will run the course. The other players will form two lines along the course with partners facing each other. One partner stands at one end of the course as guide. The other partner is blindfolded and directed through the obstacles and the people on the sides by the voice of the guide. His/her only help through the obstacles comes from trusting the guide and doing what the guide says.

Optional: If you have a large group you may want to have several courses and groups so everyone has an opportunity to play. Or you can have two guides and players at a time.

PERSPECTIVE

After everyone has had a turn, talk about the experience. How did it feel to be the blindfolded person? How did you, the guide, feel about your partner? How is this like listening to God when we have troubled times?

Sometimes when we are in trouble we think that no one cares or understands. We feel alone and confused. But the truth is that many other people go through the same kinds of problems and feel the same away.

Have the class form small groups of two or three people. Give each team a section of the newspaper and a marker. Teams are to find and tear out articles about people in trouble. They then identify what the trouble is and write it on the front of the article in big letters.

Have the class share their findings with the group, then talk about them. **Is there a common feeling in all these articles?** (Fear, depression, loneliness, misunderstanding.) **What do these people really need?** (The help of God, someone to love and guide them, some good to come out of their problems.) Professionals who help others handle grief and pain of all types find that if the person feels there is a reason for or some good that can come out of their trials, they can bear them much better.

The Bible has a message for all Christians who have troubled times. Check it out in I Peter 1:6-9. What is the message? (Everyone may have to have trials; the trials refine our faith; when we trust God in them, Jesus is praised, glorified, and honored.)

One of Jacob's sons, Joseph, found this was true in his life. Let's see how he managed his problems.

PROBE

Hand out copies of "Troubled Times" activity sheet. Keeping the same teams, have people play this game together for about ten minutes. This activity will give them a general outline of the events in Joseph's life.

Regroup for discussion. Have students follow along in their Bibles as you talk about these things. **People around him were aware that wherever Joseph was, God was there with him. God turned every bad thing that hap-**

pened to Joseph into some good because he continued to trust the Lord.

When Jacob outwardly showed his preference for Joseph, the other brothers became jealous and angry. They kidnapped him, threw him into a dry well and later sold him into slavery. **How do you think Joseph felt about being a slave?** (Sad, angry, bitter.) Joseph's reaction was to serve God and others the best he knew how. His Egyptian master, Potiphar, recognized Joseph's integrity and put him in charge of his household.

Then Potiphar's wife tried to entrap him in sexual misbehavior. Joseph identified this as a sin against God and literally ran away from the temptation. His reward for 11 years of faithful, God-honoring service was to be falsely accused and sent to prison.

A prisoner in an Egyptian jail was considered guilty until proven innocent. He might stay in prison for years before his case came to trial. In many instances, the prisoner was never given his day in court and died in the unbearable conditions of the prison.

What happened to Joseph while he was in prison? (Became an overseer of other prisoners.) Joseph quickly became known for his honest and fair dealings with others. He helped two of the Pharaoh's servants, the baker and cupbearer, to understand some strange dreams. The cupbearer promised that when he was reinstated in his job, he would speak to Pharaoh about Joseph.

When did the cupbearer tell Pharaoh about Joseph? (When the king had the dream, two years later.) After Joseph had helped him, the ungrateful cupbearer forgot all about him. One day Pharaoh was disturbed by a strange dream. Only then did the cupbearer tell him about Joseph's ability to interpret dreams. Joseph was quickly summoned to the throne room where the king asked him to tell the meaning of the dream.

Joseph focused everyone's attention on God. Rather than using the situation to make himself look good, he used it as a powerful witness to God. Pharaoh honored him as second greatest in the land and put him in charge of national plans to prepare for the coming famine.

Then one day, Joseph was face to face with his brothers, the very ones who had hated, kidnapped, and sold him into slavery. He held no bitterness towards them, but couldn't help but wonder if they had changed since last they met. He put them through several tests to find out. To his delight, he discovered that God had indeed changed his brothers and instead of mistreating a favored brother, Benjamin, they offered to give their own lives to protect him.

How did Joseph treat his brothers when he told them who he really was? (He forgave them, provided for them, loved them.) **Joseph shows how God forgives us and lavishes goodness upon us even though we have sinned against Him.**

Check out Genesis 45:6, 7. What did Joseph say about all the hard trials he had gone through? (God was really guiding him all along, God did it to save the lives of his brothers as well as others.)

PERSONALIZE

We can see God's power in these stories about Joseph. Sometimes He used miracles, dreams, or visions to direct His people. Sometimes God allowed events to happen that tested the faith of His followers.

Hand out copies of "Trust Me!" activity sheet. Select someone to read the story aloud. **We don't need miracles, dreams or visions because God guides us through His Word, the Bible.** Have students work on this activity alone, looking up the passages and using them for reference help.

Optional: If you have a shorter class time, work on this exercise as a group, with teams looking up the references and sharing their findings.

What are some principles we can draw from these references? 1) Trust in God because He has never forsaken those who seek Him. 2) As we trust Him we are to pour out our hearts to Him in prayer. 3) When we quit trusting in ourselves and put God first in our lives, He guides us through the problems to good. 4) We must not let ourselves become depressed and turn from God and praising Him. 5) Wait for God to turn the bad things into good.

What would help Todd with his problem? He should remember that God never forsakes people who trust Him. Tell God in prayer all about how he feels and ask Him for help. Put God first in his life and look for His guidance in the Bible. Stop moping and making trouble. Don't take it out on his friends, teachers, or parents. Instead, keep hoping and expecting God to bring good out of the problem.

In times of trouble we need to remember that God is in charge and may be using these problems to bless us and others.

PRAYER/PRAISE

Put the old newspapers where everyone can reach them. Have people crumple a piece of newspaper for the times they've felt alone or depressed in their troubles. Tell them to throw the pieces into the trash bag while saying, "God will help me through these times." When everyone is done, close the bag and put it out of sight.

This shows us how God can remove our sorrow and hurt in times of trouble. We can see how God was with Joseph all the way. God will be with us today if we trust and obey Him.

Troubled Times

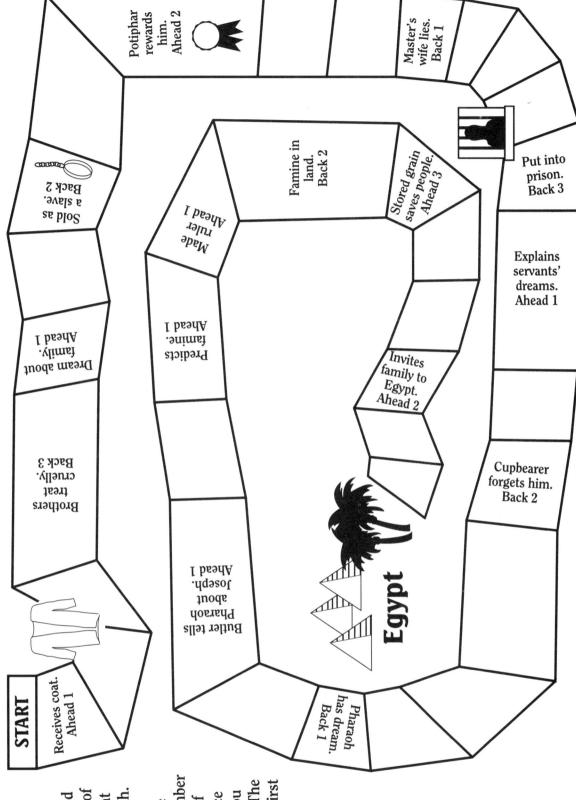

Because Joseph trusted God even when things were not going well, God brought good out of everything bad that happened to Joseph. Two may play this game. Throw a die and move the number of spaces shown. If you land on a space with directions, you must obey them. The player to FINISH first is the winner.

START

Receives coat. Ahead 1

Brothers treat cruelly. Back 3

Dream about family. Ahead 1

Sold as a slave. Back 2

Potiphar rewards him. Ahead 2

Master's wife lies. Back 1

Put into prison. Back 3

Explains servants' dreams. Ahead 1

Cupbearer forgets him. Back 2

Famine in land. Back 2

Stored grain saves people. Ahead 3

Made ruler. Ahead 1

Predicts famine. Ahead 1

Invites family to Egypt. Ahead 2

Butler tells Pharaoh about Joseph. Ahead 1

Pharaoh has dream. Back 1

Egypt

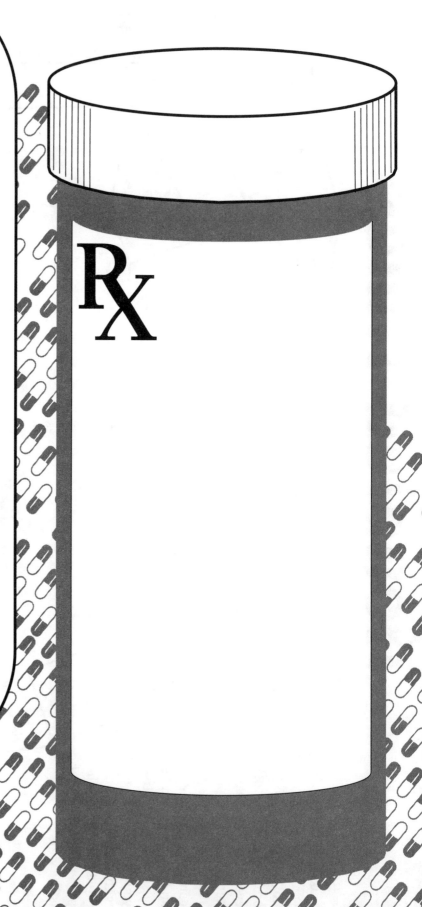

TRUST ME!

Todd got pretty good grades at school and he was getting along well with his teachers. His parents loved him and he loved them. He liked his Sunday school class and the church kids' club. His friends all got along with each other. Then—wham! Todd's dad lost his job. He told Todd, "I'm sorry, but you can't go on the class trip to the amusement park. We just can't afford it right now!"

Todd had been looking forward to the trip for several weeks. He got very upset. He felt that God had failed him so he quit reading his Bible and praying. His grades went down and he got in trouble with the teacher. At home he moped around and was rude to his parents. The Sunday school teacher had to scold him because he misbehaved. Because he was so moody, his friends left him alone.

Use the references to help you write out a prescription that would help Todd with his problem.

Psalm 9:9, 10   Psalm 27:13, 14
Psalm 42:11
Psalm 62:8   Proverbs 3:5, 6

GOD CALLS MOSES

AIM: That your students will observe how God guides, equips, and uses people to meet the needs of others

SCRIPTURE: Genesis 14:13; Exodus 2:5-10; 3:1-10; 4:1-31 (God chooses Moses to lead the people of Israel out of Egypt and keeps His promise to deliver them from bondage and be with them all the way)

PREPARATION:
1. Photocopy activity sheets—one for each student.
2. Prepare a display line and reference cards as described in PERSPECTIVE.

PRESESSION (5-10 minutes)

ACTIVITIES
* Participate in a game to learn how we can help others

MATERIALS
* Small treats such as raisins, crackers, or slices of fresh fruit—3 for each student

PERSPECTIVE (10 minutes)

ACTIVITIES
* Make a display of ways God spoke or guided people in Bible times

MATERIALS
* Bibles
* String or yarn
* Index cards and pencils
* Spring-type clothespins

PROBE (20 minutes)

ACTIVITIES
* Make a "photo" album of Moses

MATERIALS
* Bibles
* "Picture This" Activity Sheet
* Pencils, crayons or markers

PERSONALIZE (15-20 minutes)

ACTIVITIES
* Crack a code to discover ways God guides, enables, and uses us to help others

MATERIALS
* "Is That You, God?" Activity Sheet

PRESESSION

Lay out the treats where they will be available to the group. When students arrive have them join in a game. The purpose of this activity is for each person to eat three treats. But there is a catch. Players are not allowed to speak nor to serve themselves. They can only eat what someone else gives them!

Play briefly, then stop the game for a discussion using questions such as: Was this a hard game? Why or why not? How did it feel to serve others? How did you know if someone needed something? Did each person get to eat all three treats? Why or why not? How did you feel if you got less than that? More?

What do you think would have happened if you had been allowed to speak? (It would have been easy, the game would be over quickly.) **How do you think this game is like God trying to guide people?** (Sometimes you aren't sure of what the needs are, don't understand what God is saying, don't know how to determine if it is God speaking or not.)

God spoke to people in Bible times before His Word was written down. He told them what He wanted them to do and how to meet the needs of others. Let's see how some of these people received God's messages.

PERSPECTIVE

Before class today, hang up a piece of the yarn or string. Students will be hanging index cards on this later. Prepare the references that illustrate how God spoke to people in times past. Write one reference on each index card:

Genesis 3: 8, 9
Genesis 18:1-3; 22
Genesis 21:17, 18
Genesis 28: 10-13
Genesis 41:15, 16; 25
Exodus 3:1-5

Distribute reference cards. Have people look up the passage and write down the method God used to speak. Ask students to share their findings with the group.

Optional: If you have a *large group and/or a small time frame, you may choose to do this activity by having the group form small teams of two or three people.*

When they have shared, they can use a clothespin to hang up the card so everyone can see it. Answers are: face to face in the garden of Eden; as a man, face to face; angel called from heaven; in a dream; ability to interpret dreams; as an angel within a burning bush.

How do you think you would feel if God spoke to you in one of these ways? (Scared, happy, confused, upset.) **We're going to find out about one of these people today. His name was Moses.**

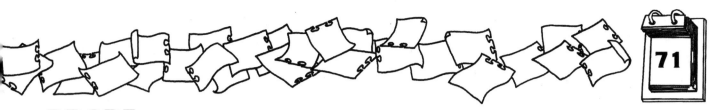

PROBE

Many years passed between the story of Joseph and the story of Moses. Joseph died at the age of 110 years. All his brothers—a whole generation—had also passed away. The children of Israel, living in Egypt since the famine, had greatly increased in numbers and wealth.

A new king now ruled Egypt. This king was not a friend of God's chosen people as the pharaoh of Joseph's time had been. He saw the large Hebrew/Israelite nation and was afraid it might take away his power. The great help that Joseph had been during the famine meant nothing to this ruler. **He decided to destroy the Israelites before they could rebel against him.**

The people were forced to become slaves. Have the group take turns reading Exodus 1:11-15 aloud. **What kind of work did the Israelites have to do?** (Make bricks and work in the fields.) Straw or grass was mixed with mud from the Nile River and then placed in molds until the bricks dried in the sun.

Cruel taskmasters beat the Hebrew people and made them work harder and faster. Frequent beatings were given to destroy their spirits. Taskmasters also had orders to kill as many slaves as necessary to keep their numbers down. **But no matter how hard the Hebrews had to work, they continued to prosper because God was with them.**

What did the fearful Pharaoh order the Hebrews to do next? Ask someone to read 1:22 aloud. (Throw all boy babies into the Nile.) **One Israelite mother, Jochebed, refused to do this.** She hid her little son for three months. When it became too difficult to hide the baby, Jochebed made a plan.

Check out Exodus 2:3 and find out what she did. (Made a waterproof basket for him and put it among the reeds on the bank of the river.) This miniature boat was woven from the tall, hollow reeds that grew along the river. It was waterproofed with natural tar, such as our asphalt. Jochebed lovingly hid the basket in the river bulrushes which grew from ten to fifteen feet high.

Who stayed on the bank, watching the basket? Ask someone to read Exodus 2:4 aloud. (Miriam, the baby's older sister.) **Why do you think she stayed?** (To watch over the baby, protect him, curiosity.) Have the group look over Exodus 2:5-10. **What happened next?** (An Egyptian princess found the basket and decided to keep him for herself.)

The princess realized the baby was facing death. She met his need by adopting him. Miriam, too, was quick to respond to the situation and used the opportunity to reunite her family legally.

What happened when Moses was older? (He went to live at the palace as an Egyptian prince.) There Moses received exactly the education he would need to help the Israelites later on. He learned the Egyptian codes of law, ritual, and standards of morality.

Even though Moses was surrounded by the riches of Egypt he didn't forget his own people. One day he saw an Egyptian beating an Israelite slave. Enraged, Moses beat the taskmaster to death and buried his body in the sand.

When Pharaoh found out about this deed, Moses ran away to the land of Midian in fear for his life. In Midian he got a job as a shepherd and married Zipporah, a daughter of Jethro, the man who hired him. They had two sons. **Moses might have felt he could never serve God now, but God had special plans for him.** The experiences he had as a shepherd in the wilderness prepared him to lead this group of Israelite nomads through the wilderness to safety.

Have the class turn to Exodus 3:1-10 and follow along. **What happened to the Israelites while Moses was in Midian?** (They cried out to God for help.) **How did God respond to their need?** (He called Moses to lead them out of slavery in Egypt to a good land.) **How did God get Moses' attention?** (Made a bush to be on fire without burning up.)

How do you think Moses felt about God's call? (Afraid, unsure, unable to do it.) God knew Moses was afraid, so He gave him three miraculous signs to prove that he was God's chosen leader. Moses was still hesitant. **What promise did God give him in Exodus 4:12-16?** (Would go with him, help him speak, teach what to say.) God even sent Moses his own loving brother to help him.

Check out Exodus 4:29-31. How did the suffering Israelites respond to Moses and **Aaron?** (Believed them.) **What did they do when they found God was concerned about them?** (Bowed down and worshiped Him.)

Distribute "Picture This" activity sheet. Let people complete this activity.

Optional: If your time is short, have people work in teams with each group doing only one or two pictures.

PERSONALIZE

(15-20 minutes)

Briefly review how God worked through Jochebed, Miriam, the Egyptian princess, Jethro, Moses, and Aaron to help meet the needs of others. **God works through people today as He did in Bible times. He wants to work through you today, too! Here are some ways He can do that.**

Hand out "Is That You, God?" activity sheets. Let someone read the directions aloud. Allow about half the time period to complete this activity. Go over the answers together.

Today we don't have to depend on miracles or dreams for guidance from the Lord. How does He guide us today? (Reading the Bible, situations, needs of others.) Sometimes a Scripture passage speaks directly to us as though God were talking face to face with us. The situations we are in provide us with opportunities to tell others about Jesus. Advice from wise Christians often shows us the needs of others and leads us to help them.

God's Holy Spirit, who lives in us when we follow Jesus, is our biggest help. What are some others? (Education and experiences.) Simple experiences of the past can also help prepare us for greater tasks in the future.

How can God work through us today? (In Sunday school, church building, grounds, our families, the elderly, shut in, sick, poor, lonely, and those in foreign countries.)

Look over this list. Is there some area where you need to be more attentive to hear God's leading? Do you need to use your education and experiences more? Do you let God work through you to help others in these ways?

PRAYER/PRAISE

Close with prayer, thanking God for His guidance. Ask Him to help you be more obedient so He can work through you to meet the needs of others.

PICTURE THIS

Make a "photo album" by drawing important events in the life of Moses. You can use simple stick figures if you prefer. The first picture is done for you.

MY BABY BROTHER, MOSES

THE PRINCESS FINDS MOSES

MY BROTHER, THE PRINCE

MOSES LEAVES EGYPT

MOSES AND HIS FAMILY IN MIDIAN

MOSES AND THE BURNING BUSH

MOSES AND I GET READY FOR PHARAOH

THE PEOPLE BELIEVE US AND WORSHIP GOD

IS THAT YOU, GOD?

Use this calculator code to discover ways God presently guides, enables, and uses us to help others.

GOD GUIDES US
when we read the $\overline{}\ \overline{1}\ \overline{8}\ \overline{1}\ \overline{}\ \overline{4}$,

$\overline{=}\ \overline{8}\ \overline{OFF}\ \overline{+}\ \overline{0}\ \overline{OFF}\ \overline{8}\ \overline{\sqrt{}}\ \overline{\div}\ \overline{=}$,

and the $\overline{0}\ \overline{3}\ \overline{ON}\ \overline{8}\ \overline{2}\ \overline{4}$ of

$\overline{MC}\ \overline{8}\ \overline{}\ \overline{4}$ Christians.

He enables us through the Holy Spirit and our

$\overline{4}\ \overline{3}\ \overline{+}\ \overline{2}\ \overline{0}\ \overline{OFF}\ \overline{8}\ \overline{\sqrt{}}\ \overline{\div}\ \overline{}$ and

$\overline{4}\ \overline{MR}\ \overline{\%}\ \overline{4}\ \overline{.}\ \overline{8}\ \overline{4}\ \overline{\div}\ \overline{2}\ \overline{4}\ \overline{=}$.

He can use us today to help others

in $\overline{}\ \overline{=}\ \overline{+}\ \overline{\div}\ \overline{3}\ \overline{0}\ \overline{M-}\ \overline{}\ \overline{=}\ \overline{2}\ \overline{7}\ \overline{\sqrt{}}\ \overline{\sqrt{}}\ \overline{-}$,

working around the $\overline{2}\ \overline{7}\ \overline{+}\ \overline{.}\ \overline{2}\ \overline{7}$ building and

$\overline{6}\ \overline{.}\ \overline{\sqrt{}}\ \overline{+}\ \overline{+}\ \overline{3}\ \overline{=}$, in $\overline{\sqrt{}}\ \overline{+}\ \overline{.}$

$\overline{5}\ \overline{0}\ \overline{X}\ \overline{8}\ \overline{-}\ \overline{8}\ \overline{4}\ \overline{=}$, with those who are

$\overline{4}\ \overline{-}\ \overline{3}\ \overline{4}\ \overline{.}\ \overline{-}\ \overline{M-}$ and $\overline{=}\ \overline{7}\ \overline{+}\ \overline{OFF}\ \overline{8}\ \overline{\div}$,

$\overline{=}\ \overline{8}\ \overline{2}\ \overline{9}$ people and those who are $\overline{\%}\ \overline{\sqrt{}}\ \overline{\sqrt{}}\ \overline{.}$,

strangers who may be $\overline{-}\ \overline{\sqrt{}}\ \overline{\div}\ \overline{4}\ \overline{-}\ \overline{M-}$, and those in

$\overline{5}\ \overline{\sqrt{}}\ \overline{.}\ \overline{4}\ \overline{8}\ \overline{6}\ \overline{\div}$ countries.

ESCAPE FROM EGYPT

AIM: That your students will show appreciation for leaders who have great faith in God

SCRIPTURE: Exodus 5:1-14:29 (Moses' faith in God's power as he leads God's people)

PREPARATION:
1. Photocopy activity sheets—one for each student.
2. Before class prepare the science oddity as described in PERSPECTIVE.

PRESESSION (5-10 minutes)

ACTIVITIES
* Choose an "all-star" team of people with great faith in God

MATERIALS
* Bibles
* Chalkboard or large piece of paper and a marker

PERSPECTIVE (10 minutes)

ACTIVITIES
* Expose a "magic" trick to reveal its true identity

MATERIALS
* Sheet of old newspaper
* Scissors and tape

PROBE (20 minutes)

ACTIVITIES
* Use an activity sheet to learn more about the way God helped the Israelites out of Egypt

MATERIALS
* Bibles
* "Faith—Can't Leave Egypt Without It" Activity Sheet

PERSONALIZE (15-20 minutes)

ACTIVITIES
* Show appreciation to leaders who have exhibited faith in God

MATERIALS
* "Acts of Faith" Activity Sheet
* Scissors, pencils, markers

PRESESSION

(5-10 minutes)

Before class, write the following on the chalk-board or a large sheet of paper. "God has asked you to manage an "All-Star" team of people who had great faith in Him. Who will you choose to be on your team?"

As people arrive, have them turn to Hebrews 11 in their Bibles and find names of possible candidates for this team. Write these names on the chalkboard or a large sheet of paper as the group gives them to you. Some examples are: Abel;

Enoch; Noah; Abraham; Isaac; Joseph; Moses; Gideon; Barak; Samson; Jephthah; David; Samuel.

Optional: If you have a longer class schedule, let the group help you identify some of the ways these Bible people demonstrated their faith in God.

We have already learned about many of the people mentioned in Hebrews 11. Today we're going to see how Moses had faith in God's power as he led God's people out of slavery.

PERSPECTIVE

(10 minutes)

Before class prepare the science oddity for a demonstration of "magic." Cut a two-inch wide strip the length of the newspaper. Turn over one end of this strip. Tape the ends together to form a loop. Lay it aside for use later in the lesson.

Belief in magic had a very strong grip on people during the time period that Moses set out to follow God's command and free the Israelites. **When Moses and Aaron went to speak to Pharaoh about releasing the Israelites from slavery, God enabled them to do great miracles to prove His power. But the Egyptian magicians were able to use evil powers to duplicate some of these first miracles and fool the people.**

With the present day emphasis on the occult, it is wise to help your students identify the differences between genuine demonstrations of God's power and false displays of mere illusionists or evil magicians. **Do you think I could fool you with a trick today?** Students will probably think they are too smart for this.

Let me show you a "magic" trick. I can cut this strip of paper down the middle and still have it remain in one piece. Gather them around so they can easily see what you are doing. Take the newspaper strip you prepared before class.

Cut it lengthwise down the center. Hold it up for all to see. Instead of having two pieces, you will have one piece which is twice as long as the first strip!

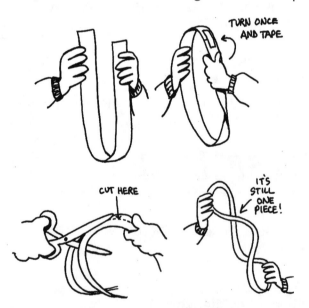

TURN ONCE AND TAPE

CUT HERE

IT'S STILL ONE PIECE!

Do you think this is magic? (Yes, no, don't know.) What you have done is to make a topological oddity known as a Möbius strip. There is nothing at all magical about this science curiosity. But it might be used to trick some naive person who believed in magic.

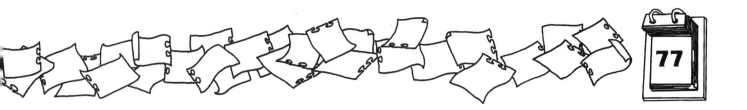

Although the evil Egyptian magicians in Pharaoh's court were able to trick people with some easy illusions, they were helpless and suffered along with the other Egyptians **when God put His power to work freeing His people to worship Him.** If the magicians had been as powerful as God, they would have reversed the plagues, not added to them.

PROBE

What did God say to Moses about speaking to Pharaoh? Have someone look up Exodus 6:1 and read it aloud. (He would do great things to make Pharaoh do His will.) Have the group find Exodus 7 and follow along in their Bibles.

To convince Pharaoh that God had sent them and meant business they showed him a miracle. What was it? (Aaron's rod became a snake.) The court magicians did some kind of illusion to make their rods look like snakes, but Aaron's snake swallowed up these snakes and then turned back into a stick.

How do you think Pharaoh felt about that? (Angry, curious, it was unimportant.) **The time had come for the miracles that God had warned would come to the Egyptians if they did not free the Israelites.**

Distribute copies of "Faith—Can't Leave Egypt Without It!" activity sheet. Divide the group into small teams to work on this exercise.

The Egyptians worshiped many false gods. These idols looked like animals, things, or part of nature. During the time the Israelites had been in Egypt some of them had also begun to worship these idols. The one, true, living God designed each of the plagues to show the people how lifeless and helpless their gods and goddesses were. Thus God dealt with the god of the Nile, Hapi; the frog god; Hathor, the cow god of Isis; Hathor, the cow goddess; and Amon-Ra, the god of the sun.

Discuss their results of the activity sheet. **How did Pharaoh react to the various plagues?** Over and over, God gave this stubborn, self-cen-

tered man an opportunity to repent and worship Him as the one, true god. But Pharaoh freely chose to continually resist God until at last God let him have his own way.

How do you think the Egyptians felt about them? (Afraid, helpless, wondered what kind of a god this Israelite God was.) Pharaoh's sinful rejection of God affected a whole nation. Whenever we sin, it always affects others, not just ourselves. **How do you think Moses felt about these demonstrations of God's power?** (Awestruck, thrilled, humble, realized how great God really was.)

At last the time to go came. People hurriedly gathered their possessions and were on their way. The people of Egypt wanted the Hebrews to leave quickly. They gave them gifts of jewelry and other possessions and hastened them along.

God went with the people. Check out Exodus 13:21, 22 to see how He showed them the way. (With a pillar of cloud by day and pillar of fire by night.) Have the group follow through Exodus 14 in their Bibles. **What did Pharaoh do after the Hebrews left?** (Changed his mind; pursued them with soldiers and 600 chariots.) **How do you think this made the Israelites feel?** (Scared; terrified.)

Moses assured the people that God would fight for them. What do you think made him so confident of that? Each step of obedience Moses had taken helped strengthen his "faith muscles." By the time Pharaoh at last released the Israelites, Moses had faith enough to lead

that vast number of people (perhaps two million) out of Egypt, headed for God's promised land. He knew he was obeying an all-powerful and trustworthy God.

Moses did as God directed him and stretched his rod over the Red Sea. Check out Exodus 14:21, 22. What happened next? (Strong wind helped the water divide and stand up like a wall on either side of dry ground.) The pillar of cloud and fire moved behind the Israelites, surrounding the Egyptians with darkness and giving the Israelites light to move. **The people of God moved across while the Egyptians remained. When His people were safe on the other side, God set about His plan to eliminate the Egyptian enemy. What did He do?** (Confused them; swept them into the sea.)

How do you think the Israelites felt about God and Moses then? Most of the next chapter of Exodus contains the beautiful song of triumph and praise to God that Moses and Miriam led the Israelites in singing. **The people were thankful that God had sent them a faithful leader like Moses.**

PERSONALIZE

(15-20 minutes)

Today God sends us faithful leaders who also have great faith in God. Who are some leaders who have helped you? While most people will be quick to mention the preacher, youth director, or Sunday school teacher, be sure to remind them of others who are sometimes forgotten. Godly grandparents or parents, other family members, friends, and acquaintances.

It has been estimated that as many as 20 Christians may be instrumental in the decision of just one person to follow Jesus. These people are important links in a chain that helps us to place our faith in God.

What are some ways you might show your appreciation to these people? (Tell them, write a note, call them, make something nice for them, help them with some chore.) Hand out copies of "Acts of Faith" activity sheet. Students can work on this individually. Encourage the group to be specific about their appreciation.

Optional: If you want to plan something special for these leaders of faith, you might think about having a coffee time or a lunch in their honor. Students could help with invitations, decorations, and food items.

PRAYER/PRAISE

Sing a verse of "Faith of our Fathers" in closing today. Encourage students to give their appreciation cards to others.

FAITH—CAN'T LEAVE EGYPT WITHOUT IT!

I carry a badge. My name is Thursday, Joe Thursday. I'm a cop. It's my job to make sure that people who want to do what's right can do it. You know what I mean. People who have faith in God and want to be free to worship Him—Israelites. Sometimes they are prevented from doing so by arch criminals. You know the type. Kings who have great power, wealth, and soldiers. Come along with me and see how God sent plagues to free His people. Look up the references and check out the miracles. The first one is done for you. Remember what to list—the facts, just the facts!

REFERENCE	PLAGUE	PHARAOH'S REACTION
Exodus 7:14–24	Blood	Evil magicians duplicate it through trickery so Pharaoh is unmoved
Exodus 8:1–15		
Exodus 8:16–19		
Exodus 8:20–32		
Exodus 9:1–7		
Exodus 9:8–12		
Exodus 9:13–35		
Exodus 10:1–20		
Exodus 10:21–29		
Exodus 11:1–12:33		

ACTS OF FAITH

God has given you leaders who have great faith in Him. What can you do so they will know you are glad for their examples of faith? Make gift tags and give them to these people. In the space beside "To" write a name. Write something you can do to show your appreciation to that person. Sign your name at the bottom of the tag.

To: _____
I can show my appreciation by:
_____
_____
_____
_____
_____
_____

To: _____
I can show my appreciation by:
_____
_____
_____
_____
_____
_____

To: _____
I can show my appreciation by:
_____
_____
_____
_____
_____
_____

To: _____
I can show my appreciation by:
_____
_____
_____
_____
_____
_____

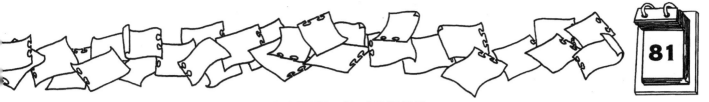

GOD GIVES THE LAW

AIM: That your students will appreciate and obey the commands that God has given

SCRIPTURE: Exodus 20:1-17 (History and meaning of the laws that God gave His people)

PREPARATION:
1. Photocopy activity sheets—one for each student.

PRESESSION (5-10 minutes)

ACTIVITIES
* Talk about why we have rules

PERSPECTIVE (10 minutes)

ACTIVITIES
* Play a game to learn more about rules

PROBE (20 minutes)

ACTIVITIES
* Read a skit to discover how the Ten Commandments affect us today

MATERIALS
* "God's Blueprint For Living" Activity Sheets

PERSONALIZE (15-20 minutes)

ACTIVITIES
* Develop a set of rules for this class

MATERIALS
* Paper, pencils
* Chalkboard or large sheet of paper, marker

PRESESSION

(5-10 minutes)

Before class time, write this question on the chalkboard or a large sheet of paper: "Why do we have rules?" As the group gathers, involve newcomers in a discussion on using some of these supporting questions. What is a rule? (The dictionary defines it as "an authoritative regulation for action or conduct.")

In what situations do we have rules? What can rules do for you? What can't they do? Are rules the same as warnings? Why or why not?

When we play games we use rules. But suppose you didn't know what the rules were and had to discover them by yourself?

PERSPECTIVE

(10 minutes)

Have students sit in a circle on the floor. One person is chosen to be "IT" and leaves the room. The rest of the group chooses a rule to use while answering questions. Examples are: Players must put their hands on their knees before answering; all girls laugh before answering and all boys cough before answering.

Ask "IT" to come back. S/he must discover the rule by asking people questions about themselves. If "IT" takes too long, people can help by intensifying the rule response.

Stop play when "IT" finds out the rule or in time to briefly talk about the game. "IT", was it hard for you to discover the rule? Why or why not? How did it feel to be the only one who didn't know the rule? How did the rest of you feel

about "IT"? Did you try hard to help him/her discover it?

How do you think you'd feel if you lived when there were no rules? (Happy, relieved, afraid.) **What do you think would happen if someone stole something from you?** (Nothing; don't know.)

When people were abused or robbed, there were no laws to help them. That was when the first rules were made. In Egypt, the king was almost a god. His word was the law and no one, not even the king himself, could cancel his law.

God set up some basic rules, the Ten Commandments, and gave them to His people to help protect individuals and insure them of their rights.

PROBE

(20 minutes)

For about two months, after Pharaoh let the people of Israel leave Egypt, they traveled through a lonely wilderness. During this time they suffered many hardships. Again and again God showed His loving care for His people. He gave them food and water. He led them with a pillar of cloud by day and a pillar of fire at night.

They arrived at the foot of a great mountain called Sinai. God told Moses to order His people to pitch their tents. Then the Israelites were told to wash themselves and their clothing. **"Be ready on the third day,"** Moses told the people. **"On that day the Lord will come down . . . in the sight of all the people."**

God's Blueprint for Living

BEN: Oh no! Why are we studying the Ten Commandments today? They're just for Bible time people, aren't they? We don't have to follow them today.

DARCY: Wrong! It might surprise you to learn that Jesus repeated nine of the Ten Commandments in His teachings. They're still good rules for life today. The first four commandments tell us how we should treat God. And . . .

BEN: And?

DARCY: And the next six tell us how to treat people. Listen and you'll find out.

READER: "You shall have no other gods before me."

BEN: What does that mean?

DARCY: It means that nothing should be more important than God. You should trust Him only.

READER: "You shall not make for yourself an idol."

BEN: I'm safe there because I've never made any wooden or stone statue or bowed down to one.

DARCY: Silly, it doesn't mean only statues. Other things can become idols or gods too.

BEN: Such as?

DARCY: Popularity, money, sports, fun. When things begin to take up too much time in our lives, then they can grow into idols. God should have first place in our lives.

READER: "You shall not misuse the name of the Lord your God."

BEN: I think I know what that means. It's not using God's name for swearing or in a joke.

DARCY: The way we use God's name shows how we really feel about Him, so . . .

BEN: So we should use it respectfully to praise or worship Him.

READER: "Remember the Sabbath day by keeping it holy."

BEN: Does that mean I should go to Sunday school and church and then just sit around and read the Bible all day?

DARCY: You couldn't sit still that long! It means that we should give God special honor and time on that day.

BEN: I get it. That's why it's a day of rest, so we don't have to hurry back to work or school but can take time to really get to know and appreciate God more.

READER: "Honor your father and your mother."

BEN: Don't tell me—I need to obey my parents and respect them.

DARCY: Exactly! God chose them to be the leaders of the family. There's only one thing we need to be careful about.

BEN: What's that?

DARCY: We shouldn't follow them in acts of disobedience.

READER: "You shall not murder."

BEN: Wow! That would be like making yourself God and deciding when someone else's life should end.

DARCY: Murder is a terrible sin. Human life is a gift from God and we should protect it.

READER: "You shall not commit adultery."

BEN: Married people should be true to each other, right?

DARCY: They should never become involved with someone else's husband or wife.

READER: "You shall not steal."

BEN: Don't take what belongs to others. Got it?

DARCY: Now you're catching on.

READER: "You shall not give false testimony against your neighbor."

BEN: That's about lying. One lie only leads to more lying. We should only speak the truth.

DARCY: Lying is trying to fool someone. It includes leaving something out of what we say—like half-truths or twisting the facts. When we tell the truth, people can trust and respect us.

READER: "You shall not covet anything that belongs to your neighbor."

BEN: Oh, oh! Does that include his video game or success?

DARCY: Coveting is another word for envying. It means not being content with what we have.

BEN: In other words, if you resent the fact that he has something you don't have, you're really telling God that He isn't supplying all your needs. Then you could get bitter and become greedy for what other people have.

DARCY: Yes. Maybe you covet his success because you don't feel appreciated by others. The best way to conquer that feeling isn't through envy, but by asking God to help you discover the good things about yourself. God can help you be satisfied with what you are and have.

BEN: You know, Darcy, this lesson wasn't bad at all. These laws are really pretty practical stuff. I'll try to pay more attention and use them as a guideline every day.

DARCY: Good for you, Ben! The Ten Commandments were given to protect the needs of each person in a responsible way. They are God's blueprint for living.

The many thousands of people in the camping area around the mountain were filled with excitement! God was going to come near them! The people bathed and washed their clothing to be ready for this wonderful event. Time passed quickly. On the morning of the third day, smoke poured from Mount Sinai. Thunder roared. A trumpet sounded. The mountain trembled.

Down below, Moses and the people watched breathlessly. It was a great occasion! Suddenly the voice of the Lord was heard. He called Moses to come up into the mountain. **On Mount Sinai, God gave Moses His rules for the Israelites. These rules are the Ten Commandments.**

Distribute copies of "God's Blueprint For Living" activity sheets. This exercise will help your students understand the meaning of the Ten Commandments as they apply to kids today. You will need three good readers to take the parts of the Reader, Ben, and Darcy. Have them read the skit aloud while the rest of the group follows along on the activity sheets.

What did the skit call the Ten Commandments? (God's blueprint for living.) **What do you think the world would be like if God hadn't given us laws for living?** (Terrible, confusing, disorderly, strong people would take everything for themselves.) In many parts of our world neighborhood, people have to live in that kind of situation daily. It is a life of the weak being preyed upon by the strong, with no recourse for help for the victims. **We can thank our heavenly Father for His wisdom and love in giving us these guidelines.**

Into what two groups may the Ten Commandments be divided? (First four are about how we should treat God. The last six are about how we should treat others.)

In the play, Ben and Darcy talked about how important God is and that you should trust only Him. What are some other things that people trust in? (Armies, weapons, money, fame, athletic ability, beauty.) **Why can't we trust in these things?** (They all fail, not lasting, change too easily.) Stock market ups and downs,

accidents which mar beautiful or athletic individuals, wars, and suicides of famous people show us that these things are certainly not stable enough to trust.

What guideline can we use to find out if something is becoming an idol to us? (How much time it takes up in our lives.) **What might be included in this list?** (Video games, TV, sports, "hanging out" at malls, gangs.) **Who should have first place in our lives?** (God.)

How should we use God's name? (With respect, to praise and/or worship Him, tell others about Him.) **What do we reveal when we use God's name?** (How we really feel about Him.)

You may have been wondering which commandment Jesus did not ask us to follow. It is the fourth commandment that says "Remember the Sabbath day by keeping it holy." The Israelites worshiped God on the seventh day of the week. Jesus Christ arose from the dead on the <u>first</u> day of the week. The early Christians, guided by the Holy Spirit, worshiped on the first day from then on. Sunday, the first day of the week, became known as the Lord's Day.

Why should we honor our parents? (Because God chose them to be the leaders of the family.)

If stealing is taking what belongs to others, what do people steal? Point out to the group that besides the regular things they name, this includes such things as shoplifting, cheating on income taxes, and goofing off on a job (stealing time from your boss).

What happens when we lie? (We cheat people out of the whole truth, try to fool them, tell only part of the story.) **Do you think we should repeat unkind things we hear about others? Why or why not?** (No. It hurts them, could only be gossip and not be true.)

What is the difference between wanting something and coveting it? (When you start to covet it, it means you resent the fact that the person has something you don't.) You may become bitter, angry with God, try to get it the wrong way.

How can we stop envying others? (Ask God to help us be satisfied with what we have.)

All the laws in our law books today are based on the rules for living that God gave in His Commandments. When lawyers are working on a case, they use these books to guide them in understanding our many laws. Today you are going to use the Ten Commandments to help you write some laws for this group.

PERSONALIZE

(15-20 minutes)

Divide the group into small teams of two to three people. Have teams think about the Ten Commandments and use them as the basis to brainstorm rules for the class. They should be as specific as possible. This should also include reasons <u>why</u> the rule should be kept. One person in each team should write down these rules and consequences.

Let teams move around the room so they are in groups and can think without being disturbed by others.

An example of these rules might be: Students should not annoy others. That is stealing their attention from the teacher and God's Holy Spirit.

Have people regroup and share their ideas with everyone. Remember that in this activity the "why?" is as important as the rule. Rules that are made simply as laws are not helpful.

List ideas on the chalkboard or a large sheet of paper. When the group has decided on which rules it wants to adopt, write them up. Make a copy of them for each student to keep as well as one copy that can be posted in the room.

Optional: If you have a copier, you may be able to do this in time to send the rules home with students. If not, hand them out in class next week.

PRAYER/PRAISE
Read the Ten Commandments in unison. **Always remember that these rules were given to help us lead happier lives by protecting the needs of each individual.**

Optional: Encourage people to memorize the Ten Commandments and know that they are found in Exodus 20.

CONQUERING THE LAND

AIM: That your students will understand that God wants us to promise to serve Him and to keep our promises to Him and others

SCRIPTURE: Joshua 1:6-9; 6:1-5, 20; 22:23 (God helps His people conquer the land He had promised to them)

PREPARATION:
1. Photocopy activity sheets—one for each student.

PRESESSION (5-10 minutes)

ACTIVITIES
* Participate in an object lesson to illustrate how God's help makes the impossible possible

MATERIALS
* Sheet of paper, dime, quarter, scissors

PERSPECTIVE (10 minutes)

ACTIVITIES
* Talk about the background history leading up to the Israelites' conquest of Canaan

MATERIALS
* Bibles
*Optional: Chalkboard or large sheet of paper and marker
*Optional: Atlas or map of Bible lands during time of Moses and Joshua

PROBE (20 minutes)

ACTIVITIES
* Discover some of the conditional promises God and the Israelites made to each other and to Rahab

MATERIALS
* Bibles
* "Promises, Promises!" Activity Sheet

PERSONALIZE (15-20 minutes)

ACTIVITIES
* Work in small groups to brainstorm and role play endings to some promises

MATERIALS
* "I Promise" Activity Sheet

PRESESSION

(5-10 minutes)

Use an object lesson to help your students better understand that with God impossible things are possible. Cut a dime-size hole in a piece of paper. Let people try to slip the quarter through the hole without tearing the paper.

After everyone has had an opportunity, show them the secret. Fold the paper in half. Put the quarter in the fold and bend the paper up as you hold it by the outer edges of the fold. With a little

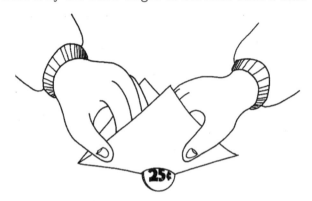

direction, the quarter slips through the dime-size hole. What's the secret? You have changed a two-dimensional shape into a three-dimensional one.

Guide the conversation: How did you feel about trying to get the quarter through the hole? Is this like some of your problems? In what way? How do you think I knew what to do in order to make the trick work? What did you think when you saw the quarter could slip through the hole? How is this like what God's help can do for you and your problems?

This deed looked impossible, but when I obeyed the instructions for doing it, the impossible became easy. Sometimes it seems impossible to solve problems we face. But when we follow God's directions, we find solutions are possible after all. That's a truth the Israelites learned as they followed God out of Egypt and into the land He promised them.

PERSPECTIVE

(10 minutes)

Briefly outline the background history, from the giving of the Ten Commandments up to going into Canaan.
1) God's people were led to Mount Sinai where God gave them laws to live by.
2) While Moses was up on the mountain talking with God, the people brought their gold jewelry which was melted. From the melted gold metal, Aaron, Moses' brother, made a golden calf. The people worshiped this idol instead of God. They were punished.
3) God gave them directions for building the tabernacle, for worship. It could be carried along as the Israelites journeyed through the wilderness.
4) Near the land of Canaan, twelve spies were sent to search the area and bring back a report. Only two men, Joshua and Caleb, had faith that

God would keep His promise and help them conquer the people.
5) Because the Israelites believed the other ten spies, the whole nation was punished by having to spend forty years in the wilderness.
6) Moses died and Joshua was chosen as leader. He had helped Moses for a long time, and he believed that God would lead the Israelites safely into the land He had promised them.

Optional: You may want to outline these points on the chalkboard or a large sheet of paper.

Optional: A Bible atlas or map would be helpful in giving a geographical picture of the places mentioned.

Just before the people entered the land of Canaan, God repeated to Joshua and the people the promise He had given to Moses. **What did**

God promise them? Have the group read aloud Joshua 1:1-4. (He assured the Israelites that He would guide them and give the land to them.) Although circumstances had changed, God had not changed. If the people worshiped and obeyed Him, He would keep His promise to them.

Many of God's promises are conditional.

Do you know what that means? Let students try to define this. A conditional promise means that the fulfillment of the promise depends on meeting a requirement. IF the Israelites would worship and obey only God, then HE WOULD give them the land. **God wants us to promise to serve Him and to keep our promises to Him and others.**

PROBE

(20 minutes)

Hand out "Promises, Promises!" activity sheet. You can fill in the blanks together. **God also gave Joshua a special promise.** Have someone read Joshua 1:7 aloud. **What was God's promise to Joshua?** (He would be successful wherever he went.) **What did Joshua have to do?** (Be strong and courageous, obey all God's law that Moses gave the people.)

Success for us today is gained in the same way as it was in the days of Joshua. We must obey God. The Israelites had God's law written on stone tablets. How do we know what God's laws are today? (Read them in the Bible.) We may not be able to see very far into the future, but when we obey God a step at a time, He blesses our way and assures us success in carrying out His purposes.

At last the Israelites arrived at the borders of the promised land. They sent two spies to look over the city of Jericho, the first city the Israelites would have to take. What did these spies discover?

Have students take turns reading aloud the story of Rahab and the spies from Joshua 2:1-13. It is generally agreed that the word used to describe Rahab as a prostitute can also mean "innkeeper." As an innkeeper with a house built into the city wall, Rahab was an ideal source of information to the Israelites.

Because God had already been working in her heart, Rahab willingly gave the spies the information they needed and protected them from the authorities of Jericho. **What did the spies promise her?** Have Joshua 2:14, 17, and 18 read aloud. (They would treat her kindly and faithfully, save all her family.)

What did Rahab need to do in order to receive that promise? (Not tell the authorities what the spies were doing, hang the scarlet cord out of the window of her house, keep everyone of her family in the house.) Because the Israelites didn't know her family, keeping them all in Rahab's house, identified by the scarlet cord, seemed the best way to insure their safety. Later, Joshua told the spies to keep their promise. Rahab and all her family were removed from the battle and kept safe near the Israelite camp.

What did God promise Joshua and the Israelites about Jericho? Have someone read aloud Joshua 6:2-5. (He would give them the city.) Jericho was a symbol of the impossible problem. It was encircled by two parallel walls. The outer wall was about 25-30 feet high and about six feet thick. The inner wall, about 12 feet away, was about 12 feet thick.

What did the people have to do in return? (Carry out God's orders completely.) And such strange orders they were! The situation must have looked utterly impossible. Imagine the skepticism the inhabitants of Jericho must have had as they watched these utterly silent people, led by priests and musicians instead of soldiers, as they marched around their city!

But God knew how to make them fear Him and

His people. After six days, their hearts must have begun to beat in rhythm to the feet of the people outside their walls.

On the seventh day, they marched around Jericho seven times. Then at last everyone shouted. The impossible happened. The walls fell down flat. The Israelites victoriously marched in and completely annihilated their enemies. They had obeyed God and He had kept His promise!

Other battles followed, but the Israelites were victorious because the Lord was on their side. What happened next? Have someone read Joshua 11:23 aloud. (Joshua took the land, it was divided among the tribes.) Only the Levites did not receive an inheritance of a section of land. As God's special helpers, they were given cities scattered throughout the whole territory.

Before Joshua died, he reminded the Israelites how the Lord had been with them, keeping His promises. He told them to keep God's law and warned them what would happen if they worshiped the false gods of the surrounding nations .

PERSONALIZE

(15-20 minutes)

God always keeps His promises to us if we believe and obey Him. When we give our word to the Lord or others that we will do something, we should also keep our promises.

Distribute copies of "I Promise" activity sheet. Divide the group into three small teams. Assign one promise to each team. Let them work on possible endings and be prepared to role play them for the entire class. Talk about their choices. Were they good or bad? Explain your answer.

Optional: If you have a large class, you may have more than three groups. In that case you *may want to have more than one group take each problem.*

God's Word tells us we have to make a choice. What is it? Have someone read Joshua 24:14, 15 aloud. (Choose to serve God or false idols.) **How we live shows people how much we really want to serve God. When we trust the Lord fully and obey each commandment He shows us, then He will keep His promises to us.**

PRAYER/PRAISE

Close by singing a verse or two of "Trust and Obey."

Promises, Promises!

_____ , if you _____

_____

then I promise _____

_____

_____ .

(Joshua 1:7)

_____ , if you _____

_____

then we promise _____

_____ .

(Joshua 2:14, 17, 18)

_____ , if you and the people _____

_____

_____

_____

_____

_____

then I promise _____

_____

_____

_____

_____

_____ .

(Joshua 6:2-5)

14A

I Promise

God wants us to keep our promises to Him and to others.
Read the story, then brainstorm and role play an ending.

PROMISE #1: Jyl promised her little sister, Amanda, that she would take her to the zoo on Saturday. Later, Jyl was invited to a party on Saturday.

ENDING:

"Amanda," Jyl said, "I . . .

PROMISE #2: Brian promised his teacher, Mrs. Carson, he would tell Kyle the class missed him last Sunday morning. Brian put it off until it was too late on Saturday night to call Kyle.

ENDING:

"Mrs. Carson," Brian said, "I . . .

PROMISE #3: Jordan promised God he would always attend Sunday school and church. He came regularly for a while, even though he was the only one in his family who came. Then a friend said, "You don't have to go every Sunday, do you?" Pretty soon Jordan missed now and then. Finally he stopped going completely.

ENDING:

"Dear God," Jordan prayed. "I . . .

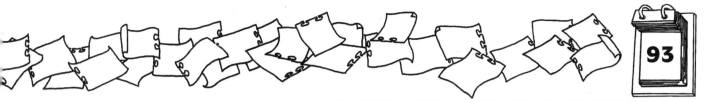

WHEN JUDGES RULED THE LAND

AIM: That your students will learn lessons from some of God's people mentioned in the book of Judges

SCRIPTURE: Judges 2:7-19; 4:1-7:25; 8:28; 13:1-16:31 (God continues to be with His chosen people even though at times they disobey Him)

PREPARATION:
1. Photocopy activity sheets—one for each student.

PRESESSION (5-10 minutes)

ACTIVITIES
* Make a "Graffiti Wall" about God's faithfulness

MATERIALS
* Large sheet of paper, markers or pencils, tape

PERSPECTIVE (10 minutes)

ACTIVITIES
* Talk about the history of the judges

MATERIALS
* *Optional: Chalkboard or large sheet of paper and marker*

PROBE (20 minutes)

ACTIVITIES
* Read a skit about Deborah, Gideon, and Samson

MATERIALS
* "Follow the Leaders" Activity Sheet

PERSONALIZE (15-20 minutes)

ACTIVITIES
* Solve a puzzle to find out some key elements in the spiritual lives of three of Israel's judges

MATERIALS
* "The Winning Combination" Activity Sheet

PRESESSION

(5-10 minutes)

As people arrive, have them help you put up a "Graffiti Wall." Fasten a large sheet of paper on the wall or bulletin board. Invite students to write comments on this "Wall" about God and His faithfulness to those who obey Him.

Optional: Since markers or pens can leak through, be sure to protect the room wall from them. You may want to put old newspapers or several layers of paper under your "Graffiti Wall."

Some ideas for this activity can be to use popular advertisement slogans and adapt them: You're in good hands with God; God's people—different is good; God—He's the real thing; God has better ideas; Relax and leave the "striving" to God. Ask the group to sit down as you read aloud their comments.

How do you think you would like school if no one was in charge or could enforce any rules? People could come when they wanted to, and there was no homework, tests or class work required? (Sounds great; confusing; like to try it.) **At first you might like this, but after a while you would find there are some disadvantages. That's the kind of situation God's people were in after they settled the land of Canaan.**

PERSPECTIVE

(10 minutes)

This was a time when there was no great leader among the Israelites. The people were supposed to follow the laws God had given them. Sometimes they did, but much of the time they disobeyed. **What kind of place do you think our world would be if everybody decided for themselves what they should or should not do?** (Wars, confusion, lots of crime, no safe place.)

The book of Judges tells us what kind of life it was when each of the Israelites did what s/he thought was right. Have students take turns reading Judges 2:7-19 aloud from their Bibles. This scripture passage gives a review of the whole period known as "the days of the judges." The judges were not magistrates but instead were mostly military leaders who led the Israelites in battle against their enemies. After each victory there was peace over the land for a while. Then God's people would disobey and begin to worship idols. Soon God would allow enemy armies to invade them. This worship of idols was the exact thing that Joshua warned his people about just before his death. It was also the thing that caused most of the trouble during this three-hundred-year period.

Very little was **written about some of the judges God raised up to lead the Israelites. You may have never even heard some of their names.** There were possibly 15 judges, 13 at least—counting Samuel, who is called the last of the judges. Often Abimelech and Eli are counted. At this time in Israel's history there was no central government or ruler. The twelve tribes operated independently of one another. However, two tribes often cooperated to battle against a common enemy.

Optional: If you have a longer class time, you may want to list the twelve tribes on a chalkboard or large sheet of paper so students can see them. They are: Reuben, Simeon, Gad, Judah, Issachar, Zebulun, Ephraim (son of Joseph), Manasseh (son of Joseph), Benjamin, Dan, Asher, Naphtali.

The first judge was named Othniel. He came from the tribe of Judah and was the nephew of Caleb, one of the twelve men sent to spy out Canaan many years earlier.

After Othniel came Ehud, of the tribe of Benjamin, and Shamgar, whose tribe isn't mentioned. Then came two judges you may have heard of. They are Deborah and Gideon.

PROBE

Deborah was the only woman judge over Israel. She had great and recognized wisdom as well as noble character and charm. People realized she was a woman who was close to God. Because of that, her captain, Barak, asked her to lead the army into battle against the Canaanites.

Gideon's name meant "great warrior," but he was so afraid of his enemies that he was hiding food when God called him to lead his people. Gideon's uncertainty led to his requests of special signs from the Lord to be sure that God would be with him when he fought the Midianites. However, once he was sure of that, he was willing to fight the great number of enemy soldiers with only 300 men.

Another judge you have probably heard of is Samson. Samson was the strongest man who ever lived. His physical strength was on record. He strangled a lion barehanded. On one occasion he killed 1,000 Philistines alone. One of his greatest performances was to carry the gates of the city of Gaza all the way to the top of a hill outside Hebron. Those metal gates probably weighed thousands of pounds, about the same size as a large van. The journey to Hebron was uphill for 38 miles!

Distribute copies of "Follow The Leaders" activity sheet. You will need four people to read the parts of Kid Toppel, Deborah, Gideon, and Manoah, Samson's father. The rest of the group can follow along on their activity sheets. Although Manoah died before the tragic end of Samson's life, his fictional view of his son's career is true to life.

Who did Deborah credit with getting the victory over the Canaanites? (God.) **How did the Lord conquer these fierce fighters?** (Made their iron chariots get stuck in mud.) The Israelites were vast underdogs because they still fought on foot with wooden weapons. This made no difference when the Lord was on their side, for He turned the Canaanites advantage to a disadvantage.

Deborah went up with Barak and the soldiers, but she did not fight. How did she show her thankfulness to God after the battle? (Sang praises to God for His help.)

What great advantage did the Midianites have over Gideon and his men? (Had fast camels to ride on.) Many times these swift and cruel people raided the fields, herds, and homes of the Israelites.

Who did Gideon say won the battle? (God.) Almost all battles were carried on during the daylight. A sneak attack in the middle of the night was a great shock to the enemy. It's no wonder the Midianites thought they were surrounded by the enemy when they saw the blazing torches and heard the earsplitting notes of the trumpets!

Who did Manoah say gave Samson his strength? (God.) **How did the Lord give Samson victory over the Philistines?** (Gave him back his strength so he could pull the supporting pillars down and make the building collapse.)

In the skit, what did Kid Toppel say about God's relationship with His people? (Even when they disobeyed, He continued to be with them; punished them when they were disobedient; helped them when they asked Him to.) **What kind of life did the people have as long as they obeyed God?** (Peaceful, good, no battles with their enemies.)

What do you think we can learn from this? (If we disobey God, He will punish us; when we ask Him for help, he gives us leaders to help save us from our enemies; will give us good, peaceful lives while we obey Him.) **Why does God do this for us?** (Because He loves us.)

Did you ever do something you were told not to do? What happened? (Were punished.) Sometimes we forget about those rules and are punished again. **Sometimes we are slow to learn our lessons.**

PERSONALIZE

Let's see what kinds of lessons we can learn from the lives of these three judges, Deborah, Gideon, and Samson. Hand out copies of "The Winning Combination" activity sheet. Ask someone to read the directions aloud. Have students work on this puzzle individually. Answers are: trusted, believed, loyal, obedient, thankful; God on their side, win, battle; strong physically, strong, temptation, friends.

There are many things we can admire about Deborah. She knew that only with the Lord's help was victory possible. She also remembered to be thankful. **Do you remember to say "Thank You" as well as "Help me" to God? What are some reasons to be thankful to God?** Let students share briefly.

Gideon learned that a small group with God on their side can win the battle. Sometimes we feel that we are all alone, when almost everyone else is doing wrong. We can be afraid to stand up for what is right. But remember that when we are on God's side, we will win the victory over Satan and his temptations. **We can lead others to victory, with God's help, just as Gideon did. What are some ways we can do this?** (Invite them to church or Sunday school, have a Bible study with them, tell them what Jesus has done for us and will do for them.)

Thinking about Samson's strength makes us want to be strong too! We need to follow the rules for good health such as eating nourishing food, and getting proper rest and exercise. Samson was very strong physically but not socially or spiritually.

What are some influences that can lead us in the wrong direction? (Bad habits, drugs, gangs, cliques, TV.) **It's very important that we choose our friends carefully. The wrong friends can get us to do wrong and get us into trouble like Samson.**

PRAYER/PRAISE

Have kids face you. **If you've ever chosen to disobey God, turn around. If you've ever asked God for forgiveness and obeyed Him again, turn back around.** Thank God for His continued love and help. Ask Him to help you obey Him.

RIGHT LINE
WITH
KID TOPPEL

Kid Toppel: Hello. My name is Kid Toppel and this is "Right Line." Today we have three people who will be sharing their experiences of God's faithfulness to His people even in times of disobedience. Deborah, you were the only woman leader God called to help the Israelites. What did you do?

Deborah: The people were disobedient and worshiped the false gods of the heathen people around them. God punished them by allowing the Canaanites to invade them. God sent Barak and me to fight Sisera, the general of the Canaanite army. Sisera had nine hundred chariots of iron and his men fought with iron weapons. But God made the iron chariots bog down in mud. He gave us a great victory over our enemies. Barak and I sang praises to the Lord for His help. I led the people for forty peaceful years.

Kid Toppel: That was a good time for the Israelites. But all too soon they disobeyed the Lord again. Gideon, you were the next leader that God sent His people. How did God use you to deliver the Israelites?

Gideon: For seven years God let the Midianites rule over us. They raided us on fast camels and took our crops and animals and mistreated us. Then the Israelites cried out to God for help and He called me to deliver them.

Kid Toppel: How did you feel about that?

Gideon: I was afraid, but God patiently convinced me. God wanted us to surprise the enemy and make the camels run away. I did as He told me. In the middle of the night, three hundred men and I surrounded the enemy camp. We won the victory with only flaming torches and trumpets because God helped us.

Kid Toppel: What a strange battle that must have been! You also led the people for forty peaceful years. Manoah, God gave your son, Samson, a special gift that helped him to defeat your enemies. Tell us about it.

Manoah: Before Samson was born, God gave us special orders to be obeyed, because He had chosen him to deliver the Israelites from the Philistines. God gave Samson great strength and for twenty years he defeated many enemies. But then they bribed a woman named Delilah to find out his secret. He told her that if his hair was cut, he would lose his power. She tricked him. He was captured. He was blinded and made to work in the prison. Later the Philistines were worshiping one of their false gods. Samson's hair had grown by then. He had regained his strength. He pulled together two of the great pillars of the building, causing it to fall. Three thousand Philistines died with him.

Kid Toppel: Thank you for sharing with us today. Although His chosen people often disobeyed Him, God continued to be with them. He punished them, but every time they asked Him for help and turned back to obey Him, the Lord sent leaders to save them from their enemies. God continues to be with people who love Him. When we pray and ask Him for help He gives it because He loves us. This is Kid Toppel signing off for "Right Line."

FOLLOW THE ◆ LEADERS

The Winning Combination

We can learn some valuable lessons from some of the leaders of God's people. Be a good B.I. (Bible Investigator) by breaking the code and discovering the secret messages.

CODE:

A	B	C	D	E	F	G	H	I	J	K	L	M	N	O	P	Q	R	S	T	U	V	W	X	Y	Z
✔	✗	✜	✦	★	✺	❁	●	♥	♣	■	✚	✪	→	▲	❖	↔	◗	▮	□	▼	↕	❄	○	◆	✳

Deborah led Israel to victory over the Canaanites.

She **[TRUSTED]** God and **[BELIEVED]** He would be with her people. She was **[LOYAL]**, and **[OBEDIENT]** to Him. She remembered to be **[THANKFUL]**.

Gideon led the Israelites to victory over the Midianites.

He learned that a small group, with **[GOD ON]** **[THEIR]** **[SIDE]** can **[WIN]** the **[BATTLE]**.

Samson defeated many of the Philistines.

He was very **[STRONG]** **[PHYSICALLY]**, but he wasn't **[STRONG]** in resisting **[TEMPTATION]**. The wrong kind of **[FRIENDS]** got him to do wrong things.

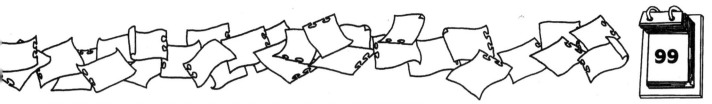

THE STORY OF RUTH

AIM: That your students will understand they will be blessed if they are faithful and helpful to the Lord and to others

SCRIPTURE: Ruth 1:1—4:17 (God blesses Ruth's life because she is helpful and faithful to Him and Naomi)

PREPARATION:
1. Photocopy activity sheets—one for each student.

PRESESSION (5-10 minutes)

ACTIVITIES
* Talk about deeds that show love, faithful-ness, and goodness to others

MATERIALS
* Old newspapers or magazines
* Chalkboard or large sheet of paper and marker

PERSPECTIVE (10 minutes)

ACTIVITIES
* Use an activity sheet to discover facts about Ruth

MATERIALS
* Bibles
* "Faith Is a Family Affair" Activity Sheet

PROBE (20 minutes)

ACTIVITIES
* Pantomime the story of Ruth

MATERIALS
* Bibles
* "Harvest of Helpfulness" Activity Sheet

PERSONALIZE (15-20 minutes)

ACTIVITIES
* Find ways you can be helpful and faithful to God and to others

MATERIALS
* Paper and pencils

LESSON 16   **UNIT THEME: GOD'S GREAT NATION**

PRESESSION

Have your students tear out stories or pictures about people doing things that show love, faithfulness, and helpfulness to others. As they do, briefly list the deeds on the chalkboard or a large sheet of paper.

Guide the conversation with questions similar to these: What was done? Who did it? What was the result? Was the helper rewarded? How? Do you think people help others so they will get something in return or just because they want to? What does it reveal about the people involved?

We never know the full purpose and importance of doing something at the time we do it. Only God can see the future and the relevance such deeds have. **But we can choose to do things that honor God. When you live in faithfulness to God and helpfulness to others, your life extends beyond your lifetime.**

PERSPECTIVE

We have been studying the stories of God's people who lived during the time when judges ruled. There was a lot of sin and trouble during those years, but there was also goodness, love, and faithfulness in the hearts of many of the people. **Our story from God's Word is about a woman who showed faithfulness to God and helpfulness to others. Her name is Ruth.**

Hand out copies of "Faith Is A Family Affair," activity sheet. Ask someone to read the directions aloud. Students can work on this fact-finding exercise individually. Be sure they understand all the words. For example: famine means a food shortage.

Optional: If you are running short of time, do this activity together.

In Bible times, there were few things worse than being a widow. Widows were left with nothing because all property went to any remaining <u>male</u> relatives. A widow had to depend on the helpfulness of others. If they chose not to be kind, she lived in extreme poverty and others often took advantage of her.

Ruth had the opportunity to return to her home and perhaps another marriage which would insure her future. However, she gave it up in order to help Naomi. Why do you think she did that? (Knew Naomi needed someone to be with her; loved her; wanted to help her.) Ruth was willing to become a "foreigner" in a strange land because she knew that Naomi needed companionship and help just to survive. The Moabite people were considered heathens and often despised by the Israelites. This, plus being a widow, made it very difficult for Ruth.

Ruth was also willing to give up the false gods her people worshiped. What did she tell Naomi about that? (Naomi's God would be her god.) **What do you think convinced her to worship God?** (Because she had experienced how real He was to Naomi.) Ruth had seen Naomi's kindness to her and knew it was really an extension of the love of Naomi's God for all people.

Check out Acts 10:34, 35. How does God feel about people like Ruth? (Accepts them; treats them all alike.) **Because Ruth was faithful and helpful to Naomi and willing to worship the one true God, God blessed her.**

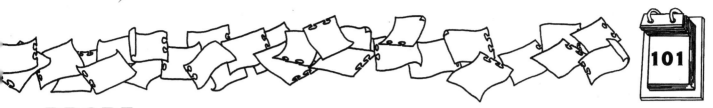

PROBE

(20 minutes)

Distribute copies of "Harvest of Helpfulness" activity sheet. This will be an activity that combines pantomime with Scripture reading. You will need four students to take the main parts of Naomi, Ruth, Boaz, and the close relative. The rest of the class can be reapers, elders, and neighbors as these groups are needed.

Clear a space for a stage. Have students stand off to the sides until it is time for their part of the pantomime. Read the story aloud, pausing to allow the participants to pantomime the action you have just read.

Optional: If you have a large group, you may have enough students to form several small groups who can be reapers, elders, and neighbors.

Optional: To make the play more enjoyable, let students wear Bible costumes or old scarves, bathrobes, etc.

Have students return to their chairs so you can talk about the story. They can follow the story in their Bibles. **What kind of work was Ruth doing to get food for Naomi and herself?** (Gleaning in the harvest field.) Israelite law said that the poor could have the grain in the corners of fields as well as pick up any grain that was dropped. This was a sort of welfare program for them.

What kind of a worker was Ruth? (Good, hard worker, kept at her job.) Even though the work was insignificant, boring, and maybe even humiliating, Ruth kept at it faithfully. **How do people often work at those kinds of jobs?** (Lazy, take lots of breaks, work only when the boss sees them.) **Because Ruth worked so faithfully at this backbreaking, tiresome job, everyone in Bethlehem soon knew what a good, helpful, faithful person she was.**

God chose some outstanding leaders like Joshua, Deborah, and Gideon, who led armies and went to battle. But not all the people He used were like that. Some of the people whom God chose to help Him were quiet and helpful like Ruth. She was consistently faithful to God in the small, daily things, and served Him even though she never led an army or spoke to great crowds of people.

Boaz was impressed with what he heard about Ruth. What did he tell his reapers about her? (Not to harm her, let her eat and drink with them, purposely pull out and drop grain for her.) **Boaz felt Ruth should be rewarded. What blessing did he give her?** Have someone read aloud Ruth 2:12. (Asked God to reward her.)

What encouragement did Naomi give Ruth when she found out that it was Boaz who had helped her? (Told her that as a near relative he had the right to ask her to marry him.) This meant a kinsman-redeemer. In Israelite culture the inheritance always went to the nearest male relative, not to the wife. A kinsman-redeemer was a close relative who volunteered to take responsibility for the dead person's family. This included marrying the widow. The firstborn son of this new marriage would be given the name of the widow's husband and inherit all of his property. In Ruth's case there was one relative closer than Boaz. But Boaz showed by his reply to Ruth that he had already been thinking of asking for the privilege of being her kinsman-redeemer.

When Boaz heard that Ruth asked him to be her kinsman-redeemer, what did he do? (Went to talk to the close relative.) Boaz was sensitive to the needs of others. He also was a man of action who kept his word. Both of these qualities made him a good choice to be Ruth's husband.

There was also a matter of buying the property that legally belonged to the men of Naomi's family. Boaz bought this land as well as obtaining permission to marry Ruth. **How did the close relative show his agreement to let Boaz be Ruth's kinsman-redeemer?** (Took off his shoe and gave it to Boaz.) Taking off the sandal in this manner was a symbol that the close relative gave up his right to walk on the land to possess it.

How did God bless Ruth? (Gave her a husband and son; chose her to be the greatgrandmother of King David and relative of Jesus.) In the time of the judges, there was much wickedness. God's people had some very sad times, but God had a great plan that He was getting ready for them. He was going to send a Savior to the world, to save the people from the punishment of their sins. Ruth had a part in that plan.

We remember Ruth because one day the Savior, Jesus, God's Son, came from descendants of her family.

PERSONALIZE

(15-20 minutes)

How do people know what you are like? (By how you act, watch what you do.) **You can be faithful and helpful like Ruth. What are some ways you can be helpful to God, your parents, friends, and others?** Be prepared to list the group's suggestions on the chalkboard or a large piece of paper. Encourage students to be as specific as possible. For example, instead of just "helping around the house," be specific: cleaning my room without being told; doing dishes; looking after my little brother when Mom is busy.

After the group has briefly named several things, hand out paper and pencils. **Let's imagine that you have just won the "Ruth Prize" for helpfulness to God and others. Write down what you did to win it.** Allow time to do this. Invite people to share their ideas. **This was just an imagination exercise but you have a** real opportunity to do something to express your faithfulness and helpfulness to God by doing something for others every day. When you do, you are really serving the Lord.

Sometimes there are sad times in our lives like those in the lives of Ruth and Naomi. We may not always have the things we would like to have. Sometimes we even lose someone who is very dear to us. **But if we are faithful and trust in the Lord, He will be with us. God will bless us and bring happiness out of our lives. He will even use them to bless the lives of others.**

PRAYER/PRAISE

Close by having people thank God for one thing the person on their right has done for them or others.

Faith Is a Family Affair

Calling all B.I.'s (Bible Investigators)! Follow the Scripture verse clues to find out more about our mystery woman. All verses are found in the first chapter of Ruth. Remember what to write in the blanks? The facts, just the facts!

A man named Elimelech, his wife, (v. 2) _____ and their two (v. 1) _____ lived in Bethlehem in Judah. Because of a (v. 1) _____ in their homeland, this family went to live in (v. 2) _____. Sometime later Elimelech died. Naomi's two sons, Mahlon and Kilion, married girls from Moab, (v. 4) _____ and _____. Within ten years, both sons died. (v. 5) _____ was lonely. One day she learned that there was no longer a food shortage back in her homeland. She decided to go back to (v. 1) _____ to her relatives and friends. Naomi's two (v. 7) _____ were going with her.

Naomi, Ruth, and Orpah had not traveled very far when Naomi stopped and spoke to her daughters-in law. "You don't have to leave your own country and travel with me to a strange land. Go back, each of you, to your (v. 8) _____. May the Lord show (v. 8) _____ to you and grant that each of you will have another (v. 9) _____. At first both girls said they wanted to return with Naomi to her (v. 10) _____. Finally (v. 14) _____ decided to stay in Moab. She kissed Naomi good-bye and walked away.

Naomi tried to talk Ruth into staying in Moab, too, but Ruth would not think of it. "Please don't urge me to (v. 16) _____ you or to turn (v. 16) _____ from you," she said. "I want to go where you go and stay where you stay. Your (v. 16) _____ will be my people and your (v. 16) _____ will be my (v. 16) _____.

Naomi realized Ruth was determined to go back to Bethlehem with her and the two women continued their journey together.

HARVEST OF HELPFULNESS

After your teacher reads the bold print, pantomime the action described in italics.

CHARACTERS: Ruth, Naomi, Boaz, close relative, reapers, elders, neighbors

When Naomi and Ruth arrived in Bethlehem, the barley harvest was just beginning. *Reapers work in field.* **Poor people were allowed to go to the fields and pick up grain that reapers left lying on the ground. Ruth went to a barley field to gather food for Naomi and herself.** *Ruth goes and works in field.* **A rich man named Boaz owned the barley field where Ruth was working. He asked who she was.** *Boaz talks to reapers.* **They told him that her name was Ruth and that she had come from the land of Moab to live with Naomi. They also told him how good she was to Naomi.** *Workers talk to Boaz.*

Boaz told Ruth to stay and glean in his field. He offered her water and food. *Boaz speaks to Ruth and shows her food and water.* **He also told his reapers to let some grain fall so Ruth could gather plenty for food.** *Boaz speaks to reapers, then leaves. Reapers and Ruth also leave. Ruth goes to Naomi.*

When Ruth got home that evening, she told Naomi all that had happened during the day. *Ruth tells Naomi about Boaz' kindness.* **Naomi was happy to hear the news. She told Ruth that Boaz was a distant relative of her family.** *Naomi happily speaks to Ruth.*

According to the customs in those times, the closest relative of Naomi's family had the first right to ask to marry the young widow, Ruth. Boaz wanted to marry her, but there was a closer relative who had to be told of the matter and given first choice. Boaz got together with this man, and they went to the elders of the city. *Boaz meets relative. They go to elders.* **To seal the bargain, according to their custom, the relative took off his shoe and handed it to Boaz.** *Relative hands shoe to Boaz.* **Then Boaz announced that he would marry Ruth. The elders and all the people who had gathered at the city gate agreed.** *Elders and people nod in agreement. Boaz goes to Ruth.*

So Boaz and Ruth were married. *Boaz and Ruth join hands.* **Later a son was born to them. They named him Obed. How happy Naomi was to have a grandson!** *Naomi joins hands with Boaz and Ruth.* **The neighbors came to see the baby and rejoiced with Naomi.** *Neighbors happily gather around Boaz, Ruth, and Naomi.* **She had been sad when she lost her husband and sons, but now she was very happy. When Obed grew up, he had a son named Jesse. When Jesse grew up, he had a son named David, who became the king!**

THE STORY OF SAMUEL

AIM: That your students will discover they can begin to serve the Lord while they are young and remain faithful all their lives

SCRIPTURE: 1 Samuel 1:1-3:21; 7:1-13 (Samuel begins as a young boy to serve the Lord and continues faithfully throughout his life)

PREPARATION:
1. Photocopy activity sheets—one for each student.
2. Prepare stickers as described in PRESESSION.

PRESESSION (5-10 minutes)

ACTIVITIES
* Make stickers of favorite Bible stories you have studied previously

MATERIALS
* 1 1/2" x 3" Self-adhesive labels—one for each student, markers

PERSPECTIVE (10 minutes)

ACTIVITIES
* Participate in an object lesson to illustrate opportunities for serving the Lord

MATERIALS
* Paper—one sheet for each student, pencils

PROBE (20 minutes)

ACTIVITIES
* Learn about Samuel from a modernized story

MATERIALS
* Bibles
* "At Your Service" Activity Sheet

PERSONALIZE (15-20 minutes)

ACTIVITIES
* Write a letter to tell others about Jesus

MATERIALS
* "The Good News" Activity Sheet

PRESESSION

(5-10 minutes)

Before class, cut apart the labels leaving the background paper on them so they won't stick to the table. Lay out markers and labels so students can easily reach them.

Invite students to design a sticker that illustrates their favorite Bible story from those you have studied previously. Some suggestions are: Joshua and the fall of Jericho; Deborah and Barak singing praises; Gideon and his men with torches and trumpets; Samson pulling down the temple; Ruth gleaning grain. Students can use either slogans or pictures to illustrate these stories.

As students work on this, guide the conversation: Why is this your favorite story? What did you like best about that person? What did you learn from the person's life?

The man we're going to hear about today was the last of the judges. He was also a great prophet. His name is Samuel.

PERSPECTIVE

(10 minutes)

Have students work in pairs. Tell one person in each pair you want him/her to write his/her name on paper. But before they do, tell them to shut their eyes while doing it. After they have written their names, they can open their eyes. Now have the other partners write their names with their eyes open.

Which was easier? (With eyes open.) **Which looks better?** (With eyes open.) **Many times when God asks us to serve Him, we shut our eyes to the opportunities around us. The results can be as bad as your writing looked. What are some things that prevent us from serving God?** (Being lazy, selfishness, pride, prejudice, not wanting to get involved.) **To be able to serve God as we should, we need to open our "spiritual eyes" and remove anything which stands in our way of doing so. This includes the idea that we are too young to serve the Lord.**

Samuel began to serve God when he was very young. Briefly outline the background for today's lesson. **Samuel's story began with a man named Elkanah and his wife, Hannah.** They lived in Mount Ephraim. Each year they went up to Shiloh to worship the Lord.

Hannah was very unhappy because she did not have any children. One day at the house of the Lord she cried as she silently prayed that the Lord would give her a son. She promised that she would give him back to the Lord to serve Him always. Eli, the priest, saw Hannah's lips moving, but he did not hear any words. He thought she might have been drinking too much wine. **The chief priest, Eli, spoke to her rather unkindly.**

How did Hannah answer Eli? Have someone read I Samuel 1:15, 16 aloud. **Eli told Hannah to go in peace and may the God of Israel grant your wish.**

God remembered Hannah's prayer, and a little son was born to her. She named him Samuel. Samuel means "asked of God." **Hannah kept her promise and gave little Samuel back to the Lord. Would Samuel be willing to serve God faithfully all his life? Are you willing to do that?**

PROBE

Distribute copies of "At Your Service" activity sheet. Have people take turns reading this modernized version of the Bible account of Samuel.

Check out 1 Samuel 2:18. When Samuel was only a little boy, what was he doing for the Lord? (Ministering before Him.) Another way of stating this is to say he was the Lord's helper.

In the New Testament, we can find out something more about children and God. Have group turn to 1 Timothy 4:12. **What can we learn from these verses?** (God can use children too.) **The Lord uses anyone who wants to learn from and serve Him.** The Lord doesn't need us to get His work done, but He wants us to serve Him because we love Him. God has no age limits. He is looking for faithful workers, regardless of their age. **Don't ever let your age be an excuse for not serving God!**

In the story, what kind of work did Sammy do to help God and Eli? (Unlocked the doors, cleaning furniture, sweeping floors.) These were not very exciting jobs but they were helpful to others. **Check out 1 Samuel 2:26. How did the Lord and other people feel about Samuel?** (He grew in favor with them.) This means that they were pleased with Samuel.

How do you think kids your age would do the kinds of chores that Samuel did? (Grudgingly, halfway, do only what they <u>have</u> to do.) **If you love God and really want to serve Him faithfully, do whatever He gives you to do, even if it seems unimportant at the time.**

How did God speak to Samuel about Eli? (With a human voice.) God spoke audibly with Samuel. **How did Samuel respond to God's voice?** (He was ready to do whatever God wanted him to do.)

Why do you think God spoke to Samuel, but not Eli? Eli had let his sons live in disobedience to the Lord. Although Eli obeyed God in other ways, he was disobedient in disciplining his sons. God chose Samuel because he was faithfully serving the Lord in obedience. God uses faithful followers regardless of age or position to give His messages to others.

When things happened as Samuel said they would, people throughout the land of Israel knew that God had chosen him to be a prophet—someone who spoke for God. The word "prophet" simply means "messenger." Prophets shared God's messages with others. Some prophets, like Samuel, were able to tell what would happen in the future.

How did God reveal himself to Samuel as he grew older? Have someone read aloud 1 Samuel 3:21. (Through His word.) In Samuel's time there was no complete Bible like we have today. However he had the books of the law to read and use for teaching others.

Optional: If you have a longer class schedule, have students name these books. They are the first five books of the Bible: Genesis, Exodus, Leviticus, Numbers, and Deuteronomy.

How does God speak to us today? (Through His Word, the Bible.) **When we read our Bibles, we should be listening for God's voice. Then we need to not only listen, but be ready to obey whatever the Lord tells us from it like Samuel did.**

PERSONALIZE

What are some ways kids your age can serve God right here in Sunday school or church? (Clean up our Sunday school classroom, help distribute lesson materials, sing for services, help with younger kids.)

Optional: If you would like to have a class service project, survey your church or Sunday school and find out what needs there are. Then brainstorm ways to meet those needs. Some examples are: have your class offer to be church greeters or ushers for a Sunday morning; get a list of shut-ins and visit with them; help the custodian empty waste baskets.)

Samuel was a great helper to the Lord by giving His messages to others. We also need to share God's message with others. The greatest message of all is to tell others that Jesus died so that God could forgive their sins and make them part of His forever family. Have you ever told anyone about Jesus?

Distribute copies of "The Good News" activity sheet. Ask someone to read the instructions aloud. **What are some things we should include in this letter?** Invite people to give their ideas. Include such things as: God's love; the separation between God and people that sin causes; how Jesus came to die in our place to pay the penalty for sin; that God raised Jesus to life again as proof that He accepted Jesus' sacrifice as the payment for sin; people can have their sins forgiven and the loving relationship between God and themselves restored when they accept Jesus as

their Savior. Students can work on this individually.

Optional: If you would like to insure privacy, have people spread out in the room where they won't disturb each other.

Optional: Be sensitive to students who may be having a hard time with this activity. Perhaps they have difficulty expressing themselves in writing. It may be that they have not accepted Jesus as their own Savior. If so, this could be the time to invite them to do so. You may want to take them aside to deal with that problem either now or after class.

Allow most of the time to work on this activity. Invite people to share their letters with the group, but remind them that people won't see their letters unless the writers want them to.

When you have accepted Jesus as your Savior you will want to follow Samuel's example of faithfully serving Him. Listen for the Lord's voice as you read God's Word and pray to Him. Tell others about God's love shown through His Son, Jesus.

PRAYER/PRAISE

Ask people to use the stickers they made in PRESESSION by putting them on their clothes, books, notebooks, balls, etc. When people ask them what they are, they can use the opportunity to tell them the Bible story and about God's love and forgiveness that everyone can receive by accepting Jesus as Savior.

At Your Service

Sammy was about three years old when his mother brought him to God's house. His parents wanted to thank the Lord for their son and give a special offering. His mother, Hannah, said to Eli, the priest, "Do you remember me? I met you once when I came here to pray. I asked God to give me a little boy. God answered my prayer and gave me Sammy. Now I want to give him back to the Lord. I want him to serve God all his life. Please take him and teach him how to be a good servant of the Lord."

So Sammy came to live with Eli and help him in God's house. Sammy helped him by unlocking the door every morning, cleaning the furniture, and sweeping the floors. Sammy loved the Lord and tried to help all he could.

One night when he was lying in bed he heard someone call, "Sammy." Sammy said, "Here I am." Then he quickly ran to Eli to see what he wanted. But Eli hadn't called him. He told Sammy to go back to bed. The same thing happened two more times. Then Eli told Sammy that if he was called again, he should tell the voice, "Speak, Lord. I'm here to serve you. I'm listening."

Sure enough, once again God called, "Sammy, Sammy!" This time Sammy said what Eli had told him. God told Sammy that Eli and his sons were disobedient and had to be punished. Even though Eli had lived a good life, he let his sons do very wicked things.

The next morning, Sammy got up and unlocked the doors. He was afraid to tell Eli the sad message he had received from God. But Eli asked what God had said. Sammy sadly told him about the punishment. Eli said, "Let God do what He thinks is best." God was with Sammy as he grew up. He continued talking to Sammy and revealing himself to him through the Bible. Before very long the things God told Sammy happened. Everyone knew that He had chosen Sammy to be His messenger. Sammy grew up and kept on telling people what God wanted them to do. Samuel, as he was now called, was a faithful and courageous leader of God's people.

One day all of God's people were gathered for a very serious meeting. They were sorry for their sins and again wanted to serve only God. Their enemies heard of the meeting. They prepared to attack God's people while they were all together in one place.

The people asked Samuel to pray for deliverance from the enemy. As the enemy marched nearer, Samuel continued to pray. He calmly continued even while the enemy closed in. Suddenly a terrible thunderstorm roared above the enemy's heads so that they didn't know which way to go. Then God's people chased them out of their land. Samuel told the people that their trust in God had been rewarded.

THE GOOD NEWS

You are writing to people who have never heard of Jesus. Write a letter that describes him and will help them know who Jesus is.

_____ ,

_____

_____

_____

_____

_____

_____

_____

_____

_____ ,

_____

THE FIRST KING, SAUL

AIM: That your students will be thankful for the abilities God has given them and use them to honor Him

SCRIPTURE: 1 Samuel 9:25-10:26; 13:1-15 (King Saul misuses his leadership to honor himself instead of God)

PREPARATION:
1. Photocopy activity sheets—one for each student.
2. Prepare room for game as described in PRESESSION.

PRESESSION (5-10 minutes)

ACTIVITIES
* Play a game to emphasize how our different gifts can be used to attain a common goal

MATERIALS
* Chair, masking tape, timer

PERSPECTIVE (10 minutes)

ACTIVITIES
* Complete a puzzle to learn how Samuel and Saul met

MATERIALS
* "The People's Choice" Activity Sheet
* Bibles

PROBE (20 minutes)

ACTIVITIES
* Read a fictional interview about Saul

MATERIALS
* "Who's Number One?" Activity Sheet
* *Optional: Two telephones (play or disconnected)*

PERSONALIZE (15-20 minutes)

ACTIVITIES
* Discover good and bad ways you can use your abilities

MATERIALS
* Paper and pencils

PRESESSION

Before students arrive, clear a space in the room. Tape a starting line on the floor. Place a chair across the room on the opposite side from this line. Have students form a relay team to help you race against the clock. Players must go from the starting line, around the chair, and back to the starting line. They then tag the next player.

Each person must move in a different manner from the others. For example they can run, hop, shuffle, walk backwards, crawl, etc. Set the timer for five minutes and see how many players can accomplish the feat before time is up.

Optional: If you have a longer time period, reset the timer and repeat the exercise, trying to better the previous time.

What did you learn from this game? (There are lots of different ways to move, everybody had to work together to beat the clock.) **What would have happened if players decided to go different directions or not tag the next person?** (The whole team would have suffered, wouldn't have accomplished the goal.)

The same thing is true for God's people. Each of you has a special ability given to you from God. You can use it to make a different and valuable contribution to help the others. In order to serve and honor God properly we all have to put our own selfish desires aside and work together as a team.

Let's see how that worked in the lives of Samuel and a man named Saul.

PERSPECTIVE

We have already studied judges such as Deborah, Gideon, and Samson. The last judge was Samuel. Like Eli's sons, Samuel's sons did not follow his good example so God could not call them to be leaders. **God's people were very unhappy. They wanted to be like the neighboring nations and have a king.**

This made Samuel very unhappy. He was sad because the people had rejected God, their true king. But the Lord told Samuel that He had chosen a young man to be the first king over His people. When God pointed him out to Samuel, he was to anoint him with oil—a ceremony that showed God had set him apart for special work.

Hand out copies of "The People's Choice" activity sheet. Because they will need to scan a lengthy Scripture passage, do the exercise together. Answers are: Israel; Saul; seer; Samuel; Benjamin; chosen; message; leader; anointed; king.

Do you think Saul was just lucky to meet Samuel? Why or why not? Nothing in our lives is really by chance or luck. God is directing our lives whether we recognize it or not. God had told Samuel about a man from Benjamin and then arranged circumstances to send Saul to meet him. Throughout our lives, in even the most common events, God gives opportunities to know more about Him and to choose to follow in His ways. He is constantly working out His purpose for us.

What was Saul doing when Samuel called him to come forward to be the king? (Hiding.) **What does that show us about Saul?** (He was humble and shy.) Saul started out at the beginning of his career with true humility, recognizing that it was God who had chosen him. However, before very long he began to take the credit for victories and other achievements. **In later years, selfish pride became his downfall. But what was he like in the years between these two extremes?**

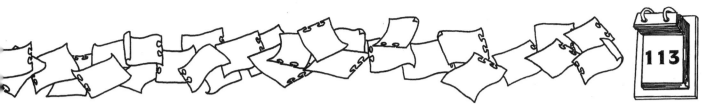

PROBE

Distribute copies of "Who's Number One" activity sheet. Choose two students to read the parts of Saul and Dan. The rest of the group can follow along on their activity sheets.

Check out 1 Samuel 10:23, 24. What did Saul look like? (Taller than others.) Saul looked like a king should look. He was tall and muscular. But the people were going to learn a lesson. Appearance can be deceiving. God alone knows what the real person inside our bodies is like.

What ability did God give Saul? (Leadership.) **How did he use it?** Saul was a true leader of men. His authority brought together men from many independent tribes and united them into one great fighting force. When it was necessary, this army could do almost impossible things.

When Saul collected his army and marched across the Jordan to help the town of Jabesh, it appears he promised a decisive intervention within twenty-four hours. This was a difficult journey, without a pause for breath to fight the cruel invaders and win a thrilling victory. When David retreated from Absalom it seems to have taken three days to accomplish a comparable march. The people never forgot that daring mission.

How did Saul misuse his God-given ability? Have students turn to 1 Samuel 15:15 and ask someone to read it aloud. (Disobeyed God and Samuel by keeping the best of the sheep and cattle alive.) **Who did Saul say disobeyed God by doing this?** (The men; army.) **Was this true?** (No.) As Adam and Eve had done long ago when God questioned them about their sin, Saul now lied to cover his sin and then blamed his disobedience on someone else. **What excuse did he give to explain this rebellious action?** (They were to be an offering for God.) **He thought that such a sacrifice would make up for his disobedience.**

Check out verses 18-21. How else did Saul disobey God and Samuel? (Brought back alive the Amalekite king, Agag.) In those days it was the custom for the conquerors to take the prisoners of war and make a spectacle of them by forcing them to march along in chains in a triumphal procession. Saul didn't let Agag live out of mercy, but to show him off as a trophy of war before the people. His pride was growing stronger with each victory God gave him.

Do people today ever defend their disobedience by giving excuses? (Yes.) **Give some examples.** One common way is to avoid telling others about God because we don't want to offend them or think they won't be interested. Sometimes we excuse ourselves saying we are too busy or don't have special Bible training to do what God calls us to do. **God isn't as interested in our ability as He is our availability.**

How did Saul refer to the Lord in verse 19? (Called Him "your God"—that is Samuel's God.) Although God had done so much for Saul, he did not really have a personal relationship with the Lord. **All Saul's actions were done out of self-will and for personal satisfaction. But all his excuses did not fool God or Samuel.**

What did Samuel tell Saul about this sacrifice? (It was better to obey than to offer a sacrifice.) Samuel spoke harshly urging Saul to look at the reasons he did what he did. If Saul only made sacrifices to God as a ritual and his heart wasn't right with God, such a sacrifice meant nothing.

Check out verse 25. **What did Saul want Samuel to do for him?** (Forgive his sin; come back with him so that he might worship the Lord.) **Do you think Saul was truly sorry for his sin?** (Yes, no, don't know.) **Verse 30 gives the real reason Saul wanted Samuel to go back with him. What was it?** (Honor him before the elders of the people and Israel.) Saul said he was sorry only because he wanted a personal favor from Samuel. He didn't want to lose face with the people. This was another example of his pride.

What warning did Samuel give Saul in verse 26? (Because Saul had rejected God, God had rejected Saul and would take the kingdom

away from him.) Saul's rebellion, lies, and pride could not be allowed to continue. God had given Saul a wonderful ability and also a responsibility. **Saul wanted the ability God gave him but refused to use it for God's purposes. Instead** he misused it for personal gain. **God has given each of us a special ability. It is different for each of us, but equally important in order to accomplish God's purpose for His people.**

PERSONALIZE

(15-20 minutes)

Hand out paper and pencils. Fold the paper in half lengthwise. **On the upper left side of the paper write "Ways I Can Honor God." On the upper right side write "Ways I Can Honor Myself." Choose one ability you have. List ways you can use or misuse this ability in the correct columns.**

Encourage students to think beyond the most visible abilities such as speaking, singing, or leadership. Other less visible abilities are things like: friendliness; helpfulness; caring for younger children; using hobbies to reach out to others; knowing how to pray for others.

Allow time to complete this activity. Invite students to share their answers with the group. To help promote this, share something personal yourself about an ability God gave you and how you can use or misuse it.

The people who have God-given abilities are God's "love-gifts" to the church. The gifts are not for personal honor or enjoyment but to prepare God's people to work in His kingdom.

PRAYER/PRAISE

Have the group form a circle, hold hands, and offer a silent prayer asking for wisdom and the willingness to use their God-given abilities to honor God and help others. **No matter what ability we have, God loves each one of us.** Go around the circle and have students say their names. Close by saying "Being different is good!" loudly in unison.

The People's Choice

Are you ready for action, B.I.'s (Bible Investigators)?
Read the story in 1 Samuel 8:19-10:24 to find the answers to
this puzzle. When you find the correct word, write it in the puzzle.

The people of [8 across] asked Samuel for a king like the other nations. This is the story of how they got one.

After looking for his father's lost donkeys for three days, [6 down] decided to return home. Before they did, Saul's servant suggested that they ask God's [6 across] in Ramah to help them.

As they were on their way, [7 down] met them. God had told Samuel that He would send him a man from the land of [4 across]. This man was the one God had [1 down] to be leader over His people.

Samuel welcomed Saul, and not only told him that the donkeys were found but also something more important. He gave Saul God's [3 across]: Saul had been chosen by the Lord to be [9 across] over His People!

The next day Samuel walked with Saul and his servant to the edge of the city. Samuel sent the servant on ahead and told Saul to stay where he was. Then Samuel [5 down] Saul leader over His people. Only the two of them knew about God's choice!

Soon after this, Samuel called all the people together at Mizpah to meet their future leader. He asked each of the tribes to pass by him. He told the tribe of Benjamin to step aside. From that group, he chose the family of Kish. Then he called for Saul to come forward.

But Saul was not there! He was hiding, perhaps because he was unused to so much attention. Some people ran to find him and brought him before the great crowd. Then the people shouted for joy over their [2 down].

So Saul became the first king of the nation of Israel and protected God's people in his kingdom.

Who's Number One?

(SOUND: Phone being dialed, two rings of phone)

SAUL: Hello.

DAN: Is this King Saul?

SAUL: Yes. Who is this?

DAN: This is Dan Lather of ASK news. I understand that you recently had a confrontation with the prophet, Samuel.

SAUL: I don't know what you heard, but I'm not to blame.

DAN: Could you give me a little background on the events that led up to this conflict?

SAUL: Sure, Dan. It all started when Samuel told me the Lord wanted me to attack the Amalekites. Then . . .

DAN: Excuse me, but didn't Samuel have more to say?

SAUL: I guess so. I wasn't paying much attention. I'm the king you know, so it's up to me to plan the battles and win them! As I was saying . . .

DAN: But didn't God tell Samuel to say He would punish the Amalekites? And also that you were to totally destroy everyone and everything that belonged to them?

SAUL: Do you want to interview me or not?

DAN: Well sure, but . . .

SAUL: Then let me finish. I and my men won the battle and went on home. That's where Samuel reached me.

DAN: Is it true that you set up a monument in your own honor?

SAUL: Well, I might have let my men praise me as they saw fit. After all, great men deserve some credit. But did Samuel even recognize my genius in such a great victory? Noooo! He just complained that the captured sheep and cattle were too noisy!

DAN: But weren't you supposed to totally destroy them?

SAUL: I explained all that to Samuel. The men took them in order to sacrifice them to the Lord. That didn't satisfy Samuel though. His next complaint was that I had brought back Agag, the Amalekite king. I started to explain that too when . . .

DAN: Is that when Samuel said, "To obey is better than sacrifice?"

SAUL: One more interruption and this interview ends! He just reacted too strongly. What does he know? He's an old man and you can't expect . . .

DAN: Didn't he also say, "Because you have rejected the word of the Lord he has rejected you as king?" Those are pretty harsh words from a man who helped you establish your position as head of the government.

SAUL: That does it! I have nothing more to say. If you want his side of the story, why don't you go talk to him? [SOUND: receiver slams down]

DAN: I would, but he's shut away, praying for you. [Hangs up phone]

THE GREATEST KING, DAVID

AIM: That your students will trust the heavenly Father to help them in times of troubles and temptations

SCRIPTURE: 1 Samuel 17:38-49; 19:9, 10; 24:8-12; 2 Samuel 1:1-4, 11, 12; 5:1-3 (David trusts in God and God is with him)

PREPARATION:
1. Photocopy activity sheets—one for each student.

PRESESSION (5-10 minutes)

ACTIVITIES
* Play charades to illustrate how physical muscles are built up

PERSPECTIVE (10 minutes)

ACTIVITIES
* Discuss how some Bible people built up their spiritual muscles

MATERIALS
* Bibles
* Chalkboard or large sheet of paper and marker

PROBE (20 minutes)

ACTIVITIES
* Observe how David learned to trust God's help through troubles and temptations

MATERIALS
* Bibles
* "Step Up to Spiritual Strength" Activity Sheet

PERSONALIZE (15-20 minutes)

ACTIVITIES
* Find ways God can help us overcome temptations

MATERIALS
* Bibles
* "Building Stronger Lives" Activity Sheet

LESSON 19   **UNIT THEME: THE KINGS OF ISRAEL**

PRESESSION

(5-10 minutes)

To get students thinking about how overcoming troubles and temptations can help us grow stronger spiritually, play a game of charades. Each person has to pantomime a different way people can build up physical muscles. Examples are: lift weights; jog; do push-ups; etc.

When a player guesses the action, s/he acts out another method. If that player has already had a turn, s/he can choose someone who hasn't so the game can continue. Participants must not duplicate techniques already done. Stop game when everyone has had a turn.

There are lots of ways we can build our-selves up physically. To be effective, all of them have one thing in common. What is it? (You have to work at it consistently.)

Building spiritual muscles is a little like that too. When we have troubles or temptations, we can ask God to help us overcome them. Each time we gain a victory over such situations, we are stronger and can deal better with whatever Satan sends us. Let's see how some of the Bible people we have already studied overcame the problems they faced with God's help.

PERSPECTIVE

(10 minutes)

Let the group help you list these Bible people and what they did in each situation. When a student gives an example, let that person write it on the chalkboard or a large sheet of paper.

Optional: While most students enjoy participating like this, be sensitive to those who may be poor spellers. Help them out gently, without calling undue attention to their problem.

Some examples are: Noah trusting God to save his family from the flood; Abraham trusting God to save Isaac and provide a sacrifice; Joseph trusting God to help him in slavery and prison; Moses trusting God to help him convince Pharaoh to release the Israelites; Joshua trusting God to give the Israelites victory at Jericho, etc. Talk about these briefly. **Not all God's people exercised their "trust muscles." God's chosen man to be Israel's first king, Saul, started out trusting God, but because of his disobedience and selfish pride, God took away the kingdom from him.**

God had already sent Samuel to Bethlehem to anoint David as the next king. David was the youngest of eight sons of Jesse. When Samuel did as God told him, the deed was done privately. The announcement about it would not be made for a long time. Afterward David went back to his work of watching his father's sheep.

Things were not going well for King Saul. Some of his servants told him it would be good to have someone play music on a harp to calm his troubled mind. King Saul agreed to this, and one of the servants suggested a shepherd boy named David who could play the harp very well. **David came and played such sweet music that soon Saul felt quite well again.**

At this time the army of Israel was at war with the Philistines. They had long been enemies of the Israelites. Now the two armies faced each other; Israel on one hill and the Philistines across the valley on another hill. **There had been no fighting for forty days. But twice a day, morning and evening, a gigantic Philistine soldier named Goliath walked out and shouted a challenge to the Israelites. What did he say?** Have students look up 1 Samuel 17:8-10 and ask someone to read it aloud. **This challenge provided David with his first opportunity to trust God and become stronger spiritually.**

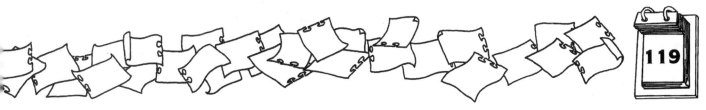

PROBE

Pass out copies of "Step Up to Spiritual Strength." Have a volunteer read the directions aloud. Depending on your time schedule, let students work on this activity individually or in pairs. Allow time to complete it. Talk about the answers together starting with number one. Students can follow along in their Bibles as you discuss. Answers are: false; false; true; false; true; false.

What might David have been tempted to do? (Think Saul's armor was better or safer.) **How did David trust God and overcome this temptation?** (He remembered how God had helped him protect his sheep in the past and used the same sling and stones he used then.) **How is that like problems we face today?** Invite students to share. It will aid you in identifying their trials and how you might encourage them to trust God to help them. Start out by sharing a problem that is similar to David's. For example: nations trusting in weapons instead of God. What do those nations need to do instead? (Stop their sin of doubting and start obeying God.)

Who did David turn to when this wicked, gigantic bully threatened him? (The Lord.) **How did David deal with this trouble?** (Turned it over to God; gave God honor for it, not himself.) **How can you overcome the temptation to brag?** (Realize that God is the one who gives us strength and courage; give Him credit for victories over sin.)

What did David do when Saul looked for him to kill him? (Asked God what to do; obeyed God's command; trusted God to protect him.) David could have given in to fear and depression, but he believed God would guide him and then followed up by obeying what God told him to do. **When you are afraid or depressed remember that trust isn't just a spectator sport. It requires your active participation in obeying what you believe is God's will for you.**

How did David deal with the opportunity to get revenge on his enemy? (Refused to take advantage of Saul; left it up to the Lord to avenge any wrongs Saul had done to him.) This same decision not to harm his enemy was repeated later when David had another opportunity to harm Saul. (1 Samuel 26:1-25) One of David's men even wanted to kill the king, but David refused to get even. Instead he gave Saul another opportunity to turn from his anger and stop trying to kill David.

How do kids your age try to get revenge on their enemies? (Spread an untrue story about them; beat them up; refuse to forgive them and keep trying to get even for everything they've done to you.) **What do you think God wants us to do about our enemies? Check out Matthew 5:43-45 to find the answer.** (Love them; pray for them.

How did David feel about Saul's death? (Was sorry; mourned for him.) **What are you tempted to do when something bad happens to someone you don't like?** (Gloat, be happy, make fun of them, tell everybody about it.) Whenever one of God's disobedient people has trouble, it is a signal to us to pray for him or her, not point fingers and condemn.

What was one of the first things David did when he became king over Israel? (Made an agreement with the people before the Lord.) The people reminded David that God had chosen him to be their ruler and guide them like a shepherd guides and cares for his sheep. David reaffirmed his commitment to obey God and carry out the Lord's will for his life and the people of Israel.

What are people tempted to do when God gives them a great honor? (Brag about it, forget who made it possible, stop obeying God and start making their own decisions.) **How do you think they should act?** (Remember how they got the honor, thank God for it, do their best to live up to His wishes.)

Because David continued to trust God in every temptation and trouble, he was able to overcome the problems that he had. When we build up our spiritual muscles a step at a time the way David did, then we too can deal with the problems that come our way.

PERSONALIZE

Let's see how well you might handle some common temptations. Distribute copies of "Building Stronger Lives" activity sheet. Choose someone to read the directions aloud. Let students work on this individually. Invite people to share their answers with the group.

In each situation follow these steps: 1) identify the temptation; 2) read what God's Word has to say about it; 3) brainstorm ways God can help you avoid the temptation; 4) choose one way and do it.

For example, go through the first situation. **What is the temptation?** (To avoid doing the dishes by hiding, pretending you don't hear, complain about it.) **What does God's Word say?** (Do things without grumbling or arguing.) **What could you do?** (Do the dishes gladly, stop mak-ing a fuss, offer to do them before Mom calls you next time.) **What way did you choose?** (Smile and stop complaining.) Discuss the other two problems in the same manner.

Probably you won't ever be challenged to fight a giant like Goliath. But sometimes you face temptations that are just as hard to battle! God will help you fight temptations and troubles and win. You can overcome temptations with God's help.

PRAYER/PRAISE

Close in prayer, asking God to help you trust Him more and give you the courage to do what is right. Thank Him for His guidance through Scripture.

Step Up to Spiritual Strength

David learned to trust God a step at a time as he faced troubles and temptations. Look up the Bible passages. Decide if the sentence is true or false and circle the correct answer.

T — When David became king over Israel, he forgot about God. — F **6**
* 2 Samuel 5:1-3 *

T — Even though Saul had hated him, David was sorry when he was dead. — F **5**
* 2 Samuel 1:1-4, 11, 12 *

T — David injured Saul to get revenge. — F **4**
* 1 Samuel 24:8-12 *

T — When Saul hunted for him, David trusted God to take care of him. — F **3**
* 1 Samuel 23:7-14 *

T — David bragged that he would kill Goliath by himself. — F **2**
* 1 Samuel 17:41-49 *

T — David depended on Saul's armor to defeat Goliath. — F **1**
* 1 Samuel 17:3-40 *

BUILDING STRONGER LIVES

Read the situation. Then use the Bible verse to decide how that person might overcome the problem with God's help.

Mom just called me to do the dishes. I'll ...
Philippians 2:14

_____
_____
_____
_____

There goes Bill with another new ball. I ...
Philippians 4:11

_____
_____
_____
_____

Janet makes me so mad. Every day I have to wait for her. I'm ...
1 Corinthians 13:4

_____
_____
_____
_____

THE WISE KING, SOLOMON

AIM: That your students will learn the importance of making wise choices

SCRIPTURE: 1 Kings 2:1-4; 3:5-10; 4:29; 10:1-7, 9, 10 (God is pleased and blesses Solomon because he trusts and obeys Him)

PREPARATION:
1. Photocopy activity sheets—one for each student.
2. Make Match Cards as described in PERSPECTIVE.

PRESESSION (5-10 minutes)

ACTIVITIES
* Play a game which emphasizes choices people can make

PERSPECTIVE (10 minutes)

ACTIVITIES
* Match Bible people with choices they made

MATERIALS
* Index cards (Match Cards)

PROBE (20 minutes)

ACTIVITIES
* Complete a newspaper to get acquainted with Solomon

MATERIALS
* "Jerusalem Journal" Activity Sheet
* Bibles

PERSONALIZE (15-20 minutes)

ACTIVITIES
* Work in small groups to make wise decisions

MATERIALS
* "Wise Guys" Activity Sheet

PRESESSION

(5-10 minutes)

To get students thinking about choices, play this game of sorting and grouping. Players will form and rearrange groups that share certain choices. Here are some examples of choices you might name: All those who like to read form one group. All who choose to bike ride in your free time form a group. All who have a daily quiet time get together. Everyone who has an extra job to earn money form a group.

Have class sit down. Talk about choices they have to make every day. Why do they choose certain kinds of friends, food, clothing, games, etc.? Which choices in life are most important? Do you think God is interested in the choices you make?

PERSPECTIVE

(10 minutes)

Prepare Match Cards by writing on index cards the names of some Bible people you have studied previously such as Eve, Abram, Esau, Joseph, Ruth, Saul, David. Make enough for half of your class.

On separate cards write a choice each of those people made. Examples are: eat fruit from a tree; take a trip; trade something for food; forgive family members; work in a field, etc.

All choices have one thing in common. They all have a result or consequence. Bible-time people also had choices to make. And like your choices, each of theirs had a consequence.

Pass out the name cards to half of the group and the choices to the other half. Have the kids with the person read the name aloud. People with choices they think match it stand up and read their cards. Discuss the choices. Were they good or bad? Why? Do you think God was interested in their choices? Why or why not?

Even great kings like David had choices to make. When David was very old he needed to choose which of his sons would be the new king. God told David in a vision that his son Solomon was to be that person. David called Zadok, the priest, and Nathan, God's prophet, and asked them to anoint Solomon king. **When David died he was buried in Jerusalem and Solomon became Israel's new king.**

PROBE

(20 minutes)

Hand out copies of "Jerusalem Journal" activity sheet. Divide the class into three groups and assign each one a story featured in this "newspaper." Teams will look up a Scripture passage and use the information in it to fill in the blanks in the article. Give them the following passages: Group one (the Queen) read 1 Kings 10:1-10; group two (temple dedication) check out 1 Kings 8:1-23; group three (dream) will find the answers in 1 Kings 3:3-15.

Teams one and two will also need someone to draw pictures of their stories. After teams have had an opportunity to complete their articles, discuss them together starting with the prophetic dream. While each team shares their findings, the rest of the group can follow the appropriate Scripture passage in their Bibles.

Why did Solomon go to Gibeon? (Offer sacrifice to God.) **Because he chose to trust and**

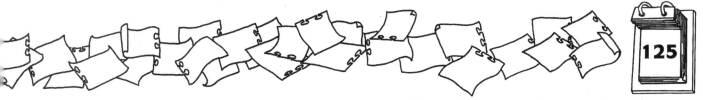

follow all of God's instructions, the Lord offered to do something for Solomon. **What was it?** (Give him whatever he wanted.) **What are some things Solomon could have asked for?** (Money, popularity, good looks, fame, health, long life.) **What did he ask for?** (Wisdom to rule the people.)

Solomon thought his decision through and asked God for wisdom to know the difference between right and wrong so he could rule the people. God was pleased with Solomon's choice.

Solomon was the wisest man that ever lived. Check out Proverbs 1:7. How did Solomon define wisdom or knowledge? (The fear of the Lord.) In this verse fear means respect or reverence for God. This kind of wisdom is an action. It means not just knowing what we should do, but also having the courage and willingness to do it because God is our king.

What quote did you find in 1 Kings 3:13? (God said: "Moreover, I will give you what you have not asked for—both riches and honor—so that in your lifetime you will have no equal among kings.") **We can see part of that honor described in the story about the temple.**

It took Solomon seven and one-half years to build the temple. The outside was made of huge limestone blocks. In the inside were beautifully carved cedar wood panels overlaid with gold and silver.

What special item was brought into the temple Solomon built for the Lord? (The ark of the covenant.) Explain that this is not the ark/boat that Noah and his family used during the flood that destroyed the world. The ark of the covenant was a wooden box overlaid with gold. On the top were two angels or cherubim with wings touching each other. Inside the box were the two tablets inscribed with the law of God, the Ten Commandments. It symbolized God's presence with Israel.

What happened when this holy box was brought into the temple? (The cloud of the glory of the Lord filled the temple so the priests couldn't continue their work in the building.) This showed that God was living in the temple in a special way. God promised to never leave the temple as long as the Israelites followed His law. **Where does God live today? Check out 1 Corinthians 6:19.** (In our bodies.)

What two things did Solomon do to dedicate the temple? (Sacrificed animals as offerings to God, prayed to God.) Solomon gathered the people to rededicate themselves as well as to dedicate the temple. His prayer was for the people and their relationship with the Lord.

What quote did you find in 1 Kings 8:23? (Solomon said, "O Lord, God of Israel, there is no God like you in heaven above or on earth below.") This summed up the history of Israel by referring to the great miracles and events that brought the people from horrible slavery in Egypt to a blessed home in the promised land.

What foreign queen came to visit Solomon? (Queen of Sheba.) Sheba was in southwest Arabia now known as Yemen. Her country was about 1000 miles away from Israel. **Why had she come?** (To test Solomon's wisdom and see how wonderfully the Lord had blessed him.)

What did she think about the reports she had heard of Solomon and God's blessings? (It was much better than what she had heard.) Solomon also built two palaces (one for himself and one for his Egyptian queen) and strong fortresses for his army. He sent out fleets of ships on three-year trading trips. They brought back gold, silver, jewels, ivory, and animals. These businesses earned Solomon about 65,000 pounds of gold a year. If gold sold for $350 an ounce, that would be $280,000,000 a year!

Not all of God's blessings are seen like these. What are some other blessings God gives to us when we serve Him faithfully? (Peace, joy, friendship, family love, good health, long life, contentment, etc.) **The Bible tells us that someday all the blessings that are seen will disappear, but these unseen ones will be the real, lasting things in Heaven.**

What did the Queen say about her visit? ("Because of the Lord's eternal love for Israel, He has made you king, to maintain justice and righteousness.") Perhaps the things that she saw and

learned about God and His people were retained.

Solomon applied some of his wisdom to write the books of Ecclesiastes, Song of Solomon, 3,000 Proverbs (wise sayings), and several of the Psalms. What should we do today if we want to have wisdom? Have group turn to James 1:5 and ask someone to read it aloud. **Remember that this kind of wisdom not only means knowing what to do, but also choosing to do it.**

PERSONALIZE

(15-20 minutes)

Distribute copies of "Wise Guys" activity sheet. Keep the same groups that worked on the newspaper and assign one situation to each group. Groups are to discuss the problem and decide on a solution. Allow about half the time for this.

Discuss each of the problems and chosen solutions. Were there other options? What are the possible consequences of the solutions? Would they help or hurt you? Others? Your relationship to God?

What most important choice will help you with all the other choices? (To love and obey God.) **You can begin now to make the right choices in life. Think through the possible** consequences to each of your choices. **If you choose to disobey God and lead sinful lives, the choice will cause you much unhappiness here on earth and separation from God in the life to come. If you choose to obey God, the choice will bring happiness here and inseparable joy in Heaven with God in the life to come.**

PRAYER/PRAISE

Close with a prayer circle focusing on the importance of making wise decisions so God will be pleased and can bless us.

JERUSALEM JOURNAL

Jerusalem, Israel   Wednesday, June 10   2 shekels

FOREIGN QUEEN PAYS VISIT

who? _____

what? _____

where? _____

when? _____

why? _____

how? _____

quote: " _____

_____."

(1 Kings 10:9)

TEMPLE DEDICATED BY KING

who? _____

what? _____

_____

where? _____

when? _____

why? _____

how? _____

quote: " _____

_____."

(1 Kings 8:23)

PROPHETIC DREAM REMEMBERED

who? _____

what? _____

_____

where? _____

when? _____

why? _____

_____

quote: " _____

_____

_____

_____."

(1 Kings 3:13)

WISE GUYS

Before you make choices do you think through the consequences? Read through the situation. Discuss it and decide on a solution.

1 Stephanie loves her younger brother, Mark, very much. But it's sometimes embarrassing when he is with her in public. He was born with a problem that causes him to talk loudly and move all the time. She was glad when one of the Bible school teachers said she would include him in her class. All the parents were invited to the closing program. Each class had a part. When Mark's class came up front to sing, he got right in the middle of the front row. Then he shouted, pointed, and jumped up and down all through the song. Stephanie was so humiliated she almost wished he hadn't come. After the program, she overhears some of the kids talking about him and calling him "Mental." What is she going to do?

2 Tony is glad when Adam invites him over to his house after school. "We'll stop at the store on the way," Adam says. "There's something I want to pick up first." They walk around the store for a while, then while they are in the school supply section Tony looks over at Adam and sees him take a bottle of whiteout solution for correcting mistakes. Adam looks around and quickly slips the bottle in his pocket. When he realizes that Tony has seen him, Adam whispers, "Have you ever tried sniffing this stuff? It gives you a real special feeling. It's great. And because you can use it at school, my folks never ask why I have it. I'll let you try it when we get home." How should Tony handle this situation?

3 It's Friday night and there is a special movie on TV that the kids mentioned at school. Your folks even say that it is a good family film. They are going to be gone for the evening and you'll be home alone. You're busy thinking about the movie and what you can eat while it's on. Then your mom says, "Didn't I hear your Sunday school teacher say you were supposed to write a special report on Solomon's temple for class? This is a good opportunity to do it since the house will be quiet and you won't be disturbed." As they go out the door, your dad says, "Don't forget that report. Your teacher is depending on you." After they leave, you pick up the Bible on the table. The movie starts in five minutes. What will you do?

WRITINGS OF THE KINGS, PSALMS AND PROVERBS

AIM: That your students will become acquainted with the books of Psalms and Proverbs and use them to find guidance for daily living

SCRIPTURE: 1 Samuel 22:1; Psalm 23; 51:3,4; 57:1, 2; 59:1-3; Proverbs 8:11; 10:2, 20; 13:22; 15:16; 16:16; 22:1 (Wisdom for daily living)

TEACHING NOTE: *Today's lesson focuses on both Psalms and Proverbs. In order to give them equal attention, the time schedule has been rearranged for today only.*

PREPARATION:
1. Photocopy activity sheets—one for each student.

PRESESSION (5-10 minutes)

ACTIVITIES
* Play a musical game that teaches about the psalms

PROBE ONE (20 minutes)

ACTIVITIES
* Participate in a choral reading from Psalm 23

MATERIALS
* Bibles
* "My Shepherd" Activity Sheet

PROBE TWO (20 minutes)

ACTIVITIES
* Match halves of several proverbs

MATERIALS
* Bibles
* "Fractured Proverbs" Activity Sheet

PERSONALIZE (5-10 minutes)

ACTIVITIES
* Rewrite a favorite proverb or psalm and make a poster of it

MATERIALS
* Paper, markers or colored pencils

PRESESSION

To get students thinking about the Psalms and the choral reading, play "Orchestra." **I am going to be the conductor and you will be the instruments. I'll use hand signals to direct you.** Divide the class into four groups.

Choose four simple sounds and signals. Each sound has a specific hand signal. For example, wiggling a finger might mean a high-pitched "ooh"; making a fist a "hmmm"; showing five fingers a growl; and raising a hand a shout of "yea!" Briefly rehearse these signals so everyone knows what they mean and makes the sounds. Now add a movement that means loudness and softness. For example, raising your other hand means louder while lowering it signifies softening it.

Conduct your "orchestra," changing the signal orders and loudness.

Optional: If you are near other groups, you may want to choose sounds that are quiet so others won't be disturbed. Even whispered sounds can be effective.

The oldest songbook in the world is the book of Psalms. Down through the years before Jesus came, the psalms were sung by God's people when they worshiped Him. **Although the people didn't make sounds like we did in our game, choirs in the temple in Jerusalem did act like an orchestra with different choirs singing or chanting lines of the song.**

PROBE ONE

Many of the psalms were written by David, the shepherd boy who became king of Israel. Have students turn to Psalm 59. **It is believed that when David wrote this psalm he was thinking about his escape from King Saul.** David prayed that God would deliver him from his enemies. David's wife, Saul's daughter Michal, helped him escape through the window. Have students take turns reading verses 1-3.

Now, Bible Investigators, can you detect what the theme is in this psalm? (God's constant love is our place of safety when evil enemies try to harm us.) **What can we learn about God from that?** (God always hears our prayers and helps us through tough times.)

When Saul and his soldiers began to hunt David, they chased him from town to town, always asking if anyone knew where he was. Once he hid in a cave at Adullam. Have someone read 1 Samuel 22:1 aloud. **Can you picture him crouching in a cave, waiting for word that King Saul had passed by?** The words in

another of David's psalms tell that story. Have students take turns reading Psalm 57:1, 2 aloud.

What word does David use to describe King Saul? (Disaster.) **What phrase does David use to show us he has confidence that God hears his prayer and will help him?** (God, who fulfills his purpose for me.)

It wouldn't be possible in one lesson to tell everything that happened in David's life. God was with him, keeping him safe from harm, and David was thankful. He became a great ruler of God's people and was admired and loved by them. He obeyed the Lord and led the people to obey also.

Once David disobeyed God's laws by deliberately ordering one of his generals into the front line of battle to be killed. Then he married the general's wife. **When his sin was pointed out, David was very sorry and asked God to forgive him. Check out Psalm 51:3, 4. Who do you think David was talking to when he wrote these words?** (God.)

Although David had really sinned against

the general and his wife, who did David say he had really sinned against? (God.) Any sin is really rebelling against God and His will for your life. No sin is too great to be forgiven if we are truly sorry for it and ask God's forgiveness. Then we must never do that sin again.

Perhaps the most beautiful and well-loved psalm is one David probably wrote when he was still a shepherd. A shepherd's life is rather lonely, and David spent his time making up songs of praise to God and singing them. Everyone around knew David's beautiful singing and harp playing.

Distribute copies of "My Shepherd" activity sheet. This is a choral reading where people talk rather than sing. Have students read it through silently several times. Assign the girls' and boys' solos in a way you think will most effectively communicate the feelings of David as he compared God's care for His people with a shepherd's care for his sheep. Practice with your students. You may want to have the two choirs (boys and girls) facing each other.

Optional: If your students are all boys or all girls, just divide the group into two choirs.

After you have done this reading as a class activity, talk about it together asking questions like these: What does the psalm mean to you today? What is the key phrase? How does the psalm make you feel about God? What character-istic of God does it reveal? What new title would you give the psalm?

King David ruled for forty years. During this time the nation of Israel was truly blessed by the Lord. The territory covered by the kingdom at this time was the largest it would ever be. The Lord helped David win the victories over all his enemies. David was called a "man after God's own heart." What do you think that means? (He wanted to do what God wanted him to do, obeyed the Lord in all things, kept God in first place in his life.)

Even as king, David was remembered as the "sweet psalmist of Israel." People never forgot his great deeds of bravery, but they remembered also his beautiful songs. For hundreds of years the psalms were the only songs sung by God's people. The verses we looked at today from the book of Psalms mean much more when we know the stories behind them.

Psalms are like the hymns we sing in church. We have songs of praise, prayer, and thanksgiving to God for His many blessings. Hymns too will mean much more when we pay attention to their messages.

Optional: If you have a longer time period let students look through hymnals and locate songs that tell stories. For example: "Away in a Manger," "Tell Me the Story of Jesus."

PROBE TWO

(20 minutes)

Thousands of years ago some of Egypt's kings were placed in tombs or pyramids when they died. There were many beautiful things put in these tombs with them. The Egyptians believed that a person would need his furniture, clothing, food, etc. in the next life. When King Solomon died he also left treasures, but they were hidden in the Bible, not a tomb. The Proverbs or wise sayings of Solomon hold some real riches for anyone who wants to take time to find them.

Pass out copies of "Fractured Proverbs" activity sheet. Have students work in pairs to do this activity. Partners can take turns looking up the passages and sharing their discoveries. Answers are: 3, 4, 6, 5, 7, 2, 1. Discuss the answers together.

What is better than rubies? (Wisdom.) Some people manage to gather great treasures. But these are worth nothing at the end of their lives.

What really counts with God? (The way a person lives, obeying God.)

The throne in the Egyptian King Tut's tomb was covered with precious jewels, gold and silver. Of how much worth are the words of a good person? (More valuable than silver or gold.)

Sometimes when very rich people die and leave an inheritance (usually money) to their children, the children use the money in a wrong way. But there is another kind of inheritance spoken of in God's Word. It can be handed down from parents to children. What is it? (Respect or a good reputation.)

An alabaster vase found in King Tut's tomb is worth a fortune. If you owned it, you would have a great treasure. But the Bible tells us that something else is worth more than treasures. What is it? (Respecting the Lord.)

Some people spend all their lives trying to get more gold or money. The Bible tells us they would spend their time better getting something else. What is it? (Wisdom.) **Do you agree with this? Why?** (Yes, money can become worthless because of stock market crashes or inflation.) Worldly wealth is only a temporary treasure.

King Tut was so rich that even the chests where his clothes were placed were made of gold and jewelry. Riches are very important to some people. What does God's Word say is more desirable (important) than riches? (A good name, good reputation, to be well thought of by others.)

These seven proverbs are just a few of Solomon's wise sayings that will help us now and in the future. There are many more waiting for you to discover them.

PERSONALIZE

(5-10 minutes)

Maybe you have a favorite from the psalms and proverbs we read. Now is your opportunity to rewrite it in a modern paraphrase and make a poster of it. Place the materials for the posters where they can be easily reached.

Invite students to share their creations with the group by having them pass them on to the person on their right. Then they read aloud the one they receive.

PRAYER/PRAISE

Close in prayer thanking God for His guidance through the Psalms and Proverbs. Remind students to take their posters home.

Fractured Proverbs

King Solomon left treasures for us in God's Word. They are wise sayings called Proverbs. They are waiting to be discovered by you. These treasures are worth more than any beautiful ornaments or jewels discovered anywhere in the world. Here are a few of them paraphrased for you. Use your Bible to help you match them up. Put the number of the last half of the Proverb by its match.

A. Proverbs 8:11

Wisdom is more precious than rubies...

B. Proverbs 10:2

Treasures gotten by doing wrong have no value...

C. Proverbs 10:20

The words of a good person are choice silver...

D. Proverbs 13:22

Good people's inheritance can be left for their grandchildren...

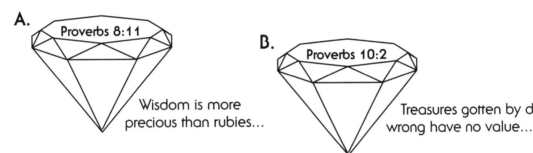

1. ...but the thoughts of the wicked have little value.

2. ...to choose understanding than silver!

3. ...nothing you desire can compare with her.

4. ...but right living will deliver you from death.

5. ...but bad people's wealth is left for good people.

6. ...to be respected is better than silver or gold.

7. ...than great wealth and much trouble.

E. Proverbs 15:16

Better to be poor and respect the Lord...

F. Proverbs 16:16

It is better to get wisdom than gold...

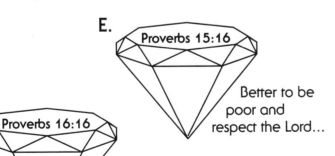

G. Proverbs 22:1

A good reputation is more important than being rich...

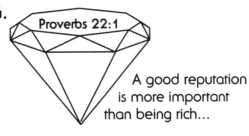

My Shepherd

All: The Lord is my shepherd,
I shall not be in want.

Girls: He makes me lie down in green
pastures,
Boy Solo: He leads me beside quiet waters,
Boys: He restores my soul.

Girls: He guides me in paths of
righteousness for his name's sake.

Boys: Even though I walk
through the valley of the shadow
of death,
Girls: I will fear no evil,
For you are with me;

Boys: You prepare a table before me
in the presence of my enemies.

Girl Solo: You anoint my head with oil;
Girls: My cup overflows.

Boys: Surely goodness and love will
follow me
All the days of my life,
All: And I will dwell in
the house of the Lord forever.

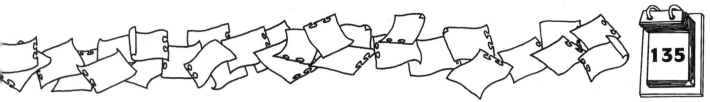
THE NORTHERN KINGDOM, ISRAEL

AIM: That your students will see the importance of remaining faithful to God even if others try to get them to disobey Him

SCRIPTURE: 1 Kings 11:26-33; Hosea 14:1; Amos 4:12; Hebrews 13:5
(A few people remain faithful to God although the nation of Israel fails to obey God's commands and is conquered and taken captive by other nations)

PREPARATION:
1. Photocopy activity sheet—one for each student.
2. Prepare obstacle course as described in PRESESSION.

PRESESSION (5-10 minutes)

ACTIVITIES
* Participate in an activity showing how outside pressures affect our obedience to God

MATERIALS
* Cotton balls—one for each student

PERSPECTIVE (10 minutes)

ACTIVITIES
* Learn about the background of the division of Israel into two kingdoms

MATERIALS
* Bibles
* Chalkboard and chalk or large sheet of paper and marker

PROBE (20 minutes)

ACTIVITIES
* Read a skit about King Jeroboam

MATERIALS
* "The Golden Calf Caper" Activity Sheet

PERSONALIZE (15-20 minutes)

ACTIVITIES
* Use an activity sheet to stress the importance of standing up for God even if no one else does

MATERIALS
* "Pressure Points" Activity Sheet

PRESESSION

Before class set up an obstacle course in your room by placing some chairs and a wastebasket in the middle of a cleared area. Divide early arrivals into teams, the Leaders and the Blockers. Have each Leader place a cotton ball on his/her head.

As latecomers arrive, continue to divide the number of people so half are on the Leader team and half on the Blockers. Station the Blockers along the raceway. Their object is to try and blow cotton balls off the heads of the Leaders.

No one is allowed to touch these balls. If a ball falls off, that Leader joins the Blockers. When a Leader completes the race, a Blocker is added to the Leader team and tries to complete the course. The team with the most members at the end of the time period is the winner.

End the game and briefly talk about it. How did you feel about the Blockers who tried to keep you from completing the race? How did it feel to have the power to stop Leaders from reaching their goal? How did you feel when you saw the other team gaining new members? How is this like situations you may get in today? Point out the pressure put on individuals by opposing groups. **Something like that happened after King Solomon died.**

PERSPECTIVE

When Canaan was conquered by the Israelites, how was the land divided? (Into twelve areas.) **Each of these areas united to form the nation of Israel when Saul became king.** Place the following list on the chalkboard:

Kingdom of Israel
Saul
David
Solomon

During the reign of David and Solomon, David's son, they continued as one nation. Then things changed. **What do you think happens when a group of states or countries, who were united to make one country, become unhappy with their leaders?** (They split into two or more groups.) **As Bible Investigators, let's find out what happened to cause the twelve tribes of Israel to divide into two groups.**

The twelve tribes of Israel had become a wealthy and powerful kingdom under their first three rulers. God had promised to be with His people as long as they were faithful. King Solomon, in spite of his wisdom, was influenced by his foreign wives to turn away from the true God and worship idols!

King Solomon noticed that a young man named Jeroboam was very brave and hard working. Solomon made him one of his officers. One day as Jeroboam was leaving Jerusalem, a prophet named Ahijah came to him. They were alone in the field. Ahijah pulled off his new cloak and tore it into twelve pieces. **Ahijah gave Jeroboam ten pieces and told him something special. What did he say?** Have students look up 1 Kings 11:31-33 and ask someone to read it aloud.

When King Solomon heard about this prophecy, he tried to have Jeroboam killed. But Jeroboam escaped and stayed in Egypt until Solomon died.

Rehoboam, Solomon's son, became the next king of Israel. He demanded so much to be paid in taxes that the people in the north rebelled. When Rehoboam sent out his tax collector, they

killed him. Rehoboam was afraid they would kill him too. From then on Rehoboam ruled over only the southern tribes of Judah and Benjamin.

Add this information to the chalkboard:

Southern Kingdom: Judah
King: Rehoboam
Northern Kingdom: Israel
King: Jeroboam

Jeroboam became the leader of the ten tribes in the north, just as the prophet Ahijah had said. However, he did not do what Ahijah had told him to do as king. Have someone read aloud 1 Kings 11:38. As you talk about him and other kings of Israel, list them on the chalkboard along with the prophets God sent to warn them. Example:

KING	PROPHET
Jeroboam	Ahijah

Suppose you were an undercover follower of God during the time Jeroboam was king. Let's listen in and find out how Jeroboam disobeyed the Lord.

PROBE

(20 minutes)

Distribute copies of "The Golden Calf Caper" activity sheet. Choose two students to read the parts of the Boss and Agent 006. The rest of the group can follow along on their activity sheets.

Optional: Let students wear dark glasses, trench (rain) coats, and disguises to act out this skit.

The kings of Israel who followed Jeroboam were all evil. God sent prophets to warn them of punishment if they did not obey Him. **Elijah was a prophet sent from God to warn King Ahab and the people to stop their wicked way of living.** Write their names in the appropriate columns.

In spite of Elijah's warnings, Ahab continued to worship the idol Baal and to do all kinds of evil. Two of Ahab's sons ruled after him, and both continued in their father's wicked ways. **Another great prophet, Elisha, followed Elijah. He too gave God's message to the kings and the people.** List Joram and Elisha.

The next kings also allowed the people of Israel to worship the golden calves. During these years more prophets were sent from the Lord with messages. List Jeroboam II and Jonah; Zecharias and Amos; Shallum and Hosea.

Finally, after about two hundred years, the punishment for their disobedience came. God allowed the king of Assyria to capture Samaria, the capital of Israel, and carry the people of Israel away as captives.

Of all nineteen kings who ruled Israel, not one was faithful to the true God. There were still some good people in Israel, however, even though they were greatly outnumbered! They followed the true God in spite of their wicked leaders.

Optional: If time permits, look up Hosea 14:1 and Amos 4:12 to find out what warnings these prophets gave the evil kings.

PERSONALIZE

Have you ever wished for the courage to stand up for what is right when everyone else is afraid? Divide the class into two teams. Distribute copies of "Pressure Points" activity sheet. Do only the top part of the page now.

Assign one situation to each group. They will have five minutes to read it over and plan how to role play it in two different ways: helpful and harmful.

Have each group act out their situation. When a group finishes both role plays, the rest of the class can vote on the options that were offered. They can use thumbs up if it was helpful and thumbs down if it was harmful.

Discuss the results together. Did the person remain faithful to God? As a result of that choice do you think s/he would be more courageous the next time? What do you think the rest of the group thought of him/her? Would they be more willing to follow the person and his/her good example in another situation?

Do the bottom half of the activity sheet individually. Talk about them together. **Why is it harder to stand for what is right when the group doesn't want to?** (Because you don't want to be different, want to be accepted by the group.)

Is it better to do what is right than be the most popular person in school? Your students don't want to be rejected by their peers. Soon, if not already, their compulsion to be accepted as part of the group will make it even harder. Be sensitive to the pressures your students are encountering and encourage them to be courageous and

strong rather than to reprimand them for following the crowd.

Do you think there are kids who would follow you if you stood up for what is right? Although situations differ, your students would probably be surprised to find that some kids really want them to stand up for the right and are willing to follow, if only they have a courageous leader.

Do you think other kids would respect you even if they didn't follow you? Even though they are too timid or peer pressure conscious to follow, most people are impressed when Christians stand up for what is right. They expect more from these believers and are disappointed if they don't live up to their hopes.

Are you really ever alone when you try to do what God wants you to do? Check out Hebrews 13:5 and 6 for a quick answer. Have someone read these verses aloud. **God will always hear and answer your prayers. He has promised to help us obey Him and will give us courage to stand for what is right even when others try to influence us to do wrong.**

PRAYER/PRAISE

Close with a circle of affirmation. One at a time, ask each person to say to the person on the left, "God can help you stand for what is right. He will never leave you alone." Finish with the group saying "Amen."

THE GOLDEN CALF CAPER

(Scene 1: Late night, under the street light on a corner in a deserted part of town) (Characters: Boss and Agent 006, both in trench coats)

BOSS: Is that you, 006? What's the code word?

006: "Faithful." Sorry, I'm a little late tonight, Boss. I've been following King Jeroboam all day and ended up on the far side of town.

BOSS: I know he's been worried about the people going down to the temple in Jerusalem to worship God.

006: Early this morning I followed him to Gold-Finger, the goldsmith in Idol Alley. Seems he had ordered two golden calves. I overheard him say to put one in the city of Dan in the north and the other in Bethel in the south.

BOSS: Sounds like our tip was right. He's up to something all right. But what? Stick with him, 006, and keep me posted.

(Scene 2: Same street corner, one week later)

BOSS: 006?

006: "Faithful," Boss. I followed another tip and . . .

BOSS: And?

006: Today Jeroboam called some of his henchmen to the palace. He made them priests even though they're not from the tribe of Levi as God commanded.

BOSS: Something big is going on here. I wouldn't be surprised if he even made a new feast day.

006: Funny you should mention it because that's exactly what he did next.

BOSS: Anything more on the golden calves?

006: Word on the street is that he's going to go ahead and try to get the people to worship those statues by saying they are the gods that brought them out of Egypt.

BOSS: Why the old rebel! Don't let him out of your sight, 006. Meanwhile I'll keep praying that people out there will come to their senses and realize this is all a bunco scam to fool them.

(Scene 3: Same street corner, one month later)

006: Boss, have I got news for you!

BOSS: The code word?

006: "Faithful." The action's going down. This afternoon Jeroboam offered sacrifices and burned incense in front of one of those golden calves!

BOSS: Wow! He's leading the people of Israel to sin against their heavenly Father. Sure as anything God will have to punish such widespread disobedience to His commands. Our only hope is that a few people will remain . . .

006: Faithful, Boss. Faithful!

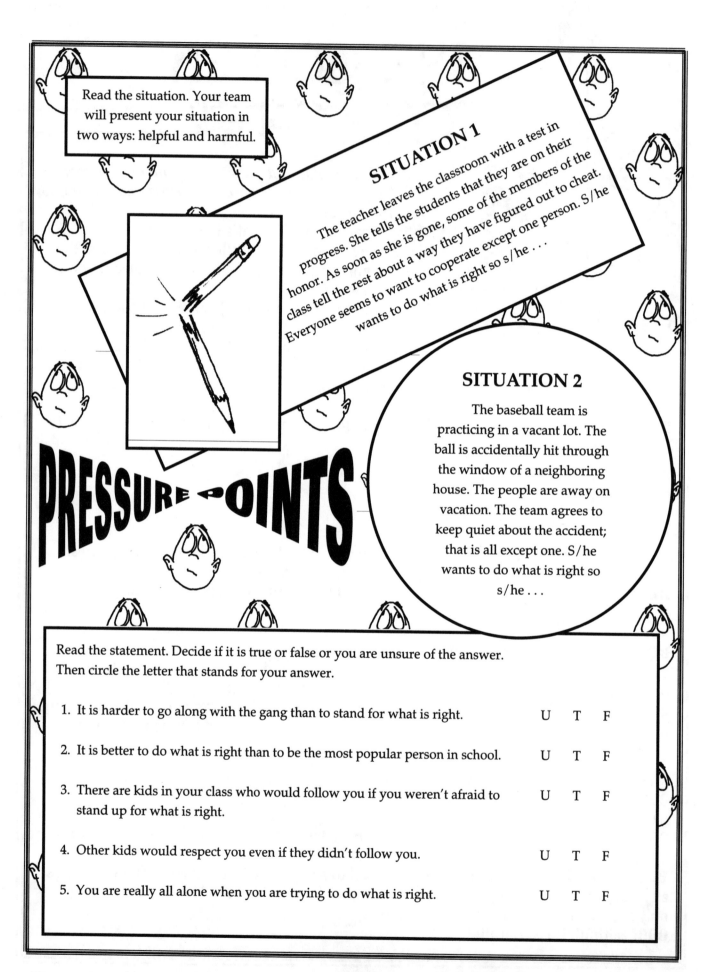

Read the situation. Your team will present your situation in two ways: helpful and harmful.

SITUATION 1

The teacher leaves the classroom with a test in progress. She tells the students that they are on their honor. As soon as she is gone, some of the members of the class tell the rest about a way they have figured out to cheat. Everyone seems to want to cooperate except one person. S/he wants to do what is right so s/he . . .

SITUATION 2

The baseball team is practicing in a vacant lot. The ball is accidentally hit through the window of a neighboring house. The people are away on vacation. The team agrees to keep quiet about the accident; that is all except one. S/he wants to do what is right so s/he . . .

Read the statement. Decide if it is true or false or you are unsure of the answer. Then circle the letter that stands for your answer.

1. It is harder to go along with the gang than to stand for what is right.　　U　T　F

2. It is better to do what is right than to be the most popular person in school.　　U　T　F

3. There are kids in your class who would follow you if you weren't afraid to stand up for what is right.　　U　T　F

4. Other kids would respect you even if they didn't follow you.　　U　T　F

5. You are really all alone when you are trying to do what is right.　　U　T　F

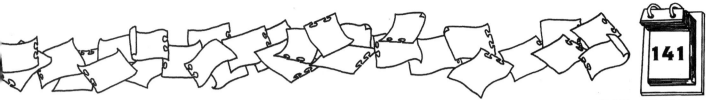

THE SOUTHERN KINGDOM, JUDAH

AIM: That your students will realize that if they are faithful to God and His teachings, God is able to use them to bless others

SCRIPTURE: 1 Kings 12:1-17; Isaiah 1:4; 10:21; Micah 6:8

PREPARATION:
1. Photocopy activity sheets—one for each student.
2. Prepare a set of matching game cards as described in PRESESSION.

PRESESSION (5-10 minutes)

ACTIVITIES
* Play a game to become familiar with the names of Judah's kings and prophets

MATERIALS
* Index cards

PERSPECTIVE (10 minutes)

ACTIVITIES
* Make a pop-up map to see how the kingdoms were divided

MATERIALS
* "The Divided Kingdom" Activity Sheet
* Crayons, markers, or colored pencils, scissors

PROBE (20 minutes)

ACTIVITIES
* Use an activity sheet to learn more about some of the kings and prophets of Judah

MATERIALS
* Bibles
* "Mixed-Up Monarchs and Puzzling Prophets" Activity Sheet

PERSONALIZE (15-20 minutes)

ACTIVITIES
* Imagine you are a child leader and make a list of things you want to do

MATERIALS
* Bibles
* Paper and pencils

PRESESSION

(5-10 minutes)

Cut index cards in half and write the following names on them, making two cards of each name: Rehoboam, Asa, Jehoshaphat, Joash, Amaziah, Uzziah, Jotham, Hezekiah, Josiah. Mark the other side of these cards with the letter K. These were all kings over Judah.

Make a second set of cards in the same manner with these names: Obadiah, Joel, Isaiah, Micah, Nahum, Zephaniah, Jeremiah, Habakkuk, Daniel, Ezekiel. On the other side of these cards put the letter P. These were all prophets of Judah.

As people come, give a set of matching cards to every two to four, alternating sets of kings and prophets. Tell groups to shuffle the cards and place them name down on the table. Players take turns by turning over two cards and reading the names on them. If they match, they can be removed and the player keeps them and takes another turn. If they don't match, they are turned name down again and the next player takes a turn. Continue playing until all the matches have been made. The players with the most cards are the winners.

Optional: If you have a longer time schedule, have groups exchange cards with other groups so teams get a chance to match both kings and prophets.

The game you just played used the names of some of the kings and prophets who lived in the southern kingdom of Judah. What was the name of the king of Israel who ruled over the ten tribes in the northern kingdom of Israel? (Jeroboam.) **Let's take a closer look at that northern kingdom on a map.**

PERSPECTIVE

(10 minutes)

Distribute copies of "The Divided Kingdom" activity sheet. **Where is the capital of our country?** (Washington, D.C., Ottawa, Canada.) **Has it always been there?** If no one knows give an example. When the United States was divided for a time into the Union and the Confederacy, there were two capitals: Washington, D.C., and Richmond, Virginia.

When the whole nation of Israel was under the rule of King David, Jerusalem was the capital. Have students find the temple at Jerusalem on their maps.

When the nation divided, the northern kingdom had to have a capital. First it was in Shechem, then moved to Tirzah. Finally Samaria was picked and it remained their capital until the northern kingdom ended. Have students find Samaria on the map.

Briefly review some of the facts from last week's lesson. All the kings of Israel who followed Jeroboam were all evil. God continued to send prophets to warn them of punishment if they would not follow His commands. **Elijah was sent to warn wicked King Ahab and Queen Jezebel.** He had a confrontation with the evil priests of the false god, Baal, at Mount Carmel. There God proved to the people He was the only living, true God. Have people find Mt. Carmel on the map.

The prophet Elisha followed Elijah. When Elijah was taken up to heaven in a fiery chariot in a whirlwind, Elisha continued to warn the wicked kings. Have students find the picture of Elijah and Elisha.

Students can color the map, cut along the dotted lines, and fold up the pictures of Jerusalem, Samaria, Mt. Carmel, and Elijah and Elisha. The rest of the pop-up pictures will be done in PROBE.

In our last lesson we reviewed what happened during the history of the northern kingdom of Israel. Now we will learn what was happening at the same time in the southern kingdom of Judah.

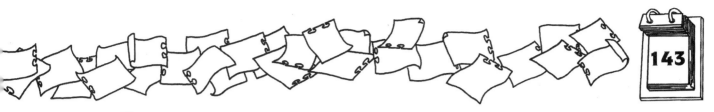

PROBE

Rehoboam, Solomon's son, was to be crowned king over all of Israel. A large group headed by Jeroboam had an offer for him. What was it? Invite students to turn to 1 Kings 12:4 and ask someone to read it aloud. **What happened after that?** Have people take turns reading verses 5-17 aloud.

During the days of Solomon the worship of heathen idols had begun to spread. This situation grew worse under Rehoboam and the people were led to sin against God. Students can find the picture of Baal worship on their maps, cut, and fold it up.

When the people of Judah forgot God's laws, they began to do all kinds of wicked things. Their punishment soon began. The history of Judah is very much like the history of Israel. But there were some very important differences. All nineteen of the kings of Israel were wicked. **Eight of the twenty rulers of Judah were good.** They followed the commands of God. They were good leaders who encouraged their people to also be obedient to God. **Because they were faithful to God and His teachings, God was able to use them to bless others.**

Another difference was that the kings of Israel were from many different families. The kings of Judah all descended from David's family. Hand out copies of "Mixed Up Monarchs and Puzzling Prophets" activity sheet. **Look at this list of kings. All of them were descendants of King David. They were good kings who tried to obey God.** Have students work individually to unscramble the names.

Go over the mini-descriptions of each king pointing out the way God used them to bless His people. Be sure to say their names aloud so your class can recognize them when they hear them again. Two of these kings were only children when they began to rule. Joash was seven years old and Josiah was only eight years old.

Before and after some of the good kings, there were wicked rulers. Often when a good king began to rule, he had to get rid of the worship of idols and other evil practices in which the wicked king before him had led. So the nation of Judah went back and forth between obeying and disobeying God.

God sent prophets to Judah, just as He sent them to Israel. Let's read two brief messages from the prophets to the people. Have two people look up Isaiah 1:4 and Micah 6:8 and read them aloud. **Now look at the list of prophets on your activity sheet. These prophets warned the people of punishment to come if they continued to be disobedient.**

Have students unscramble these names. Go over the mini-descriptions of each prophet pointing out the way God used them to warn His people. Be sure to say their names aloud so your class can recognize them when they hear them again.

The punishment for Judah was to be the same as that for Israel—captivity. The nation of Judah lasted nearly a century and a half longer than Israel. You might think that Judah would have learned a lesson from Israel, after seeing Israel taken captive into foreign lands. But Judah also disobeyed more than they obeyed.

The words of the prophets came true, and from time to time Judah was invaded by armies from Egypt and Babylon. King Nebuchadnezzar of Babylon carried off captives to his country in three different invasions. The third time he broke down the walls of Jerusalem and burned the temple and palaces. The third time, Jeremiah, a prophet who lived during the last days of the kingdom of Judah, foretold that the captivity would last for seventy years. Have people cut and fold back the two pictures of the captivity that are on their pop-up maps.

God had preserved the descendants of King David from generation to generation and they ruled for four hundred years. Then the kingdom came to an end. But God planned for another kingdom that was still to come. It was

not an earthly one. **God promised that one day all the world would be blessed by an obedient person whose family could be traced all the way back to King David, and even farther, to Abraham. Who was this person?** (Jesus.)

What is a remnant? (A small, remaining part of something, a piece left over.) **What did the prophet Isaiah say about a remnant in Isaiah 10:21?** (A remnant of the people of Jacob, God's people, would return to God.)

Whenever the kings were faithful to God and led their people to obey Him, the people were blessed. That's still true today.

PERSONALIZE

(15-20 minutes)

Why does God punish His people? Check out Hebrews 12:10, 11. (So we can share in His holiness, become holy like He is.) **Can punishment ever be good for us?** (Yes, no, unsure.) Although it is very painful at the time, discipline helps us stop doing wrong and start doing right.

God's prophets told the people of Israel and Judah how to be faithful to God. How can we learn what God wants us to do today? (Read the Bible, prayer, advice of other Christians.)

Imagine you are a young leader like Joash or Josiah. Make a list of five things you want to accomplish. What are they? Use Micah 6:8 for a guideline. If you were rewriting this verse for today you might say something like this: The Lord wants you to be fair to others, love being kind to them, and humbly trust and obey God.

Distribute paper and pencils and let students work at this individually. Invite them to share their lists with the group when they are done. **God is pleased when we willingly obey Him. Then He can use us to bless others by showing them the only loving, heavenly Father who loves and forgives His children.**

PRAYER/PRAISE

Say a prayer of thanksgiving for God's forgiveness and desire to show us His love, even when we are disobedient.

THE DIVIDED KINGDOM

Here is a map showing how the land was divided into two kingdoms, Israel and Judah. Color the map. Cut along the dotted lines of the pictures and fold up on the solid lines to make a pop-up map.

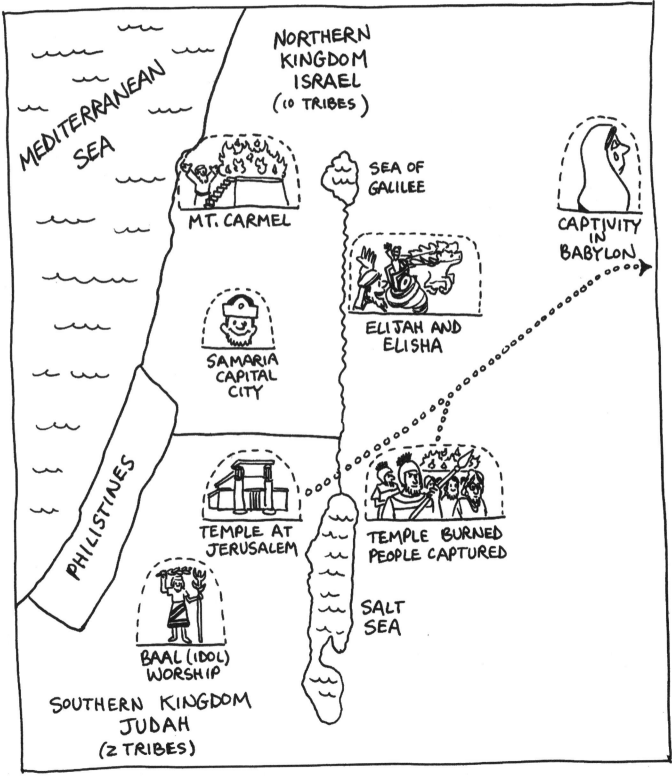

MIXED-UP MONARCHS & PUZZLING PROPHETS

Sammi Shovel was learning some of the kings and prophets of Judah, but he's run into a problem. While he was out of the room, a wind blew all the letters around. Now everything is mixed up. Can you help him straighten them up so he can finish his lesson? Use the Word Bank if you need help.

KINGS OF JUDAH

MOLNOOS _____
rich, wise man

BEHRMOOA _____
heavy taxes

SAA _____
defeated Ethiopians

THAJPHSOEHA _____
religious education

HASJO _____
repaired the temple

ZAMAHIA _____
conquered Edomites

HUZAZI _____
builder, farmer, warrior

MOTHAJ _____
godly builder

ZEHEKAHI _____
restores worship and Passover

HIASJO _____
cleaned temple and restored obedience to
God's laws

PROPHETS OF JUDAH

HIDABOA _____
Edom's doom

LEJO _____
locust plague and punishment

HAISAI _____
God's salvation through Messiah

HIMAC _____
God wants right living, love

MANHU _____
comfort, Assyria destroyed

PHEZHINAA _____
Judah's judgment and blessing

MERJHEIA _____
gloom and doom because of sin

KABKUHKA _____
questions unpunished evil

LINADE _____
visions and faith

KELZIEE _____
Jerusalem punished by Babylon

KINGS	KINGS	PROPHETS	PROPHETS
JOTHAM	SOLOMON	ISAIAH	JOEL
REHOBOAM	JOSIAH	OBADIAH	NAHUM
JEHOSHAPHAT	HEZEKIAH	EZEKIEL	HABAKKUK
AMAZIAH	JOASH	JEREMIAH	ZEPHANIAH
UZZIAH	ASA	MICAH	DANIEL

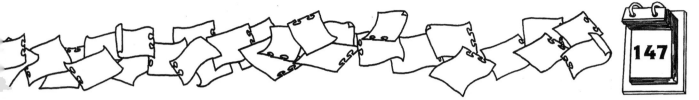

CAPTIVITY

AIM: That your students will realize that although God allows His people to be punished, He is still with those who trust Him and promises to help them

SCRIPTURE: Daniel 1:3-20; 6:1-28 (God allows His people to be taken captive but is with those who trust Him and promises they will return to their homeland)

PREPARATION:
1. Photocopy activity sheets—one for each student.
2. Prepare balloons for the balloon burst as described in PRESESSION.

PRESESSION   (5-10 minutes)

ACTIVITIES
* Preview events from the captivity of Judah in Babylon

MATERIALS
* Balloons, slips of paper—one for each student
* Straight pins, or unbent paper clips

PERSPECTIVE   (10 minutes)

ACTIVITIES
* Experience an emotional story of a captive in a strange land

MATERIALS

PROBE   (20 minutes)

ACTIVITIES
* Take part in a rap about Daniel

MATERIALS
* Bibles
* "Daniel, Diets, and Darius" Activity Sheet

PERSONALIZE   (15-20 minutes)

ACTIVITIES
* Rewrite a warning from Jeremiah

MATERIALS
* "Modern Prophet" Activity Sheet

PRESESSION

Before class, write events from the lesson on slips of paper. You will need one event for each student. Use things like: a prophet warning people of God's punishment; someone refusing to eat some food; a man taking treasures from one country back to another; a hand, writing a message on the wall; someone being thrown into a den of lions; someone praying for others, a prisoner being marched away. (Insert the slips of paper into the balloons, blow them up, then tie the balloons shut.)

As students arrive, let them choose a balloon and burst it by poking it with a pin or the end of an unbent paper clip. People quickly line up. They must pantomime the action described on their slip of paper. The pantomime is done in the order that the students are standing, even though it's mixed up. The rest of the group try to guess what action, story, or Bible person the pantomimes describe.

Was it easy to guess the story or person from the clues? (No, Yes.) Why? (Everything was mixed up, the major events like the lion's den gave it away.) How is that like understanding what God is doing in the lives of His people? Our view of history is very limited. We can only see one thing happening at a time. It seems like a puzzle, all jumbled up and not making much sense. God can see the beginning, the ending, and everything in-between. It is all a part of His plan for His people. What do you think it was like for the people of Judah who were taken captive?

PERSPECTIVE

Close your eyes, relax, and listen while I tell you a Bible story. Don't answer the questions aloud, but just think about them. Imagine you are part of the story.

An enemy army has conquered your country. They are taking you as a captive. You are being taken from your home and moved to a place hundreds of miles away. You remember how the enemy soldiers fought with your army. The battles were noisy and fierce. Many people were wounded and killed. You're not even sure your father is still alive. You haven't seen any of your family since the war. How do you feel? [Pause]

Your feet are sore. You are hungry and wish you could stop for a meal and rest. You keep thinking how good it would be to sleep in your own bed in your own home again. What are you feeling? [Pause]

You remember how God's spokesman told your people that an enemy would capture them and rule for seventy years. He said that it was because the people had dis- obeyed God. And now everything has happened just as he said. How do you feel about these events?** [Pause]

Even the rich treasures from God's house have been brought to this country. What do you think of God's allowing this to happen? [Pause] **How do you feel about Him?** [Pause]

You are now living as a prisoner in a strange land where the language, the customs—the whole way of living—is different from what you knew. The people don't even worship God like you do. They expect you to change your ways and live like them. How do you feel about that? [Pause] **You choose to continue praying to God. What will you pray about/for?** [Pause] **Your name is Daniel.**

Have students open their eyes and talk about this story. Use the questions within the story for discussion. **Do you think Daniel doubted God or felt abandoned by Him? Let's see if we can find out how Daniel reacted to the hard situation he was now in.**

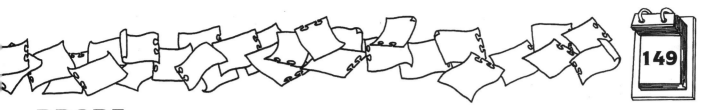

PROBE

(20 minutes)

Distribute copies of "Daniel, Diets, and Darius" activity sheet. Allow time for the students to read through this rap silently. Ask for volunteers to take the parts of God, Daniel, Belshazzar, and the Babylon Princes. The rest of the group can be the chorus that keeps the rhythm and theme going.

Optional: This rap can be done with handclaps or finger snaps to help kids keep the beat better. It is based on a rhythm of four beats. The words to be accented are underlined for you.

After the rap has been read, look over the Biblical accounts and note some of the details of these stories. **Check out Daniel 1:3-20. What were some of the things that the Babylonian king did for or to Daniel and his friends?** (Gave them a home in his palace, taught them his language and literature, gave them food and drink, new names.) The names the boys were given were names associated with the Babylonian idols. **Why do you think the king did all these things?** While seeming to be giving special privileges, the king really intended to force these young servants of God to conform to the heathen standards of Babylon.

Read verse 8. What did Daniel decide? (Not to defile himself with the royal food and wine.) Daniel knew that these items had been offered to the false gods first. They were also things God had told His people not to eat.

Daniel asked for permission to eat vegetables and drink water for ten days. What happened at the end of that period? (The boys were found to be healthier than the others, were allowed to continue their diet.)

Look at verse 20. **How did God bless Daniel and his friends for obeying Him in this matter?** At the end of the three-year training period, the king found that they were ten times better than all the other wise men of his kingdom.

Meanwhile King Nebuchadnezzar invaded Judah a second and a third time. The second time he brought ten thousand more captives back to Babylon. These people were not treated as slaves but were allowed to have homes, farm the land, and enjoy most of the privileges of other subjects of the king. While looking like real benefits, these advantages were designed to make the people conform to Babylonian culture and religion. They were all attempts to turn the people from the one true God to worthless idols. **An idol is anything that has first place in your life. What are some idols people worship today?** (Money, fame, popularity, TV, sports, themselves.) **Whenever these kinds of idols receive more attention than God, we are just as disobedient as these heathen people.**

Among these new captives was a prophet named Ezekiel. Ezekiel received many strange visions of the glory of the Lord, foretold the final destruction of Jerusalem, and many other events of importance. The final prophecies about Jerusalem came true. During the last invasion, the temple and palace in Jerusalem were burned and the city was left in complete ruin.

In Babylon, Daniel continued to serve as an official during the leadership of several kings. He was there for seventy years and remained true to God all that time. One of the kings he served was Belshazzar. Have students turn to chapter 5 of Daniel and skim through it for answers.

What evil thing was Belshazzar doing at his feast? (Drinking wine out of the golden goblets from God's temple and praising their carved idols.) **Whose hand do you think it was that wrote on the wall?** (God's.) **Check out verses 26-28. What did Daniel say the handwriting meant?** (God would end Belshazzar's kingdom, the king was not good enough to escape punishment, the kingdom would be divided between the Medes and the Persians.) **Look at verse 30. What happened to Belshazzar?** (He was killed that night.)

The new king, Darius, saw how wise and fair Daniel was and promoted him to chief of the three presidents over the land. How did

the princes of Babylon feel about Daniel? (Jealous, angry, wanted to get rid of him.) These wicked men found that Daniel was such a trusting and obedient man to God that the only way they could bring a charge against him was to tie it in with his faithfulness to God.

Turn to Daniel 6:10. **What did Daniel do about the king's law that no one could pray to any god or man except him?** Prayed to God as he always did.) **Check out verse 16. What did the king have to do to Daniel?** (Throw him in a den of lions.) **What did God do for Daniel because he remained faithful to the Lord?** (Sent an angel to shut the lions' mouths.) **Daniel showed his faith during all the years of the captivity of his people. Soon after the Medes and Persians took Babylon they let the captive Jews return to their own land.**

PERSONALIZE

(15-20 minutes)

God's people were taken into captivity because they disobeyed God's law and worshiped false gods. God sent spokesmen like Jeremiah to the people to warn them of their punishment. What do you think would happen if God chose you to be a spokesman like him? Hand out copies of "Modern Prophet" activity sheet.

Let volunteers read the directions and the Bible passage aloud. Allow students time to identify the promise and paraphrase the message in a modern version. If you have time, have students share these with the group.

God is still looking for faithful people like Jeremiah and Daniel. Even if you are surrounded by temptations as they were surrounded by idol worship or threatened by people who don't want you to worship God, you can still be faithful to the one true God.

PRAYER/PRAISE

Sing "Dare to be a Daniel" or close with a prayer circle asking for courage to trust God. Thank Him for keeping His promises.

GOD:	My **prophet**, Isaiah, **once** fore**told** that the **treasures** of the **kingdom**, all the **silver** and the **gold**; along with the **people,** and the **royal** fami**ly**, would be **hauled** off to **Bab'lon** in cap**tivity**. A **hundred** years **later** I **called** on a **man**, "Jere**miah**," I **said**, "you'll be **my** spokes**man**. Please **tell** all the **people** that for **seven**ty **years**, Nebuchad**nezzar**, the **king**, will **cause** lots of **tears**."
CHORUS:	Just **trust** in **God**, He's **there** with **you**, He'll **keep** His **promises**, He's **al**ways **true**.
BOYS:	**Dan**iel, Hana**niah**, Mi**shael**, and Aza**riah**, all **four** Hebrew **boys**, were **chosen** for their **poise**. Each was **given** a **diff**erent **name** and a **chance** for **fame**. So **to** the king's **pal**ace, they all **came**.
CHORUS:	Just **trust** in **God**, He's **there** with **you**, He'll **keep** His **promises**, He's **al**ways **true**.
DANIEL:	We were **picked** for special **training**, but the **food** was very **paining**. There was **meat** that God **said**, "Don't **eat** it—not a **shred**. And the **wine**, that's **served** with **ev**ery **meal** has been **offered** to their **god**; an **idol** that's not **real**." We **had** to make a **choice**, so our **decision** we did **voice**. Then **God** blessed us **greatly**, gave us **wisdom** that was **weighty**.
CHORUS:	Just **trust** in **God**, He's **there** with **you**, He'll **keep** His **promises**, He's **al**ways **true**.
GOD:	A **second** and a **third** time, my **pe**ople **paid** for **their** crime. E**zekiel** my **prophet** told the **people** to **stop** it. Nebuchad**nezzar** burned **Jerus'lem** . . .
DANIEL:	Being a **captive** was **troublesome**.
CHORUS:	Just **trust** in **God**, He's **there** with **you**, He'll **keep** His **promises**, He's **al**ways **true**.
DANIEL:	I **served** Bab'lon's **kings** for **many** a **year**, I **stayed** true to **God** and His **Word** I did **revere**. One **night** the **king**, Bel**shazzar** by **name**, used our **temple** vessels as **cups**. Oh **shame**!
BELSHAZZAR:	The **fingers** of a **hand** wrote a **message** on my **wall**. I was **scared** half to **death** and for **Daniel** sent a **call**.
DANIEL:	It **means**, my **king**, that your **days** are **through**. The **Medes** are **coming**, and they're **looking** for **you**! You've **mocked** the **Lord**, they'll **kill** you **tonight.** Your evil **deeds** are **offensive** in His **sight**!
CHORUS:	Just **trust** in **God**, He's **there** with **you**, He'll **keep** His **promises**, He's **al**ways **true**.
DANIEL:	The **new** king, **Darius**, made me **chief** of **staff**.
BABYLON PRINCES:	He **said** he'd **acted** on **our** be**half**. We were **mad** so we **made** up a **plan** to get **rid** of **Daniel**, the **Lord's** faithful **man**.
DARIUS:	Oh **Daniel**, I'm so **sorry** to **say**, since you **prayed** to your **God**, I must **lock** you **away**. Way down **deep** in the lions' **den**, will your **Lord** help you **out**? Will I **see** you **again**?
DANIEL:	He **will**, my **friend**, just you **wait** and **see**. The **Lord** hears my **prayers**. In the **morning** I'll be **free**.
CHORUS:	Just **trust** in **God**, He's **there** with **you**, He'll **keep** His **promises**, He's **al**ways **true**.
DARIUS:	Let **all** people **know**, within this **land**, that **Daniel's** God should be **wor**shiped.
DANIEL:	**Amen**!
CHORUS:	Just **trust** in **God**, He's **there** with **you**, He'll **keep** His **promises**, He's **al**ways **true**.

Modern Prophet

Bible Investigators: Jeremiah was only a boy when God called him to give messages to His people. Can you identify the promise in this message that the prophet Jeremiah gave the faithful people of his day? Write your answer on the lines below the passage.

• •

"For I know the plans I have for you . . . plans to prosper you and not to harm you, plans to give you hope and a future. You will seek me and find me when you seek me with all your heart. I will be found by you, declares the Lord, and will bring you back from captivity. I will gather you from all the nations and places where I have banished you, declares the Lord and will bring you back to the place from which I carried you into exile."

—Jeremiah 29:11, 13, 14

The promise is: _____

_____

_____

Now write a similar message that God might want to give people today.

_____

_____

_____

_____

_____

_____

_____

_____

_____

RETURN

AIM: That your students will let God work through them and be good leaders and examples to others

SCRIPTURE: Ezra 1:5-7; Haggai 2:4; Zechariah 8:9; Nehemiah 1:1-2:20; 4:1-20, 27; 6:15; 12:27 (God works through Nehemiah to help His people rebuild the walls of Jerusalem)

PREPARATION:
1. Photocopy activity sheets—one for each student.
2. Prepare situation cards as described in PERSONALIZE.

PRESESSION (5-10 minutes)

ACTIVITIES
* Join in a game to learn about leadership

PERSPECTIVE (10 minutes)

ACTIVITIES
* Decode messages from Ezra, Haggai, and Zechariah

MATERIALS
* Bibles
* "Information Please" Activity Sheet

PROBE (20 minutes)

ACTIVITIES
* Use an activity sheet to discover how a good leader handled pressure from his enemies

MATERIALS
* Bibles
* "Go Lay a Brick" Activity Sheet

PERSONALIZE (15-20 minutes)

ACTIVITIES
* Brainstorm ways God can use you to be good leaders and examples to others

MATERIALS
* Situation cards
* 3 sheets of paper and pencils
* *Optional: large sheet of paper and a marker*

PRESESSION

To help your students think about the big part leaders have in influencing others, play this movement game. Choose one person to be leader. Gather the rest of the group (followers) into a single line behind the leader. The leader makes a motion that is passed down the line. For example the leader raises both arms or tilts his/her head back.

The object of the game is to follow the person ahead of you—not the leader individually. The first follower mirrors the leader, the third follower mirrors the second follower, the fourth follower mirrors the third follower and on down the line. Leaders must stay in one place. Add new players to the follower line as they arrive. Change leaders frequently so other players can have a turn.

Optional: If you have a longer time period, you could try a variation. Split the group into two lines with leaders facing each other. The second leader will mirror the first and on down both lines. You can add more leaders and follower lines as desired.

Talk about the game. How did it feel to be a leader? A follower? Who did you have to depend on to play the game right? What would happen if the person ahead of you gave the wrong motion? How is this like following a leader in real life? **Leaders are very important. As long as we follow a good leader, everyone is safe and good things can be accomplished by the group. But if our leader is bad and doesn't care about his/her followers, the whole group suffers. Today we're going to see how that worked out for the Jews when they returned to their homeland as God had promised.**

PERSPECTIVE

God's prophets had foretold the captivity of God's chosen people. But they also said that God's purpose for them had not ended. In the first year that Cyrus, king of Persia, ruled Babylon, he made a proclamation that the people of Judah could return to their homeland and rebuild the house of the Lord. He suggested that those who did not go should give freely of silver, gold, and other possessions to help those who returned. **Ezra, the prophet, told about this plan.**

Can you imagine how these people must have felt as they came to the city of Jerusalem? They were both happy and sad: happy because they were home in Judah and sad because their beautiful city now lay in ruins.

The people built a new altar where the old one had been and began to get ready to rebuild the temple. But they soon met trouble from the Samaritans and the building stopped for several years.

God called Haggai and Zechariah to be His prophets. They were to encourage the people to finish the rebuilding they had started. The people had built comfortable homes for themselves but God's house was still unfinished.

What did these men have to say? Hand out copies of "Information Please" activity sheets. Read the directions aloud. Allow time for people to finish this activity. Answers are: heart, house, Lord, silver, gold, freewill, temple, Jerusalem, strong, work, with, hands, temple, built.

The people resumed their building with enthusiasm, and in just a few more years the temple was finished! A dedication service was held, such as the dedication led by King Solomon when the first temple was built. It was a great day for God's people! **About a hundred years went by, and although the temple had been rebuilt, the walls and gates of the city were still in ruins. Then God called a new leader to help His people. The man's name was Nehemiah.**

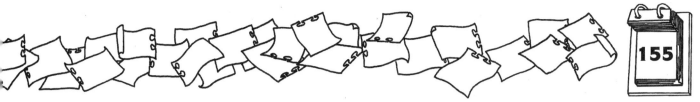

PROBE

Nehemiah was a Jew who lived in Persia. He was a cupbearer to the king in the palace at Shushan. One day Nehemiah's brother and some others from Judah came with an urgent message. Nehemiah was very unhappy when he heard that the Jews were having trouble. Because the walls of Jerusalem had not been rebuilt, the people there had no protection from their enemies.

Nehemiah cried and prayed to God. He wanted to do something to help his people. The next time Nehemiah performed his duty to the king, he had a very sad look on his face. The king noticed this and asked him why he was so unhappy.

Nehemiah told him that the city of his people was destroyed many years ago and the walls and gates had never been rebuilt. Now the people were in danger from their enemies. The king asked him what he wanted to do about it. Nehemiah asked for permission to go back to Jerusalem and help rebuild it. God answered Nehemiah's prayers and gave him permission to return to Jerusalem.

Nehemiah arrived in Jerusalem along with captains and horsemen. When the Jews' enemies, Sanballat and Tobiah, heard of his arrival they were furious. At first they did nothing. For three days Nehemiah stayed quietly in Jerusalem so as not to arouse suspicion. At night Nehemiah rode all around the city looking and planning.

On the fourth day he went to the priests and rulers of the city. Nehemiah told them that God would be with them and that the king had given help. The people became very enthusiastic and said, "Let us start rebuilding!"

Sanballat and Tobiah immediately started trouble. Bible Investigators, see if you can find out what these two troublemakers did and how the good leader, Nehemiah, dealt with them.

Distribute copies of "Go Lay A Brick" activity sheet. Divide the group into three teams and assign a passage to each team. Allow about eight minutes to complete their investigations. Discuss the tactics Tobiah and Sanballat used and how Nehemiah countered them.

In chapter 4 verses 1 through 9, who caused the trouble? (Sanballat and Tobiah.) What did they do first? (Made fun of the Jews and the wall.) What did Nehemiah do? (Prayed to God about it.) What did they do next? (Plotted to fight them.) What did Nehemiah do? (Prayed again and posted a guard.)

What do these verses show us about how good leaders handle tough situations from these verses? (They pray to God and ask for His help, are watchful against sneak attacks by our enemy—Satan.)

What did Nehemiah say? (Asked God to hear their prayer, turn the enemies' insults back on themselves, punish the enemies because they insulted the builders.)

Continue debriefing the teams using the questions on the activity page.

Ask someone to read aloud Nehemiah 6:15. How long did it take to rebuild the walls of Jerusalem? (Fifty-two days.) How do you think it was possible to do such a huge job in such a short time? (Because God helped the builders, they didn't let anything stop them from fulfilling God's plan.)

When the work was all finished, a ceremony was held to dedicate the rebuilt walls. Check out Nehemiah 12:27. How did the people celebrate? (Brought the Levites—the temple helpers—back to Jerusalem, sang and played songs of thanksgiving.)

After this project, Nehemiah had another job to do. He wanted to get his people to change their bad ways of living. He led them in returning to the worship of God, as the law of Moses had taught.

Nehemiah was a good leader. He not only told the people what to do, but was also a good example to them.

PERSONALIZE

(15-20 minutes)

Before class prepare three situation cards by writing the following on index cards: Team 1: How can God work through you at home? At school? Team 2: How can God work through you when you're on the playground? In your neighborhood? Team 3: How can God work through you in this class? In the worship service?

God worked through leaders like Nehemiah to bring blessings to many people. How can God work through you?

Have students work in the same three teams they were in for the PROBE activity. Give each team one situation to work on. **Write down as many ways as you can think of for each place. Then we'll meet in one group and share our lists.**

Encourage students to make them as creative and new as possible. Remember that your emphasis is on the quantity of ideas, not the quality. You can always pick out the best ideas later.

After all the teams have had a chance to present their ideas, go over the list again and pick one good suggestion for each situation.

Optional: If you desire, you can list these best ideas on the chalkboard or a large sheet of paper. You may even decide to pick one overall idea and use it as an outside-class project.

You need a leader to follow all through your life on this earth—someone who will lead you to do the right things and keep you safe from harm. You will find that the Lord is the best leader, and the only one who can lead you to a heavenly home. If you are a faithful follower of the Lord, someday you may become a leader of God's people.

PRAYER/PRAISE

Pray the following prayer, pausing after each line to let students repeat it: **God, thank you for good leaders. Help me to be a faithful follower. Be my leader throughout this life on earth and lead me to my heavenly home. Amen.**

Information Please

Bible Investigators, decode the following words to complete the verses. Use the letters on the telephone buttons. The vowels are given to help you, but you will have to choose which letter to use.

CODE:

1	ABC 2	DEF 3
GHI 4	JKL 5	MNO 6
PRS 7	TUV 8	WXY 9

EZRA 1:5-7

Then everyone whose __ E A __ __ God had
          4   7 8

moved—prepared to go up and build the

__ O U __ E of the __ O __ __ in Jerusalem.
4   7   5 7 3

All their neighbors assisted them with articles of

__ I __ __ E __ and __ O __ __ , with goods and livestock, and with
7 5 8 7   4 5 3

valuable gifts, in addition to all the __ __ E E __ I __ __ offerings.
                               3 7   9 5 5

Moreover King Cyrus brought out the articles belonging to the

__ E __ __ __ E of the Lord, which Nebuchadnezzar had carried away
8 6 7 5

from __ E __ U __ A __ E __ and had placed in the temple of his god.
     5 7 7 5 6

HAGGAI 2:4

But now be __ __ __ O __ __ all you people of the land, and
         7 8 7 6 4

__ O __ __ . For I am __ I __ __ you, declares the Lord Almighty.
9 7 5   9 8 4

ZECHARIAH 8:9

Let your __ A __ __ __ be strong so that the __ E __ __ __ E may be
       4 6 3 7   8 6 7 5

__ U I __ __ .
2 5 7

Go Lay a Brick

Read the verses shown and fill in the answers. All verses are from the book of Nehemiah.

	4:1-9	4:10-15	4:16-20
WHO caused the trouble?			
WHAT did they do?			
HOW did Nehemiah and the people overcome the problem?			
HOW should a good leader handle this kind of situation?			
WHAT did Nehemiah say?			

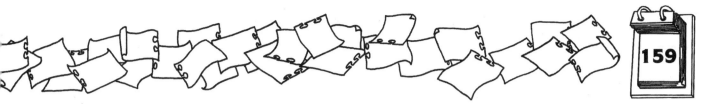

PROPHECY OF THE MESSIAH

AIM: That your students will understand that prophecies were fulfilled when Jesus came and that His perfect life and sacrifice were part of God's great plan of salvation for all people

SCRIPTURE: Malachi 4:5, 6; Jeremiah 23:5, 6; Isaiah 9:6, 7; Micah 5:2; Hosea 3:5; Amos 9:8; Matthew 2:1, 2; 11:12-14; 21:9-11; Luke 1:31-33; John 14:27; 17:24; Acts 3:13, 14, 25, 26 (Christ's coming to earth as the Savior was God's plan from the beginning)

PREPARATION:
1. Photocopy activity sheets—one for each student.
2. Prepare a "Jesus" jigsaw puzzle as described in PRESESSION.
3. Make Bible reference slips as described in PROBE.

PRESESSION (5-10 minutes)

ACTIVITIES
* Put together a jigsaw puzzle of Jesus

MATERIALS
* "Jesus" puzzle

PERSPECTIVE (10 minutes)

ACTIVITIES
* Talk about telescopes and compare them with Old Testament prophecies about the Messiah

MATERIALS
* *Optional: Binoculars or a telescope*

PROBE (20 minutes)

ACTIVITIES
* Match Old Testament prophecies with the prophets who made them
* Do a word search to highlight key words from the prophecies

MATERIALS
* Bibles
* "Looking Ahead" Activity Sheet

PERSONALIZE (15-20 minutes)

ACTIVITIES
* Use an activity sheet to discover how to receive God's salvation

MATERIALS
* Bibles
* "The Roman Road To Salvation" Activity Sheet

PRESESSION

Before class make a jigsaw puzzle of Jesus. Glue a large picture of Jesus on a piece of cardboard from the back of a cereal box or writing tablet. Cut it in several pieces depending on the age of your class. Fewer large pieces for younger students and more small pieces for older ones.

As students arrive let them put the puzzle together as you guide the conversation to the prophecies about Jesus. What is prophecy? (Messages from God.) Prophets were able to tell the people God's message. Sometimes they even told what would happen in the future.

How did Old Testament people describe the Savior that God would send to save them from their sins? What were some of the names they used for Him? What did they think He would do? What kind of a person were they thinking He would be like?

The puzzle pieces seemed unrelated and not worth much alone. But what happened when you put all the pieces together? (They made a complete picture of Jesus.) **Some of the Old Testament prophecies about the Savior seemed curious and separate from the whole plan of God to save His people. However, when we fit them together we find that they also make a complete picture of Jesus.**

PERSPECTIVE

(10 minutes)

Have you ever looked through a pair of binoculars or a telescope? Display the telescope or binoculars if you have them. Let students take turns looking at objects through them. **If you would go to Mount Palomar in California you would see the world's largest optical telescope.** The mirror on this telescope is two hundred inches across, and it reflects the light given off by objects (stars) that are billions of light-years away. Light travels at the rate of 186,000 miles per second. A light-year is the distance that light travels in one year. Some telescopes are built to study and take pictures of the sun. Others measure the distance between stars. By using telescopes, scientists are learning more and more about the great universe God created.

Even though telescopes are powerful instruments, they cannot be used to look into the future and tell what will happen years ahead. Only God, who created everything and everyone, knows what will happen in the future. He knew from the very beginning that people would need a Savior.

Check out John 17:24. Where was Jesus in the beginning? (With God.) God knew from the very beginning that people would need a Savior. **But many things were to happen and thousands of years were to go by before the great event of the coming of the Savior to the world.**

PROBE

Before class write down the following references on slips of paper: Matthew 11:12-14; Matthew 21:9-11; John 14:27; Matthew 2:1, 2; Luke 1:31-33; Acts 3:13, 14, 25, 26. To save time, hand them out to six people at the beginning of class and have them look up the passages and be prepared to read them later in this section of the lesson.

If we had time to review the entire Old Testament, we would see how every event pointed toward the coming of the Savior. As time went on, God continued to tell His people, through the prophets, about the Messiah. How the Hebrew people hoped for the day when the Messiah would come!

After the prophet Malachi had finished his work for the Lord, there were no more prophets and no more messages from God for about four hundred years. During this time the people had God's written Word, the books of the Old Testament to study.

As the people of the day studied the books of prophecy, they realized more and more that God was planning to send Someone to them—Someone who would be a King, a Prophet, a Servant, a Teacher, and a Savior. None of the prophets gave the whole message, but many of them gave part of it. When these parts were put together, an important future event was seen, but not very clearly. There was still a great mystery about the coming of the Messiah.

Let's look at some of the prophecies that were read by God's people long ago. Distribute copies of "Looking Ahead" activity sheet. Have students use their Bibles to look up the passages on the activity sheet. Do only the matching exercise at this time. **We'll share our answers when you are done.** Answers are: 6, 3, 2, 1, 5, 4.

Be sensitive to any students who may have difficulty in finding the various books mentioned.

Optional: You may want to have students work in pairs, teaming a person who knows the Bible with one who does not. If you need to do this, try to keep it upbeat and not call attention to the Biblical illiteracy of any individual.

As you discuss these Old Testament passages, call to your students' attention their fulfillments in New Testament texts by having people read aloud the passages they looked up earlier. **Malachi is the last book in the Old Testament. He spoke about a messenger like Elijah who would prepare the people's hearts for God's Chosen One. Who was this messenger?** Have the person who looked up Matthew 11:12-14 read it aloud. (John the Baptist.)

Jeremiah spoke about the descendant of David who would come and rule the earth. Who was this person? Have Matthew 21:9-11 read aloud. (Jesus.)

The book of Isaiah is full of prophecies about the coming Savior. Who brought peace to the hearts of people everywhere and deserves the title of The Prince of Peace? Ask the person who has John 14:27 to read it aloud. (Jesus.)

Bethlehem was a small town of little importance, yet God spoke through the prophet Micah and said it would be the birthplace of God's Savior. Who was born there? Have the person who looked up Matthew 2:1, 2 read it aloud. (Jesus.)

The prophet Hosea said that the Messiah would be great as David was. Who was this great ruler? Ask to have Luke 1:31-33 read aloud. (Jesus.)

Who was the person who came from the family of Abraham to bless the whole world? Have the person who looked up Acts 3:13, 14, 25, 26 read the verses aloud. (Jesus.)

Let students finish the word search. It will help reinforce the key words from the prophetical passages you just studied together.

Although these prophets lived at different times and brought messages to various people, all of their messages about the Savior were fulfilled in one person—Jesus. During

the four hundred years when there were no new messages from God, the people waited for the coming of one who was to be their king. They were thinking of an earthly king who would help them defeat their enemies and make their nation great again. They did not fully understand the meaning of the prophecies.

One name Christ was given was "Emmanuel," meaning "God with us." God himself was going to live among His people and show them the way He wanted them to live. Then He would become the sacrifice for their sins. **This was all part of God's great plan of salvation.**

PERSONALIZE

(15-20 minutes)

When God wants His people to learn something, He doesn't give them the knowledge all at once. He gives them a little at a time. They can think about what they learned and then understand just a little more as they go along.

God wants us to learn more and more about Him and His Son, Jesus. He wants us to understand His plan of salvation for the world.

Distribute copies of "The Roman Road to Salvation" activity sheet. Go over it together. Invite your kids to express what they do understand and answer any questions they may have. Try to clear up any misunderstandings. Sin broke the loving relationship people had with God. Salvation is the way of restoring it again.

No amount of good deeds or church going will ever pay for your sin. Only a perfect, sinless person can do that. Jesus is that person and He has already paid the penalty for <u>your</u> sin. When you

believe that and accept His gift of forgiveness, then life that will never end is yours. You become a part of God's forever family.

Direct your class's thought toward accepting Jesus as their Savior.

Optional: You may want to have a helper stay with your class while you deal privately with students who want to make a decision to follow Jesus.

If students have previously accepted Christ, they can turn their papers over and write a brief prayer of thanksgiving to God, their heavenly Father.

PRAYER/PRAISE

Close the lesson with a circle prayer. Students hold hands and form a heart instead of a circle. Have them repeat in unison, "Thank you, God, for making it possible to be part of your forever family."

Looking Ahead

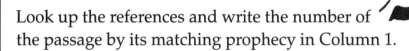

Look up the references and write the number of the passage by its matching prophecy in Column 1.

○ God would send a messenger like Elijah to prepare the hearts of the people for the Messiah.

○ A descendant of David would come and rule the earth.

○ A child would be born who would be known as "Wonderful Counsellor, the Mighty God, the Everlasting Father, the Prince of Peace."

○ The Savior would be born in the small town of Bethlehem.

○ A king would come who would be as great as David was.

○ God would not allow His people to vanish completely.

1. Micah 5:2

2. Isaiah 9:6, 7

3. Jeremiah 23:5, 6

4. Amos 9:8

5. Hosea 3:5

6. Malachi 4:5

The word bank has some words from these prophecies. Use them to find the words in the puzzle. They might be up and down, across, or even diagonal!

RIGHTEOUSNESS ❑
HEARTS ❑
PEACE ❑
BLESSING ❑
MESSENGER ❑
COUNSELLOR ❑
SAVIOR ❑
MIGHTY ❑
ELIJAH ❑
FATHER ❑
BETHLEHEM ❑
DAVID ❑
PREPARE ❑
PRINCE ❑
KING ❑
LORD ❑

```
K T P R Q Z K T H O L J R
A E L I B C M A W K Q O Z
T R O G M Y J M A R I Q B
H A B H S I U E G V D N V
F P M T L C Y S A B C Z G
S E L E V T R S Z W K I S
V R C O U N S E L L O R Q
B P K U B E C N I R P E B
A B D S F Y L G W X Y H E
Q O L N C U T E Z P R T T
Y F R E N S T R A E H A H
O I Z S S T E Q J A P F L
L C Q S V S R Z W C S D E
U Z Y T H G I M N E J E H
D A V I D L B N Z A K F E
B I V D R O L D G W Q S M
```

The Roman Road to Salvation

Look up the passages and follow the road to salvation. You will find that God has lovingly provided a way for you to become part of His forever family.

JESUS IS BORN

AIM: That your students will understand that Jesus is the Lord who is to be obeyed above all others and is the Savior of all who do so

SCRIPTURE: Matthew 1:18-21; 2:1-20; Luke 1:26-33; 2:1-38; John 3:16 (Events surrounding the birth of Christ)

PREPARATION:
1. Photocopy activity sheets—one for each student.
2. Prepare "Savior gifts" as described in PERSPECTIVE.

PRESESSION (5-10 minutes)

ACTIVITIES
* Compare Christmas hymns and carols about the birth of Christ to learn more about what "Savior" and "Lord" mean

MATERIALS
* Song books that contain Christmas carols or hymns

PERSPECTIVE (10 minutes)

ACTIVITIES
* Learn about God's gift of the Savior to all people

MATERIALS
* "Savior gifts"—small boxes or envelopes, bows or stickers, copies of John 3:16—one for each student
* *Optional: wrapping paper*

PROBE (20 minutes)

ACTIVITIES
* Complete a story about the birth of Jesus

MATERIALS
* Bibles
* "A Savior, Christ the Lord" Activity Sheet

PERSONALIZE (15-20 minutes)

ACTIVITIES
* Plan how to tell someone the good news about Jesus

MATERIALS
* Good News—For Everybody!" Activity Sheet

PRESESSION

As students arrive, have them look through the books to find Christmas songs that refer to Jesus as Lord and Savior. See how many they can find. Let them help you list the titles of these songs on the chalkboard or a large sheet of paper.

Talk about the meaning of "Savior" and "Lord." God sent His Son to earth to show people as well as tell them how to live. A Savior is someone who saves people from danger. Jesus would give His life as a perfect sacrifice to save people from death and the punishment for their sins.

The word "Lord" means one who is in control. When God's Word tells us that Jesus is Lord, it means that He has power and authority over everyone and everything! Since He is our Lord, we must obey what He tells us. The New Testament is filled with His teachings and examples, His commands and promises. We learn from what He said and did while He was on earth. **Jesus came to be Savior and Lord. He wants to be *your* Savior and Lord!**

PERSPECTIVE

Before class, prepare "Savior gifts" for each pupil. Make one copy of John 3:16 for each pupil and cut it apart in phrase strips like this:

For God so loved the world

that He gave His one and only Son

that whoever believes in Him shall not perish

but have eternal life John 3:16

Place these in small boxes or envelopes and decorate them like gifts.

Optional: You need not use wrapping paper. Small bows or stickers will be enough to make them look like gifts.

We know from reading the story of God's chosen people in the Old Testament that a great many of them disobeyed God's teaching and worshiped idols. But down through the years there also remained a faithful group. These Jews believed that God would send them a leader, a Savior. But most of them had in mind a military or political leader who would win their country back from the Romans.

God had given certain men the message about the coming of the Savior hundreds of years ahead of time. They did not know when this event would take place, but they knew many other things about it. They knew the Savior was to be called Wonderful Counsellor, the everlasting Father, and the Prince of Peace. These men were called "Prophets." **The right moment finally came for Jesus to make His appearance on earth.** The one who knew exactly the right time for the coming of the Savior is the one who knows all things. He is God, our heavenly Father.

Let students open their "gifts" and put the phrases of the verse in the correct order. Discuss the meaning of the verse.

Why do you think it was wrapped as a gift? **The Savior is a gift because God gave His one and only Son. A gift is something you don't have to pay for. But you do have to accept it!** To accept Jesus is to believe in Him and obey Him. Do you believe that Jesus is the Son of God? Will you obey His commands? Will you take Jesus as your Savior and Lord?

Optional: even though the last lesson included an opportunity to accept Jesus as their Savior, don't neglect this further opening. Be loving, caring, and sensitive to any child who may still not have established a personal relationship with Jesus.

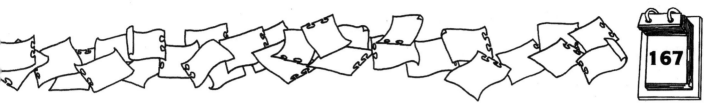

PROBE

(20 minutes)

Distribute copies of "A Savior, Christ the Lord" activity sheet. Read aloud the directions at the top.

Have students open their Bibles and turn to Matthew 1:18-21 and 2:1-20. Ask volunteers to take turns reading. Then have the group turn to Luke 1:26-33 and 2:1-38 and also read them aloud. The rest of the group can follow along in their Bibles. They can fill in the blanks in the story as they go along.

Optional: If you have a longer time period, let your students pantomime the story.

Although this story is a very familiar one, it is a very special one because the birth of Jesus was special. Let's look at some of the things that make it so special.

Jesus lived before He was conceived or born. For all of us life begins at conception when cells from both the father and the mother combine to start a new life. Check out John 1:1, 2 to find out when life began for Jesus. (He was with God in the beginning.)

Jesus had no human father. Although his mother, Mary, was human, God alone was the father of Jesus. Check it out in Matthew 1:18.

The birth of Jesus was announced by angels. Several times in this story we see how God used angels to tell people about His Son's birth: Mary, Joseph, the shepherds.

A star indicated His birth. The wise men from the east studied the heavens nightly, but only at the birth of Jesus did this very special star appear. It also led them all the way to the place where Jesus was.

Joseph and Mary were from a special family. God had promised that the Savior would be born from the family of King David. Both Mary and Joseph were descendants of King David.

The shepherds and flocks of sheep in the story were special. They were the men who cared for the temple flocks which were used for sacrifices.

Even the gifts the wise men offered were special. Jesus' parents were so poor that they could not even afford a lamb for an offering in the temple when He was presented there. But God provided three types of gifts through the wise men who came to worship the little King of the Jews.

Gold symbolized royalty, a gift fit for a king. Frankincense was mixed with the offerings of priests and used for worship. Perhaps it was a sign of the priestly role the Savior would take in salvation. Myrrh was a gift of suffering. It was used to ease pain and anoint the bodies of the dead.

Yes, Jesus was a special baby and He came to live a special life as our Savior and Lord.

PERSONALIZE

If you have received Jesus as your Savior and Lord that is good news! How much good news? Let's see if we can list some of the things that Jesus does for you. List the following on the chalkboard or a large sheet of paper:

Jesus loves you. This is an unconditional love which means that you don't have to be "good" to earn it.

He forgives your sins. His sinless life, death on the cross, and resurrection to life again paid the debt for your sins.

He makes you a member of God's forever family and gives you a home in Heaven. He gives you eternal life. That means life that will never end.

He guides your life. You can learn from Him how God wants you to live so you can best enjoy life and honor God. **He answers your prayers and helps you in every situation.**

Good news like that is too good to keep to yourself. What are some ways you can share this good news with others?

Hand out copies of "Good News—For Everybody!" activity sheet. Initially talk about the questions together in general terms. **Who can we tell about this good news?** (Friends, family, ball team, scout troop, neighbors, classmates, people in our town, country, nation, people in other lands.)

What can you tell? Briefly refer to the list you made earlier of good news about you and your relationship with Jesus.

Where can you tell? (In your home, classroom, playground, camp, school, the mall, streets, hospitals, nursing homes, homeless shelters.)

When can you tell? (Anytime, day or night, especially when people are lonely, frightened, friendless, in trouble.)

How can you tell? (By speaking to them, letters, tracts, telephone, bumper stickers, T-shirts, skywriting, posters, banners, TV, books, by the way you live—praying, reading the Bible, respecting my parents, treating others kindly.)

Now have students work on this activity sheet individually and invite them to give specific plans that they will personally try to do. To be really effective, have them limit this plan to one person or two at the most. For example: Tell my friend, Kyle; Jesus helps me when I'm sad; on the playground; the next time we play ball together again; I'll treat him kindly and tell him face to face.

Don't neglect foreign missions in this planning. Many career missionaries testify that it was when they were young children that God called them to service in other lands. Missionary agencies need people from every walk of life: artists, writers, farmers, mechanics, teachers, as well as nurses, doctors, and evangelists. If God doesn't call you to other countries, you can still pray for the missionaries, write letters to them, make things for them, and send money to help them. Help your students to be well informed about the opportunities, needs and outreach into all the world.

PRAYER/PRAISE

Close with a prayer of thanksgiving to God for sending His one and only Son to be our Savior.

Encourage people to memorize John 3:16 if they haven't already done so.

A SAVIOR, CHRIST THE LORD

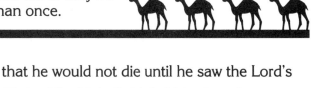

Follow the story and fill in the blanks. Use the word bank
if you need help. Some words may be
used more than once.

In a town near Jerusalem a woman was told about the coming birth of the Savior. She was the wife of a priest who served in the temple at _____. She was also the relative of Mary. Later she gave birth to a son, named _____ who had already been chosen by the _____ to prepare the way for the Savior. The name of this woman was_____.

In the town of _____ the coming birth of the Savior was announced to a young woman. She was visited by an _____ who told her that she was to be the mother of _____. Her name was _____. Her husband also knew about the one to be born. _____ was told this by an angel in a dream. When this baby was born, He was to be named _____ which meant "the Lord saves."

A group of _____ near the town of _____ knew when the long-awaited Savior came. They were watching their flock of _____ when an _____ appeared and gave them the good news.

In the city of Jerusalem a man named _____ knew that the Savior had been born. The _____ _____ told him

that he would not die until he saw the Lord's Christ. The Holy Spirit led him into the _____ on the day when the baby _____ was brought in, as the custom was, for presentation before the Lord. He took the baby in his arms and praised God because he had seen the one who was to save the people.

An elderly woman, Anna, who was a _____ came at the same time. She too gave thanks to the Lord for the _____ and told everyone about him.

The _____ _____ in the East knew about the one who was born _____ of the _____. They saw His _____ and followed it. They stopped in Jerusalem to ask where this child had been born. Jealous King _____ was troubled because he thought a new king would try to take his place. He didn't know that _____ was to rule a heavenly, not an earthly, kingdom. He wanted the men to bring him word when they found the child, but God warned them in a _____ to go home another way. When they had presented their gifts to the new king and _____ Him, they went back to their homes.

WORD BANK

prophetess	angel	king	Jesus	Holy Spirit
John	Elizabeth	dream	Simeon	Herod
Bethlehem	child	Nazareth	star	Joseph
wise men	temple	sheep	Jews	shepherds
Lord	Jerusalem	Mary	dream	worshiped

GOOD NEWS
FOR EVERYBODY!

WHO can you tell?

_____
_____
_____
_____

WHAT can you tell?

_____
_____
_____
_____

WHERE can you tell?

_____
_____
_____

WHEN can you tell?

_____
_____
_____
_____

HOW can you tell?

_____
_____
_____
_____

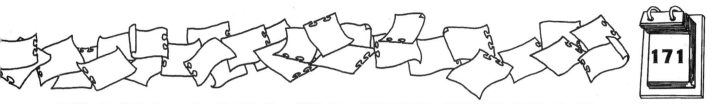

JESUS GOES TO THE TEMPLE

AIM: That your students will be encouraged to follow the example of Jesus who did the work of God, His Father

SCRIPTURE: Luke 2:40-52 (The boy Jesus is prepared to do the work of God, His Father, in everything He says and does)

PREPARATION:
1. Photocopy activity sheets—one for each student.
2. Prepare materials for four-leaf clover bookmarks as described in PERSPECTIVE.

PRESESSION (5-10 minutes)

ACTIVITIES
* Talk about family trips students have taken

MATERIALS
* Old calendars or magazines with pictures of different parts of the country or other countries

PERSPECTIVE (10 minutes)

ACTIVITIES
* Make four-leaf clover bookmarks to illustrate how Jesus grew

MATERIALS
* Green, white construction paper, scissors, crayons or markers, glue
* Carbon paper, pattern, pencils

PROBE (20 minutes)

ACTIVITIES
* Read a skit about Jesus in the temple

MATERIALS
* Bibles
* "I Witness News" Activity Sheet

PERSONALIZE (15-20 minutes)

ACTIVITIES
* Play a board game to learn ways boys and girls can work for the Lord now

MATERIALS
* "Following Jesus' Footsteps" Activity Sheet
* Buttons—one for each student, pennies—one for each group playing

PRESESSION

Choose pictures that are very colorful and show lots of scenery. Lay out the pictures so early arrivals can look through them. As they do, guide the conversation towards family outings.

Where did you go? What did you do? What did you like best? Would you do anything differently? Why? What would you like to do the next time? Where would you like to go next? Perhaps one or more people have gotten lost from their parents. Have them tell about it.

If you have students who have not had the opportunity to travel like this, include them by having them share about a family gathering or special-day celebration. The Jewish people had many special family celebrations.

We have already talked about the time **when God's people were looking forward to the coming of a Savior and we have learned about the time when Jesus, the Son of God, was born. But Jesus didn't stay a baby.**

King Herod, because of his jealousy, ordered that all boy babies two years old and younger were to be killed. Joseph and Mary had to take the baby Jesus to Egypt to save Him from a cruel death. There they stayed until Herod died. When they returned to their homeland, they lived in the town of Nazareth in Galilee. This is the town they left when the emperor of Rome required everyone to register for taxes in the city of his ancestors. **Nothing more is known of Jesus' life until He was twelve years old, and the only story of Jesus' boyhood is found in the book of Luke.**

PERSPECTIVE

Before class cut white construction paper into strips 3" wide and 8" long. Cut green construction paper into 3" by 4" sections. Make enough of both colors for every member of your class.

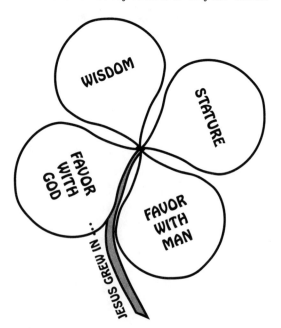

Enlarge the pattern below (double it) and make several to use as patterns so students can make four-leaf clovers from the green pieces.

Check out Luke 2:52 to see what he was like. (Grew in wisdom and stature, and in favor with God and men.) Even though Jesus was a special person, God's one and only Son, He lived and grew like we do. Have students make the bookmarks and print one part of the verse on each leaf. Guide the conversation during this time to thoughts about Jesus as a boy. If He were born in their lifetime, what do you think His favorite food would be? Would He be in sports? If so, which one/s? Continue in this manner emphasizing that even though He was God's Son, Jesus was also human like your juniors. He had friends, played games, went to school, and obeyed His earthly parents.

Let's find out what happened during those silent years when Jesus was a boy.

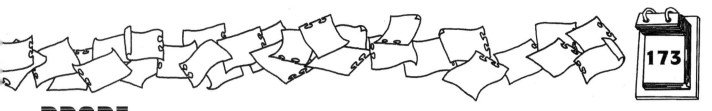

PROBE

(20 minutes)

Each year the Jewish men came together in Jerusalem to attend three special feasts: Passover, Pentecost, and the Tabernacles or Booths. Most of the time, entire families traveled together and made the Passover a sort of family reunion. When a Jewish boy was twelve he would be allowed to join his father in the temple worship services.

Hand out copies of "I Witness News" activity sheet. Ask for volunteers to read the parts of the announcer, Matthew, Mark, Luke, Mary, and Jesus. The rest of the class can follow along on their sheets.

How excited Jesus must have been the year he was twelve. From now on He would be allowed to go with Joseph to the temple feasts three times a year! At age twelve, Jesus would be considered almost an adult. He was considered old enough to be responsible for keeping God's law. Boys that age were considered more like a boy of eighteen today.

Have students turn to Luke 2:41-52 in their Bibles.

What was the holiday Jesus and His parents were going to celebrate in Jerusalem? (Passover.) It was probably a beautiful spring day when they started out. The trip from Nazareth to Jerusalem was more than eighty miles, and the people had to walk or ride on donkeys. They joined together in caravans for protection from robbers.

The Passover was followed by a seven-day celebration. On the first day each Jewish family killed a lamb. They prepared certain other foods according to God's commands. They feasted and thought about how good God had been to their ancestors in helping them to escape from slavery in Egypt.

Also during that time some of the nation's best religious teachers held public classes in the temple. They would probably be debating about when God's Messiah would come. This is probably what caught Jesus' attention and prompted Him to stay behind in Jerusalem.

Finally the time of worship and celebration was over. It was time for Jesus and His family to return to Nazareth with their friends. Once again the caravan was formed and the people set out on their long journey. Why didn't Mary and Joseph miss Jesus until the first evening's stop? (Thought He was in the group with them.) Women and children usually traveled at the front while the men brought up the rear. A twelve-year-old boy could be with either group. Because of this, Mary and Joseph each thought Jesus was with the other one.

When evening came after the first day of travel, the caravan stopped. Each family prepared for the night's rest. Mary and Joseph expected Jesus to come any minute. But Jesus did not come. Mary and Joseph searched throughout the caravan, but no one had seen Jesus. Mary became very upset. Perhaps she was afraid that she had not taken as good care of this special God-given child as she should have. What did Mary and Joseph do when they couldn't find Jesus in the caravan? (Turned back to Jerusalem and began to search for Jesus there.)

When they found Him at last, among the noted teachers, they were very surprised. Not only was He listening to them talk, but Jesus was also asking and answering questions. The teachers were shocked at the depth of understanding Jesus' comments revealed. This incident is the first hint we have that Jesus realized He was God's Son. Even so, He did not reject His earthly parents, but willingly went with them and obeyed them. Jesus grew normally, like other healthy children.

PERSONALIZE

He grew in four ways. Check out Luke 2:52. What were they? (Wisdom, stature, favor with God, favor with man.) Jesus, like other children, grew both physically and mentally. Have someone look up James 1:5. **How can we grow in wisdom?** (Ask God to give it to us.) **Have you ever asked God for wisdom? What happened?** Invite students to share any experiences they have had. Encourage them to turn to their heavenly Father whenever they need wisdom. He gives wisdom generously to those who truly trust Him to do so.

Did Jesus have any brothers or sisters? Check out Matthew 13:55, 56. (Yes, James, Joseph, Simon, Judas, and some sisters.) These were all children of Mary and Joseph, which made them half-brothers and sisters to Jesus. He grew stronger in body just like they did. He was the oldest boy in the family and was raised along with his half-brothers and sisters in normal ways.

Jesus grew socially. This means that He got along with other people and was liked by them. What are some things you do that help others and make them like you? (Be friendly, treat them nice, show you care about them, share your things with them, tell them about your best friend, Jesus.)

Jesus also grew spiritually. That means that He pleased and was loved by God. What are some things you do that make God like you? (Respect Him, love Him, read His Word, talk to Him in prayer, tell others what He has done for me.)

Distribute copies of "Following Jesus' Footsteps" activity sheet. Divide the class into small groups of two to four people to play this board game. Use differently shaped or colored buttons for playing pieces and pennies to determine moves. **When you land on a space with directions, you must do what they say.** Allow several minutes for playing this game. It will reinforce specific ways your students can follow Jesus' example.

To be all that God wants you to be, you need to develop in the same areas that Jesus did.

PRAYER/PRAISE

Close with a prayer of thanksgiving for the example Jesus gave us of how to grow and please others and God. Repeat Luke 2:52 together.

Remind people to take their four-leaf clover bookmarks home and use them in their Bibles as a reminder of how to have a balanced life.

Witness news

ANNOUNCER: Good evening and welcome to the six o'clock news. Tonight we have a special in-depth report from our "I" team about a missing boy. For a background check we call upon our historical reporter, Matthew.

MATTHEW: This is a twelve-year-old boy we're talking about. His name is Jesus and He was reported missing a few days ago. His parents, Mary and Joseph, made the trip here to Jerusalem along with friends and family from the Galilean city of Nazareth. For a week they celebrated the Passover together. The family rejoined the caravan and set out to return to their home. They noticed Jesus was missing the first evening.

ANNOUNCER: Is that when they talked to officials?

MATTHEW: No. They supposed Jesus was with the rest of the children or other relatives. But after a thorough search throughout the caravan they became very worried. Mary decided they would have to go back to Jerusalem and look for Him there.

ANNOUNCER: Thank you, Matthew. Now we go to our reporter at city hall. Mark, how did the authorities react to the story of this missing person? Do they suspect foul play in this situation?

MARK: Actually, there has been very little if any reaction to this case. The government officials are Romans and have very little interest in missing Jews whatever their age. They are treating this as a runaway.

ANNOUNCER: Have the parents been pretty upset about this? It seems that in a city as large as Jerusalem there could be many bad endings to this story.

MARK: So far, they've been hopeful. But you're right. As tense as things are here with the Roman government concerned about the possibility of an upset by Jewish Zealot patriots, anything could have happened to Jesus.

ANNOUNCER: Thank you, Mark. Now let's turn to our on-the-spot correspondent, Luke. How are things going there?

LUKE: I've been with the boy's parents, Mary and Joseph, for the past three days as they have carried on a relentless search for their son. At the present time we're back at the temple where they last saw Jesus. Mary has noticed a group of religious teachers sitting here with a boy and is headed over to talk to them. Hold on . . . I can't be sure, but I think she's just found her son.

ANNOUNCER: Luke, can you give us more details on that?

LUKE: Yes. Both Mary and Joseph now identify the boy as Jesus. It seems He has been sitting here listening to the teachers and asking and answering questions. I'll try to get a little closer and catch Mary's comments.

MARY: Son, why have you treated us like this? We were terribly worried about you. Your father and I have been anxiously searching for you.

JESUS: Why were you searching for me? Didn't you know I had to be in my Father's house?

LUKE: Well, that's the story. Back to you in the studio.

ANNOUNCER: Thank you, Luke. The missing young man, Jesus, is safe and now on His way home with His parents. He does, however, leave us to wonder what He meant by calling the temple His father's house. This is your Channel 7 news anchor saying goodnight.

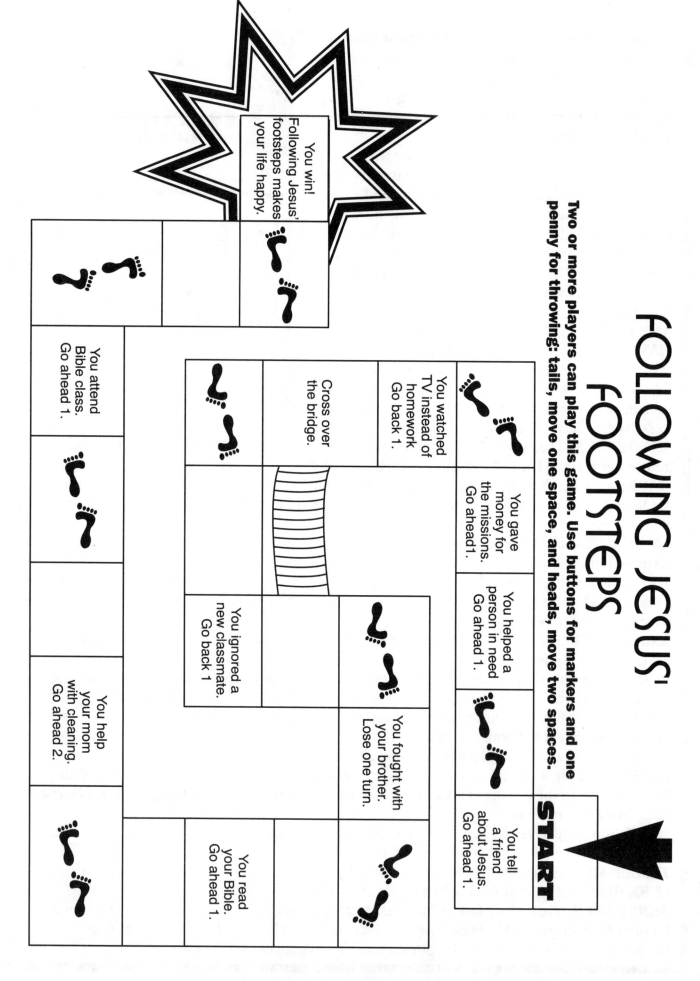

FOLLOWING JESUS' FOOTSTEPS

Two or more players can play this game. Use buttons for markers and one penny for throwing: tails, move one space, and heads, move two spaces.

START — You tell a friend about Jesus. Go ahead 1.

You fought with your brother. Lose one turn.

You helped a person in need. Go ahead 1.

You gave money for the missions. Go ahead 1.

You read your Bible. Go ahead 1.

You ignored a new classmate. Go back 1

Cross over the bridge.

You watched TV instead of homework. Go back 1.

You help your mom with cleaning. Go ahead 2.

You attend Bible class. Go ahead 1.

You win! Following Jesus' footsteps makes your life happy.

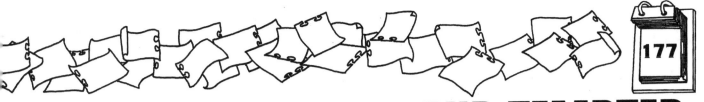

JESUS IS BAPTIZED AND TEMPTED

AIM: That your students will realize Jesus can help them in times of temptation because He withstood Satan's temptation

SCRIPTURE: Matthew 3:13-17 (Jesus is baptized and resists the devil's temptation)

PREPARATION:
1. Photocopy activity sheets—one for each student.
2. Write directions for the designing activity as described in PRESESSION.
3. Prepare a "Vote Wall" as described in PERSONALIZE.

PRESESSION (5-10 minutes)

ACTIVITIES
* Draw designs that show how you feel about temptations

MATERIALS
* White paper—one sheet for each student, crayons or markers
* Chalkboard or large sheet of paper and marker

PERSPECTIVE (10 minutes)

ACTIVITIES
* Learn about Jesus' baptism by deciphering a code

MATERIALS
* "For Example" Activity Sheet

PROBE (20 minutes)

ACTIVITIES
* Identify a "sound bite" from a Scripture passage
* Use an activity sheet to learn more about the temptation of Jesus

MATERIALS
* Bibles
* "The Winner and Still Champion" Activity Sheet

PERSONALIZE (15-20 minutes)

ACTIVITIES
* Use a "Vote Wall" to discuss temptation

MATERIALS
* Bibles
* Pencils

PRESESSION

Before class write these directions on the chalkboard or a large sheet of paper:

1. Pick a color and use straight lines to express types of things that are a temptation to you. (For example—chocolate, buying new clothes or sports equipment.)

2. Pick a color and use one uninterrupted line that shows how you feel about things that tempt you to disobey God.

3. Pick a color and use any design that describes how you handle those kinds of temptations.

4. Pick a color and use any pattern that represents how you think Jesus might handle those same temptations.

Give a sheet of paper to each early arrival. Lay the crayons or markers where they can be easily reached. Have students fold their paper in half horizontally and half again to form four sections. Invite students to use these portions to complete the activity shown on the chalkboard.

Optional: If desired you can enlarge this part of the lesson by having students share the results with the group, letting them explain their thinking. Invite them to tell how they felt as they worked on the project.

Talk about temptations. Are they the same for different people? Why or why not? What causes temptations?

Do you think Jesus was ever tempted to do something wrong?

PERSPECTIVE

Distribute copies of "For Example" activity sheet and read the directions. Have students take turns reading Matthew 3:1-16 aloud. The activity can be done together to save time. Students can fill in the blanks as they follow the story in their Bibles. The answers to this activity are all given backwards. For example the answers for the first sentence are "true messenger, God, years."

Jesus was thirty years old when He set out from Nazareth to be baptized by John. John was the embodiment of the Old Testament prophet Elijah, preparing people for the coming of the Messiah, God's chosen one.

Why was John surprised when Jesus asked John to baptize Him? Because John recognized Jesus as the Savior, the Son of God, he did not feel worthy to baptize Him. Check out Matthew 3:11. Jesus was the very person John had been telling the people about—the person whose sandals John did not feel fit to untie!

Why did Jesus tell John to go ahead and baptize Him? (It was proper for them to do all that God had commanded. If Jesus left out only one command, He would be sinning.

The Holy Spirit came as a dove to Jesus and God's voice spoke from Heaven declaring His love for, and pleasure in, His Son. How do you think that made Jesus feel? (Glad, awestruck, humble.) This affirmation from God united the Godhead in a manner reminiscent of what they had enjoyed before Jesus was born on earth. The Holy Spirit (dove), Father (voice), and Son (Jesus) were together again to initiate the ministry Jesus was to have on earth.

Jesus set an example for His followers in baptism. He knew that people needed a physical symbol to reaffirm their decision to confess their sins, turn away from them, and start following God wholeheartedly. When people make an outward declaration of their faith in God like this, they are much more apt to stick with it in hard times. **Although He was sinless, Jesus identified with sinners in His baptism. He was our example of obedience to all of God's commands.**

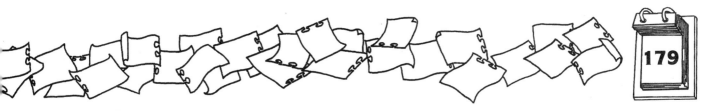

PROBE

(20 minutes)

Have students take turns reading aloud Matthew 4:1-11. Tell them to listen for a "sound bite." This is a short phrase, expression, or quote, which catches the listener's attention. **Did you discover the sound bite? What was it?** (It is written.) **Where was it written?** (In God's Word, Old Testament Scriptures.) Point out that Jesus wasn't the only one who said this. Satan also used the phrase, but the verse he used with it was used incorrectly.

Warn your students that oftentimes people try to get us to do something by giving us convincing reasons why we *should* do it. It isn't enough to memorize Scripture. You also have to use it in the right way. Satan separated the verse from its complete setting.

It is very important that people understand the general principles that Scripture discloses; the whole picture of how they should live—not just single verses. But even knowing the principles of Scripture is not enough. The most important thing is to *obey* them!

Hand out copies of "The Winner And Still Champion" activity sheet. Students can work on this exercise individually. The answers are: b, a, c, b, b, a, b, c.

Why do you think Satan waited until Jesus was alone and hungry to tempt Him? (Jesus was weakest then, less able to fight the devil.) Satan is not a fair opponent. He often takes advantage of us in those areas where we are the most vulnerable.

Was there a real need for bread? If so, why was it wrong for Jesus to turn the stones into bread? That would have been doubting that God was able to provide for His needs. We can depend on our heavenly Father to supply the things we really need to carry out His plans.

Why was it wrong for Jesus to jump off the temple and call upon God to protect Him? God is a sovereign Lord. He is not a mere magician whose purpose is to fulfil all our selfish desires. We are never to try and control Him just to do a special favor for us.

Jesus was born to be King of Kings and Lord of Lords. The whole world will belong to Him. Why would it have been wrong for Him to have received it when Satan offered it to Him? This would have meant not only worshiping someone who did not merit worship but also taking a shortcut to complete the work God had for Jesus. Trying to do God's work in our time and with our power never works.

Do you think Satan ever offers people today something similar to this offer to Jesus? If so what is the offer? Satan often tempts people with offers of fame, money, material goods, or popularity. However Satan doesn't really care about helping people. He just wants to get them to disobey God.

PERSONALIZE

Before class write the following statements on four different pieces of paper. Put one statement on each sheet.

1) Temptation is sin.
2) It is all right to satisfy our natural desires.
3) Satan never tempts us in areas where we are strong.
4) Because Jesus never sinned, He can't understand or help us when we are tempted.

Attach these papers to one of the walls in your room. Let your students move around to read the statements and vote on them. If they agree, they write "yes;" disagree, "no;" and "not sure" if they are undecided. Allow time for them to vote, then discuss the questions.

Is temptation sin? (No.) Temptation by itself is not sin. Jesus was tempted and yet never sinned. Sin is when we give in to temptation and disobey God. When we learn this fact, then it will be easier to reject the temptation and escape from it.

Is it all right to satisfy our natural desires? Natural desires such as hunger, rest, and sex are all built into people by God. They are not wrong. But a great deal depends on how and when we satisfy those desires. When we individually try to determine those times and methods we can get into trouble. We need to trust in God and He will satisfy our desires in the right way and time. Jesus did not give in to Satan on this issue and use God's power to provide food for Himself. After the temptation, God sent angels to provide for Jesus and help Him.

Does Satan ever tempt us in areas where we are strong? (Yes.) Most of us think that it is only in the areas where we are weakest that Satan tries to tempt us and get us to disobey God. But areas where we are strong can also be attacked.

The apostle Peter was very outgoing and a spokesman for God. He made a wonderful declaration that Jesus was the Christ, the Son of God. Yet, only a short time later when Jesus was arrested, Peter swore he didn't even know Jesus. Satan had tempted Peter in one of his strong areas and Peter gave in and disobeyed God.

Jesus never sinned, so how can He understand or help us when we are tempted? While it is true that Jesus never sinned, it is not true that He was never tempted by Satan to disobey God. Today's lesson points that out clearly. The fact that He was tempted in all ways is exactly why He can and will help us when we are tempted. Have two people look up Hebrews 2:18 and Hebrews 4:15 and read them aloud. These verses offer us help and understanding when we are tempted to do wrong. **We must be prepared for temptation at all times. When it comes, we must focus on Jesus and His loving power to defeat Satan and give us victory over temptation.**

PRAYER/PRAISE

Close with a prayer of thanksgiving for Jesus' example of obedience to God's commands in baptism and His understanding help to us in temptation.

FOR EXAMPLE

A good teacher shows us how to do something as well as tells us. Read Matthew 3:1-16. What really happened when Jesus got baptized? Decode the words to find out.

People came to hear John the Baptist because he was the first _____ _____ from
EURT   REGNESSEM

_____ in 400 _____. John told them they needed to _____ their _____ and turn
DOG   SRAEY   SSEFNOC   SNIS

from sin toward God. He told the crowds of people they should be baptized because it showed

they wanted to _____ doing _____ and start doing _____ . When Jesus came to
POTS   GNORW   THGIR

John to be baptized, John didn't want to do it because Jesus was _____ and John didn't
RETAERG

feel _____ . Jesus didn't really need to be baptized because He had _____
DEIFILAUQ   REVEN

_____ . But He said John should baptize Him because Jesus wanted to be an _____
DENNIS   ELPMAXE

of _____ to God. When Jesus came up out of the water, the _____ came
ECNEIDEBO   YLOH TIRIPS

down in the form of a dove to Him. A voice from _____ said, "This is my _____,
NEVAEH   NOS

whom I love; I am well _____ with Him."
DESAELP

29A

THE WINNER AND STILL CHAMPION

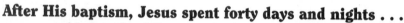

Read Matthew 4:1-11. What really happened when Satan tempted Jesus in the wilderness? Circle the letter of the phrase that best finishes the sentence.

After His baptism, Jesus spent forty days and nights . . .
a. preaching to the followers of John the Baptist.
b. going without food and praying about the work God wanted Him to do.
c. choosing twelve men who would help him do God's work.

Satan waited until Jesus was very weak from lack of food to . . .
a. try to get Him to disobey God.
b. help Him.
c. try and kill Him.

First, the devil tried to get Jesus to turn stones into . . .
a. the children of Abraham.
b. angels to help Him.
c. bread to eat.

Jesus told Satan that . . .
a. people should work hard to feed themselves.
b. obeying God's words and commands was more important than food for the body.
c. only God could feed people in the wilderness.

Then Satan suggested that Jesus should . . .
a. ask God to protect Him from sickness and death.
b. jump off a high place so God would send angels to protect Him.
c. ask God to help Him assemble an army to overthrow the Roman government.

Jesus knew the devil had used God's Word in a wrong way and said . . .
a. people shouldn't do something foolish and harmful just to dare God to help them.
b. that God's Word didn't say that.
c. He was afraid of heights.

The devil told Jesus that if Jesus would worship him, he would . . .
a. never bother Him again.
b. make Him ruler of the world.
c. leave the people of earth alone.

Jesus told Satan . . .
a. the devil didn't have the power to do it.
b. He didn't trust him to keep his promise.
c. we should worship and obey only God.

JESUS CHOOSES HIS APOSTLES

AIM: That your students will discover they have talents and skills to use for Jesus

SCRIPTURE: Matthew 10:2-8; Mark 2:14; Luke 6:13, 15, 16; John 1:43-45, 47; 20:24-29
(Jesus calls many kinds of workers to help Him in His ministry)

PREPARATION:
1. Photocopy activity sheets—one for each student.
2. Prepare a puzzle as described in PRESESSION.

PRESESSION (5-10 minutes)

ACTIVITIES
* Solve a puzzle to learn the names of the twelve apostles

MATERIALS
* Bibles
* Chalkboard or large sheet of paper and marker
* Pencil and paper—one for each student

PERSPECTIVE (10 minutes)

ACTIVITIES
* Use a game card to identify God-given natural talents people possess

MATERIALS
* "Talent Time" Activity Sheet

PROBE (20 minutes)

ACTIVITIES
* Use an activity sheet to learn more about the twelve men Jesus chose to be His special helpers

MATERIALS
* Bibles
* "Meet the Apostles" Activity Sheet

PERSONALIZE (15-20 minutes)

ACTIVITIES
* Take part in an object lesson to see how God can use our talents when we work together

MATERIALS
* One 8 1/2" x 11"sheet of white paper
* Marker or pencil, glue, pair of scissors
* Red paper—one sheet for each student plus one extra

PRESESSION

(5-10 minutes)

Before class time, place the names of the twelve apostles on the chalkboard. Omit letters as shown below:

```
_ _ T _ _
_ _ _ R E W
J _ _ _ _ S (son of Zebedee)
_ O H _
_ _ I L _ _
_ _ _ _ _ O L O _ _ _ _
T _ _ _ _ S
_ A T _ _ _ _
_ A M _ _ (son of Alphaeus)
_ _ A D D _ _ _ _
S _ _ _ N
J _ _ _ S
```

To get people thinking about the apostles, let early arrivals look up Matthew 10:24 and fill in the missing letters. Provide pencils and paper for this opening activity. The answers are Peter, Andrew, James, John, Philip, Bartholomew, Thomas, James, Thaddaeus, Simon, Judas.

See if anyone can tell you something specific about these Bible men. **Jesus knew He needed helpers to tell others about God's plan of salvation. He chose twelve men to do this.** These men would have the job of spreading the most important message the world had ever heard. **God gave each one of these helpers different talents that would enable Him to use them and complete this task.**

PERSPECTIVE

(10 minutes)

There is a distinction between spiritual gifts and natural abilities. In this lesson we are going to focus on natural talents.

How well do you know your classmates? What talents has God given them to help spread the good news about Jesus to others? Distribute copies of "Talent Time" activity sheet. Ask a volunteer to read the directions aloud. This activity will allow your students to know each other better and to be made aware of their own God-given natural interests and abilities. Spend most of the time in this section of the lesson in completing the exercise.

Optional: Just for fun, see if anyone had five spaces filled vertically, horizontally, or crosswise.

Did you find out some new things about each other? Did the game reveal some interests and abilities of your own? People are often not conscious of areas where they have special interests or natural gifts until someone else makes them aware of them. God has given us those interests and talents and wants us to use them to honor Him and help others.

Who were the twelve men that Jesus chose to help Him? Have the group say their names in unison.

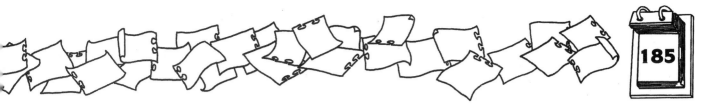

PROBE

(20 minutes)

The apostles were ordinary people, like many of the ones in our own church. They were a varied group from many different walks of life. They had only one thing in common—the desire to follow and serve Jesus.

First of all, Jesus let His multitude of followers know about them by calling them out of the crowd and appointing them as twelve special helpers and called them "apostles." "Apostle" is a Greek word meaning "someone who is sent out." The entire crowd of disciples knew that the twelve were to be His special messengers.

Now we know their names, but let's find out more about them. What interests and talents did they have? Pass out copies of "Meet the Apostles" activity sheet. Divide the class into small groups of two or three people. Depending on the size of your class, assign each of these Bible Investigator teams part of the puzzle to solve by looking up the reference/s and filling in the blanks. Answers are: Andrew, Peter, Bartholomew, John, Judas, Matthew, Philip, Simon, Thomas, Thaddaeus, James (Zebedee), James the less (Alphaeus).

When you are done, we'll talk about your discoveries. Expand your students' discoveries by sharing some of the following background sketches of the apostles.

Andrew was a fisherman. His home was Bethsaida. He was always eager to bring others to Jesus. Jesus said He would make him a fisherman of people's souls.

(Simon) Peter was Andrew's brother and also a fisherman. Whatever he did, he did it thoroughly, whether it be recognizing Jesus as the Messiah or denying he even knew Him. Jesus recognized that Peter would become a rock in his faith after he received the Holy Spirit.

Bartholomew (Nathaniel) was honest and direct. Although he first rejected Jesus because He came from Nazareth, Bartholomew later called Him the Son of God. Jesus said Bartholomew was an honest man and a true son of Israel.

John was a fisherman and often called "the disciple Jesus loved." Although Jesus called him a "son of thunder" because of his short temper, He knew John would later become known for his love for others.

Judas came from the town of Kerioth which gave him the added name of Iscariot. He was not only in charge of the money for the group but also helped himself to it when he desired. Jesus continued to reach out to Judas with loving forgiveness right up to the time of His betrayal. After Jesus' arrest, Judas gave the betrayal money back to the priests and killed himself.

Matthew (Levi) was a tax collector in Capernaum when Jesus called him to become a follower. He gave a feast in Jesus' honor. Matthew gave up his crooked ways of extortion and found true friendship and forgiveness with Jesus.

Philip was also a fisherman from Bethsaida. He had an inquiring frame of mind that caused him to wonder about Jesus' miracles and the purpose of Jesus' ministry. He was always eager to bring others to Christ.

Simon was a member of the Zealots. They were a radical group of patriots who worked to overthrow the Roman government. He found that the kingdom Jesus offered was far superior to any earthly one and gave up his subversive plots to follow the King of Kings.

Thomas (Didymus) had courage as well as doubts. It was Thomas who suggested the apostles should go with Jesus to Bethany when Lazarus was sick, even though it might mean death for all of them. Jesus did not criticize him for his unbelief but reached out to prove Himself to Thomas.

Thaddaeus (Judas or Lebbaeus) is a shadowy figure with little background information available. In two lists of the disciples he is called Thaddaeus, and in others he is Judas. This is probably because people might have confused him with Judas Iscariot.

James (son of Zebedee) was the brother of John and also a fisherman. Like John, he possessed a short temper which later turned to solid commitment to Jesus. He was the first apostle to be martyred for his faith.

James (son of Alphaeus) was also called the less or the younger to distinguish him from James the son of Zebedee. Little more is known about him.

Did you notice that Jesus recognized the natural interests of each man and showed him how it could be used to honor God and help others? For example, four of the men were fishermen. Jesus identified their interest and called them to be fishers of men. They knew how to be patient until the fish were hooked, how to work together to pull up and empty the net, how to work hard, depend upon God in severe storms, and also spend long, boring hours mending nets and repairing the boats. **Jesus used their natural talents and interests and turned them into valuable tools for the work God wanted to do. When the Apostles used their talents and worked together, they spread the Gospel to every part of their world.**

PERSONALIZE

(15-20 minutes)

Jesus didn't demand or force the apostles to follow Him. He invited them to be co-workers with Him in the greatest project of all times. God won't force you to follow Him either. But He gave you your special talents and wants you to use them to honor Him and tell others about Jesus.

Display the white paper. **Let's make a card to show people how much God loves them.** Fold the paper in half like a card. Ask for three volunteers to help you. Give one person the scissors, one the glue, and one the marker. **What would happen if I asked only one of these people to make the card?** (Couldn't do it.) **What would happen if they all worked together?** (Could make the card.) Have the helpers complete the card by cutting out a red heart, gluing it on the outside of the card, and printing "God loves you!" on the inside page.

Distribute the red paper and have each person tear a heart shape from it. **Think about the blocks you signed in our talent game. Choose one of your interests or talents and write it on the heart. Below it, write one way you could use it to honor God and help others.** Allow time to complete this activity.

God has given each one of you special talents. We can thank Him for the talents He has given us and also those of other people. We can use our different abilities and work together to help others and honor God.

PRAYER/PRAISE

Close with an "answering machine" prayer. **Jesus has called and left you a message. It is "Come, follow me." What answer will you give Him?** Have each student turn their paper activity hearts over and write a brief prayer to be left for God.

TALENT TIME

Ask questions to help you discover talented people. Try to find someone who is interested in or has one of the gifts listed below. Have him/her sign the square. See how many unrecognized talents you can identify.

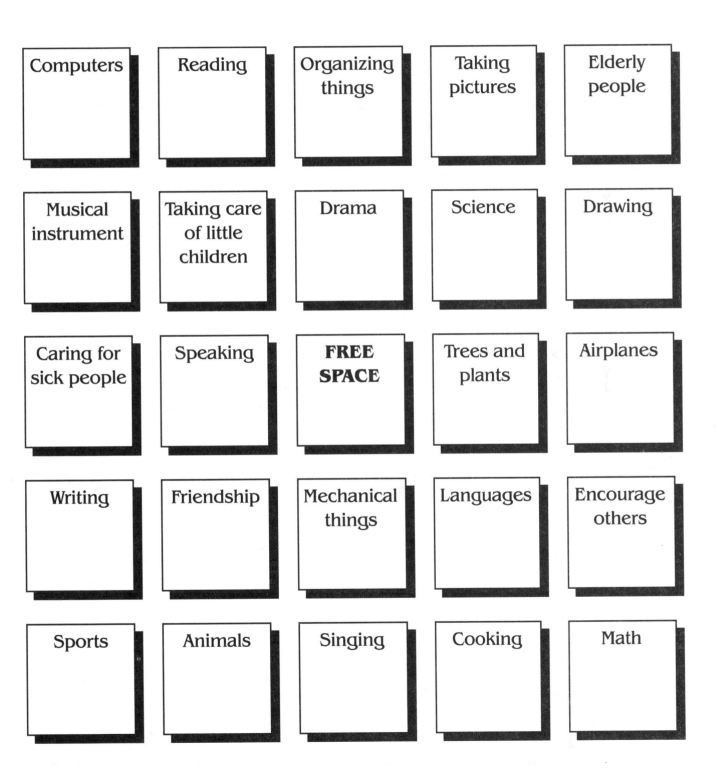

Computers	Reading	Organizing things	Taking pictures	Elderly people
Musical instrument	Taking care of little children	Drama	Science	Drawing
Caring for sick people	Speaking	**FREE SPACE**	Trees and plants	Airplanes
Writing	Friendship	Mechanical things	Languages	Encourage others
Sports	Animals	Singing	Cooking	Math

Meet the Apostles

Read the description and unscramble the letters to discover the name. Check the references if you need help.

I brought my brother to Jesus. I also brought the boy whose lunch Jesus blessed and multiplied to make it feed a huge crowd. My name is RAN-WED _____. (John 1:40, 41; 6:8, 9)

Jesus blessed me because I confessed my faith in Him. But later, I said I didn't even know Jesus. I am sometimes called "the mouth" of the apostles. My name is MONIS REETP _____.

(Matthew 16:16; Mark 14:66-71)

I am also called Nathaniel. Philip told me about Jesus. The Savior praised me highly. My name is THROLMWEBAO _____. (Luke 6:14)

I am a son of Zebedee. Along with Peter and James, I had the privilege of seeing Jesus transfigured. I wrote a Gospel about Jesus. My name is NOJH _____. (Matthew 4:21)

I was the only apostle who was not from Galilee. I kept the money for the apostles. I'm the one who is remembered for a wicked deed. My name is SADJU _____. (Luke 22:1-5)

I was a tax collector. I was also known as Levi. One of the four Gospels is written by me. My name is TAWTHEM _____. (Matthew 9:9)

I told Nathaniel about Jesus. Like him, I live in Bethsaida. One time I brought some Greeks to Jesus when they were looking for Him. My name is LIPHIP _____.

(John 1:45; 12:20-22)

I have the same name as one of the other apostles. People remember me because I am a member of a very patriotic group of Jews called Zealots. My name is NISMO _____. (Luke 6:15)

I was also called Didymus. I am the apostle who wanted proof that Jesus had risen from the tomb. My name is MOTHSA _____. (John 20:24-28)

I asked Jesus why He showed himself to us, but not to others. I have also been called by the names of Lebbaeus and Judas. My name is DADASEUTH _____. (John 14:22; Matthew 10:3)

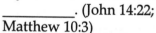

I am also a son of Zebedee. Jesus called my brother and me "sons of thunder." I was with Jesus when He was transfigured. My name is SAMEJ _____. (Mark 3:17)

I am the son of Alphaeus. I have the same name as one of the other apostles. My name is often given as MAJES the less because I am younger than the other apostle. _____. (Matthew 10:3)

JESUS BRINGS GOD'S MESSAGE

AIM: That your students will apply the truths of Jesus' Sermon on the Mount to their lives

SCRIPTURE: Matthew 5:14-16, 43-48; 6:1-4, 19-24; 7:12, 24-29 (Jesus gives many great lessons in His Sermon on the Mount)

PREPARATION:
1. Photocopy activity sheets—one for each student.

PRESESSION (5-10 minutes)

ACTIVITIES
* Play a secret word game

PERSPECTIVE (10 minutes)

ACTIVITIES
* Take part in a choral reading

MATERIALS
* Bibles
* Candle
* "Light of The World" Activity Sheet

PROBE (20 minutes)

ACTIVITIES
* Decipher a code to discover some of the important principles in the Sermon on the Mount

MATERIALS
* Bibles
* "God's Message" Activity Sheet

PERSONALIZE (15-20 minutes)

ACTIVITIES
* Observe and participate in some object lessons that illustrate how Christians are the lights of the world

MATERIALS
* Matches, aluminum foil
* Candles—one for each student and two for yourself
* Candle holder

LESSON 31   **UNIT THEME: JESUS, THE LORD**

PRESESSION

To get your students thinking about Christians as lights in the world, let early arrivals try to guess a secret word. The word is "light." Players can ask you general questions about the word. Examples could be: Is it alive? How big is it? What color is it? Can it talk? After a few minutes tell the group what it is.

Talk about light. What does it do? What happens to growing things if they don't have it? What effect does it have on our work, play, or daily life?

Share the following story with the group:

Many years ago, a rich man built a beautiful church. When it was finished and people came to see it, one man suddenly asked, "Where are the lights? You have forgotten the lights!"

The man smiled and said, "No, I have not forgotten the lights. Each person who comes to worship service will be an example for all to see. When people come into the building, they will light a lamp from a large candle in the entrance and carry it to their seats in the church. When everyone is here the lamps will make the room very bright. If people stay away their places will be dark because their lamps will not be lighted."

Jesus said something special about lights in His Sermon on the Mount.

PERSPECTIVE

After Jesus had chosen the twelve apostles from among His followers, He came down to the mountainside to teach the huge crowd there. He gave lesson after lesson on how to live a life pleasing to God. **His sermon was called the Sermon on the Mount, because it was preached on a mountainside.**

Hold up one of the candles. **The purpose of a candle is to give light. What would you think of someone who puts a lighted candle under a basket?** (They were silly, it defeats the purpose of the candle.) **No, instead people place lighted candles where they can give light to rooms.** Have the group turn to Matthew 5:14-16 in their Bibles and follow along as you read it aloud. **Jesus compares a person's life to a candle. Others can see the way a person lives. Jesus doesn't want us to hide our good deeds from other people. He wants us to show others how to live by the way we live.**

Hand out copies of "Light Of The World" activity sheet. Let people read it over silently several times. Assign people to take the different parts.

Vocal combinations used in choirs can be used in choral readings. Have people mark volume changes or parts assigned as solos and duets. Read it through with your students several times and make adjustments if necessary.

Optional: If you have a longer class period, consider presenting your choral reading for another group. You can prerecord it or perform it live for another class or a church service.

What are some ways we hide our lights? Sometimes Christians are silent when they should speak out for Jesus. Other times we are so much like non-Christians that there is no difference between us. In that way we deny Jesus. Sin can come between us and God and dim our lights. When we pay no attention to the needs or questions of others about the Lord, we also hide our lights.

What happens when we let our lights shine? (Others praise our heavenly Father.) **Jesus said many more things in the Sermon on the Mount as He explained to the people what God expected of them.**

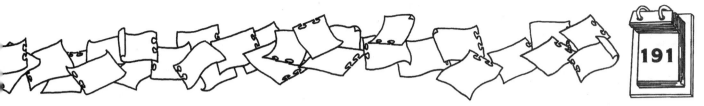

PROBE

(20 minutes)

Distribute copies of "God's Message" activity sheet. Ask someone to read the directions aloud. Students can work on this individually. Answers are: light, shine; love, enemies; time, energy, treasures, heaven; God's kingdom; faith, God, blessings; others, do for you.

The Old Testament taught the rule of "an eye for an eye." This new teaching of Jesus was radical to the Israelites. **Is it easy to love your enemies? Why or why not?** (No. The normal reaction is to strike back and get revenge.) Jesus is saying that it is more important to be just and fair than taking the law into our own hands and demanding justice. But when we allow God to work through us and love them, even our enemies can see God's light shining through us.

Some people spend all of their time and energy working hard and saving all their money or accumulating "things." Why should we store up treasures in Heaven instead? (Material things don't last, only heavenly values last.) Most people spend their time and money on things that interest them. That's what Jesus meant when He said, "Where your treasure is, there your heart will be also."

What did Jesus say we should put first in our lives? (God's kingdom.) Jesus said that if we try to please God first we will find that the necessary things of life will also be provided.

Does worrying about something help? (No.) **What does worrying do to us?** Worry can make us physically sick and places importance on the problem instead of God. We get so absorbed with it that we aren't sensitive to the needs of others or are too troubled to carry out God's plans for us.

When we love and trust our heavenly Father we will realize that He loves us too and wants to do good things for us. He wants us to come to Him first with our requests because He has the knowledge of how to best help us. We

often ask God for things for ourselves and others, but we must also thank Him for all He does and is for us each day.

What does the Golden Rule say in the Bible? (Matthew 7:12) (We should do to others what we would have them do to us.) It is hard to make the first move to treat others kindly and with love. We would much rather wait for them to take the initiative. But God loved us while we were still sinners, and we are to also let Him love others, even our enemies, through us.

Jesus compared people who heard His words with two builders. Check out Matthew 7:24-27. What was the difference Jesus was emphasizing? Both people heard Jesus words. The real difference between them was that one put them into practice and the other did not.

What happened to the house of the wise man when the storm came? (His house didn't fall.) **What happened to the house of the foolish man when the storm hit?** (His house fell with a great crash.)

Hearing or learning God's message is not enough. We need to obey it.

Huge crowds followed Jesus as He came down from the mountain. The people were awestruck at His teaching. Other teachers just repeated the law of Moses and quoted traditional sayings. Jesus didn't need to quote others. He was the Word of God in human form. The wonderful words of His Sermon on the Mount are considered the greatest teachings the world has ever heard.

What a different world we would have if Christians really did the things Jesus said to do instead of just talking about them. An old saying is "You are the only Bible some people ever read." Unbelievers watch our lives to see if we walk our faith as well as talk it. What do they see in each of us? **Now you have heard Jesus' words. It's up to you to follow His teachings!**

PERSONALIZE

(15-20 minutes)

Place a piece of aluminum foil on the table. Light a match. **This match is like the Holy Spirit. When you become a Christian the Holy Spirit enters your life. He empowers you to shine for God.**

Use the match to light one of the candles and hold it over the foil. Now light a second candle and hold the two candles sideways over the foil so one flame is about 1 1/2" above the other flame. **Sometimes we hide our light. Sometimes sin makes it go out.** Blow out the lower flame. The lower candle will now relight itself. **When we are really sorry and ask for forgiveness, Jesus is ready and able to relight the heav-enly light of the Holy Spirit and restore us to shine for God.** Put away one candle and place the other in a stand.

PRAYER/PRAISE

Turn off the lights and darken the room. Have everyone sit holding an unlit candle. Take the lit candle. Turn to the person on your right. **(Name), you are the light of the world.** Light his/her candle. S/he turns to person on the right and repeats, "(Name), you are the light of the world. Proceed until all students have been named and have lighted candles.

Close by singing "This Little Light of Mine."

LIGHT OF THE WORLD

Girl solo: (softly) You are the light of the world.

Boy solo: (gaining strength) You are the light of the world.

Girls: A city on a hill

Boys: Cannot be hidden.

All: (confidently) You are the light of the world.

Boy Solo: Neither do people light a lamp

Girl Solo: And put it under a bowl.

Boy Duet: Instead they put it on its stand

Boys: And it gives light to everyone in the house.

Girls: (emphatically) Everyone!

All: You are the light of the world.

Girl solo: In the same way

Girl Duet: Let your light shine before men,

Girls: That they may see your good deeds

Boys: And praise your Father in Heaven.

Girls: (joyfully) Praise you, Father!

Boys: (joyfully) Praise you, Father!

Girls: (slightly softer) You are the light,

Boys: (fading) You are the light,

All: (whisper) You are the light of the world.

God's Message

CODE:

	1	2	3	4	5	6
1	A	B	C	D	E	F
2	G	H	I	J	K	L
3	M	N	O	P	Q	R
4	S	T	U	V	W	X
5	Y	Z				

Example: 12 = B
(Read vertical number first.)

Hi there, Bible Investigators! Can you decode the sentences below and uncover some of the wonderful teachings from Jesus' Sermon on the Mount? If you need help, look up the Scripture references.

Let your ‾26‾ ‾23‾ ‾21‾ ‾22‾ ‾42‾ ‾41‾   ‾41‾ ‾22‾ ‾23‾ ‾32‾ ‾15‾ .   (Matthew 5:15, 16)

‾26‾ ‾33‾ ‾44‾ ‾15‾   your   ‾15‾ ‾32‾ ‾15‾ ‾31‾ ‾23‾ ‾15‾ ‾41‾ .   (Matthew 5:44)

Spend your ‾42‾ ‾23‾ ‾31‾ ‾15‾   and   ‾15‾ ‾32‾ ‾15‾ ‾36‾ ‾21‾ ‾51‾

laying up ‾42‾ ‾36‾ ‾15‾ ‾11‾ ‾41‾ ‾43‾ ‾36‾ ‾15‾ ‾41‾   in

‾22‾ ‾15‾ ‾11‾ ‾44‾ ‾15‾ ‾32‾ .   (Matthew 6:20)

Seek ‾21‾ ‾33‾ ‾14‾ ‾41‾ '   ‾25‾ ‾23‾ ‾32‾ ‾21‾ ‾14‾ ‾33‾ ‾31‾   first.   (Matthew 6:33)

Have ‾16‾ ‾11‾ ‾23‾ ‾42‾ ‾22‾   to ask ‾21‾ ‾33‾ ‾14‾   for His

‾12‾ ‾26‾ ‾15‾ ‾41‾ ‾41‾ ‾23‾ ‾32‾ ‾21‾ ‾41‾ .   (Matthew 7:7-11)

Do to ‾33‾ ‾42‾ ‾22‾ ‾15‾ ‾36‾ ‾41‾   what you want them to ‾14‾ ‾33‾

‾16‾ ‾33‾ ‾36‾   ‾51‾ ‾33‾ ‾43‾ .   (Matthew 7:12)

31B   ©1993 by The Standard Publishing Company. Permission is granted to photocopy this page for ministry purposes only—not for resale.

JESUS SHOWS HIS POWER

AIM: That your students will worship Jesus as the Son of God and trust Him to care for them in fearful times

SCRIPTURE: Matthew 8:18, 23-27; 14:22-33; Mark 4:35-41; Luke 8:22-25 (Jesus causes the wind to cease and walks on water)

PREPARATION:
1. Photocopy activity sheets—one for each student.
2. Make a list of common fears as described in PRESESSION.

PRESESSION (5-10 minutes)

ACTIVITIES
* Talk about common fears

MATERIALS
* Chalkboard and chalk or large sheet of paper and marker

PERSPECTIVE (10 minutes)

ACTIVITIES
* Share personal experiences of God's help in fearful times

MATERIALS
* Bibles

PROBE (20 minutes)

ACTIVITIES
* Read a fictional newspaper about Jesus calming a storm

MATERIALS
* Bibles
* "Tiberian Times" Activity Sheet

PERSONALIZE (15-20 minutes)

ACTIVITIES
* Bibles
* Finish writing a story about Peter and Jesus walking on water

MATERIALS
* "Believe It Or Not" Activity Sheet

PRESESSION

(5-10 minutes)

Before class, list these or similar fears on the chalkboard or a large sheet of paper: dark, heights, tight spaces, monsters, death of parent, nuclear war, storms, fires, dogs, serious illness, rejection, loss of money.

As students arrive today ask them to help you with a question. **What do these things have in common?** (They are all common fears people have.)

Why do you think we are afraid of these things? (Can't control them, they can change our lives, they have to do with the unknown, hurt us.)

What or who can help us when we are fearful? (Parents, doctors, pastors, youth workers, authority figures such as police or government, God.)

PERSPECTIVE

(10 minutes)

What does fear do to people? Fear often paralyzes people. They cannot carry on a normal life because the fear consumes their thoughts and actions. It causes us to concentrate on the fear. When that happens we have difficulty hearing God or carrying out His plan for our lives.

Have you had any experience when God helped you in a fearful time? What happened? Encourage students to talk about their fears. Let your students talk freely and informally. Be sensitive and sympathetic. Do not belittle any story that they tell. Everyone is usually afraid of something. Our fears may differ, but they affect us much the same nonetheless.

To get the group started, share some experience you have had in which you were very frightened. Or, perhaps, you can share the experiences of a Christian friend who was frightened. Tell how that person's prayer was answered.

Optional: If you have difficulty sharing something personal, you can use the following story.

Once an English missionary named Mr. Scott was traveling through the jungles in India to reach some people who had never heard of Jesus. He carried no weapons, just his Bible and his violin. After walking for many days, he found himself in a clearing. Suddenly he was surrounded by natives with their spears pointed right at his heart! He breathed a prayer, took his violin, and began to play and sing, "All Hail the Power of Jesus' Name." When he opened his eyes, the warriors had lowered their spears and many of them had tears in their eyes. Mr. Scott stayed and taught them about Jesus. When he left they begged him to return. This man prayed and the Lord saved him by His mighty power.

Check out Psalm 50:15. What does the Lord tell you to do in times of trouble? (Call upon Him.) **What promise does He give you?** (He will deliver me.) **What should you do when God helps you?** (Honor Him.) **Let's see how Jesus' apostles put this promise into action.**

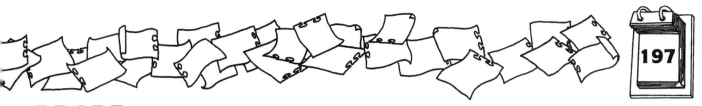
PROBE

(20 minutes)

When Jesus began His ministry of teaching and healing, people came from everywhere to be made well and to listen to Jesus. One day four men brought a sick friend to Jesus by lowering him from the roof into the room where Jesus was. Jesus healed the man and forgave his sins. **By His power, He showed that He was the Son of God.**

Great crowds followed Jesus wherever He went. **One day after speaking to a multitude of people Jesus and His disciples crossed the Sea of Galilee. A storm swooped down on them suddenly. Let's imagine you lived in the lakeside town of Tiberias then. What do you think the local newspaper might say about what happened next?**

Distribute copies of "Tiberian Times" activity sheet. Ask for volunteers to read the different articles aloud.

The Sea of Galilee is like a bowl of water, situated in a valley surrounded by hills. It is a relatively small lake thirteen miles long and seven wide. The shore's surface is 680 feet below sea level. While most scholars think the depth is about one hundred fifty feet, some have estimated it from eighty to seven hundred feet deep.

The winds blow from the north down towards the Dead Sea. They can become violent with little or no warning by clouds or rain. Tempests are caused by wind alone. Waves up to twenty feet high (two and one-half stories tall) can whip up and make the sea very dangerous. The gospel writers knew this and used a word meaning "earthquake" to describe the storms. When a storm struck in all its fury, the Sea of Galilee was indeed a treacherous place!

Four of the apostles were career fishermen. They knew how to read the signs of approaching storms and would not have set sail if they had seen one coming. But this one came upon them with no warning. They were seagoing men who had been in storms and survived before, but this one was so violent that they felt certain that the boat was going to sink and they were all going to drown.

How is this weather storm like the stormy times of our lives? The fears we have are like storms in our lives. They threaten to defeat us. We often experience our worst times when we don't expect them. People tend to keep a watch out and prepare themselves for trouble when they see its signs. But the unexpected storms of life can take us off guard and destroy us. Those are the times when we need to call upon God most of all.

Where was Jesus while the storm threatened the apostles? (Asleep in the back of the boat.) **How do you think it was possible for Jesus to sleep so soundly during this terrible tempest?** (He knew that as God's Son He had power over everything—including winds and waves.)

What did this experience teach Jesus' followers? (To trust Him, that He was more than a man, He was the Son of God and worthy of their worship.)

What do you think we can learn from this story? (The same things.) **When you have those kinds of experiences you can do either one of two things. You can think that Jesus doesn't really care about you or want to help you. That lets fear and worry conquer you. Or you can call upon Him and trust Him to calm the storm and deliver you. One day, the apostle Peter found that out personally.**

PERSONALIZE

Have students find Matthew 14:22-33 in their Bibles. They can take turns reading these verses aloud. Hand out copies of "Believe It or Not" activity sheet. This exercise gives a Bible situation and a starter to the story. People can work on completing the story, writing it as if they are Peter. If they need help, they can refer to the Bible account. Spend about ten minutes finishing the story.

Optional: If time permits, invite students to share their stories with the group. Be upbeat and supportive with people who do this. Don't compare their creative writing efforts, but stress that just as Matthew, Mark, and Luke differ in their literary viewpoints so do your students.

The important thing in this activity is not to have polished writing but as reinforcement for students so they can see that Bible people were like them and that the Lord's help is the same for us today as it was in Peter's time.

Peter was impulsive and reacted in faith to Jesus' assurance that He was not a ghost but a real person. What happened after Peter started walking on the water to Jesus? (He began to sink in the water.) **Check out Matthew 14: 30. Why did this happen?** (Peter looked at the wind and waves and began to be afraid.) **How did Jesus help Peter?** (He reached out His hand and caught him.) **Whenever you are afraid, don't be distracted by the storm around you. Keep your eyes on Jesus. Remember that He will be with you and help you.**

Jesus is God's Son. **The apostles knew this and worshiped Him.** They knew this because of the wonderful miracles He did. We can read about these miracles, but we also read that Jesus died for us, came back to life, and went to Heaven to prepare a place for His followers.

Jesus deserves our worship because He is God's Son. What are some ways you can worship the Lord? Be sure to include these means in your discussion: singing hymns of praise; by listening attentively to God's Word and thinking about its meaning; by bringing gifts of money to be used in the Lord's work; when we bow in prayer to God and pray in the name of Jesus; when we give our lives to serve the Lord.

Do you believe that Jesus is God's Son? Do you worship Him? If you answer "yes" to the first question, then surely you need to answer "yes" to the second.

PRAYER/PRAISE

Lead with a prayer of thanks to God for Jesus' power to help you in the stormy times of your life. Make this an "add-a-thought" prayer of thanks. Start out the prayer and let students each add a phrase to it. **Thank you, God, for Jesus' power to help me . . .** After all people have prayed close the prayer. **We worship you, Jesus, because you are worthy of praise and honor and glory.** Have everyone say, "Amen."

TIBERIAN TIMES

Tiberias, Galilee   Wednesday, July 15   5 shekels

TEACHER STOPS STORM

The popular teacher and healer, Jesus, is reported to have stopped a dangerous storm on the Sea of Galilee last night by simply speaking. If this is true, the question people are asking is, "What kind of man is this that even the wind and waves obey His voice?" Time will tell.

APOSTLES: WE THOUGHT WE WERE GOING TO DROWN!

The twelve apostles of Jesus said that they had been on the other side of the lake where Jesus taught and healed the people. "Jesus suggested we go to the other side. He was exhausted and fell asleep in the back of the boat."

Suddenly a storm hit the Sea of Galilee and the apostles were terrified. Without warning, the wind roared down one of the valleys that border the lake and raised twenty-foot waves which threatened to swamp the boat and plunge them to the depths of the lake's bottom 150 feet below.

They quickly awoke Jesus. "We asked Him to help us because we were going to drown," said a spokesman for the group.

"Jesus asked why we were afraid. Then He stood up and rebuked the wind and waves saying, 'Be quiet!'"

An eyewitness in another boat nearby reported that immediately the wind stopped and the water became perfectly calm over the entire lake. "It was as if He had power over nature itself!" the sailor said.

Public Opinion Poll

Today's question: "Who do you think Jesus really is?"
John: The Son of God.
High Priest Caiaphas: The Prince of Demons.
Centurion Rufus: A mighty Lord.

YOU: (Your opinion) _____
_____
_____
_____
_____
_____

Tiberian Weather:

Tuesday: Sunny and warm.
Wednesday: Chance of showers.
Thursday: Gale force winds.

INDEX

Believe It Or Not!

What if you were Peter? You have just come home after a boat trip with the other apostles and are telling your family about your experience.

"What a night! I've been a fisherman all my life, but I've never seen anything like it. I can still scarcely believe it really happened! While we were on the lake last night, a bad storm came up. The boat was having trouble because of the wind blowing up huge waves.

"In the early hours of the morning we suddenly saw someone walking toward us. He was walking on top of the water! We were terrified because we thought it was a ghost.

"Then the person immediately said, 'Don't be afraid. It is I, Jesus.'

"I called to Him and said, ". . .

Finish this story

_____

_____

_____

_____

_____

_____

_____

_____

_____

_____

_____

JESUS SHOWS HE CARES

AIM: That your students will follow in Jesus' footsteps of love and serve others

SCRIPTURE: Matthew 9:18-35; Mark 5:22-43; Luke 8:41-56 (Jesus serves others with love and compassion: brings a girl back to life; heals a sick woman, two blind men and a demon-possessed mute)

PREPARATION:
1. Photocopy activity sheets—one for each student.

PRESESSION (5-10 minutes)

ACTIVITIES
* Find stories of people in need and talk about the needs

MATERIALS
* Old newspapers, pencils or markers

PERSPECTIVE (10 minutes)

ACTIVITIES
* Brainstorm general ways we can show our care for others and serve them

MATERIALS
* Chalkboard and chalk or large sheet of paper and marker

PROBE (20 minutes)

ACTIVITIES
* Read a skit about Jesus serving others

MATERIALS
* Bibles
* "For All I Care" Activity Sheet

PERSONALIZE (15-20 minutes)

ACTIVITIES
* Find specific ways to help people in need

MATERIALS
* "Help Wanted" Activity Sheet

PRESESSION

Invite early arrivals to look through the old newspapers for headlines or articles about people in need. They can tear these out. After the group has assembled, have them take turns reading these headlines or articles aloud. Work together to identify what the specific need is. Have the person who found the item write that need on the top of it. **How do you feel when people are in need?** (Answers will vary.)

PERSPECTIVE

Most of us feel sorry for needy people. Feeling sorry for others is a beginning, but in order to show people we care we need more than pity. The bigger question is "Do you feel sorry enough to do something about it?"

Why do you think people don't try to serve others more often? (Afraid they'll do something wrong, don't want to get involved—law suits, afraid they'll get hurt emotionally, too self-centered to think about others.) The word "service" as it is used today usually refers to what people want rather than what they *give*.

How do you think Jesus feels about needy people? (Has compassion for them, loves them, wants to help them.) Serving others because He loved them was the very heart of what Jesus did every day. His desire for us is to follow His example and do the same.

What are some general rules we can make about how to show others we care? Invite students to help you list these. They can write them on the chalkboard or a large sheet of paper. Some good guidelines could be like these: do errands for them, be good friends, pray for them, find out their needs and explore ways to meet them, offer to help in any way possible and let them choose the way that's best for them, give them hope by telling them how Jesus helps you.

Serving others in these ways may mean doing things you don't particularly like to do. It may also take time from yourself to spend it on another person.

Showing you care might even mean involving grown-ups or professional helpers such as doctors or counsellors. For example a student trying to help another student with a drug problem or abuse from home needs to know this is beyond their power. They need to include family or professionals. Promises to keep those kinds of secrets may need to be broken. A student who really wants to help the hurting person must reveal the secret to a trusted adult who has the experience and power to help.

Jesus had many busy days. They were often filled with kind deeds for others as He continued to carry out His Father's will. During the short time that Jesus spent on the earth, He put something worthwhile into every minute of every day.

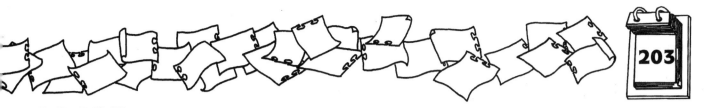

PROBE

Let's take a look at one particular day in the life of Jesus. Hand out copies of "For All I Care" activity sheet. This fictional program interviews some of the people Jesus loved and served. You will need people to read the parts of the host, Jairus, the woman, blind man, and mute man. Have the rest of the group follow along on their activity sheets and be ready to discuss it.

Have students turn to Matthew 8:18. **How did Jesus respond to Jairus' need?** (Quickly, calmly, went willingly.)

What happened on the way to Jairus' house? (A woman touched Jesus' coat.) **How did Jesus react to her?** (He asked her to identify herself and then tell her problem.) **How do you think the woman felt before she touched Jesus?** (Sad, suffering, desperate, believed He could help her, determined to get near Him.)

This woman's extreme need drove her to do the unexpected and reach out and touch Jesus' clothes. In Bible times women who had a sickness like hers were considered unclean. Rabbis (teachers) would never allow an unclean person to touch them. This woman's action must have raised some eyebrows from people in the crowd! But instead of condemning her for her action, Jesus assured her He cared and showed it by healing her.

Check out Mark 5:36. What did Jesus say to Jairus when the messenger told him his daughter was dead? (Not to be afraid, but believe in Him.) The messenger told Jairus there was no longer any need to have Jesus come. Because of the climate and lack of methods to preserve the body, burial was usually on the same day as the death. Jesus loved Jairus and responded to his feelings of despair. He offered Jairus comfort and hope.

What was going on at the house when Jesus and Jairus arrived? (People were mourning by wailing and playing sad songs on flutes.) In Bible times mourners were professional people, usually women. They were paid to come weep, make eulogies, and play funeral dirges.

What did these mourners do to Jesus when He told them to leave because the little girl was only asleep? Ask someone to read Mark 5:40 aloud. (Made fun of Him.) Jesus tolerated this insult just so He could help Jairus and his family.

What does verse 41 say Jesus did when He was in the room with the dead girl? (Took her by the hand and told her to get up.) **Why do you think Jesus took her by the hand?** (To show how much He cared about her, because she needed help to get up, don't know.) Not only were dead people unclean but to touch a dead body made the other person unclean as well. Jesus had such great power that He could have just spoken to the girl and she would live again. But He put His sympathy for Jairus and his family into action and physically demonstrated His love and compassion.

Look in verse 43. What did Jesus do after the little girl stood up? (Told her parents to give her something to eat.) It's always a good sign when a sick person wants something to eat. It means they are getting better. Jesus not only had power from God, He had human common sense.

Have students turn back to Matthew 9:27-31. **What happened after Jesus left Jairus' home?** (Two blind men asked Him to heal them.) These men were not only hopeful, they were determined. They followed Jesus right inside a building. **How did Jesus show His love and sympathy for these men?** (He restored their sight.)

How do you think the man who couldn't speak felt after Jesus healed him? (Happy, relieved.) Demons are real. They have power to hurt people, but Jesus' power is far greater and He always uses it for good!

Check out verse 34. What did the Pharisees say about Jesus' power? (His

power came from the prince of demons.) **Why do you think they said this?** (Jealous of Jesus, their beliefs about God were challenged, were afraid of losing control over the people.) **Jesus did not let criticism or humiliation stop Him from serving others. He let God use Him to love and help the needy around Him. We need to follow His example.**

PERSONALIZE

(15-20 minutes)

Hand out copies of "Help Wanted" activity sheet. This gives six situations about needy people. Students are to pick one specific way to show their love for the person having the problem.

Optional: If you are short on time, do this activity by dividing the class into several small groups and assigning each team one or two problems.

When the activity is completed talk about it together. Encourage your students to be as specific as possible in their answers. It is often easy to just spout generalities that never get done. Getting down to specific deeds leads to real action, not just words.

For example: You could let Amber confide in you. Sometimes just sharing our troubles with someone makes them easier to handle.

Running errands such as getting her groceries, mowing the lawn or dusting could benefit crippled Mrs. Hunt. Visiting frequently would help her loneliness.

Being the first person to approach a new classmate with friendship can lead to great relationships later. Offering to introduce them to your friends or show them around school can also help.

Looking directly at a hearing disabled person and speaking slowly and carefully can be more helpful than just turning up your voice volume.

Assuring Kaitlin that what's inside is more important than her clothes, shows her you care. Speaking up for her as a person rather than joining with kids who make fun of her clothes can also help.

People are all important to Jesus. He doesn't care if the person comes from a minority background. Openly standing with Alex instead of picking on him is a good way to show love and service.to God.

Loving and serving others involves an element of risk. You might get your feelings hurt or be criticized by others for it. But it is well worth it when you see people's needs met and they praise God for His help given through you.

PRAYER/PRAISE

Lay out the news items that you used in Presession. Have students each take one and pray a sentence prayer about it. Close by asking God to guide and use your students to love and serve others as Jesus did.

For All I Care

Host: Welcome to our show, "The Man in the Street." Today we've been following Jesus. Let's talk to some of the people who helped to make this a busy day for Him. Jairus, you are the ruler of the synagogue. Would you tell us what Jesus did for you today?

Jairus: I'll be glad to. It started out to be a terrible day. My little girl was dying. I asked Jesus to come and touch her. I believed that if He did, she would be well.

Host: What did Jesus do?

Jairus: He and His disciples came to my house. But when they got there, my child was already dead. It was dreadful. Mourners were everywhere, wailing and playing sad songs on flutes. Jesus told them to stop. He said she wasn't dead but only sleeping. They all laughed at Him.

Host: Did Jesus leave then?

Jairus: No. He told me not to be afraid but believe. Then He brought three of His disciples into the room. My wife and I went with them. He walked over to the bed and took my daughter's hand. He said, "Little girl, get up!" I can hardly believe what happened.

Host: What did happen?

Jairus: She stood up! Jesus gave life to our daughter. He really cares about people in need.

Host: That was really fabulous. Thank you, Jairus. Now let's talk to someone else Jesus helped. I noticed that this lady right here stopped Jesus on His way to the home of Jairus. What was that all about?

Woman: For twelve years I've been suffering from a terrible disease. I spent all my money on doctors. But instead of getting better, I only got worse. I decided that if I could just touch the hem of Jesus' coat I would be healed.

Host: And did you do that?

Woman: I sure did. Then Jesus stopped and asked who had touched Him. I was afraid, but I came and knelt at His feet and confessed that I was the one. I told Him the whole story.

Host: What did Jesus say to that?

Woman: He told me to go in peace. My faith had made me well.

Host: Next Jesus helped two blind men. Sir, what did Jesus do for you and your friend?

Blind Man: We asked Him to have mercy on us. We believed He could give us back our sight. Jesus touched our eyes and we could see! We're going to tell everyone that Jesus uses His great power to serve others.

Host: Thank you. Before we leave, let's talk to one more person. Sir, I saw some people bring you to Jesus. What did Jesus do for you?

Mute Man: I had a demon that took away my ability to speak. I wanted to talk to my friends and family but I couldn't.

Host: Jesus must have healed you, or you wouldn't be talking to us now.

Mute Man: That's right. He drove the demon out and now I can speak again. It's wonderful!

Host: You've heard it right here, folks. Jesus has great power. And what's more important is that He uses it in love to serve others. Tomorrow we'll have more examples of Jesus' love and compassion.

HELP WANTED

Look at each of the situations below. Then write one thing you can do to show the person you care and want to help.

1. Amber's parents are getting a divorce. She is really sad and worried about what will happen to her.

_____

2. Mrs. Hunt lives next door to you. She is an elderly widow who has arthritis. She has no family near by.

_____

3. Brant is new in school. He is very shy and having a hard time making friends. You are in the same class with him.

_____

4. David has a hearing disability. He has trouble hearing what people say. Some of the kids are making fun of him.

_____

5. Kaitlin's family stays at a shelter for the homeless. They can't buy trendy items. Many of her clothes are secondhand.

_____

6. Alex is from a minority group. He wants to join the team but some of the other kids don't want him.

_____

JESUS IS CHRIST, THE SON OF GOD

AIM: That your students will understand the importance of confessing that Jesus Christ is the Son of God

SCRIPTURE: Matthew 16:13-18; Mark 9:2-10 (Peter calls Jesus the Son of God; Jesus is transfigured on the mountain)

PREPARATION:
1. Photocopy activity sheets—one for each student.
2. Write discussion question as described in PRESESSION.

PRESESSION (5-10 minutes)

ACTIVITIES
* Discuss who Jesus is

MATERIALS
* Chalkboard and chalk or large sheet of paper and marker
* 3 x 5 index cards—one for each student

PERSPECTIVE (10 minutes)

ACTIVITIES
* Talk about confessing Jesus through music

MATERIALS
* Hymnals or chorus books

PROBE (20 minutes)

ACTIVITIES
* Read the story of Peter's confession of Jesus as the Son of God and Jesus' transfiguration
* Match items about Jesus
* Write a commercial promoting Jesus as the Son of God

MATERIALS
* Bibles
* "The Son Of God" Activity Sheet

PERSONALIZE (15-20 minutes)

ACTIVITIES
* Determine some ways you can confess Jesus by words and actions

MATERIALS
* "I Confess" Activity Sheet

PRESESSION

(5-10 minutes)

Before class, write this question on the chalkboard or a large sheet of paper: Who do you think Jesus is?

Have students write their answers on 3 x 5 cards. They should not put their names on the cards. When they are finished, they can fold the cards in two and place them in a box. Mix them up.

Draw them out one at a time and share them with the group. Are there any two alike? Why do you think they are each a little different? Is there a common definition in the whole group? If so, what is it? Would it make any difference if it was Jesus himself who asked you that question?

One way that shows who we think Jesus is is through the music we sing about Him.

PERSPECTIVE

(10 minutes)

What is your favorite chorus or song about Jesus? Let students share briefly. Discuss their choices. Why do you like it best? Read over the words carefully. What does it say about Jesus? Do you think about those words when you sing it or are you mostly enjoying the music or rhythm?

Many times Christians are so familiar with the hymns and choruses that they never really make a special effort to think about what they are singing. It has been said that more flippant comments are made about Christ through our singing than any other way. We must guard about being careless in our music and not meaning what we sing. Impress your juniors with the need to really think about the words they sing.

Their words can either honor and glorify Jesus as God's Son or be sung carelessly as if we take Him for granted and treat Him in a slap-on-the-back, old-pal, insincere manner. It is better not to sing something we don't mean than to sing it just because everyone else is. That kind of singing is in reality a lie and a disservice to the Lord. **Because He is God's Son, Jesus deserves only our highest worship and praise.**

Optional: If you have more time, sing one or more of the group's favorite songs that glorify Jesus.

People during Jesus' lifetime had many opinions about who He was. They had some guesses that were often wrong.

PROBE

(20 minutes)

Have students turn to Matthew 16:13-18. They can take turns reading this passage aloud. **Who did the people think Jesus was?** (John the Baptist, Elijah, Jeremiah or one of the prophets.) John the Baptist had been killed by King Herod. Many people thought Jesus was John, who had come back to life. Elijah was a man of God who prophesied during the time of

King Ahab. He did not die because God took him to Heaven in a whirlwind. When the Jews saw Jesus perform miracles some of them were sure that He was Elijah, who had come back to earth. Some of the Jews also thought that Jeremiah would return to earth one day. **All these guesses made by the people who saw Jesus, or heard about Him, were wrong.**

Who did Peter say Jesus was? (The Christ, the Son of the living God.) **Who did Jesus say revealed this to Simon Peter?** (His heavenly father.) **What was the "rock" upon which Jesus was going to build His church?** (Peter, don't know, this confession.) Jesus did not mean He was going to build His church on Peter but on the truth of his confession. This solid foundation of truth would make it impossible to destroy Christ's church.

After Peter made his great confession, Jesus had some sad news to tell the apostles. Check out verse 21 to discover what it was. (He must suffer many things, be killed, raised to life again.) Now that they truly understood and believed that Jesus was God's Son, they must begin to learn that it was part of God's plan to have His Son die for the sins of the world. This explanation of God's plan was necessary because the apostles still believed, as did the people, that God's Son, the Christ, would be a military leader. Instead He came to be a suffering servant.

Have the class turn to Mark 9:2-10 and take turns reading it aloud. **What happened to Jesus while He was praying on the mountain?** (He was changed, His face and clothing became dazzlingly white, two men came to talk with Him.)

Who were the two men who talked with Jesus? (Moses and Elijah.) Moses represented the law, and Elijah represented the prophets. This was the sign that Jesus was the fulfillment of the Old Testament law and the prophetic promises of the Messiah, the Christ, God's Son.

What did Peter want to do? (Build three shelters—one for Moses, one for Elijah, and one for Jesus.) **Why do you think he said this?** (Didn't know what to say, was frightened, felt he should do something to honor the occasion.) Peter saw Moses, Elijah, and Jesus as equals.

How did God respond to Peter's offer? (He covered them with a cloud, told them only Jesus was His Son and they should listen to Him alone, took away Moses and Elijah.) God wanted him to realize Jesus was superior to the other two. His response to Peter's offer was immediate and impressive. He said, in no uncertain terms, that Jesus was His Son, His *beloved* Son. Because of

that Jesus had full divine authority and the apostles should listen to Him to know how to live and know God.

Why do you think Jesus told Peter, James, and John not to tell anyone what they had seen until He had risen from the dead? (It would only confuse people, cause too many people to follow Him to see more miracles like the transfiguration.) Jesus had not yet finished the work He had come to do—die for the sins of all people. Before He did that, this incident would only confuse people who didn't understand God's plan of salvation.

Why do you think they discussed among themselves what "rising from the dead" meant? (They didn't know anyone who had done it, didn't believe in life after death, I don't know.) At this point, the apostles didn't understand the suffering, death, and resurrection of the Christ. They wouldn't be able to explain to others what they, themselves, did not understand. As Jews, the apostles were familiar with the belief in resurrection after death because it was taught by the Pharisees. But the problem was that they couldn't get the connection between Jesus' death and His claim to be the Christ, God's Son.

Check out Mark 8:32 and 33. Peter loved Jesus and wanted to protect Him from suffering. Peter meant well but his attempt to stop Jesus from discussing His suffering and death was a temptation from Satan. To His followers it was unthinkable that the Messiah would suffer and die. Jesus pointed out to Peter that this way of thinking was from a human point of view, not from God's.

Distribute copies of "The Son Of God" activity sheet. Divide the class into small groups of three or four people. Let these teams work on the activity, using the research from the references to write their commercials. Answers to the matching exercise are: 4, 4, 16, 7, 14, 8, 12, 10, 9, 1, 6, 11, 2, 5, 15, 13. Invite teams to share their commercials with the class.

Optional: If you have a longer class period, record these commercials on tape or video. Your students will really enjoy hearing and seeing themselves!

PERSONALIZE

(15-20 minutes)

Who is Jesus to you? Is He merely a good teacher like the men who founded other religions? Or is He someone special and unique? If we believe that Jesus really made the claim to be the only Son of God, it means He was one of three things: a man who was exactly who He claimed to be; an imposter and a liar; or someone who was mentally ill and didn't know what He was saying. Which of these three do you think He is? **If you decide Jesus is God's Son, is He your Savior and Lord?**

What does it mean to confess your faith in Jesus by your actions, as well as by your words? Sometimes words alone are not enough. Actions give weight to our words by showing in a tangible way that we mean what we say.

Distribute copies of "I Confess" activity sheet. Students can work on this individually. When they are finished, invite them to talk about their choices. For example, you could confess Christ in the first situation by telling the offender that Jesus is your best friend, God's Son, and it hurts you and God when he uses Jesus' name in anger. You could do this actively by walking away when your teammate swears.

In situation two you could ask your friend if s/he really listened to the words of the song and considered what they would mean if carried out. Then tell your friend that life is a gift from God who wants us to protect it, not destroy it. Actively you could play some popular Christian music instead.

In situation three you could actively enter the group of people ridiculing Sue and tell them you also went to church and Bible class regularly. You could also invite them to attend with you and offer to pick them up the next week.

Optional: If you have a longer class time, have students role play these situations.

PRAYER/PRAISE

Close in prayer, asking God to help us confess Jesus Christ as His Son openly as we have opportunities. Thank Him for sending Jesus to be our Savior and Lord.

THE SON OF GOD

Imagine that Jesus asked you to write a commercial that promotes Him as the Son of God. Choose at least two of the verses in each section for background research. Read the references and then pick the word or phrase that fits that Bible passage and write the number on the line beside it. When you are finished, work up a sixty-second commercial to sell Jesus to the world as the Son of God.

APPLICANT'S NAME: *JESUS*

QUALIFICATIONS:

Matthew 4:24 _____

Matthew 8:26 _____

Matthew 9:24, 25 _____

Matthew 14:25 _____

John 6:11 _____

John 10:17, 18 _____

John 10:25 _____

John 10:28 _____

Hebrews 4:15 _____

REFERENCES:

Matthew 14:33 _____

Matthew 27:54 _____

Mark 1:1 _____

Mark 3:11 _____

Luke 1:35 _____

Luke 3:22 _____

Galatians 2:20 _____

COMMERCIAL:

_____

_____

_____

_____

_____

_____

_____

_____

_____

_____

_____

_____

WORD BANK

1. apostles
2. evil spirits
3. stop a storm
4. heals the sick
5. angel
6. Roman soldier
7. walks on water
8. gives eternal life; take it back
9. without sin
10. gives eternal life
11. Mark
12. does miracles
13. Paul
14. feeds hungry people
15. God the Father
16. raises people from death

I Confess

Read each situation. Decide how you could confess Christ either by words or by deeds. Write it on the lines provided.

Situation 1:

One of the players on your team swears a lot. He frequently uses the names of God and Jesus. How can you confess Christ in this situation?

_____

_____

_____

_____

Situation 2:

You are spending some time with a friend who is really into heavy metal music. You aren't familiar with it but start to listen to the lyrics. One of the most popular songs is about going out and killing policemen. You know that this is the opposite of what Jesus wants His followers to do. How can you handle this problem?

_____

_____

_____

_____

Situation 3:

You hear a group of classmates making fun of Sue because she attends church and Bible class regularly. You go to a different church than she does but are also a regular attender. How can you confess Christ?

_____

_____

_____

_____

THE TRIUMPHAL ENTRY

AIM: That your students will be encouraged to honor Jesus as King of kings and Lord of lords by their words and deeds

SCRIPTURE: Zechariah 9:9; Matthew 21:1-11 (The prophecy of the Messiah; Jesus enters Jerusalem)

PREPARATION:
1. Photocopy activity sheets—one for each student.
2. Make a secret word list as described in PRESESSION.

PRESESSION (5-10 minutes)

ACTIVITIES
* Play a game about entertaining honored guests

PERSPECTIVE (10 minutes)

ACTIVITIES
* Read and discuss how people honored Jesus

MATERIALS
* Bibles

PROBE (20 minutes)

ACTIVITIES
* Read a skit to learn about Jesus' triumphal entry into Jerusalem

MATERIALS
* Bibles
* "Great Expectations" Activity Sheet

PERSONALIZE (15-20 minutes)

ACTIVITIES
* Take part in a matching game to determine ways you can honor God

MATERIALS
* "Make Way For The King" Activity Sheet— one for every two students
* Scissors

PRESESSION

Before class prepare a list of words for a password game. Use words that are associated with honoring important people. Examples are: banquet; food; cleaning; parade; banner; invitation; speech; crowd; balloon.

Team up early arrivals in pairs. Whisper a word to one partner in each team. They will then give their partners one word clues to help them guess the secret word. When a secret word is guessed, give them another. Have partners take turns giving clues and guessing answers.

After several minutes of play, guide the conversation to center upon honoring important guests. Use questions such as: What does your family do when company is coming? If the company will be staying overnight, what extra things might be done? What part do you have in these preparations? Have you ever been present when an important person comes to visit your city or town? How did people feel about the guest? What did the city do to honor the guest?

In the days when Jesus lived on the earth He was very popular with many people.

PERSPECTIVE

Ask for volunteers to look up these passages and be ready to read them: Luke 5:29; Luke 19:5, 6; John 12:1, 2; John 12:3; Mark 14:3.

Read Luke 5:29. **How did Levi [Matthew] honor Jesus?** (Gave a banquet in His honor, invited his friends to the banquet for Jesus.) Read Luke 19:5, 6. **How did Zacchaeus honor Jesus?** (Took Him into his house as a guest, welcomed Him gladly.)

Read John 12:1, 2. **This family was very close to Jesus. What did they do for their special guest?** (Gave a dinner in His honor.) **Check out verse 9. What made this an unusual meal?** (Lazarus was there with them, he had been raised from the dead by Jesus.) Sometime earlier, Lazarus had died and Jesus had brought him forth alive from the tomb four days after he had been buried. Crowds came to the home of Lazarus that day, not only to see Jesus, but to see the man who had been brought back to life.

Read John 12:3. **How did Mary honor Jesus?** (Poured expensive perfume on His feet and wiped them with her hair.) One of Jesus' disciples, Judas, the treasurer of the group, was very critical of what Mary had done. He asked why the perfume wasn't sold and the money given to the poor. Jesus explained to Judas that Mary had honored Him in this way to show her love.

The next day, Jesus and His disciples left Bethany and went into the city of Jerusalem. Let's find out what happened that day.

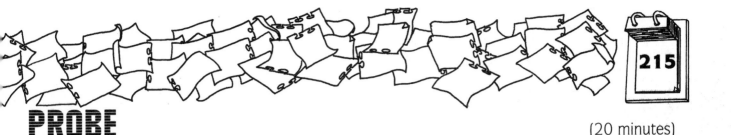

PROBE

(20 minutes)

Hand out copies of "Great Expectations" activity sheet. (p. 217) You will need two people to read the parts of Darbra Falters and Enos. **The rest of you can follow along on the activity sheet and listen carefully so you can help us talk about it afterwards.**

Who was Zechariah? (A prophet.) **What does "prophet" mean?** (A spokesman or messenger from God.) Have people turn to Matthew 21:1-11.

In the skit why did Enos say both **the donkey and the colt were borrowed?** (Because the colt had never been ridden before and the donkey wanted to stay near her baby.) In Old Testament times important people often rode donkeys. But when Jesus lived on earth, the donkey was a symbol of labor and peace. It was the beast of burden for ordinary people.

What did the great crowd of people want to do for Jesus? (Honor Him as king.) When you honor a person, it means you show respect to someone who is worthy. Jesus had been teaching and healing during His three years of ministry among the people. He was loved by thousands of them as a teacher, friend, and helper. Now He was being honored as the king for whom God's people had waited hundreds of years.

How did they show their honor? (Spread their cloaks on the road, waved palm branches, shouted blessings on Jesus.)

Look back through this Scripture passage. What names are used for Jesus? (Lord, king, Son of David, prophet.) **Jesus was a prophet, but He was more than that. Lord means "master." King means "ruler of all."**

"Son of David" was the name given to God's promised Messiah/King. Jesus was called Son of David because he was descended from the line of David. **Many Jews believed that God's Messiah/King would be the kind of king who would overthrow Rome's control and set up a Jewish kingdom.**

In the skit, why did Enos think Jesus chose to ride on his donkey rather than a horse or in a chariot? (To show the people He wasn't going to be that kind of a king.) **Instead of setting up an earthly kingdom, Jesus came to set up an everlasting spiritual one by overthrowing sin.**

In the skit, what did Darbra think could happen if Jesus set up that kind of kingdom? (People would cause trouble for Jesus.) Because they were looking for a military leader the people paid no attention to the real meaning of Jesus' fulfillment of prophecy.

What was the quote Enos gave from Jesus at the end of the skit? (I came to serve and give my life for others.) Because Jesus came to be a suffering servant who would pay the penalty for all sin, the Jews turned against Him and urged His death.

Jesus' triumphal entry into Jerusalem is remembered and celebrated each year as Palm Sunday. God wants people to offer genuine praise and heartfelt worship, not only on this day, but on all days. No doubt Jesus is more pleased with those who honor Him by the things they do and say every day, not just on special days set aside for worship.

When we realize how great Jesus really is, we will give Him all honor and praise. Let's make way for the king in our hearts and find ways we can honor Him.

PERSONALIZE

Pass out copies of "Make Way For The King" activity sheets. Ask someone to read the instructions aloud. Have people work in the same teams they did during the password game in PRESESSION.

After about half the time allowed, discuss the ways we can honor God.

It is important to put God first in your life. A good rule to go by is every time you begin to do or say something, think to yourself, "Will this bring honor or dishonor to Jesus, the King of kings?"

Keeping Sunday as a day to think about and worship God is a good way to honor the Lord. But going to church or Bible class on the first day of the week does not make up for dishonoring Jesus on other days of the week.

You need to be honest in all things. If you are dishonest in even the smallest things, people will learn not to trust you in bigger ones.

It is very easy to ask God to give us things or help us in times of trouble, but we often forget to thank Him for answers to our prayers or tell others how He helped us.

Which do you think people pay more attention to, your words or your actions? (Actions.) That is why it is important that both words and actions are consistent with each other. Saying you love Jesus and then hating somebody for whom He died is contradictory.

Setting aside money and material gifts for God are important. Although Jesus' kingdom is an eternal, spiritual one, it needs money and material items to make it work. Printing Bibles in other languages or feeding starving people in another land require money.

Using God's name respectfully means more than not swearing. Jokes made about God are as bad as swearing. Respectful use includes praising and worshiping Him.

We need to clear out false pride and be a humble servant of God. We should not take any glory for ourselves. **What does it mean to be humble?** (Meek, gentle, submissive.) **To be humble is to put others ahead of yourself. It is not bragging or boasting about who you are; the possessions you have; or your accomplishments.** The opposite of humble is proud. It is all right to "take pride" in your work and do your very best. But taking all the credit for yourself means thinking too highly of yourself and not giving Jesus the praise He deserves. **We can't wave palm branches or spread our coats in Jesus' way today, but we can give Him praise and honor and glory.**

PRAYER/PRAISE

Close with a circle prayer. Go around the circle, having each student add one "praise-phrase" to a prayer to God. They are to ask nothing for themselves but simply offer praise to God. For example: I love You and will use my talents to praise You; thank You for each day; praise You for sending Jesus to die for my sin.

Darbra Falters:	Let's welcome our next guest, Enos the donkey man. Enos, would you like to tell our audience what happened to you today?
Enos:	I'll be glad to. This morning I was thinking about how people said that Jesus, the great prophet, was coming to Jerusalem for the Passover.
Darbra:	Do you mean the man some people say could be the Messiah?
Enos:	That's the one. Anyway, while I was doing my chores, two men came. They wanted to borrow my donkey and her colt.
Darbra:	Did they say what they wanted them for?
Enos:	They just said the Lord needed them and would send them back right away.
Darbra:	Did you know who they meant by the Lord?
Enos:	I figured it had to be Jesus. I mean, why else would I have been thinking about Him right at that moment?
Darbra:	Couldn't that have just been a coincidence?
Enos:	I don't think so because the next thing that came to mind was the prophecy Zechariah made five hundred years ago about the Messiah. You know the one, "See, your king comes to you, gentle and riding on a donkey, on a colt, the foal of a donkey." I'm sure God sent these men to me.
Darbra:	What did you do then?
Enos:	I untied the animals and went with the men to see what would happen. We walked until we got to a crowd of people surrounding a man. It was Jesus all right. Well, they put their cloaks on the colt. Sarah, that's my donkey, crowded right up close to her colt. Guess she was afraid he'd act up, never having been ridden before, you know. It was really exciting.
Darbra:	Tell us about it.
Enos:	People were lined up all along the way. Some of them spread their cloaks on the road, while others cut branches from the trees and spread them on the road. They were all shouting so loud I got a headache.
Darbra:	What were they saying?
Enos:	Hosanna to the Son of David! Blessed is He who comes in the name of the Lord! I tell you, it sent chills right down my spine!
Darbra:	It sounds as if they believe Jesus is the Messiah/King God promised to send. If that's so, then Jesus could be our national leader who will overthrow the Romans and restore Israel to its former glory. You were close to Him today. What do you think about that, Enos?
Enos:	Somehow I don't think that's what Jesus meant. If He was going to be that kind of king, He wouldn't have borrowed my donkeys. He would have ridden a horse or in a chariot. Donkeys are just a sign of work and peace. They sort of belong to us ordinary people.
Darbra:	Then what was the purpose of today's demonstration?
Enos:	I'm not real smart like the priests and scribes, but I think Jesus decided that today, with all the people gathered in Jerusalem, was the perfect place and time to announce that He was going to be a different kind of king with a different kind of kingdom.
Darbra:	The people won't like that. They might even cause trouble for Jesus. Well, Enos, thank you for sharing your story with us. Do you have any last words for us?
Enos:	Jesus said, "I came to serve and give my life for others." Now, that's my kind of king! I'll follow Him from now on.

GREAT EXPECTATIONS

MAKE WAY FOR THE KING

Cut the cards apart. One person takes all the reference cards. The other person takes all the phrase cards. Player one reads a verse aloud. Player two picks a card s/he thinks matches it and reads it aloud. The game is over when all cards are matched.

REFERENCE CARDS	PHRASE CARDS
"I will praise you, O Lord my God, with all my heart; I will glorify your name forever." Psalm 86:12	Put God first in your life.
"Give thanks to the Lord, for he is good; his love endures forever. Let the redeemed of the Lord say this." Psalm 107:1, 2	Keep the Lord's day as a day of rest from everyday jobs. Instead, worship God and think about His blessings to you.
"Honor the Lord with your wealth, with the firstfruits of all your crops." Proverbs 3:9	Be honest in all things.
"A truthful witness gives honest testimony." Proverbs 12:17	Thank God for all the good things He does for you and tell others about them.
"O Lord, our God, other lords besides you have ruled over us, but your name alone do we honor." Isaiah 26:13	Obey God's Word as well as hear it. Make sure your actions are the same as your words.
"Call the Sabbath a delight and the Lord's holy day honorable . . . honor it by not going your own way." Isaiah 58:13	Set aside money and material gifts for God's work in spreading the good news about Jesus and helping the needy.
"Do not think of yourself more highly than you ought, but rather think of yourself with sober judgment." Romans 12:3	Use God's name respectfully.
"Dear children, let us not love with words or tongue but with actions and in truth." I John 3:18	Clear out false pride and be a humble servant of God.

THE LAST SUPPER

AIM: That your students will understand the meaning of the Lord's Supper

SCRIPTURE: Matthew 26:20-30, 36-42; Mark 14:15-26, 44, 45; Luke 22:14, 15, 19, 20; John 13:3-15; 18:12; 1 Corinthians 11:23-25 (The events of the night Jesus was betrayed)

PREPARATION:
1. Photocopy activity sheets—one for each student.
2. Make a set of cards for the concentration game as described in PRESESSION. Make one set of cards for every two to four students.
3. Prepare list of phrases for time line as described in PERSPECTIVE.
4. Copy problem cards as described in PERSONALIZE.

PRESESSION (5-10 minutes)

ACTIVITIES
* Play a game of concentration using words identified with the Lord's Supper

MATERIALS
* 3" x 5" cards for concentration game, scissors

PROBE (20 minutes)

ACTIVITIES
* Read the story of the Last Supper
* Solve a puzzle about the Lord's Supper

MATERIALS
* Bibles
* "The Last Supper" Activity Sheet

PERSPECTIVE (10 minutes)

ACTIVITIES
* Complete a time line of the events of the day Jesus was betrayed

MATERIALS
* Bibles
* Chalkboard and chalk or large sheet of paper and marker
* "A Day In Time" Activity Sheet
* Scissors, tape

PERSONALIZE (15-20 minutes)

ACTIVITIES
* Work in teams to find solutions to problems arising during Communion

MATERIALS
* Two 3" x 5" cards for problems

LESSON 36   **UNIT THEME: JESUS, THE SAVIOR**

PRESESSION

Prepare cards for the concentration game by cutting 3" x 5" cards in half and writing the following words on them, thus making two cards of each word: Communion; Eucharist; Last Supper; Lord's Supper; Passover; cup; bread; betray; remembrance; sacrifice; worship; salvation; prayer; disciples.

As students gather, give a set of the concentration cards to every two to four people. Have them shuffle the cards and place them facedown on the table. Players take turns turning over two cards and reading the words printed on them. If they match, players remove and keep them and take another turn. If not, players turn them face down and the next players take a turn. Continue playing until all matches have been made. Players with the most cards are the winners.

Take out the cards "Communion," "Eucharist," and the "Lord's Supper" and lay them face up on the table. What do these words have in common? (They are all names for this sacrament.)

The name Lord's Supper is the name given to this observance because Jesus started it.

The Last Supper refers to the Passover meal Jesus ate with His disciples. It was His last meal on earth.

"Eucharist" is a Greek word meaning "gratitude" or "thanksgiving." It is often used because by partaking of it we thank God for Jesus' sacrifice for us.

"Communion" means sharing in the Lord's Supper because through it we commune or have fellowship with God and other believers. **Each of these terms helps us think about Jesus' perfect sacrifice as He took the punishment for all the sins of all people. That sacrifice came at the end of a very busy week in Jesus' earthly life.**

PERSPECTIVE

Before class today prepare a mixed-up list of phrases that will be used in the time line activity. On the chalkboard or a large sheet of paper write the following phrases:

Soldiers arrest Jesus
"One shall betray me"
Prayer in Gethsemane
In remembrance of Jesus
Passover meal
Jesus washes feet
Judas betrays Jesus
Last Supper ceremony

Be sure that students can easily see the list. **As we studied last lesson, on the first day of that week Jesus was honored by great crowds as He entered Jerusalem.** The next day, Jesus went into the temple and drove out the money changers and the people doing the trading. He said that God's house was a house of prayer. Jesus continued to teach the people and answer their questions. He told them that He would be going to Heaven soon, but that someday He would return.

All during this week the enemies of Jesus plotted against Him. They were afraid to capture Him because He was so popular with the crowds. Then one of His own close followers gave in to the devil's tempting and offered to lead the soldiers to Jesus in a place where no crowds would be gathered. He was paid thirty pieces of silver (the price for buying a slave) in advance for this terrible deed. (Today that would be worth only about $4.80!) All he had to do was to wait for the right moment to betray the Son of God.

Meantime Jesus and the others were thinking about preparation for the yearly

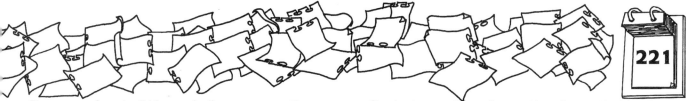

Passover feast. "Where shall we prepare the Passover?" some of Jesus' disciples asked. Jesus told them to go into the city of Jerusalem and follow a man carrying a pitcher of water. "Ask the owner of the house where the guest chamber is in which the Master will eat the Passover with His disciples. The man will show you a large, upstairs room."

The apostles followed Jesus' instructions. The meal that they prepared included a lamb, killed and roasted according to strict regulations; unleavened bread, herbs, and wine. The feast was held each year to remember God's goodness in delivering the Jews from slavery in Egypt.

Pass out copies of "A Day in Time" activity sheet. Do this exercise together. Have volunteers look up the passages and read them aloud.

Students can then choose the phrase that best describes the picture and action and write it on the line at the top of each section of the time line. Correct answers are:

Passover meal
"One shall betray me"
Last Supper ceremony
Jesus washes feet
Prayer in Gethsemane
Judas betrays Jesus
Soldiers arrest Jesus
In remembrance of Jesus

Students can cut the time line out and tape it together at the dotted line.

Let's take a closer look at the events of that night.

PROBE

(20 minutes)

Have the group turn to Mark 14 and take turns reading verses 17-26. Jesus and His apostles dipped their fingers in a common bowl, because eating customs in Bible times were different from ours. A large bowl of meat was passed from person to person. Each one cut off a piece of meat with a sharp knife, then ate it with his fingers. Pieces of bread were broken from a loaf and dipped into the broth. Then the moistened bread was eaten with the fingers.

Jesus was very sad as He told His friends, "One of you is going to betray me." Check out John 13:26. Who did Jesus say would do this terrible deed? When Jesus gave Judas this piece of bread dipped in the broth, He was repeating a Jewish custom of singling out an honored guest at a meal. It was as though Jesus was giving Judas one last chance to turn back from his betrayal, confess his sin, and accept Jesus' forgiveness.

Two of the foods on the table, used at every Passover feast, were flat cakes of unleavened bread and cups of wine. At the end of the meal

Jesus took the bread and the cup and blessed them and gave them to His disciples. From that time on these two items were to have a very special meaning to the followers of Jesus.

Bread is an important food that is eaten in every land. Grapes may be grown in nearly every climate and the juice of grapes or wine is drunk in some countries in place of water. Jesus said that the bread represented His body, and the liquid in the cup represented His blood. Each time His followers ate the bread and drank of the cup they were to remember His sacrifice to take away the punishment for all sins.

Distribute copies of "The Last Supper" activity sheet. Students can work on this individually. Answers are: twelve, hymn, betray, blood, Passover, disciples, covenant, sin, Judas, cup, upper, Olives, bread.

After their last supper together, Jesus and His friends sang a hymn and went out to the Mount of Olives. The sacrifice of which Jesus had spoken was soon to take place.

Ask a volunteer to read aloud Matthew 26:36-

222

38. **What kind of a mood was Jesus in?** (Sad, sorrowful, troubled.) Have another volunteer read verses 39 and 42. **What did Jesus ask God to do for Him?** (Take the suffering away from Him, have His will in Jesus' life.) The "cup" that Jesus mentions here is the portion of agony He would shortly suffer as He was separated from His heavenly Father by taking the punishment for all the sins of all the people. Although He was sinless, Jesus willingly chose God's plan knowing it included this terrible grief.

Suddenly the quiet scene was changed! A band of soldiers and other men invaded the peaceful garden! In the lead was Judas. His face looked hard and cruel in the light of the torches and lanterns carried by the armed men. Their weapons flashed as beams of light flickered over them. Judas stepped up and identified Jesus to the mob by kissing Him.

The apostles looked to Jesus, possibly expecting Him to strike these wicked people dead. But Jesus stood there quietly. He was bound and led away captive in the darkness. He went willingly to give His life.

PERSONALIZE

(15-20 minutes)

Before class write these problems on two 3" x 5" cards.

#1: Chad is a Christian. He wants to remember Jesus' death during Communion. Sometimes when Chad is trying to think about Jesus, other thoughts come into his mind. What can Chad do about this?

#2: Sara is a Christian who partakes of the Lord' Supper. But afterwards she often whispers to the girls with whom she is sitting. If Sara is truly a follower of Jesus, what should she be doing during this time?

Jesus asked His followers to eat the bread and drink the fruit of the vine in remembrance of Him. When Christians meet together to worship in the Lord's Supper, the most important part of the service is communing with Jesus, their Lord and Savior. This part of worship should never become just a routine, but cause us to be closer to Jesus each time we meet around His table.

Divide the class into two teams. Have each team discuss one problem and share their thoughts with the whole group.

Every time we partake of the bread and the cup we are to be thankful for the salvation that Jesus brought to us.

PRAYER/PRAISE

Close with a prayer thanking Jesus for His sacrifice for us. Ask Him to help you remember His sacrifice whenever you partake of the Lord's Supper.

A Day in Time

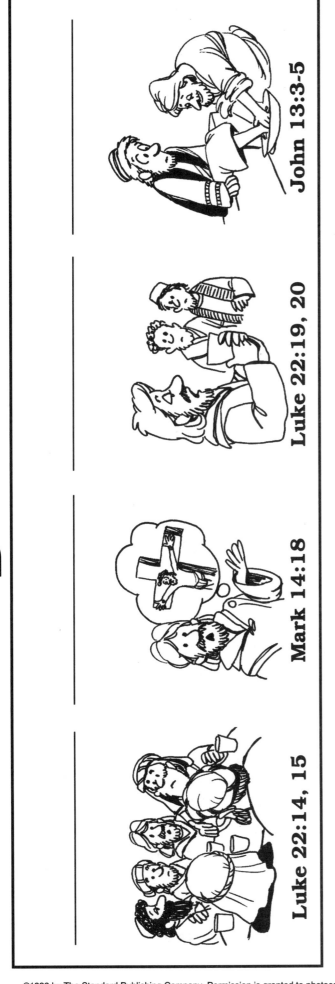

John 13:3-5

Luke 22:19, 20

Mark 14:18

Luke 22:14, 15

1 Corinthians 11:23-25

John 18:12

Mark 14:44, 45

Matthew 26:36, 39

THE LAST SUPPER

Check out Mark 14:15-26 and Matthew 26:20-30 to find the answers.

How many disciples ate the last supper with Jesus?
T

What did they sing after the meal was finished?
H

What did Jesus say Judas would do to Him?
E

What did the cup represent?
L

What was the name of this particular feast?
A

By what name were the twelve men often called?
S

T Jesus said His blood was the new what?

For the remission of what was His blood shed?
S

Who dipped his hand in the bowl when Jesus did?
U

P From what did the disciples drink?

In what kind of room did they meet?
P

E To what mount did they go later?

What represented Jesus' broken body?
R

JESUS IS CONDEMNED TO DIE

AIM: That your students will realize that each person must accept or reject Jesus as God's Son

SCRIPTURE: Deuteronomy 22:23; Mark 14:53, 55-65; 15:1-15; Luke 20:22-25; John 3:16; 18:36; 19:12; James 4:17 (Jesus, the sinless Son of God, is condemned to death)

PREPARATION:
1. Photocopy activity sheets—one for each student.
2. Make a list of terms and definitions as described in PRESESSION.

PRESESSION (5-10 minutes)

ACTIVITIES
* Learn about terms used for court trials by playing a matching game

MATERIALS
* Chalkboard and chalk or large sheet of paper and marker

PERSPECTIVE (10 minutes)

ACTIVITIES
* Discuss court procedures and prominent people in the trial of Jesus

MATERIALS
* Chalkboard and chalk or large sheet of paper and marker

PROBE (20 minutes)

ACTIVITIES
* Finish a play about the trial of Jesus

MATERIALS
* Bibles
* "On Trial" Activity Sheet

PERSONALIZE (15-20 minutes)

ACTIVITIES
* Make a personal decision about Jesus

MATERIALS
* Bibles
* "What Will You Do With Jesus?" Activity Sheet

PRESESSION

Before class divide the chalkboard or a large sheet of paper into two columns. Use the captions "Terms" and "Definitions" to head these columns. Under "Terms" write: judge; trial; jury; witness; defendant; evidence; sentence; charges; lawyer; supreme court. In the second column write the following definitions: person trained in law who represents someone in a trial; person who saw or heard something; formal examination of the facts of a case; decision or punishment; highest court in the land; group of people who hear evidence and decide the outcome; public official who hears and decides cases; something which applies to a point in question; accused person; accusations against a prisoner. Be sure to mix up the definitions.

As the group gathers, have students help you match terms and definitions. Students can come forward and draw lines that connect each correct pair.

Have you ever been in a courtroom or witnessed a trial scene on television? If people have, let them share briefly. **Trials were held in Bible times, too.**

PERSPECTIVE

As you talk about the court procedures and prominent people in the trial of Jesus, write underlined words on the chalkboard.

When Jesus lived on earth, the highest Jewish court in the land met in Jerusalem and was called the <u>Sanhedrin</u>. The Sanhedrin had seventy-one members, including the high priest, who was its presiding officer. The court normally met inside the temple's outer walls. On special occasions it met in the high priest's palace.

The Jewish high priest was named <u>Caiaphas</u>. <u>Annas</u>, his father-in-law, was high priest until the Romans removed him from the office and put Caiaphas in his place. For this reason, the Jewish people considered both men as high priests. Jesus was first brought to Annas and then taken to the section of the palace where Caiaphas lived. Because the chief priests, elders, and scribes were determined to get rid of this leader who had taken away their followers, they were in hopes of discovering a quick way to find Jesus guilty and pronounce the death sentence on Him.

The Jews were under Roman rule. When the council passed the death sentence, the members could not carry it out without the permission of the Roman governor, <u>Pilate</u>. When Pilate learned that Jesus was from Galilee, he sent Him to <u>Herod</u> because Herod ruled the region of Galilee for Rome. However, Herod sent Jesus back to Pilate for sentencing.

Jesus was actually tried six times before His death on the cross: at night before Annas in the high priest's palace; a small group of Jewish leaders with Caiaphas later that same night; in front of the whole Sanhedrin at dawn; early in the morning before Pilate in his home; later by Herod at his palace; lastly, sent back to Pilate at the judgment hall.

Let's investigate this trial closer.

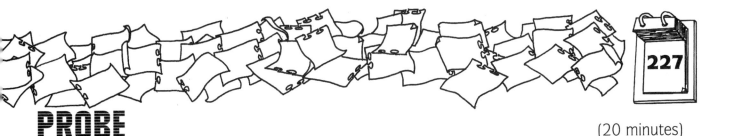

PROBE

(20 minutes)

Hand out copies of "On Trial" activity sheet. Students can work on this exercise in pairs.

Optional: If you have a longer time period, read and/or act out this play. You will need people to read the parts of the narrator, High Priest, Jesus, and Pilate. The rest of the group can be the Crowd. A few simple costumes such as robes or pieces of cloth for shawls, head coverings, and belts will add to the feeling of reality.

In their haste to find Jesus guilty, the Sanhedrin tried to find men who were willing to tell lies about Jesus at the trial. The problem was that none of these liars could agree on their stories! They finally found two men who similarly testified that Jesus said He would destroy the temple of God and build it in three days. Jesus had not been talking about the temple building, but about His death and resurrection. The temple He referred to was His body in which God lived.

Why do you think Jesus refused to answer the high priest's question about that statement? (It was too hard to explain; it was a foolish accusation; the high priest didn't care about an answer but only to convict Jesus.)

When Jesus answered "I am" to the question about being the Christ, the Son of God, He used a term that was very familiar to the Jews. God told Moses to tell the Hebrew slaves in Egypt that "I Am" had sent him. Jesus used it to declare His godly, royal nature. To the Jews this declaration was blasphemy—declaring to be equal with God. It was a crime punishable by death. However, because He really was the only Son of God, what Jesus said was true. Only Pilate, the local head of the Roman government could put Jesus to death. And the Jews knew Pilate would not consider this religious "crime" grounds for crucifixion.

The Jews were very anxious to have Jesus die by Roman crucifixion because of several reasons. It would mean that Jesus was a rebel and a criminal, not a king. The people would blame the Romans, not the Sanhedrin, for His

death. **Check out Deuteronomy 22:23. What does it say about someone hanging on a tree (cross)?** (They are under God's curse.) In this form of death the Jewish religious leaders thought they could convince the people that God cursed, not blessed, Jesus.

The Jewish leaders had to make up some reasons that would cause Pilate to condemn Jesus to death by crucifixion. They at last decided on three accusations against Jesus: 1) He claimed to be a king; 2) encouraging the people not to pay taxes to Rome; 3) starting riots against the government.

Bible Investigators, let's check out these false accusations and find out the truth. Read John 18: 36. What did Jesus say about being a king? (His kingdom was not of this world; His kingdom was from another place.)

In that same verse what did He say about riots? (If His kingdom was of this world, then His servants would fight to help Him.) But since Jesus was not a worldly king, there would be no riots against Rome.

Read Luke 20:22-25. **What did Jesus say about paying taxes to Rome?** (Pay to Caesar [the Roman ruler] what belongs to him.) Jesus even had Peter go fishing to obtain money to pay His and Peter's taxes! [See Matthew 17:27.]

Pilate became convinced that Jesus was innocent of all crime and had been brought to trial only because the Jewish religious leaders hated Him. Still Pilate turned Jesus over for death by crucifixion. Check out John 19:12 to find out why Pilate did this. (They threatened Pilate that if he let Jesus go, he was not a friend of Caesar.) This threat to his political career was what caused Pilate to give in to the Jewish crowd. He would rather save himself from trouble with the government than save the sinless, innocent, Son of God from death.

How do people feel when others make fun of them because they believe in Jesus? (Sad; afraid; like giving up following Jesus.) It is often easier to take the easy way out and yield to the pressure of those who don't love Jesus than to stand up for what we know is right. **Check out James 4:17. What does God say about a person who knows what is good and doesn't do it?** (The person sins.)

Pilate was not the only person who had to decide about Jesus. Everyone has to make a decision about what to do with Him.

PERSONALIZE

(15-20 minutes)

Distribute copies of "What Will You Do With Jesus?" activity sheet. Have students work on this exercise individually.

Optional: If you have a shorter time period, do the first part of this activity together.

All the people listed in the first part of this activity made choices about Jesus. What did they all choose? (To reject Him.)

Read the next paragraph on the activity page aloud. Emphasize that each of your students has to make a choice. Help them to see that their decision is not only a choice for now but it has eternal results. Because this is such a strong personal judgment, allow students more privacy by letting them move to more secluded areas of the room if they desire. Be sensitive to people who may be confused about this activity. Be prepared to help them whether it be to explain the way a person becomes a Christian or to pray with them as they make their choices.

Students who have already made a choice to follow Jesus can write a personal thank-you prayer to Jesus in the space provided at the bottom of the activity sheet.

PRAYER/PRAISE

Have a volunteer read aloud John 3:16. Close with a moment of silent prayer and meditation. People can repeat the above verse silently, inserting their names instead "the world" and "whoever." For example, "For God so loved Kevin that he gave his one and only Son, that Kevin who believes in him shall not perish but have eternal life." Use this time to let the group reflect on Jesus' love and sacrifice for them.

Complete this play about the trial of Jesus. On each blank line, write the correct information. The first line is done for you as an example.

ACT 1
Palace, the home of the High Priest
Mark 14:53-65

Narrator: The chief priests and the whole Sanhedrin were looking for evidence against Jesus so that they could put Him to death, but they did not find any. Many testified *falsely* against Him, but their statements *did not agree*. (v. 56)

High Priest: Are you not going to _____? (v. 60)

Narrator: But Jesus remained _____ and gave ____ _____ (v. 61)

High Priest: Are you the _____, the _____ of the _____ ____? (v. 61)

Jesus: ____ ____, and you will see the Son of Man sitting at the right hand of the _____ ____ and coming on the clouds of Heaven. (v. 62)

Narrator: The high priest tore his _____. (v. 63)

High Priest: Why do we need any more _____? (v. 63) You have heard the _____. (v. 64) What do you think?

Sanhedrin: He is worthy of _____. (v. 64)

Narrator: Then some began to _____ at Him; they blindfolded Him, _____ at Him with their _____ and said "_____!" And the guards took Him. (v. 65)

ACT 2
Home of Pilate, Roman Governor
Mark 15:1-15

Narrator: Very early in the morning, the chief priests, elders, teachers of the law, and the whole Sanhedrin _____ Jesus, _____ Him away and _____ Him over to Pilate. (v. 1)

Pilate: Are you the _____ of the _____? (v. 2)

Jesus: _____, it is as you say. (v. 2)

Narrator: The _____ _____ accused Him of many things. (v. 3)

Pilate: Aren't you going to _____? See how many things they are _____ you of. (v. 4)

Narrator: But Jesus still made no reply, and Pilate was _____. (v. 5) It was the custom at the Feast to release a prisoner whom the people requested. A man called _____ was in prison with the rebels and had committed _____ in a riot.(v. 7) The crowd came up and asked _____ to do for them what he usually did. (v. 8)

Pilate: Do you want me to _____ to you the _____ of the _____? (v. 9)

Narrator: But the _____ _____ stirred up the _____ to have Pilate release _____ instead. (v. 11)

Pilate: What shall I do, then, with the one you call the _____ of the _____? (v. 12)

Crowd: _____ Him! (v. 13)

Pilate: Why? What _____ has He _____? (v. 14)

Crowd: (louder) _____ Him! (v. 14)

Narrator: Wanting to _____ the crowd, Pilate _____ Barabbas to them. He had Jesus _____, and handed Him over to be _____. (v. 15)

37A

WHAT WILL YOU DO WITH JESUS

Each person who hears about Jesus has to make a decision. A person can't be undecided. Look up and read each passage, then determine what the people involved decided to do about Jesus. Circle the A if they accepted Him or the R if they rejected Him.

Caiaphas
(John 18:14)
A   R

Pilate
(John 19:16)
A   R

Sanhedrin
(Matthew 26:66)
A   R

Herod
(Luke 23:11)
A   R

Chief Priests
(Matthew 27:20)
A   R

Jews
(John 19:14-15)
A   R

Accept Him Or Reject Him?

What will you do with Jesus? Either you believe that Jesus is the Son of God with power and authority to rule over you and accept Him, or you reject Jesus as God's Son and refuse to obey Him.

If you decide to be a follower of Jesus, you will belong to a great group of Christians around the world who obey Him and honor Him, trying to live the way He wants them to live. If you decide not to accept Christ's invitation, you reject Him.

Pray about this decision. Then write your choice on the line below.

I_____Jesus as the Son of God, my Lord and Savior.

_____

(sign your name here)

If you have already made your decision to be a follower of Jesus, write a thank-you prayer to Him.

Dear Jesus,_____

_____

_____

JESUS' DEATH AND RESURRECTION

AIM: That your students will see that Jesus' death on the cross fulfilled God's promise of salvation and His resurrection gives the promise of eternal life

SCRIPTURE: Matthew 27:28-31, 46-54; 28:1-8; 1 John 5:11; 1 Corinthians 6:14; 15:3, 4 (Jesus dies and is raised to life again)

PREPARATION:
1. Photocopy activity sheets—one for each student.

PRESESSION (5-10 minutes)

ACTIVITIES
* Learn more about places mentioned in the biblical account of Jesus' death and resurrection

MATERIALS
* *Optional: a map or pictures of Jerusalem as it was during Jesus' trial and death, pictures of Golgotha and the garden tomb*

PERSPECTIVE (10 minutes)

ACTIVITIES
* Match up words or phrases and meanings associated with the Scripture lesson

MATERIALS
* "Meet Your Match" Activity Sheet

PROBE (20 minutes)

ACTIVITIES
* Work in teams to write an account of Jesus' death and resurrection

MATERIALS
* Bibles
* "60 Minutes" Activity Sheet

PERSONALIZE (15-20 minutes)

ACTIVITIES
* Express what Jesus' resurrection means to you

MATERIALS
* Paper—one sheet for each student, pencils
* *Optional: copies of the song, "He Lives"*

PRESESSION

Place reference materials where students can see them easily as they gather for class. **In recent years, many thousands of people have visited the land where Jesus lived. Perhaps you know someone who has made such a trip and has taken pictures. Photos and descriptions help us picture in our minds the way things may have looked.** Let students look at this material.

Optional: If it is impossible to find a map or pictures, simply share the descriptions of these locations with your class.

When Jesus was brought to Pilate by the Jewish leaders, He was kept in the Roman soldiers' barracks called Antonia Fortress next to the temple. It stood on a cliff nearly 75 feet high. Huge towers, between 75 and 100 feet tall, stood at each of its four corners. Some scholars think that Jesus was tried before Pilate on the pavement here. If so, it was here that the soldiers made a crown of thorns and put it upon Jesus' head. They put a reed in His hand and bowed before Him saying, "Hail, King of the Jews!" Then they spit on Him and hit Him on the head.

After that He was led through the streets of Jerusalem by soldiers. The city streets were very narrow and not streets as we often think of them. They were paved with stones and went up and down stairs frequently. **The path that Jesus took is often referred to as the "Via Dolorosa" or "Way of Sorrow."** Jesus was forced to carry His cross on His shoulders. Because He was weak from the beatings He had received, He had difficulty carrying it. The soldiers forced a man named Simon, visiting from the North African city of Cyrene, to carry the cross for Jesus.

Golgotha was a hill outside the city of Jerusalem. There are two theories why this site was called the "Place of the Skull." Because people were executed here, skulls might have lain around. Or the hill itself may have been shaped like a skull. The location was near the public highway so that everyone could see the criminals put to death. Jesus was crucified here between two thieves.

The hillsides around Jerusalem are made of limestone. Joseph of Arimathea, a member of the Sanhedrin and a secret follower of Jesus, had a burial place cut into the limestone and prepared for his own death.

PERSPECTIVE

Distribute copies of "Meet Your Match" activity sheet. Students can work on this activity individually. Answers are: 3; 5; 8; 6; 1; 10; 9; 12; 11; 2; 4; 7.

What do you think it would have been like to have been in Jerusalem when all these things were going on?

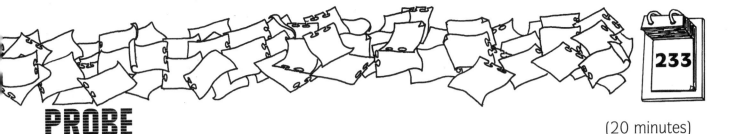

PROBE

(20 minutes)

Today we are going to do a Bible-times version of "60 Minutes." Divide the group into four teams. Team one will present the facts of Jesus' crucifixion and death. Team two will write up "interviews" with witnesses who were there. Team three will report on the Jewish and Roman leaders' comments and reactions to Jesus' death. Team four will write a follow-up report on His resurrection.

Hand out copies of "60 Minutes" activity sheet. . Ask a volunteer to read aloud the directions at the top of the page. To avoid overlap, stress that each team is to do only the specific task it is assigned based on the Scripture portion given. Have each team choose one person to be a secretary and write down the findings of the team. These notes can be written on the back of one of the activity sheets.

Optional: The two longest portions of this activity will probably be the first and last. Because they are the most involved you may choose to place better students on these teams. This will allow students who have more difficulty to take care of the easier and shorter sections of the report.

Allow about ten minutes to be spent on writing the team reports. Then split the remaining time between presentations and discussion. One person can be the "reporter" from each team. Discuss the facts presented.

Crucifixion was a horrible way to die. The upright part of the cross was a pole with the top tapered to a point. It was permanently set in the execution area. A wooden crossbar fit over the tip of this pole. It weighed about 125 pounds and was carried to the death site by the criminal. The person was then nailed to the cross at his wrists and feet.

Roman soldiers who were hardened to these horrible scenes of death were placed in charge to certify that the criminals were executed according to law. It was an everyday task for them and often a long, boring one. They made the time go faster by dividing up the prisoners' clothes among themselves by casting lots to determine who got to keep them.

Crowds lined the streets of the city to watch the criminals carry their crosses to the death sites. They followed and stood around Golgotha watching the people die and making comments. Some, like the Jewish leaders, made fun of Jesus. Others, like the Roman centurion and one of the men crucified with Him, recognized that Jesus was no ordinary man but the Son of God just as He claimed.

Several unusual things happened at Jesus' death. A great darkness covered the land for the three hours He was on the cross. A great earthquake occurred at the moment of His death. At the cemetery, many godly dead people came back to life. They entered the city and appeared to many people.

The huge cloth curtain that divided the Holy Place and the Holy of Holies in the temple was split from top to bottom. Only the priests could enter the Holy Place. The High Priest alone could enter the Holy of Holies and then only once a year. Now Jesus' death opened it to all who wanted to worship God.

But this darkest day in the history of the world was not the ending. Instead it was the beginning—for Jesus' followers then and throughout the years since then. One of the wonderful things that happened that day was that Joseph of Arimathea openly admitted he loved and obeyed Jesus. Joseph asked Pilate's permission to bury Jesus' body. Lovingly he wrapped it in a new linen cloth and spices for burial and placed it in his own new tomb in a beautiful garden near Golgotha.

The Jewish leaders forced Pilate to send Roman soldiers to watch the tomb where Jesus was buried. They thought this would prevent the disciples from removing Jesus' body from the tomb and claiming He had risen from the dead. Little did they know that a great miracle was about to take place.

Several of the women who followed Jesus hurried to the tomb very early on the first day of the week. They were bringing spices to anoint Jesus' body. There they found the huge stone covering the entrance to the burial chamber rolled aside. The stone was rolled away from the tomb; not to let Jesus out, but to let His followers in. The women were met by angels, an empty tomb, folded wrappings from the body, and the wonderful news that Jesus was alive and wanted to meet with His disciples!

Jesus met with many of His followers after His victory over death and the grave. They talked with Him, walked with Him, and even ate with Him. His resurrection made possible eternal life for all who would follow Him.

PERSONALIZE

(15-20 minutes)

If Jesus had not conquered death, we would have no hope. If we have no hope of eternal life, life on this earth would have no real purpose or meaning. But because of Jesus' victory over death, we can face hard times and many problems while living on this earth. What are some things that Jesus' death and resurrection mean for His followers? Have students help you make a list on the chalkboard. Some examples are: the certain hope of never-ending life with God for His followers; Jesus kept His promise about rising to life so we can trust Him to keep <u>all</u> His promises; because Jesus rose from the dead, we will live after death too; Jesus' death and resurrection prove that God accepted His sacrifice to pay for our sins; because Jesus was a real part of history, our world's end doesn't need to be tragedy but joyous redemption.

What does Jesus' resurrection from death mean to you? Hand out sheets of paper to the group and allow them time to answer this question. Encourage your students to make their answers as personal and specific as possible. For example: "I have leukemia. Now I don't need to be afraid of what will happen to me after I die. I know Jesus will take me to live with Him in Heaven forever where I won't hurt or cry anymore."

Optional: If you have time, ask volunteers to share their answers with the class.

The leaders of all other religions are buried in tombs and remain dead. Christianity is the only religion that has a risen from death, ever-living leader. That is good news indeed!

PRAYER/PRAISE

Close by having everyone read 1 Corinthians 6:14 in unison.

Optional: Sing the song "He Lives" as a praise song to Jesus.

Meet Your Match

Ready to go, Bible Investigators?
Write the number of the definition
in Column 2 by its match in Column 1.

____ a. mocked

____ b. Cyrene

____ c. Golgotha

____ d. wine . . . gall

____ e. casting lots

____ f. charge

____ g. gave up His spirit

____ h. curtain of the temple

____ i. centurion

____ j. tomb

____ k. deception

____ l. worshiped

1. like "throwing dice" to decide something

2. place where dead person's body was buried

3. made fun of

4. lie

5. native of a city in North Africa

6. medicine to ease pain

7. praise and honor given to God

8. "Skull," place of crucifixion

9. died

10. accusation against a criminal

11. leader of one hundred soldiers

12. material dividing the Holy of Holies and the Holy Place in the temple

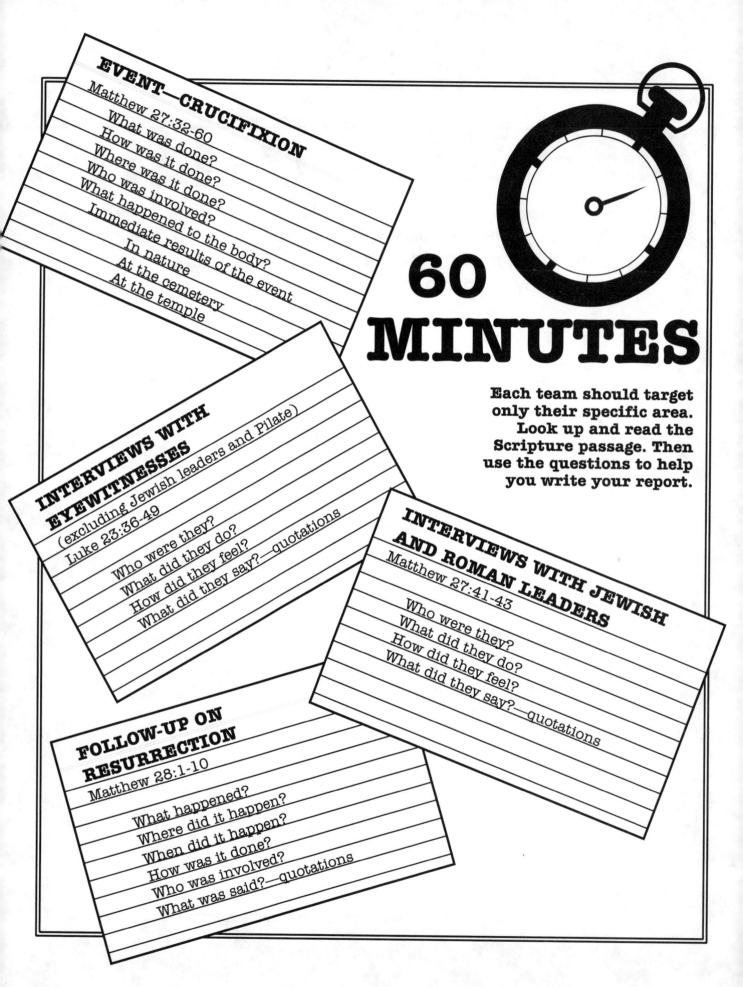

EVENT—CRUCIFIXION

Matthew 27:32-60

What was done?

How was it done?

Where was it done?

Who was involved?

What happened to the body?

Immediate results of the event

In nature

At the cemetery

At the temple

60 MINUTES

Each team should target only their specific area. Look up and read the Scripture passage. Then use the questions to help you write your report.

INTERVIEWS WITH EYEWITNESSES

(excluding Jewish leaders and Pilate)

Luke 23:36-49

Who were they?

What did they do?

How did they feel?

What did they say?—quotations

INTERVIEWS WITH JEWISH AND ROMAN LEADERS

Matthew 27:41-43

Who were they?

What did they do?

How did they feel?

What did they say?—quotations

FOLLOW-UP ON RESURRECTION

Matthew 28:1-10

What happened?

Where did it happen?

When did it happen?

How was it done?

Who was involved?

What was said?—quotations

THE GREAT COMMISSION

AIM: That your students will accept the Great Commission and pass the gospel along to others

SCRIPTURE: Matthew 28:8-10, 18-20; Mark 6:7-13; 16:9, 10, 15, 16; Luke 24:13-15; Luke 24:13-25, 33-42; John 20:24-29; 21:1-6; Acts 1:1-12; 1 Corinthians 15:6, 7 (Jesus appears after His resurrection, gives His followers the Great Commission, and ascends into Heaven)

PREPARATION:
1. Photocopy activity sheets—one for each student.
2. Prepare secret word cards as described in PRESESSION.

PRESESSION (5-10 minutes)

ACTIVITIES
* Use a code to discover a secret word that is a key to the lesson and talk about its meaning

MATERIALS
* 3" x 5" cards—one for each student

PERSPECTIVE (10 minutes)

ACTIVITIES
* Discuss missionaries supported by your church

MATERIALS
* Optional: pictures, maps, or other information about missionaries supported by your church

PROBE (20 minutes)

ACTIVITIES
* Solve a mystery to find out to whom Jesus appeared after His resurrection

MATERIALS
* Bibles
* "By All Appearances" Activity Sheet

PERSONALIZE (15-20 minutes)

ACTIVITIES
* Use an activity sheet to learn more about the Great Commission and how you can carry it out

MATERIALS
* Bibles
* "The Great Commission" Activity Sheet
* Copies of the words of the hymn "We've a Story to Tell to the Nations"

PRESESSION

Use 3" x 5" cards to make secret word cards. On each card write the following:

Code: B = A; D = C

Secret Word:

D P N N J T T J P O

Make one card for each student and have them work on them as they arrive. The secret word is commission. **What do you think this word means?** (Don't know; cut given to salesman; government committee in charge of something; order.) **When Jesus was ready to return to** His Father in Heaven, He gave His twelve apostles a special order or command. This is referred to as the Great Commission. Have someone read Mark 16:15 and 16 aloud.

Can you identify a familiar word in that word "commission?" (Mission.) A **mission is a special task given to a person by an authority. What are the people who go on a "mission" for Jesus called?** (Missionaries.) **How much do you know about the special missionaries our church supports?**

PERSPECTIVE

If you have pictures, maps, or other information about these missionaries, let the group look at them as you discuss the missionaries. Talk about individuals. Have you ever met them? Where do they work? What type of work do they do? Do their children go to English-speaking schools or attend national schools with the citizens of the country? What type of food do you think they eat? What might they do for fun?

Optional: If you have time, pray for each one of them by name, mentioning their particular needs. Remind your students to pray for these missionaries each day.

Optional: Use pictures of these people and maps of the countries where they work to make a room bulletin board to encourage student participation.

Optional: Get a list of the names and ages of the missionary's children. Start a class project where your students can choose a child and become pen pals with him/her.

Have you ever been excited over getting to see someone—a favorite relative, a good friend from camp, or a neighbor who moved away, someone you thought that you would never see again, or at least not for a long time? Let your group respond briefly. **If so, then you know how Jesus' friends must have felt when they saw Him die on the cross and heard that He was alive again.**

PROBE

In that dark hour when Jesus was crucified, the apostles and other followers were very sad. They did not realize Jesus would be raised from the dead. They feared that the enemies of Jesus would be after them, too, and so they shut themselves in a room in Jerusalem. At that time they had no hope.

Distribute copies of "By All Appearances" activity sheet. Have students form pairs and work together to complete this exercise. **When you are done, we will talk about the people**

together. You can share some of the following information with your class.

Mary Magdalene was a woman from whom Jesus had driven seven demons. She thought that someone had stolen Jesus' body. When she saw Jesus, she didn't recognize Him. She thought He was the gardener. How delighted she must have been when she realized it was Jesus who was talking to her!

The book of Mark tells us that the other women to whom Jesus appeared were Mary, the mother of James, and Salome. After they met Jesus they joyfully hurried to tell His disciples that Jesus was alive and going ahead of them into Galilee where they would see Him.

Cleopas and his friend were on their way home to Emmaus from Jerusalem. They were sad because of Jesus' death. They evidently knew about the empty tomb, but didn't believe that Jesus was alive and the importance of that fact to their futures. Jesus took the time to explain how the Scriptures applied to himself and the events surrounding His ministry, death, and resurrection. It was only at the end of their journey that they recognized Him. When they did, they rushed back to Jerusalem to tell the other disciples.

The Gospels don't tell us details about Peter meeting Jesus. But the important thing is that Jesus was concerned about Peter after his denial and wanted to assure him he was forgiven.

When Jesus suddenly appeared among them in the locked room in Jerusalem, the ten disciples and His other followers were terrified. They thought Jesus was a ghost. They wavered between joy and doubt. To prove His reality, Jesus ate a piece of broiled fish while they watched.

Although Thomas was one of the twelve, he was not present when Jesus appeared to the others on the night of His resurrection. But when Jesus appeared and singled him out by showing him the wounds in His hands and side, Thomas made a mighty declaration of faith, calling Jesus "My Lord and my God."

When Jesus first appeared to the seven disciples fishing on the Sea of Galilee, they did not recognize Him. It was only after He told them how to miraculously fill their empty net to overflowing that they understood He was Christ. On this same occasion, Jesus had prepared breakfast for them on the beach. He spent special time with Peter and helped him work through his denial and reinstated him to full commitment to Jesus and His plan for mankind.

Jesus' resurrection brought a new command from Him to His disciples. He told them that He had been given all power and authority. They were to carry on His work on earth now that He was going back to be with His Father. They were to go and make followers of all nations, baptizing them and teaching them to obey everything He had commanded them.

Later, Jesus appeared to five hundred followers at one time. This vast number of witnesses was reliable proof that He was alive.

The James mentioned in 1 Corinthians 15:7 is the half brother of Jesus. Although he had not believed in Jesus before the resurrection, now James not only joined the disciples but became an outstanding leader of the church in Jerusalem.

At last, after forty days, Jesus left His followers to return to His Father in Heaven. Two angels promised that some day He would return visibly and physically to the earth and the people He had died to redeem.

Check out Acts 1:12. What did the followers of Jesus do after Jesus was taken into Heaven? (Returned to Jerusalem.) They went back to the upstairs room where they were staying to await the coming of the Holy Spirit, as God promised through Jesus.

Earlier in His ministry, Jesus had given His disciples a commission to go out by twos and preach and heal the people of Israel. They obeyed Him. Now they were being sent into all the world. Let's look more closely at what Jesus told them to do.

PERSONALIZE

Have students turn to Matthew 28:18-20 and read it in unison. Hand out copies of "The Great Commission" activity sheet. Students can complete this top section as a group.

The work Jesus assigned His followers was to be done in a definite way. They were to begin where they were [Jerusalem and Judea], spread out to the half Jews around them [Samaria], and continue to the non-Jewish people [the ends of the earth.]

Joyfully, the apostles obeyed Jesus' command. The book of Acts tells us of their active lives in the service of Christ. The apostles were hardworking, conscientious men; but they were only human. In their short lifetime they could not possibly have traveled around the entire world to preach and teach and baptize people into Christ. But the apostles certainly made a good start. The people they taught went out and taught others, and the Word of God was passed along from generation to generation. **What do you think would happen if one generation would fail to teach the next about Jesus?** (There would be no more Christians; people would die as sinners and be separated forever from God.)

Let's look at the rest of the activity sheet. Have people work on this exercise individually.

World Christians are people who look at and love the world the same way God does. They believe that God made everyone and loves them all. They see all people equally in need of the salvation Jesus provides and desire to have the good news about Him told to everyone.

World Christians obey Jesus' last command by learning about other people and countries in their world. They find out where the countries are and what the special needs of the people are.

World Christians don't just pray for God to "bless the missionaries," but learn the individuals their church supports. They also pray for them regularly being specific in their requests and thanks. And even if they can't go to other countries to tell others about Jesus, they give money to help those who do.

You don't have to wait until you're a grown-up to do what Jesus wants you to do. Begin now to spread the good news. Then perhaps when you are older, you'll prepare to carry out the Lord's work in another land.

PRAYER/PRAISE

Close by reading or singing the words of the hymn, "We've a Story to Tell to the Nations."

By All Appearances

In each blank space write the name or group to whom Jesus appeared.

The first by whom the living Lord was seen
Was a woman named Mary _____.
                          (Mark 16:9)

Other _____ too, the risen Christ did meet;
They worshiped at their Master's feet.
                          (Matthew 28:8-10)

_____ and a friend, along the way
Met Jesus on His resurrection day.
                          (Luke 24:13-25)

Then _____ saw the risen savior too;
His Master's promise had come true.
                          (Luke 24:34)

To the _____ Jesus showed His face,
And at their table found a welcome place.
                          (Luke 24:33-42)

To help sad, doubting _____ understand
Jesus showed the nail-print in His hand.
                          (John 20:24-28)

Seven _____ fishing by Him were told
How to get all their net would hold.
                          (John 21:1-6)

On a mountain where they could see Him well
To his _____, Jesus said, "Go and tell."
                          (Matthew 28:18-20)

_____ of the brothers saw, as Jesus said,
That He was risen from the dead.
                          (I Corinthians 15:6)

No doubt _____ felt joy and fear
When he saw the risen Lord so near.
                          (I Corinthians 15:7)

The _____ who saw the Lord rise to the sky
Knew that Jesus' followers need never die.
                          (Acts 1:1-11)

39A

The Great Commission

Jesus gave His followers a command before He returned to Heaven. It is found in Matthew 28:18-20. It directs us to:

_____

_____

_____

_____

Use this code to discover ways you can carry out this Great Commission. Write the words on the lines above the code.

A, E, I, O, U = ✧

C = ⊷	D = ♣	H = ★	J = ▲
K = ✳	L = ✚	M = ✈	N = ✿
P = ■	R = ▶	S = ⊠	T = ✕
V = "	W = ✾	X = ●	Y = ☉

1. _____ to my friends and relatives about _____ and _____
  ✕ ✧ ✚ ✳   ▲ ✧ ⊠ ✧ ⊠   ✧ ✿ " ✧ ✕ ✧

them to study and worship with my church.

2. Become a _____ _____ .
  ✾ ✧ ▶ ✚ ♣   ⊷ ★ ▶ ✧ ⊠ ✕ ✧ ✿

3. _____ about other world _____ and their _____ .
  ✚ ✧ ✧ ▶ ✿      ⊷ ✧ ✧ ✿ ✕ ▶ ✧ ✧ ⊠

Find out where they are and what their special _____ are.
  ✿ ✧ ✧ ♣ ⊠

4. Learn about individual _____ and _____ for them
  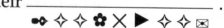   ■ ▶ ✧ ☉

regularly.

5. Give _____ to help with _____ _____ .
  ✈ ✧ ✿ ✧ ☉   

PETER PREACHES ON PENTECOST

AIM: That your students will tell others the good news about Jesus

SCRIPTURE: Matthew 28:19, 20; Luke 24:49; Acts 2:1-42 (The Lord works through Peter and the other apostles to spread the good news of His kingdom)

PREPARATION:
1. Photocopy activity sheets—one for each student.
2. Prepare clues for the Bible Investigator assignment as described in PRESESSION.
3. Make answers for a quiz game on Peter as described in PERSPECTIVE.

PRESESSION (5-10 minutes)

ACTIVITIES
* Find two promises and a command from God

MATERIALS
* Bibles
* Chalkboard and chalk or large sheet of paper and marker

PERSPECTIVE (10 minutes)

ACTIVITIES
* Participate in a balloon burst quiz on Peter

MATERIALS
* Quiz balloons—minimum of 10 or one for each student

PROBE (20 minutes)

ACTIVITIES
* Complete a skit of Peter and John talking about Pentecost

MATERIALS
* Bibles
* "Man Alive!" Activity Sheet

PERSONALIZE (15-20 minutes)

ACTIVITIES
* Work in teams to find ways to reach others with the good news about Jesus

MATERIAL
* "Think Tank" Activity Sheet

PRESESSION

Before class write this on the chalkboard:
Bible Investigators! Can you find these things?
A PROMISE—Luke 24:49
A COMMAND—Matthew 28:19, 20
A PROMISE—Matthew 28:20

As the group gathers let them look for these items in their Bibles. Have slips of paper available for them to write down their answers.

Guide the discussion afterwards using these questions: What was the promise? Who made it? Who was it promised to? Is it conditional—does something have to be done in order for the promise to be fulfilled?

After Jesus went back to Heaven to be with His Father, the apostles returned to Jerusalem. One of those who waited for Jesus to fulfill His promise of the Holy Spirit was Peter. How much do you know about Peter?

PERSPECTIVE

Prepare answers for a balloon burst quiz on Peter by writing the following on strips of paper: rock; Andrew; fisherman; apostles; Christ; denied; water; Pentecost; Jerusalem; two. Before class, insert the strips and blow up the balloons.

Optional: If you have less than ten students, give two balloons to some of them. If you have more than ten students, make duplicates of the slips so there will be one slip and balloon for each student.

Let students select balloons and burst them by poking them with pins or the ends of unbent paper clips. Read the statements and let students answer with the word that completes the sentence.

If more than one person has the correct word let them all give it.

1. **Peter's name means** (rock).
2. **His brother's name was** (Andrew).
3. **His occupation was** (fisherman).
4. **He was chosen as one of the twelve** (apostles).
5. **He confessed that Jesus was the** (Christ), **the Son of the living God.**
6. **He** (denied) **Jesus three times.**
7. **He tried to go to meet Jesus when Jesus walked on the** (water).
8. **He preached the sermon on the Day of** (Pentecost) **when three thousand became followers of Jesus.**
9. **He became one of the leaders of Christ's church at** (Jerusalem).
10. **In his later years, he wrote** (two) **books of the New Testament.**

In Jerusalem the apostles waited together as Jesus had told them for the promised Holy Spirit. Jesus told His followers that the Spirit would come to help them as they introduced the gospel message to the world. Prayerfully, the eleven apostles had chosen Matthias to replace Judas who had betrayed Jesus. Now these twelve men waited eagerly for the Spirit to come to give them the wisdom and power to do the job that God had given them to do. **Let's see what happened on the day the Holy Spirit came.**

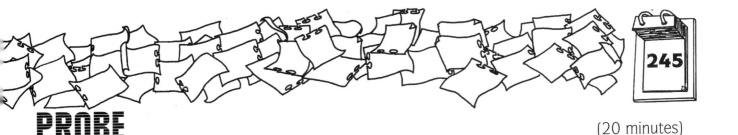

PROBE

(20 minutes)

Distribute copies of "Man Alive" activity sheet. Have students work in pairs to finish this exercise. Answers are: Holy Spirit; wind; tongues, fire; nation, languages, wine; Joel; name, Lord, saved; miracles, wonders, signs; death, you, Lord, Christ; do; repent, baptized, sins, forgiven; Holy Spirit; plead; three thousand; Pentecost, teach, fellowship, bread, pray.

Optional: If you have a longer class period, let the group read this skit aloud. Choose two students to take the parts of Peter and Andrew. The rest of the class can follow along on the activity sheets.

What special day was it when God sent the Holy Spirit to the apostles? (Pentecost.) This was a Jewish holiday that came fifty days after the offering of the barley sheaf at Passover. Its name, Pentecost, means "fifty." Like Passover it was one of the three great pilgrim festivals when the city was filled with Jews from nations other than Israel. Even Gentiles who had accepted Judaism were there. It was a family celebration where all members came together. Some scholars have estimated there may have been up to two and one-half million people in Jerusalem for Passover. For the followers of Jesus, it was fifty days since Jesus' resurrection.

Have volunteers read aloud Acts 2:5-8. **Why do you think God sent the Holy Spirit on this special holiday when Peter had an international audience?** (So they could all hear about Jesus at one time; take the message back home with them.) Unlike Passover, Pentecost was celebrated only <u>one</u> day. It was this one crucial day when people were gathered from every nation that God sent the Holy Spirit to start the apostles out on spreading the gospel to all nations. God used this miracle to show that salvation is to <u>all</u> people regardless of their race, color, nationality, sex, or age.

Check out Acts 2:24. What was one of the very first things Peter told the people about Jesus? (That God had raised Him from the dead.)

Perhaps many of the Jewish worshipers had stayed during these fifty days between Passover and Pentecost. The events of Jesus' trial and crucifixion were still fresh in their memories. Now these apostles who were witnesses of Jesus' resurrection and ascension were able to proclaim the highest proof that what Jesus had claimed was true. He was indeed the only Son of God, their Messiah/Christ!

In the skit, what did Andrew say showed that the audience understood Peter's message? (They asked what they should do.) **What did Peter tell them?** (Repent and be baptized to have their sins forgiven.) We must not only be sorry for our sins, we need to do something about them. Only when we confess our sins, let God forgive them, and are determined to not do them again, can we really live as Jesus wants us to. Only then can we have God's help to guide us. Then He can work through us to carry out His plan for all people just as He did through the apostles.

What happened to the three thousand people who believed about Jesus? Ask a volunteer to read verse 41 aloud. (They were baptized.) This baptism showed that they were choosing to obey Jesus and wanted to be a part of His followers.

Check out verse 42. What four things did the early Christians do together? (Devoted themselves to the apostles' teaching, to the fellowship, to the breaking of bread, and to prayer.) "Baby" Christians need to grow. When new believers are in a group, they have a better chance to do that as they learn from more mature Christians.

What do you think is meant by the "breaking of bread"? This refers to Communion services held to remember Jesus' sacrifice for sin. These services were modeled after the Last Supper Jesus had with His apostles on the night He was betrayed.

In the skit, Peter said that Pentecost was the beginning of God's church. What is the church?

(People who follow Jesus; building where they meet.) The word "church" is from a Greek word meaning "called out assembly." The church of God is like a family where believers are all brothers and sisters who have a common father—God. In the Bible it is compared to a body where members have different jobs but all work together.

Peter and the other apostles were willing to speak out for Jesus. We must be willing to confess Christ's name before others too.

PERSONALIZE

(15-20 minutes)

Divide the group into three teams. Hand out copies of "Think Tank" activity sheet. Ask a volunteer to read the directions. Assign one problem to each group. Explain that in a think tank, the members all contribute. They try to think of as many new ways to do something as they can. Encourage these teams to come up with as many ways as they can to solve their assigned problems. Have teams select someone to be a secretary and write down the ideas. Allow about five minutes to let the teams finish this part of the exercise and choose one idea to role play.

When teams have worked out their role plays have them present them to the group. Always encourage students who take part in these mini-dramas. In that way they will be more likely to participate in similar activities in the future. If students are having a hard time playing one person, suggest they reverse roles. You might want to step into a role yourself if people are having a difficult time. End the role plays when the point is made or people are stuck.

Discuss the role plays using questions like these:

How did you feel playing the part of the Christian(s) trying to help the person with the problem? What do you think the problem person was feeling? Why did the characters act the way they did? Why do you think the characters reacted the way they did? Why is it so easy for Christian kids to ignore kids who have these kinds of problems? What could we do to help carry out God's plan and reach hurting kids like these?

If you have never accepted Jesus as your Savior and Lord, you should consider making that great choice now. If you are already a Christian, you should tell others of God's plan of salvation.

PRAYER/PRAISE

Close in prayer where you go around the class with each person adding one word to a prayer, such as "thanks, " "help," or name of a person to reach with the love of God.

Read Acts 2:1-42 and use the clues to fill in the missing words.

PETER: Wow! What a day this turned out to be—talk about excitement and surprises! I'm really tired tonight.

ANDREW: You have reason to be. I never heard you talk to people about Jesus like you did today. What a change there is in your life!

PETER: You know as well as I do that the change in all of us is because of the _____ _____ who came and filled us this morning.(v. 4)

ANDREW: You're right. I didn't know what to think when I heard that sound like a violent _____ in the house.(v. 2) Then I saw those _____ of _____ on everyone.(v. 3) And suddenly we were all talking different languages. It's no wonder people came to find out what was going on.

PETER: They were from every _____ (v. 5) and they heard us in their own _____. (v. 6) It was such a miracle I don't understand how the people of Jerusalem thought we had had too much _____!(v. 13)

ANDREW: Well, you certainly set them straight in a hurry. How did you happen to use that verse from the prophet _____?(v. 16)

PETER: I just suddenly remembered it. It must have been the Holy Spirit who told me about it. Wasn't that a wonderful promise that everyone who called on the _____ of the _____ would be _____?(v. 21)

ANDREW: Great! You really told them clearly how Jesus had proved He was God's Son by all the _____, _____, and _____ He did.(v. 22)

PETER: It was all true.

ANDREW: Then you told the people that although they were the ones who put Jesus to _____, God had planned it long ago.(v. 23) When _____ said that God raised Jesus from death and that He is alive again at God's side and is both _____ and _____, I wanted to jump and shout "Hallelujah!"(v. 36)

PETER: God put a real love for the people in my heart. I never felt like that about people before. Instead of trying to protect myself from harm, I only wanted to help them know Jesus like we do.

ANDREW: The message must have gotten through, because they wanted to know what to _____.(v. 36)

PETER: I just told them what Jesus told us: "_____ and be _____ in the name of Jesus Christ so your _____ can be _____."(v. 38)

ANDREW: And to think that if they do they too will receive the _____ _____ like we did.(v. 38) What a wonderful promise that is.

PETER: I just felt that I had to _____ with them to save themselves from all the evil around them.(v. 40)

ANDREW: Just think of it—people accepted your message and were baptized. Do you know, there must have been about _____ _____ added to the number of Jesus' followers today!(v. 41)

PETER: Yes, God has done great things through us. From now on people will remember this day, _____, as the beginning of God's church.(v. 1) These believers in Jesus will grow as they listen to us _____, have _____ with each other, break _____ in remembrance of Jesus' sacrifice for sin, and _____ to God, their heavenly Father. (v. 42)

Think Tank

Suggest ideas of how you can carry out God's plan and help out the person in the problem. After everyone has had a chance to make a suggestion, choose one and role-play it for the group.

Problem 1:

Enrico has just come to this country. He grew up in a nation where the government wouldn't let the people learn about God's great plan of sending Jesus to be the Savior of the world. Enrico doesn't speak your language very well yet. You don't speak his language at all. He smiles hopefully at you and your friends as you pass by on your way to church.

Problem 2:

Allison is physically disabled. She uses a wheelchair and has difficulty getting around. She is often left out of activities and is lonely. Often she wishes she had a good friend to love her. She has never gone to church or heard very much about Jesus.

Problem 3:

Ty's parents are divorced. He lives with his mom who has to work full-time. Ty works hard at home to help her and his younger sister out. He can't afford a Bible so he hasn't read about how Jesus came to be his friend and Savior and restore his relationship with his heavenly Father.

PETER AND JOHN PREACH

AIM: That your students will have faith in God's power and bravely follow the Lord

SCRIPTURES: Acts 3:1-4:21 (Peter and John use the miracle of healing through God's power as an opportunity to preach bravely about Jesus)

PREPARATION:
1. Photocopy activity sheets—one for each student.
2. Make the basis for the acrostic as described in PRESESSION.

PRESESSION (5-10 minutes)

ACTIVITIES
* Help make an acrostic on showing courage in serving Jesus

MATERIALS
* Chalkboard and chalk or large sheet of paper and marker

PERSPECTIVE (10 minutes)

ACTIVITIES
* Hear a story about a brave Christian
* Talk about times you were brave

PROBE (20 minutes)

ACTIVITIES
* Participate in a rap to learn more about Peter and John's brave preaching

MATERIALS
* Bibles
* "Take Courage" Activity Sheet

PERSONALIZE (15-20 minutes)

ACTIVITIES
* Choose the best way to courageously witness for Jesus

MATERIALS
* "Have Courage—Will Witness" Activity Sheet

PRESESSION

Before students arrive, write "COURAGE" vertically down the middle of the board. Be sure to leave room on either side to add other letters.

As students gather have them help you make an acrostic showing courage in serving Jesus.

Each letter in the word "COURAGE" becomes the first letter of a word or phrase of your choosing OR one of the letters inside a word or phrase. For example, Call a friend and invite him to Bible class or preach a sermon.

PERSPECTIVE

Read or tell this story to your class.

"You can't get away from us now."

The street gang formed a tight circle around Mary. She looked around. Everywhere she turned were boys with angry faces. She hadn't noticed them until they had surrounded her. Now it was too late to escape. She stood her ground and turned back to the ringleader. "What do you want?"

"We're tired of your coming down here to preach about Jesus. You give the girls and younger kids ideas we don't like. So now we're going to make you pay for it."

He stepped closer. In his hand he held a rope. Tied to the end of it was a big rock. He began to spin it around his head, closer and closer to Mary's face. "Will you give up and quit while you can?"

"No." Mary stood still. Although the rock whizzed closer she refused to move. She never stopped staring into the boy's face. Her lips moved silently in prayer.

"Go away and never come back!"

Still Mary held her ground. The rock scraped her forehead and blood ran but she never blinked or showed fear.

As suddenly as he began, the boy
dropped the rope. **"You're a brave girl! From now on you can come down here and nobody will bother you. We'll see to that!"**

Mary's heart was racing so hard she was afraid the gang could hear it. She tried to swallow the big lump in her throat. "Then show me how brave <u>you</u> are. Come to my Bible study tomorrow night."

The next night, to Mary's surprise, the entire gang showed up and stayed throughout the meeting.

The Mary in this story was Mary Slessor. She later became a pioneer missionary to Nigeria on the western coast of Africa. All through her life she bravely obeyed Jesus and used every opportunity to tell others about Him.

Optional: If you can tell this story rather than read it, you will have attention from your students.

Have you had times when you were brave and told others about Jesus? Let students share their experiences briefly. Today we're going to learn about a time when two of Jesus' apostles, Peter and John, were courageous and used an event that showed God's mercy to tell others about Jesus.

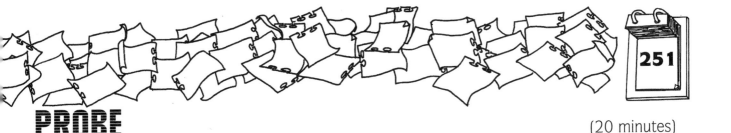

PROBE

Hand out copies of "Take Courage" activity sheet. This skit is written as a rap which means that it is a rhyming poem done to a four-beat rhythm. The words to be accented are underlined for you.

Assign people to read the parts of Peter, John. The rest of the class can be divided into small groups to take the parts of the chorus, crowd, and priests. Allow the group to read the skit over silently a few times before they read it aloud. You will probably find it much easier if the class keeps the rhythm going by clapping or snapping fingers.

Have students turn to Acts 3:1-4:21 for a discussion time. **What were Peter and John going to the temple to do?** (Pray to God.) There were three main times of prayer when devout Jews went to the temple. The one at three o'clock was the last of these three. Although Peter and John were followers of Jesus, they still kept these prayer times.

The lame man was sitting by one of the main gates of the temple where he could be seen by the most people. **What do you think the lame man thought would happen when Peter told him to look at him?** (Get money from Peter.) Because he was lame from birth, there was little for him to do to earn money except to beg.

What did Peter offer him instead of money? (The use of his legs again.) **How did the man feel about this gift?** (Thrilled; happy; jumped and walked around to show his joy.) **Who did he thank for it?** (God.) **What do you think the lame man's praise to God showed about where he thought the miracle had come from?** (He recognized it was God's power, not Peter's, that made him well.) When someone helps you, you should remember to thank him/her. And when God blesses you, don't forget to thank and praise Him too!

How did Peter say the lame man was healed? (By the power of Jesus; by faith in Jesus.) Peter made it very plain that it was not his, nor John's power, but that of Jesus that did

this miracle. He was actually saying that by believing in the authority Jesus has, as God's Son, the Holy Spirit can work powerfully through people to produce miracles.

Check out Acts 3:13-21. What four things did Peter tell the crowd about Jesus Christ? (Who Jesus was; that they rejected and killed Him; God brought Him back to life again; they needed to repent and let Jesus take away their sins.) Peter saw his opportunity and took advantage of it to clearly and briefly lay before the people the story of Jesus.

Why did the priests, temple guard, and the Sadducees arrest Peter and John? (They didn't want them talking about Jesus.) The Sadducees were a sect of Judaism that did not believe in the resurrection. The leaders of Jewish religion were the ones responsible for Jesus' arrest, trial and death. They thought they were through with Jesus when they killed Him. Now here were two of His followers who not only claimed that Jesus was the Messiah but that God had raised Him to life again. When Peter said that the people must repent and obey Jesus, this was a direct threat to the authority of these leaders who thought more of their own power and positions than they did of obeying God. They responded by quickly throwing the two men into jail.

Look at Acts 4:4. What happened while Peter and John were in jail? (The number of followers of Jesus increased by 2000, going from 3,000 to 5,000.)

How did Peter and John act the next day when they were brought before the Jewish high court, the Sanhedrin? (They courageously witnessed for Jesus.) How surprised these leaders must have been when instead of being on the defensive, Peter and John boldly proclaimed that only Jesus was able to save people from their sin!

What did Peter and John say about not speaking or teaching about Jesus anymore? (They had to do what God wanted; were going to continue speaking about the true things they had seen and heard.) **Peter and John had to decide whether to obey the voice of man or the voice of God. They were determined to obey God and carry out Jesus' command to** take His message to all nations. How about you? Will you choose to obey God and tell others about Jesus—even when it requires great courage?

PERSONALIZE

(15-20 minutes)

Distribute copies of "Have Courage—Will Witness" activity sheet. Ask a volunteer to read aloud the directions and the situation. **Work on this activity by yourselves. When you are done, be ready to talk about your choices.** Allow about half the time period to do this. Have students share their answers and reasons with the group.

Several of your students may choose the first option as the best way because they don't have to openly admit they were the guilty person. **Why do you think choice number 1 is the best one?** (You are witnessing for Jesus by offering to pay and also by writing the comment about why Christians want to do the right thing.) Point out that while this option will help pay for the repair work, it doesn't really make the best use of the opportunity to witness. **Do you think writing a witness like this is as good as telling someone personally why Christians obey God?** Why or why not?

How many of you chose option 3? Why do you think this is the best decision? To many students this is the safest and least confrontational. It is also the least helpful. **Why do you think people often choose this kind of way to handle difficult situations?** It allows the person to seek God's forgiveness and not get personally involved. However, it also ignores the opportunity for a personal witness.

Those of you who chose option 2, why did you think this was the best way to obey Jesus? While it requires real courage to face the possibility of undeserved criticism, it also gives your neighbor a chance to ask you why you admitted the accident and are now willing to help make things right. It is a perfect occasion to tell him about Jesus and what being a Christian is really all about. **Just like Peter and John, we must have faith in Jesus and bravely use every opportunity to tell others about Him.**

PRAYER/PRAISE

Close with prayer asking God for help to bravely witness for Jesus to others.

PETER: About three o'**clock** on **one** fine **day**, we were **headed** to the **temple** to **kneel** and **pray**.

JOHN: We **entered** the **gate** and a **beggar** called to **us**. He **wanted** some **money** and he **made** quite a **fuss**.

PETER: I **said**, "I **don't** have **silver** or **gold**, but **something** much **better** than **money** to **hold**. In the **name** of **Jesus**," I **said**, "rise and **walk**." A **crowd** was **gathering**, they **stood** around to **gawk**.

JOHN: Then **Peter** took his **hand** and **pulled** him to his **feet**. He **jumped** right **up** and **walked** in the **street**.

CHORUS: Be **brave** now, **Peter**. And **John**, you be **bold**. God **sends** times like **this** so **others** can be **told**.

CROWD: We **all** saw him **walking** and **praising** God. We **rubbed** our **eyes** and **said**, "That's **odd**. Is **this** not the **beggar** who was **lame** from **birth**? Whose **name** did they **use**, that it **has** such **worth**?"

PETER: It's **Jesus**—the **name** that we **used** to **heal**. All of **you** had Him **killed**, but His **res**urrection's **real**. God **raised** up His **Son** to be **Lord** of **all**. Re**pent** all of **you**, and on **His** name **call**.

JOHN: Then **all** at **once** the **priests** arrested **us**. They **hauled** us off to **jail** and be**gan** to **discuss**.

CHORUS: Be **brave** now, **Peter**. And **John**, you be **bold**. God **sends** times like **this** so **others** can be **told**.

PRIESTS: By **whose** **authority** did you **heal** that **man**? Come **on**, speak **up**, say it **loud** if you **can**.

JOHN: The Holy **Spirit** helped us **know** what to **say**. He **gave** us **courage** as on **Pe**ntecost **Day**.

PETER: It's **Jesus**, the **Messiah**, whom you **nailed** to the **cross**. But **God** raised Him **up**. It was **Sa**tan's **loss**. By **Je**sus' **name** this **man** can **stand** right **here**. His **name** will **save** you, so **take** some **cheer**.

PRIESTS: What **shall** we **do**, for a **miracle** has been **done**? The **man** has been **healed**. See him **jump** around and **run**! We'll **threaten** them **hard** and **warn** them not to **speak**. This **man** called **Jesus** makes our **power** look **weak**!

CHORUS: Be **brave** now, **Peter**. And **John**, you be **bold**. God **sends** times like **this** so **others** can be **told**.

JOHN: To **listen** more to **you** than to **God** on **high**? You must **judge** for **yourselves**, but our **Lord** we can't **deny**.

PETER: We're **going** to **speak** the **things** that are **true**—what we **saw** and **heard** and **just** told to **you**.

JOHN: They **let** us **go**, for they **couldn't** punish **us**. They **knew** if they **did**, the **crowd** would make a **fuss**.

CROWD: Let's **praise** the **Lord** for **all** He has **done**! And **praise** Jesus **too**, God's **own** dear **Son**!

CHORUS: We **thank** you, **Peter** and **John** so **bold**. God **sends** times like **this** so **others** can be **told**.

HAVE COURAGE—WILL WITNESS

Read the situation. Circle the best way to use it to witness for Jesus.

Your neighbor doesn't like Christians. He says they don't really live the way they talk. You accidentally broke his window while playing ball. No one saw you do it. You are really sorry and want to follow the Lord and tell others about Him. You decide to:

1. Write an unsigned note apologizing for the broken window. Add, "Christians want to do the right thing because they obey Jesus." Put some money in it to help pay for the damage and leave it in his mailbox.

2. Tell him that you broke the window accidentally. Offer to pay what you can and work out the rest of the damage expense by doing chores for him.

3. Ask God to forgive you. Tell your parents about it and ask them to pay the neighbor for the damage. Say you will pay them back out of your allowance or by doing jobs for them.

Why do you think this is the best choice? Write your reason on the lines.

_____

_____

_____

_____

Use this space to illustrate your choice.

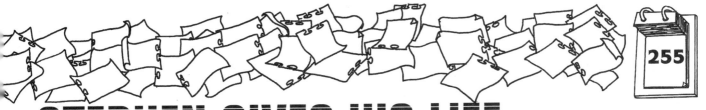

STEPHEN GIVES HIS LIFE FOR THE FAITH

AIM: That your students will be encouraged to be truthful and faithful to Jesus until death

SCRIPTURE: Acts 6:1-15; 7:1-60 (Stephen is not afraid to speak the truth and becomes the first to give his life for the faith)

PREPARATION:
1. Photocopy activity sheets—one for each student.
2. Make the base message and secret code cards as described in PRESESSION.

PRESESSION (5-10 minutes)

ACTIVITIES
* Crack a code to discover a message about faithful Christians

MATERIALS
* Shelf paper, 3" x 5" cards, tape
* *Optional: a copy of Fox's Book of Martyrs, By Their Blood, or any other information about martyrs*

PERSPECTIVE (10 minutes)

ACTIVITIES
* Learn more about the background of Stephen

MATERIALS
* Bibles
* "Getting The Facts Straight" Activity Sheet

PROBE (20 minutes)

ACTIVITIES
* Read a skit about Stephen's death

MATERIALS
* Bibles
* "The Deacon Who Disappeared" Activity Sheet

PERSONALIZE (15-20 minutes)

ACTIVITIES
* Share experiences about telling the truth
* Help make a list of tips on how to faithfully tell the truth

MATERIALS
* Chalkboard and chalk or large sheet of paper and marker
* Small rock
* *Optional: some type of crown*

PRESESSION

Today you are going to put a secret message on the wall. The message is: "A martyr is someone who was killed for being a witness for Jesus." You will be writing some of the letters of this sentence on cards for the students to add to the coded statement. Because of that, you will need to leave space lines like the illustration below. On a large piece of shelf paper write:

A MARTYR __S
S_M_O_E _HO W_S
_IL_ED FO_ B_IN_
A _HRIS_I_N.

Write one missing letter on each 3" x 5" card, making sure there is at least one for each student. Tape the shelf paper on the wall where students can easily reach it.

Optional: If you have more than this number of students, you will have to leave out more letters. If you have fewer, let them draw more than one card.

As students arrive have them draw cards. Explain that they have to tape the missing letters on the wall in order to crack the code and discover the secret message. After the group has solved the message, talk about martyrs. The word "martyr" was originally a Greek word that meant "witness." But as time went on it came to be widely used to mean anyone who was killed for being a Christian. **Do you know of anyone who was a martyr?** Most scholars agree that all of the apostles, except John, became martyrs because of their witnessing for Jesus.

Optional: If you have a longer time period and were able to obtain information about martyrs, allow students to look at it.

The first man to become a martyr in the early church was a godly man named Stephen.

PERSPECTIVE

In the early church the apostles felt that they should spend their time teaching and praying. But soon, because of the large number of people who were joining the group of Jesus' followers, other jobs needed to be done as well.

Hand out copies of "Getting The Facts Straight" activity sheet. Ask someone to read the directions aloud. Students can do this page individually. **What was Stephen chosen to do?** (Help in the distribution of food to the widows.) **Why did the group choose him?** (He had great faith and was full of the Holy Spirit.) Point out that although this job seemed to be a rather menial one, the believers felt that the men chosen for it should be godly, faithful men. This is true no matter what duty the Lord calls a person to do in His church—whether it be to lead in worship or help keep the building clean.

Stephen was an outstanding Christian man. People listened when he spoke. He talked about Jesus at every opportunity, and the Holy Spirit helped him.

Every church needs good leaders to help do the Lord's work. Some people are chosen to watch over God's people. They are like shepherds who watch the flock. **Another group chosen to work with these people take care of the many business matters of the church.** They see that the building is kept in repair and take care of the many details of the work of the church. **Today as in the early days of the church, people of good reputation, spiritual people, are needed as workers for the Lord.**

Optional: If you have a longer period of time, mention some names of leaders in your congregation.

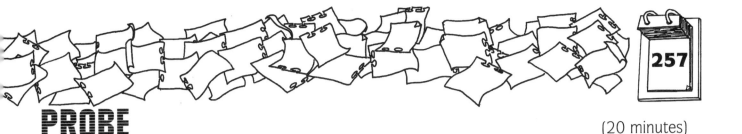

PROBE

(20 minutes)

Stephen's trouble started at the Synagogue of the Freedmen. These were Greek-speaking Jews who had been freed from slavery. Stephen also spoke Greek and probably went there to tell the people the good news about Jesus.

Soon some of the well-educated members started arguing with him. Have students look back over the Scripture passages they studied in PERSPECTIVE. **Why do you think these people got angry with Stephen?** (Didn't want to hear they were sinners who needed a Savior; were jealous of him.)

These men did not believe in Jesus as God's Son, and possibly they thought Stephen wouldn't have a chance against them. However, the Holy Spirit helped him, and he spoke with such wisdom and power that those men couldn't say a thing. They became enraged when they were defeated in an argument. They were also jealous because people began listening to Stephen instead of them. **The angry Jews decided to do something to silence Stephen.**

Distribute copies of "The Deacon Who Disappeared" activity sheet. Choose two of your best readers to take the parts of Agent 006 and Boss. Have them read the skit aloud while the rest of the class follow along on their activity sheets. **What was the plan to stop Stephen from speaking the truth about Jesus?** (Arrest him; bring him before the Jewish Supreme Court; have false witnesses lie about him.)

Check out Acts 6:14. What did these false witnesses testify about Stephen? (He said that Jesus would destroy the temple and change the customs Moses had handed down to them.)

The majority of the ruling party of the Sanhedrin were Sadducees. This Jewish sect believed only in the laws of Moses. This meant that speaking against Moses was equal to blasphemy and punishable by death.

In his reply to the Sanhedrin, Stephen mentioned several great men of God. Look through chapter 7 and let's list them on the board. These men were Abraham, Isaac, Jacob, Moses, Joseph, Joshua, David, and Solomon. This speech showed that Stephen founded Israel's history on Moses' writing.

Ask someone to read aloud verses 51-53. **What did Stephen accuse the Sanhedrin of doing?** (Persecuting the prophets; betraying and killing Jesus, God Messiah; not obeying God's law.) **How did they react to this charge?** (They were furious; refused to listen; dragged him out of the city; killed him with stones.)

Stephen was brave to continue his message when he knew that his words didn't please the crowd. He also knew that this group had the power to kill him. As he was dying, what did he ask the Lord to do? (Receive his spirit into Heaven; not blame his enemies for killing him.)

Stephen was the first Christian to die for his faith in Jesus. No doubt Christians took Stephen's body and buried it. Perhaps as they buried it they thought, "He was the first one of us to be killed. But he won't be the last. Will the rest of us be as loyal to our Master as he was?" How faithful do you think you would be to tell others the truth about Jesus? Let this be only a question for thought.

PERSONALIZE

Have students sit in a circle on the floor. **This will be our sharing circle. I'd like someone to volunteer to be a Share Starter and comment on this question: Have you ever been afraid to tell the truth?** If it is difficult to get the discussion started, share a personal experience briefly about this yourself. After all those who want to share about this question have done so, continue in the same manner with these questions: Have you ever lost a friend because you told the truth? Have you ever wished someone had not told the truth? Have you ever been glad because someone did tell the truth?

Let this sharing time lead naturally into a group discussion about truth covering questions like these: What is truth? Why is it important? What does telling the truth have to do with being faithful to Jesus?

Why don't people often not like to hear the truth about Jesus? (They don't like to hear that they are sinners or are doing wrong.) **Why do you think people are afraid to speak the truth about Him?** (They don't want anyone to dislike them or be angry with them.) Have your students help you make a list of timely tips on how kids their age can faithfully tell the truth.

If you make a habit of telling the truth now you'll be able to stand up to the big tests later on in life. Like Stephen, you won't be afraid to speak the truth, even if it means giving up your life.

Ask the group to turn to Luke 23 and read verses 34 and 46. **What did Jesus do just before He died?** (He prayed, asking forgiveness for the enemies who were putting Him to death; asked God to receive His spirit.) **Just before Stephen died, he also prayed to God. Check out Acts 7:59, 60.** What did Stephen pray? (Jesus to receive his spirit; not to hold this sin against them.) **Stephen followed the example of His Lord, even as he died. He was truly "faithful unto death."**

Read aloud Revelation 2:10. **What promise does this verse give?** (God will give a crown of life to those followers who are faithful to death.) **Yes, God has promised to reward His followers like Stephen who are faithful to Jesus even if they become martyrs for being truthful. And God always keeps His promises!**

PRAYER/PRAISE

Hold up the rock so others can clearly see it. **Let this rock remind you of the price Stephen paid for being faithful. But also remember that if you are truthful to Jesus even to death, He will give you a crown of life.** Pass the rock to the student closest to you. Have people pass the rock to each other and silently reflect on this truth.

Optional: Use a crown also and have students consider the reward for faithful Christians.

Getting the Facts Straight

Ready, Bible Investigators? The main facts of Acts 6:1-15 are paraphrased below, but they are listed in the wrong order. Be good detectives and number the facts in the order they occurred.

Read Acts 6:1-7 and number these facts 1-6.

____ The apostles told the whole group to pick seven men to be in charge of distributing the food.

____ More and more people were becoming followers of Jesus including both Jews who spoke Hebrew and those who spoke Greek.

____ The Twelve apostles gathered all the followers of Jesus together.

____ The Greek-speaking Jews complained that their widows were not getting their share of the food each day.

____ The apostles laid their hands on the men.

____ The group chose Stephen because he was a man with great faith and full of the Holy Spirit.

Read Acts 6:8-15 and number these facts 7-12.

____ Stephen's face looked like the face of an angel.

____ False witnesses testified against Stephen.

____ Some Jews began to argue with Stephen.

____ Stephen did great miracles and signs among the people.

____ Stephen was arrested and brought before the Jewish Supreme Court.

____ Enemies of Stephen persuaded some men to tell lies about him.

THE DEACON WHO DISAPPEARED

(Scene 1: Late night, under the street light on a corner in a deserted part of town) (Characters: Boss and Agent 006, both in trench coats)

BOSS: Is that you, 006? What's the code word?

006: "Truthful." I'm really glad to see you, Boss. I've got a lead on this case.

BOSS: Great! I've got to tell you this disappearing deacon business has really had me down. What did you find out?

006: Remember those Jews who were always arguing with Stephen? Well, seems they secretly made a deal with some shady characters to tell lies about him. I'm positive they're behind his disappearance. But what their plan is remains a mystery.

BOSS: Sounds like you're on to something all right. Stick with it, 006. We'll get to the bottom of this yet.

(Scene 2: Same street corner, one week later)

BOSS: 006?

006: "Truthful," Boss. Things are starting to fit together. Word on the street is that these crooks nabbed Stephen and brought him before the Sanhedrin. They charged him with blasphemy and speaking out for Jesus. Then the hoods they hired lied about him. But Stephen faithfully told the truth.

BOSS: What happened?

006: He reminded them about how God had led and cared for the Jews from the time of Abraham. Then he accused them of refusing to listen to the truth about Jesus. He charged them with killing Jesus, their Messiah, and disobeying God.

BOSS: No! That must have made them furious.

006: It sure did, Boss. An informant told me they were so mad they ground their teeth. Then Stephen boldly told them he saw the glory of God and Jesus standing at God's right side.

BOSS: Go on. What happened then?

006: They shouted to drown him out and covered their ears so they couldn't hear him. Then they took him out of the city and threw stones at him until he was dead.

BOSS: Murder, eh? So that's what happened to Stephen. How tragic!

006: That's not the end, Boss.

BOSS: There's more?

006: Yep. The really terrific thing is that as he was dying, Stephen prayed for Jesus to receive his spirit. Then he asked the Lord to not blame his enemies for his death.

BOSS: Wow. What a way to die! Bravely telling the truth about Jesus even when it meant his death. Faithfully following Jesus' example when he died. The Bible's right. If Jesus' followers are faithful to death, He will give them the crown of life. What we need are more believers who are . . .

006: Truthful, Boss. Truthful!

PHILIP PREACHES IN SAMARIA

AIM: That your students will be encouraged to tell others how Jesus can deliver them from sin

SCRIPTURE: Isaiah 53:7, 8; Acts 6:5; 7:4-8; 8:26-38 (The early Christians and Philip feel the urgency of the task Jesus gave them to bring others to Him for salvation)

PREPARATION:
1. Photocopy activity sheets—one for each student.

PRESESSION (5-10 minutes)

ACTIVITIES
* Identify places mentioned in the story of Philip and the Ethiopian official

MATERIALS
* Bibles
* *Optional: Map of Bible lands or modern day nations showing Jerusalem, Samaria, Gaza, (Israel) and Sudan (Africa)*

PERSPECTIVE (10 minutes)

ACTIVITIES
* List the main events of Jesus' life

MATERIALS
* Chalkboard and chalk or large sheet of paper and marker

PROBE (20 minutes)

ACTIVITIES
* Read about Philip and the Ethiopian official
* Discover some principles you can use to bring others to Jesus

MATERIALS
* Bibles
* "Philip's Principles" Activity Sheet

PERSONALIZE (15-20 minutes)

ACTIVITIES
* Create a tract about Jesus that will help others come to Jesus for salvation

MATERIALS
* "The Story of Jesus" Activity Sheet

PRESESSION

Before class, display the map where it can easily be seen. As the group gathers center the conversation on Philip and his willingness to bring others to Jesus for salvation.

Have you ever taken a long hike? Why? Let students share briefly. Point out that in most cases they took the hike because they knew there was something special to see or do. **Would you hike many miles to a deserted spot simply because you believed God wanted you to go? The Bible tells us about a man who did just that. His name was Philip.**

Who was Philip? Ask someone to look up Acts 6:5, 6 and read it aloud. This man was not the same as the apostle Philip. Philip, like the first martyr, Stephen, was chosen to help oversee the food distribution to the early church in Jerusalem. Also like Stephen, Philip was a godly man filled with the Holy Spirit.

After Stephen's death, there was a terrible persecution against the church. What group was behind this oppression? (The Jewish leaders.) **Many Christians had to leave Jerusalem to escape capture and possible death. Philip left Jerusalem to preach in a city in Samaria.** Point out Samaria. This area is northwest of Jerusalem.

Some scholars believe that the city Philip went to was Sebaste. It was a Hellenistic or Greek-speaking city whose citizens were Jews who had come from all parts of the Roman Empire. Since Philip was also Hellenistic, he would be accepted easily.

Southwest of Jerusalem a well-traveled route took travelers through a beautiful fertile valley just north of Mamre where Abraham first lived. This was near the place where the Hebrew spies brought enormous bunches of grapes back to Joshua. A spring of water known as the "Fountain of St. Philip" is located there where tradition has it that Philip baptized the Ethiopian official.

From there the road continued southwest across the coastal plain to Gaza. Gaza was a city near the coast of the Mediterranean Sea.

Finally, the road wound down into Egypt and Ethiopia. This ancient Ethiopia was not the country of Ethiopia as we know it today. Instead it was what is now Sudan. It was located in Southern Egypt and also known as Nubia. The people were Negroid, but had adapted Egyptian culture completely and were ruled by a succession of queens, each with the title of Candace.

Philip was soon to visit several of these areas as he faithfully carried out Jesus' command to tell others the good news of salvation.

PERSPECTIVE

What things do you think Philip told people about Jesus? Let students come up and write their suggestions of various events from the life of Christ on the board. List them as briefly as possible. Events could include: Born in Bethlehem; Spent some time in Egypt; Visited the temple at age 12; Baptized by John at age 30; Preached and healed people for three years; Arrested and tried before the Jewish council; Died for the sins of all people; Buried in Joseph's tomb; Came from the tomb alive; Appeared many times to His followers; Ascended into Heaven after forty days; Now King of kings and Lord of lords; Coming again to earth.

Since the Hellenistic Jews used a Greek version of the Old Testament called the Septuagint, Philip would probably tell them that Jesus is God's own Son, the Messiah, the one whose birth was foretold by Isaiah and other prophets.

While Philip was in Samaria he won many people to the Lord. He did miraculous signs, drove out evil spirits and healed many people. **One day, an angel of the Lord gave him an important message from God.**

PROBE

(20 minutes)

Have students take turns reading aloud Acts 8:26-38.

Who did Philip find when he got there? (An Ethiopian official, in charge of the queen's money.) The Hebrew word "eunuch" means officer. The title doesn't necessarily suggest physical conditions. There were married eunuchs.

What was the man reading? (The book of Isaiah.) **What did Philip do for the man?** (Explained the passage he was reading and told him about Jesus.) **What happened when Philip did that?** (The man believed and asked Philip to baptize him.)

What do you think happened when the man got back to his home? (He probably told others about Jesus.) **When Jesus went back to Heaven, He told His followers to tell others about Him. That includes us today. Let's see if we can learn something from this story about how to do that.**

Distribute copies of "Philip's Principles" activity sheet. **When you are finished with this activity, we'll talk about it.** Answers are: 1. Talk about Jesus everywhere you go; 2. Be alert for the Holy Spirit's guidance; 3. Obey God's plan for you; 4. Bravely reach out to someone different than you; 5. Begin with the person's interest; 6. Use the Bible to tell about Jesus; 7. Tell the Gospel simply; Trust God to take care of the new believer.

Optional: If you have a shorter time period, save the word search at the bottom of the activity page for later. Students can take it home to finish if necessary.

Did it make any difference to Philip where he was when he talked about Jesus? (No.)

Think about the place where it is hardest for you to talk about Christ. For many people their families are that place. For your students it might be when they are with peers. **Ask God to help you to also speak out for Jesus there.**

What do you think Philip thought about the message he received from God? Why? (It was strange. Because it didn't give a reason; meant leaving a successful preaching ministry; was a long way to go.) Point out that Philip was alert to the Holy Spirit's leading and recognized the message was from God even though it didn't tell Philip what to do when he got there.

What did he do about it? He followed it even if he didn't understand why. **Why do you think the Ethiopian official was there at the same time as Philip?** (Coincidence; God planned it; don't know.) **God's timing is perfect. We can trust His plan even when we don't understand it.**

Why do people hesitate about approaching someone different from themselves? (Afraid they'll be rejected or made fun of; don't know what to expect; have preformed ideas about them.) When God directed Philip to a man from a totally different culture it was the birth of cross-cultural missions.

How did Philip begin to tell the man about Jesus? (Began with what he was reading which was about Jesus.) Encourage your students to follow the same pattern when they are witnessing and begin with the person's interest.

Which part of the Bible was the Ethiopian man reading? (The Old Testament; Isaiah 53.) The entire Bible points to Jesus so we can use all parts of it to tell others about Christ.

Why do you think the Gospel should be kept simple? (So you don't confuse people; helps them understand it better.) A good witness doesn't have to know the entire Bible to tell others about Jesus. However, knowing key verses is helpful because you probably won't have a concordance handy to find the verses you need. The Holy Spirit will bring these verses to your mind once you have stored them in your brain and heart.

What happened to Philip after he baptized the Ethiopian official? (He was suddenly taken away from the man.) Philip never saw this important man again. Over and over again in the book of Acts we read how the evangelists had to leave new believers and go on to other places. God took care of these baby Christians and strong churches grew up everywhere the Gospel was told. **We can trust God to lead and bless our witnessing today as He did for Philip long ago.**

PERSONALIZE

(15-20 minutes)

Suppose you are visiting a country that has never heard of Jesus. Would you know how to tell them about Christ? Hand out copies of "The Story Of Jesus" activity sheet. Select someone to read the directions aloud. Briefly review the list of events from Jesus' life that you made earlier. These and other events can be used in this activity. Allow time for students to complete this tract.

Optional: If you have a longer period encourage students to share their creations with the whole class.

In the early days of the church, Christians told others about Jesus even when they knew they might die if they did. Why do you think they did that? (Because they loved Him and wanted to obey Him; knew they would go to

be with Him in Heaven if they died anyway.) These people wanted to win others to Him. They knew that a person can be saved only through Jesus and so they told everyone.

Winning others to Christ is not only done by preaching to crowds. The Christian faith is also spread as believers share the good news about Jesus with one or two friends at a time. If we really believe God loves us, we shall have to tell others about it.

PRAYER/PRAISE

Close in prayer asking God to provide opportunities to share the Gospel with others. Ask for His guidance and courage to tell others about Christ.

Phillip's Principles

Principles are general tips or clues on how to do something. Bible Investigators, can you unscramble these sentences to discover some of these tips on how to bring others to Jesus for salvation?

1. _____
   .OG UOY EREHWYREVE SUSEJ TUOBA KLAT

2. _____
   .ECNADIUG S'TIRIPS YLOH EHT OT TRELA EB

3. _____
   .UOY ROF NALP S'DOG YEBO

4. _____
   .UOY NAHT TNEREFFID ENOEMOS OT TUO HCAER YLEVARB

5. _____
   .TSERETNI S'NOSREP EHT HTIW NIGEB

6. _____
   .SUSEJ TUOBA LLET OT ELBIB EHT ESU

7. _____
   .YLPMIS LEPSOG EHT LLET

8. _____
   .REVEILEB WEN EHT FO ERAC EKAT OT DOG TSURT

Find and circle these key words in the puzzle. They might be up, down, across, or even diagonal!

JESUS	INTEREST
TALK	BIBLE
ALERT	TELL
GUIDANCE	GOSPEL
OBEY	SIMPLY
PLAN	TRUST
REACH	CARE
DIFFER	BELIEVER

```
P G Q M B T N J E S U S S L
D U C E V I W A R Z N H E G
E I F O Y L P M I S Q P L N
L D F R S C E T R U S T Z Q
M A L F H P V S N O G M K D
Y N U W E Y E F G C T Z L E
T C K B L R S O T D R A A P
R E N O A I N T E R E S T X
E X B C Q F P T Z N V O M G
L D I T H X R L S Q E A H B
A G B U V O B E Y P I C P T
V S L Y S T N R H G L O L N
W E E X L L E T U W E T A S
H C A E R B Z Q A G B P N X
```

THE STORY OF JESUS

You want to reach out to people who have never heard of Jesus. Use the spaces provided to create a handout about Him that will help them trust Him as their Savior. You can write or draw your ideas.

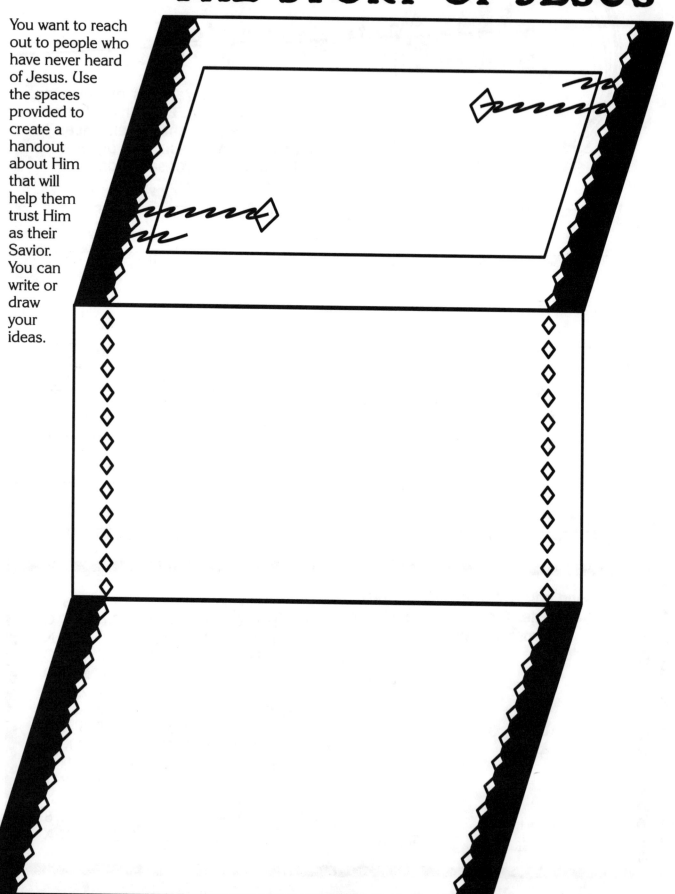

GOD CALLS PAUL

AIM: That your students will understand people can be changed by trusting and obeying Jesus and that Jesus can use them

SCRIPTURE: Acts 9:1-22 (Paul is changed by the power of the Gospel and is used mightily by the Lord)

PREPARATION:
1. Photocopy activity sheets—one for each student.

PRESESSION (5-10 minutes)

ACTIVITIES
* Play a game emphasizing change and our memories

PERSPECTIVE (10 minutes)

ACTIVITIES
* Talk about changes in people's lives

PROBE (20 minutes)

ACTIVITIES
* Participate in a skit about Paul's conversion
* Identify four basic changes in Paul's life

MATERIALS
* Bibles
* "Change For The Better" Activity Sheet
* Chalkboard and chalk or large sheet of paper and marker

PERSONALIZE (15-20 minutes)

ACTIVITIES
* Use finger puppets to role play people who have been changed by Jesus

MATERIALS
* "The Next Step" Activity Sheet
* Scissors, tape

PRESESSION

As students gather, have them form pairs and move into an empty spot in the room. Have partners face each other looking at hair, clothes, jewelry, etc. Then partners turn their backs to each other and make three changes in their looks. This could be by putting glasses on upside down, untying a shoestring, rolling a sleeve up, or a sock down. When both have done this, they face each other and try to point out the changes the other has made. When they have completed this, have players change partners and repeat, making three changes again. End play after several minutes or everyone has had at least one opportunity to play.

Optional: If you have an uneven number of students, team up with one student to make a pair.

How many changes could you remember? Let students share briefly. **Our memories can be very choosy. We tend to remember only the things that we want to or that affect us the most.**

PERSPECTIVE

Get your students to thinking about changes the Lord can bring by guiding the conversation. **What is the biggest change you ever had?** Allow students to share their experiences. You may choose to start this time by telling about the changes you made such as conversion, a job, graduation, marriage, or moving. Point out that before changes occur, people have to make choices. For example you had to choose to accept the job, share your life with another person, or complete the work required to graduate. Also ask questions such as these: How did you feel about those changes? How did others react to them? How did they act towards you because of them? Do you think the changes were worthwhile? Why? Why not? Did you pray about them?

In the early days of the church, people had many changes because of their choices to follow Jesus. Some gave up houses and lands, others had to leave loved ones behind, and still others gave up positions of power and authority. **But all of them knew that any change was worthwhile for the sake of belonging to Jesus. The apostle Paul was such a man. Following Jesus made many changes in his life. One of these was his name, which was changed from Saul to Paul.**

"Saul" means request or seek. This was an appropriate name for a man who wanted to seek God's blessing on his life at all costs. The problem was that Saul sought that blessing by doing the wrong things.

"Paul" means little. After he met Jesus and discovered it was not only Christians, but the Lord he was persecuting, Saul was humbled. His decision to follow Jesus had a deep effect on him. His name was changed to Paul.

The first thing God had to do was change Saul's feelings about Jesus.

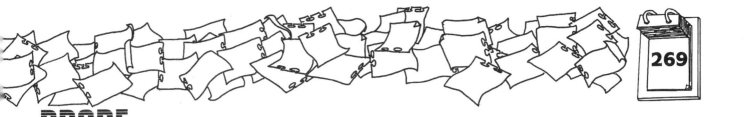

PROBE

Have someone read aloud Acts 8:3. **What did Saul do to the followers of Jesus?** (Put them into prison.) **What does that show us about his attitude towards Christians?** (He hated them.) **Towards Jesus?** (He didn't believe in Him.) Saul was a Pharisee. These were the Jews who tried to show their love for God by keeping God's commandments and doing good deeds. Saul studied under the best teachers and had a great knowledge of the laws found in the Old Testament. **Saul thought that Jesus and the Christians were trying to destroy the laws that God had given to the Jews so he set out to destroy the church.**

Hand out copies of "Change For The Better" activity sheet. Choose three people to play the parts of Darbra, Nathan, and Ananias. While they are reading the skit, the rest of the group can follow along on their activity sheets.

Saul fiercely waged violent attacks against the Christians in Jerusalem. But he couldn't destroy the church. Look up Acts 8:1. What happened to the Christians? (They scattered throughout Judea and Samaria.) **Check out Acts 9:2. Where did Saul want to go to arrest Christians?** (Damascus.) **Damascus was a city about 175 miles northeast of Jerusalem. Why do you think Saul wanted to go that far away to persecute them?** (To gain a bigger reputation; thought that might stop them forever; didn't want any Christians to get away from him.)

What stopped him from carrying out his plan? (He was struck down with a blinding light from Heaven; became blind; met Jesus.) **Saul said he heard a voice. Whose voice was it?** (Jesus.) Look at Acts 9:5. **What did Saul call Him?** (Lord.) **That term shows that Saul now had a new relationship with Jesus. This was the first change in Saul's life.** Write the numbers 1 through 3 vertically on the board. Opposite number 1 list "Relationship with Jesus."

How do you think Saul felt when he realized it was Jesus that he had been persecut-ing? (Afraid; upset; confused.) When the voice identified Himself as Jesus, reality hit Saul hard. If Jesus was God, his actions were based on the wrong concept of serving God by persecuting Jesus' followers! He had thought he was attacking people who dishonored God. Now he learned that <u>he</u> was the one guilty of showing great disrespect and hurting the Lord.

What happened to Saul after the light and voice were gone? (He was blind; had to be led into Damascus.) **How did Saul act after he was led into Damascus?** (He didn't eat or drink anything for three days.)

Why do you think he reacted that way? Just imagine how humiliating this experience must have been for Saul! He had come filled with spiritual pride, planning to be the great conqueror taking rebellious followers of Jesus as his prisoners. Instead he was blind and had to be led like a little child into the city to wait until Jesus gave him more instructions.

Have someone read Acts 9:11. **What did Saul do while he waited for Jesus to tell him what to do next?** This turn of events was a traumatic shock to his entire being. He devoted his time to thinking about what had happened and praying for wisdom to understand what it all meant to him now and in the future.

In the skit, Ananias said he was terrified when the Lord told him to find Saul and help him regain his sight. What did the Lord say to reassure him it would be all right? (He had chosen Saul to serve Him.)

Check out Acts 9:17. What did Ananias call Saul when he prayed for him? (Brother.) **What does that show us about Ananias?** (He was willing to believe that Saul was really changed; accepted him as a fellow believer in Jesus.)

What do you think would have happened if Ananias had been unwilling to change his mind about Saul and disobeyed God's command to him? (God would have found someone else to go to Saul.)

What did Saul do next? (He was baptized; ate and regained his strength.) **From that time on, Saul, now called Paul, preached about Jesus as powerfully as he had persecuted the Christians. This was the second change in his life.** List "Message" opposite number 2 on the board.

Paul became the messenger God chose to lead in winning the non-Jews to Christ. This **was the third change in his life.** List "Goal and direction" opposite number 3.

What was Paul like before God called him? Have someone read aloud Acts 9:1. (Violent; breathed out murderous threats; threatening.) **After he began to follow Jesus, his life was changed to one of love, kindness, and forgiveness.**

PERSONALIZE

(15-20 minutes)

Sometimes we think certain people are so bad that the Lord can't change them. But when people trust and obey Jesus, miracles occur and their lives are changed around like Paul's. Other times we choose to remember only bad things about someone and think that person could never be used by the Lord. But again the story of Paul shows us that isn't true.

Distribute copies of "The Next Step" activity sheet. Choose someone to read the directions aloud. Divide the group into pairs and have each team take one situation to work on. Have people cut out the appropriate puppets and tape them together at the back. Using these puppets they can role play the endings to each problem.

After pairs have an opportunity to work out their solutions, have them share them with the group. Remember to talk about the role plays using questions like these: How did you feel in that role? Were any changes expected? Accepted? Do you think the Christian followed God's plan? Did s/he do anything to help the other person's relationship to the group?

Paul changed from an enemy of the church to a great preacher of the Gospel. He trusted and obeyed Jesus and was used mightily by the Lord. God can change people today as He did Paul. How can the Lord use you to spread His Word?

PRAYER/PRAISE

Think of someone who needs changing. It may even be you. Then ask God to work a miracle and not only change but use that person to tell others about Jesus. Allow time for silent prayer. Close by reading Acts 1:8 in unison.

Darbra Falters: Welcome to our show. You've all been hearing about Saul of Tarsus and his violent attack on the Christians. Today our guests are people who have been close to him and can tell us more about Saul. Let's welcome Nathan.

Nathan: Glad to be here, Darbra.

Darbra: Nathan, you were one of the men who traveled with Saul to Damascus. What was the purpose of that trip?

Nathan: Well, in Jerusalem Saul had been arresting Christians and hauling them off to prison. When he heard that some of them were living in Damascus, he went to the high priest and got permission to go and arrest all of them there.

Darbra: Something happened on the way to that city that dramatically changed Saul's mind. Tell us about it.

Nathan: We were nearing the city when a dazzling light from Heaven flashed all around Saul. He fell to the ground. We heard a noise but didn't see anyone. He said a voice asked why Saul was persecuting Him. Saul asked whose voice it was. He told us the voice said He was Jesus. Then Saul said that Jesus commanded him to go into the city and he would be told what to do later.

Darbra: How strange! What happened next?

Nathan: Saul got up, but when he opened his eyes he was blind. We had to take his hands and lead him into Damascus because he was helpless.

Darbra: What did you do then?

Nathan: We realized the trip was ruined, so we went back to Jerusalem. When we left him, Saul had been blind for three days and hadn't had anything to eat or drink. It was really sad.

Darbra: Thank you, Nathan. Well audience, as you can see something or someone really stopped Saul in his tracks. Perhaps our next guest can give more information. Let's welcome Ananias.

Ananias: Thank you, Darbra.

Darbra: Ananias, you are a follower of Jesus and live in Damascus, correct?

Ananias: That's right, Darbra.

Darbra: How did you get mixed up with Saul?

Ananias: I was at home when the Lord asked me to go to a certain house and ask for Saul of Tarsus. I was told he was praying and in a vision had seen me come and give him back his sight.

Darbra: How did you feel about that, knowing Saul's intention was to persecute all Christians?

Ananias: I was terrified at first. But the Lord said He had chosen Saul to tell the Gentiles and people of Israel about Jesus. That gave me confidence so I hurried out to find Saul.

Darbra: What happened when you found him?

Ananias: I put my hands on Saul and told him that the Lord Jesus sent me so he could see again and be filled with the Holy Spirit. Instantly something like scales fell from his eyes and he could see. He got up and I baptized him. Then he ate and regained his strength. Since then he's preaching in the synagogue and convincing many Jews that Jesus is the Christ. He is really a changed man.

Darbra: That's truly a powerful story. Are miracles still possible today? The story of Saul seems proof positive that God can help any person change for the better and even use him. That's our show for today. Tune in tomorrow when our guest will be Aeneas, a former paralytic from Lydda.

44A

THE NEXT STEP

Read each situation and think about what the person should do. Cut out the finger puppets and tape the ends of the bands together. Use the puppets to act out the situations and possible endings.

Situation #1: Ty has been making fun of Brant and the other kids in Bible Club for a long time. At tonight's meeting the youth leader brought Ty and announced that he accepted Christ at a Bible study recently. During the snack time Ty walks over to Brant.

Ty: I'm sorry for how I've acted in the past. But I really do love Jesus now and want to follow Him. Do you think the kids can accept me as a member of Bible Club?
Brant: You were really hard on us before. I don't know about the other kids but I . . .

Situation #2: Amber is usually with a group of girls who are pretty wild. Lately Rachel has been thinking a lot about her and wishing she knew Jesus. Now she has the feeling that the Lord wants her to invite Amber to go along to Bible camp with her. After praying about it she does it.

Amber: You really want me to go with you to a Bible Camp? Why?
Rachel: Because . . .

PAUL AND BARNABAS

AIM: That your students will be encouraged to become world Christians and help spread the gospel around the world

SCRIPTURE: Acts 13:1-14:27 (The Holy Spirit guides the church at Antioch to send Paul and Barnabas to preach the gospel in other places)

PREPARATION:
1. Photocopy activity sheets—one for each student.

PRESESSION (5-10 minutes)

ACTIVITIES
* Make a montage of people around the world

MATERIALS
* Old magazines with pictures of the world's people, large sheet of paper, scissors, glue

PERSPECTIVE (10 minutes)

ACTIVITIES
* Talk about missionaries

MATERIALS
* Optional: Chalkboard and chalk, or large sheet of paper and marker

PROBE (20 minutes)

ACTIVITIES
* Read about a missionary trip of Paul and Barnabas
* Trace the journey on a map

MATERIALS
* Bibles
* "Missionary Journey of Paul and Barnabas" Activity Sheet
* Crayons or colored markers, pencils

PERSONALIZE (15-20 minutes)

ACTIVITIES
* Compare true and false statements about missions and missionaries

MATERIALS
* "Mission Facts and Fiction" Activity Sheet

PRESESSION

Before class write *Be My Witnesses* at the top of the large sheet of paper. Use old copies of magazines such as *National Geographic* for pictures. Lay these, scissors, and glue where students can easily reach them.

As your students arrive, have them cut out pictures of people showing as many different cultures, races, and occupations as possible. Let the group arrange these in a montage on the background sheet and glue them on.

Before Jesus went back to Heaven, He gave His followers a special command. Have the group read Acts 1:8 in unison. **It takes courage to be witnesses and speak out for Christ. Missionaries are brave people.**

PERSPECTIVE

Guide the conversation using questions like these: Have you ever met any missionaries? Where did they live? What kind of work did they do? What were they like? What impressed you about them?

Optional: If neither you nor your students have personally met a missionary, use questions you would like to ask one. Examples are: What do you do? What kinds of food do you eat? Do your children go to schools with the nationals? Do you have pets? What do you do for fun? What do you like best about being a missionary? What is the hardest thing? What is the one thing you would like to have us pray about the most? You may want to list these on the board.

Our story today is about some missionaries in the early days of the Church who spoke out for Jesus.

PROBE

Hand out copies of "Missionary Journey of Paul and Barnabas" activity sheet. Students will trace the journey on this map, locate towns, and add a key word or phrase to help them remember what happened there.

After Stephen's death, Christians from Jerusalem were scattered in many places, among them the city of Antioch, capital of Syria. Can you find that city on the map? There are two cities named Antioch on this map. Be sure students locate the one in Syria, to the far right of the map. People of many nations lived in this city. **Many of the Greeks living in Antioch heard the gospel from these newly arrived Christians and believed and turned to the Lord.**

The church in Jerusalem decided to send one of the leaders, Barnabas, to Antioch to preach and teach. Because many people were added to the church, he got Paul to help with the Lord's work there. They taught the people for a year. The followers of Jesus were called Christians for the first time in Antioch. Have the group write (Christians) beside the city.

The Holy Spirit had some special work for

Paul and Barnabas to do. Ask for volunteers to read aloud Acts 13:1-4. **A young man named John Mark went with Paul and Barnabas on this first trip to preach the gospel.** John Mark was a nephew of Barnabas. **Where did they start their journey?** (Seleucia.) Have students draw a line from Antioch down to Seleucia.

Ask someone to read aloud verse 5. **Where was their first stop?** (Salamis on the island of Cyprus.) Draw a line from Seleucia to Salamis. Write (first stop) beside Salamis. **Check out verse 6. Where did they go next?** (Paphos.) Draw a line from Salamis to Paphos. **Who did they meet there?** (Bar-Jesus, a Jewish sorcerer and false prophet.) This man tried to stop the governor, Sergius Paulus, from hearing the gospel, but Paul, filled with the power of the Holy Spirit, struck Bar-Jesus blind. Write (Bar-Jesus) beside Paphos.

From Paphos the travelers went to Perga. Draw a line up to Perga. **For some reason John Mark left them there and returned to Jerusalem.** Write (John leaves) beside Perga.

Paul and Barnabas went on to another city named Antioch. Draw a line to Antioch. **Angry Jews here persecuted them and they left for Iconium.** Write (persecution) near Antioch and draw a line to Iconium.

Look up Acts 14:3. What special things did Paul and Barnabas do in Iconium? (Miraculous signs and wonders.) Write (miracles) near Iconium. **But again they had to leave because of persecution. They went on to Lystra.** Draw a line from Iconium to Lystra.

In Lystra the people thought Barnabas and Paul were gods. When the disciples stopped the crowd from worshiping them, some Jews from Antioch and Iconium came. Check out Acts 14:19, 20. What did they do? (Threw stones at Paul.) Write (gods-Paul hurt) near Lystra. Where did they go next? (Derbe.) Draw a line from Lystra to Derbe. **In Derbe they won a large number of followers to Jesus.** Write (followers) near Derbe.

Read verse 21. **What happened next?** (Returned to Lystra, Iconium, and Antioch.) Draw new lines back to these cities. In each of these cities they preached, established churches, and ordained men to carry on the work.

Have people take turns reading verses 24-26. **How did Paul and Barnabas end their trip?** (Went back through Perga and sailed from Attalia back through Seleucia and Antioch, Syria.) Write (return home) near Attalia. Draw a line to follow this trip.

Paul and Barnabas were brave missionaries. They experienced hardships as well as adventure and personal satisfaction. Above all, they continually spoke out for Christ. How much do you know about mission work and missionaries today? Let's find out.

PERSONALIZE

(15-20 minutes)

Distribute copies of "Mission Facts and Fiction" activity sheet. Have a volunteer read aloud the directions. **Only do the questions now. We will do the bottom section later.** Allow three to five minutes to complete the questionnaire.

Who is a missionary? (Answers 1 and 2.) **Are you a missionary?** It has been said that every person is either a missionary or a mission field. If you are a follower of Jesus you have been given the Great Commission from Christ and are therefore called to be a missionary. **You don't have to go live in another country to tell others about Jesus. Begin where you are.**

Who is a world Christian? (Answers 1, 2, and 3.) Especially in these days of world trade there is a need for Christians to have a global outlook and see the world's people as their mission field. This eliminates national barriers and prejudices. **It reinforces the Great Commission Jesus gave His followers to witness about Him "to the ends of the earth."** (Acts 1:8)

What is the truth about cross-cultural missionaries? (Answer 1.) Being a cross-cultural missionary doesn't necessarily mean going to a foreign land. It does mean working with people who have a different culture and language. In this day of immigration from shattered nations that may mean people right in your neighborhood.

How old do you have to be to be a missionary? (Any age.) Many missionaries decided to become one when they were children. **Much of the word today is in large cities.**

Who can be a missionary? (Answers 1, 2, 3, 4.) Mission agencies can use people with these four qualifications and many more besides. **Any person who really wants to be a missionary can be used either on the foreign field or right at home.**

How can you help missionaries? (Answers 1, 2, 3.) **Like you, they have times of discouragement. They welcome letters of encouragement and friendship.**

How should you pray when you pray for missionaries? Pray as specifically as possible mentioning special needs, opportunities, weaknesses, etc. **The only way to have specific information is to learn about individual people.**

How much money do you think you have to send to help missionaries? Let students give their answers. God uses whatever we give to Him and multiplies its use for others. For example: For the cost of a hamburger, you can share vaccinations for seven children—so they won't get measles; for the cost of an ice cream cone, you can share high protein food for ten hungry children for one day.

Perhaps even more important than giving money for missions is giving your time and talent. Have the group return to the bottom section of the activity page.

Are you ready and willing to become a world Christian and help spread the Gospel around the world? Think about the ways you can help. Briefly review these. **Choose one area as a goal you can set. Then write some ways you can reach that goal.**

For example: Goal: Become informed about a country or people and their needs. 1. Use a map to locate the area. 2. Read everything I can about that country, people. 3. Get information about their needs: hunger? homes? Bibles? missionaries? 4. Learn about their religion. 5. Get on a missionary newsletter list about that country or people.

Optional: Check with your minister or the U.S. Center for World Mission—non-denominational—1605 Elizabeth St., Pasadena, CA 91104

PRAYER/PRAISE

Take this pledge home as a reminder. Every day ask God to help you begin now to be a world Christian and missionary for Jesus. Remember, you are old enough now to tell others about Jesus everywhere you go! Ask God to bless each student and help them keep their pledge.

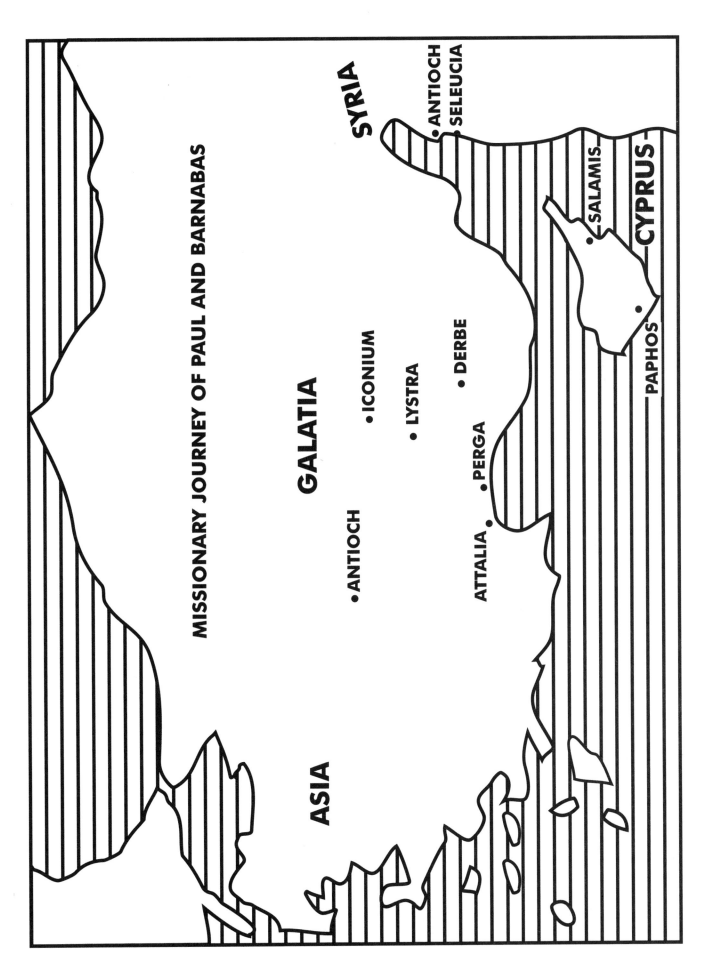

MISSIONARY JOURNEY OF PAUL AND BARNABAS

SYRIA

• ANTIOCH
• SELEUCIA

SALAMIS •

CYPRUS

PAPHOS •

GALATIA

• ANTIOCH

• ICONIUM

• LYSTRA

• DERBE

• PERGA

ATTALIA •

ASIA

MISSION FACTS AND FICTION

Read the statements. Choose the correct ending and circle the number. Be alert! There may be more than one correct answer.

A missionary
1. is anyone who loves Jesus and wants to be His follower.
2. is someone who tells others about Jesus.
3. has to go live in another country.

A world Christian is a follower of Jesus who
1. looks at and loves the world the same way God does.
2. believes God made everyone and loves them all equally.
3. believes that all people need the salvation Jesus provides.

Cross-cultural missionaries
1. bring the good news about Jesus to people with a different culture and language.
2. have to move to a different country to work with the people there.
3. must send their children away to school.

A missionary
1. has to be an adult.
2. can be any age.
3. wears outdated clothes and lives in mud huts.

Missionaries can be
1. mechanics.
2. computer specialists.
3. farmers.
4. preachers.

A world Christian
1. needs to go overseas to serve Jesus.
2. learns about people who are different.
3. tells others about Jesus everywhere he or she goes.

You can help missionaries by
1. writing them letters.
2. praying for them.
3. sending them money.

MY PLEDGE:

I will be a world Christian and help to spread the Gospel around the world by

GOAL: _____

_____

_____

_____

PAUL AND SILAS IN PRISON

AIM: That your students will have faith in God in times of stress and turn to Him in prayer

SCRIPTURE: Acts 16:16-40 (Paul and Silas trust in the power of the Lord, even though they are put in jail for obeying Him)

PREPARATION:
1. Photocopy activity sheets—one for each student.

PRESESSION (5-10 minutes)

ACTIVITIES
* Find pictures or stories of people in difficult circumstances and identify their problems

MATERIALS
* Old newspapers or magazines,
* Chalkboard and chalk or a large sheet of paper and marker

PERSPECTIVE (10 minutes)

ACTIVITIES
* List questions people in difficult situations might ask God

MATERIALS
* White paper—one sheet for each student

PROBE (20 minutes)

ACTIVITIES
* Read about what happened when Paul and Silas trusted the power of the Lord
* Finish the story

MATERIALS
* Bibles
* "The Praising Prisoners" Activity Sheet

PERSONALIZE (15-20 minutes)

ACTIVITIES
* Play a board game suggesting how to pray in stressful situations

MATERIALS
* "Prayer Path to Power" Activity Sheet
* Buttons—one for each player; pennies—one for every two students

---

LESSON 46   **UNIT THEME: THE CHURCH GROWS**

PRESESSION

(5-10 minutes)

Today while the group gathers, have students use the old newspapers or magazines to find and tear out articles or pictures of people having tough times. Have them identify the problem and write it at the top of their selection.

Invite the group to help you make a list of these problems on the board. Examples are: out of work; illness; flood destroyed crop; house burned down; robbed; accident.

What are some problems you have? Let people suggest their tough times and write their ideas on the board. Be sensitive to your students' problems. Even if they seem minor to you, they are major to them. Their struggles may even be so intense that it is hard to voice them.

If you have difficulty getting students to express their problems, start by sharing one of your own. It will help your students to realize that adults also have difficulties. **All people have stressful problems at some time in their lives.**

PERSPECTIVE

(10 minutes)

Think about a tough time in your life. Write down five questions you would have liked to ask God about. Maybe you are even having one of these times now. Allow about five minutes for this. Examples are: Why doesn't God help me? What did I do to deserve this? How can this be part of God's plan for me? Why did this happen when it did?

Encourage people to share their questions. Share something yourself. It will aid your juniors in identifying with you as a person, not just "the teacher." It will help them understand that it is all right to question God about our circumstances. When we ask questions honestly and trust God to answer them they often lead to rock-solid faith in Him.

Have you ever prayed for faith to overcome fear or stress? What happened? Encourage discussion by the group then add an experience of your own. Stress that even though we question God about tough times, He is always ready to help us in them. He might not remove the problems but He never leaves us to face them alone. His power is released through our prayers.

After Paul and Barnabas finished their first missionary journey, Paul took another trip. This time he took a Christian named Silas with him. One day they were walking along the streets of Philippi on their way to a quiet place by the river to meet other followers of Jesus. But before they got there, something strange happened.

PROBE

(20 minutes)

Distribute copies of "The Praising Prisoners" activity sheet. (p. 283) Have students take turns reading the story aloud while the rest of the group follow along on their activity sheets. After they have read the directions about finishing the story have them look up Acts 16:33-38 and read it.

Be sure they understand that they are to write the ending in the first person, using "I" and "me." This is the same way as the fictional story is writ-

ten—as if the jailer was telling the story.

Optional: If you have a longer period, encourage people to share their endings. If your time schedule is tight, then omit sharing.

Why do you think Paul didn't want the demon in the slave girl to tell the truth about who he and Silas were? (Don't know; she was not a Jew; it would make it look like the demon and Jesus' followers were connected in some way.)

Check out Acts 16:19. What was the real reason the men were angry with Paul and Silas and had them arrested? (They could no longer make money from the slave girl's fortune telling.) Just as today, people wondered what would happen in the future. They were willing to pay to find out. But the truth is that no one but God really knows what will happen in the future. **Look over verses 21-24. What did the Roman rulers do to Paul and Silas?** (Beat them with rods again and again; threw them in jail.) **What was the jailer told about these prisoners?** They were dangerous and should be carefully guarded. **How did he go about doing that?** (He put them in the inner cell and fastened their feet in the stocks.)

To help your students understand the tough situation Paul and Silas were in, share some of this following information about prisons and prisoners during New Testament times. A cell in Philippi was tiny, dark, and airless. It had no toilet and so the smell was dreadful. Prisoners were fastened in stocks which may have been holes in a stone floor [which prevented them from lying down or sleeping] or iron bolts attached to wooden posts [which made them lie spread-eagled on the cold, damp floor.]

Because prisoners were considered guilty until proven innocent, they were thrown into jail until the time of their trial. Sometimes they were in cells with murderers, robbers, and even the insane.

How do you think Paul and Silas felt about this kind of undeserved treatment? (Terrible; angry; confused; wondered why God let it happen to them.) **Why do people in tough situations sometimes feel God is picking on them?** (Because they think they didn't do anything to

deserve it; it is unfair; think they should only have good things from God.)

How did Paul and Silas act when they were mistreated like this? (They sang hymns and praised God.) **Why do you think they could act like that?** (Trusted God; don't know; knew God could help them.)

Check out Romans 8:28, and 38, 39 for a clue to their behavior. What do these verses tell us about tough times? (God will turn bad things to good for us; nothing can separate us from the love of God in Christ.)

Why do you think the other prisoners were listening to Paul and Silas? (They hadn't heard any prisoner ever praise God before.) Just think of the witness this must have been, to not only the jailer but to these prisoners!

What happened when Paul and Silas reacted this way to their undeserved punishment? (God sent an earthquake to free them.) **When we praise God in even the toughest times, it releases His power to work in and through us.** Not only were Paul and Silas set loose from their bonds, but also all the rest of the prisoners. When we trust God and pray to Him in trouble, others are also blessed.

How did the jailer respond when Paul and Silas told him everyone was still there? (Rushed in and knelt before them; asked what he had to do to be saved.) **What does this show us about him?** (Recognized they were servants of the living God; believed they could tell him how to personally know God; they were different from other prisoners.)

How did Paul and Silas help the jailer? (Told him about Jesus; helped him follow Jesus' command and be baptized.) **What did he do for them?** (Took them home; washed their wounds; fed them.)

Would knowing this story be helpful to you in times of stress? Why or why not? (Yes. It is an example to show us how God can help us when we trust Him and ask Him to help us; we don't need to worry because He knows our problems and will help us.) **Let's see how this example works out in real life today.**

PERSONALIZE

In tough times the most important thing is our reaction towards them. Will we trust God no matter what happens or lose faith in Him? Will it leave us better or bitter?

Hand out copies of "The Prayer Path To Power" activity sheet. This board game will help your students put into practice what they have been learning about trusting God in tough times. Ask a volunteer to read aloud the directions. Have the group form small teams of two to three people. Allow about half of your time for them to play the game. Regroup for debriefing.

How did the verses help you know what to pray about? (They were specific; gave promises from God for us to claim; pointed out where the people were wrong or right.) Most of the fictitious people in this game were in circumstances where they had no control over the stress. This is usually true for us also.

Point out that when the people reacted negatively and refused to trust the Lord, they were also cutting themselves off from His power to change them and/or the circumstances. This kind of bitterness can destroy people.

When people focus on how they will react to the tough situation, they grow spiritually and learn God is able to help them more than they realized before the situation. That growth is what makes them better, not bitter.

After this difficult time, Paul and Silas knew that God was with them everywhere and would turn even the worst situations into times of rejoicing and blessing—for themselves and others. If they had never been in that prison, the jailer and his family would never have come to know Jesus as their Savior and Lord! **When we trust God and continue to praise Him in difficult times He not only helps us, but uses us to bless others.**

PRAYER/PRAISE

Have the class read Romans 8:37 in unison. Close with praise to God for His power for those who have faith in Him and turn to Him in prayer.

THE PRAISING PRISONERS

I am the head jailer of the prison here in Philippi. Today there was a riot in the city. Two men, Paul and Silas, were arrested for teaching things that are not right for us Romans to do. But I heard that they had only driven an evil spirit out of a poor slave girl who told fortunes. She kept following them saying they were servants of the most high God and were telling people how to be saved. I think her masters caused the riot because they were furious at losing the money they made from her.

A crowd of people turned the men over to the Roman rulers who beat them with rods again and again. Then the prisoners were turned over to me. I was told they were very dangerous and needed to be carefully guarded. The officials told me I would be killed if they escaped, so I put them in a cell deep in the prison and pinned their feet down between large wooden blocks.

About midnight I heard something. It was Paul and Silas. They were praying and singing songs of praise to their God. The jail got quiet as the other prisoners listened to them.

Suddenly there was a strong earthquake. It shook the jail's foundation and broke open the doors of the cells. All the prisoners' chains came loose. I was sure everyone had escaped and knew the Romans would kill me for letting Paul and Silas get away. I drew my sword and was about to kill myself. Paul quickly called out, "Don't harm yourself! We are all here!"

Shocked, I called for lights and rushed inside. I was confused but realized these men were different from any others I had ever met. I had to find out why. I knelt down before Paul and Silas. "What must I do to be saved?" I asked. What would their answer be? What strange power caused the great earthquake? Are these men really servants of the most high God. What will happen next?

Read Acts 16:33-38 and write the surprising ending to this story as if you are the jailer. If you need more room, use the back of this page.

_____

_____

_____

_____

_____

_____

_____

_____

46A

THE PRAYER PATH TO POWER

Two or more players may play this game. Use buttons for markers and a penny for determining moves; tails, move one space, and heads, move two spaces. If you land on a space with a Bible verse, look it up and read it aloud before moving as it directs.

START

Tim's mother is very sick. He prays... James 5:16 Go ahead 1.

Mitch sasses Dad, then asks God to help him study. Mark 11:25 Go back 1.

Jyl's parents are getting a divorce. She prays... Psalm 27:10 Go ahead 2.

Marissa worries about everything. 1 Peter 5:7 Go back 1.

DETOUR ↑

Adam tells God what he wants God to do. James 4:3 Take detour.

Kids tease Taya for praying at meals. She prays... Colossians 3:17 Take an extra turn.

Jessica is in a new school. She prays... Hebrews 13:5 Go ahead 1.

Tony quits praying because his dad loses his job. Romans 12:12 Lose 1 turn

Shawn's best friend lies about her. She prays... 1 Peter 3:9 Go ahead 1.

Brett listens to others instead of God and tries drugs. Hebrews 2:18 Go back 3.

Wendy thinks she is not pretty. She prays... 1 Peter 3:3, 4 Go ahead 2.

Cory doubts that his sins are really forgiven. 1 John 1:9 Go back 2.

FINISH

PAUL IN ATHENS

AIM: That your students will be ready to speak for Jesus when opportunities arise

SCRIPTURE: Acts 17:16-34 (Paul takes advantage of an opportunity to preach about Jesus in a pagan city)

PREPARATION:
1. Photocopy activity sheets—one for each student.
2. Prepare list of terms as described in PERSPECTIVE.
3. Optional: If desired, make play dough as described in PRESESSION.

PRESESSION (5-10 minutes)

ACTIVITIES
* Make a clay sculpture to illustrate things people worship

MATERIALS
* Clay or play dough
* *Optional: homemade play dough*
          —see PRESESSION

PERSPECTIVE (10 minutes)

ACTIVITIES
* Identify terms used in the Bible lesson

MATERIALS
* Large sheet of paper and marker
* Seven 3" x 5" cards, tape
* *Optional: map showing Athens, Greece*

PROBE (20 minutes)

ACTIVITIES
* Work in a team to discover truths about the Bible lesson

MATERIALS
* Bibles
* "Mission Possible" Activity Sheet

PERSONALIZE (15-20 minutes)

ACTIVITIES
* Make a chain reaction of ways to witness for Jesus

MATERIALS
* "Speak Up!" Activity Sheet

PRESESSION

If you desire to use a homemade play dough, make it before class. Create this easy-to-store play dough by using 1 1/2 C salt, 1 1/2 C water, 3C flour. Mix ingredients together until it is the consistency of bread dough. If it is too sticky, add a small amount of flour. Divide the dough into small portions and mix in a few drops of food coloring to make different colors. Store in a tightly-covered container in the refrigerator.

As students arrive give each one a small amount of clay or play-dough. **Mold the clay into a statue of anything you want.** As they work on these statues, guide the conversation using these questions: Have you ever been to a museum where there were many statues? What were they images of? What would it be like to see a whole city full of images? What do you think it would be like to worship statues like that?

Encourage people to present their creations and explain what they illustrate. This may be diffi-cult for non-artistic students, but assure students you are more interested in their ideas than their style.

During the time the apostle Paul lived, people worshiped many images. They thought these idols were responsible for bringing them blessings or punishments. They worshiped them by bringing gifts such as food and flowers, burning sacrifices and even killing human babies. They thought these things pleased their "gods."

Check out Romans 1:18, 19, 22, and 23. What did God think about this? (Was angry with them, because they foolishly worshiped these things.)

Our story today is about a city that had nearly as many images for worship as peo-ple. They even had one statue that was ded-icated to "the Unknown God!"

PERSPECTIVE

Before students arrive, write these terms verti-cally on a large sheet of paper: Athens; syna-gogue; marketplace; philosophers; Epicurean; Stoic; Areopagus. Leave room behind each term for a 3" x 5" card. Display this sheet on a wall so your students can tape on the definitions.

Write one of these matching definitions on each card: central city of culture in Greece; Jewish place of worship; public square where people liked to meet; thinkers searching for truth; people who believed pleasure was the most important thing in life; people who believed life should be lived with-out feelings; group of important city leaders.

Mix up the cards and invite seven volunteers to draw one. Read each term aloud. Then explain it. Students who have the matching card may come forward and tape it in the correct place.

Athens, Greece was the central city of culture and knowledge hundreds of years before the time of Christ. It had thousands of memorials to false idols.

Optional: If you have a map, show the location of Athens.

Because Paul had a Jewish background, he went first to the synagogue to tell the Jews and God-fearing Greeks about God's Son Jesus, the Messiah.

In Athens the people went to the marketplace to listen to people express their opinions on all kinds of things. This public square was a good place for Paul to begin his ministry in this pagan city.

The philosophers were Greeks who were known for thinking about everything. They loved to talk

about and listen to new ideas and teachings.

The Epicureans believed that the most important thing in life was pleasure. One should find happiness in mental quiet and have no fear of the gods. They denied the resurrection fiercely. The Stoics believed that you should accept all things in life with a cheerful shrug, showing no emotion at all.

The Areopagus was a group of leaders in the areas of religion and morals. They thought of themselves as the keepers of teachings on new religions and foreign gods. The place where they met was also sometimes referred to as the Areopagus.

The people in Athens desperately needed to know about the one true God and His Son, Jesus. So the Lord sent a man who talked about Jesus everywhere he went.

PROBE

(20 minutes)

Distribute copies of "Mission Possible" activity sheet. Ask a volunteer to read the directions aloud. Divide the group into three teams. Assign one set of problems to each team. Have them move to a separate area so they can more easily work on the assignment. **We'll talk about your discoveries after your investigation.**

Who was the secret agent God sent? (Paul.) Paul was waiting in the city of Athens for Silas and Timothy to join him. In the meantime he was moved to action by the idolatry that surrounded him.

Who were some of the people Paul brought God's message to? (Jews; God-fearing Greeks; Stoic and Epicurean philosophers.) **What gods were most of the people worshiping?** (Idols; even the unknown god.) Paul noticed not only the statues, but also the temples and altars throughout the city. In the Parthenon there was a 38 foot high statue of Athena made of gold and ivory.

How did Paul carry out his assignment? (Reasoned with Jews; disputed with philosophers; explained God's message to Areopagus.) Paul didn't assume that these religious people knew the Lord personally. He basically followed "Philip's Principles" [see lesson 43]. He started with their interest—religious worship. Then he gave an example—the statue "To the unknown god." He went on to explain that the living God he served was their unknown god. Finally he led the people to make a choice about Jesus, God's Son and the Savior of the world. **We would be wise to follow Paul's example.**

How did the people respond to Paul's message? (Called him a babbler; sneered; became followers and believed.) **How do you think Paul felt about those who called him names?** (Sad; angry; prayed for them.)

Not everyone who hears the story of Jesus will choose to believe it and follow Him. But even one person makes it worthwhile! Paul did not live to see his efforts pay off, but today we know the results of Paul's work.

Paul was one of the most courageous people who ever lived. He never hesitated about speaking up for Jesus. Have you ever had an opportunity to speak up and tell someone about Jesus? If not, here is the chance now.

PERSONALIZE

(15-20 minutes)

Pass out copies of "Speak Up!" activity sheet. Choose someone to read aloud the directions. Stress that the students are to give only the first sentence they would say.

I will read aloud the situation. Then you will have one minute to complete the sentence.

When they have done this they are to fold the paper down accordion-pleat style so their answer does not show. Then they will pass it on to the person on their right. After all the situations have been done, have people pass the paper one more time so they don't have their own.

Share answers and discuss possible results following them. For example: In situation 1 you might say, "Let's make a circle around him and offer to be his friends." From there you could go on and tell him about your best friend, Jesus.

In situation 2 you could speak up and say, "Come over to my house and you can drink pop and listen to some of my new tapes." When you are there you could play a Christian tape and talk about the words in the songs.

Situation 3 offers you the chance to say, "I know somebody who will find out." Then you could tell your friend about God and why you want to follow Him and not take things that aren't yours.

When you are asked about reading the Bible you can say, "Why don't we read some of it together so you can see why I read it?" That gives you an opportunity to read the story of Jesus to your sister.

Situation 5 is a great chance to say, "Jesus isn't dead, but alive." Then you can share the story of His resurrection with your friend.

In situation 6 you might answer, "Prayer helps because the Lord is alive and wants to help His followers who trust Him." You could follow this with some examples of other prayers God has answered for you.

Optional: Encourage them to follow the same game plan Paul did. If you have time, briefly review this plan: 1) Start with their interest. 2) Give an example. 3) Explain God's plan for salvation through His Son, Jesus. 4) Lead the people to make a choice about Jesus.

Optional: If you have a longer time period, choose one situation and ask volunteers to act out the situation.

God gives us many opportunities to speak up for Him every day. Ask Him to help you identify them. Then use the courage He gives and tell others about Jesus.

PRAYER/PRAISE

Have each team pray together asking God to help them be courageous and speak up for the Lord.

Invite students to take their statues home as reminders of people who need to hear about Jesus.

Mission Possible

"Good day, Bible Investigators. The people in Athens are held as hostages by God's enemy, Satan. God sent a secret agent on a mysterious assignment to them. Your mission, should you accept it, is to find out the answers to the questions given below. Begin by following the clues in Acts 17:16-34. Should you or any member of your team decide to follow this agent's example, God will give you courage, the words to say, and a reward in Heaven. This reward will never be destroyed."

TEAM 1

1. Who were some of these people? (vs. 17, 18)

2. What gods were they worshiping? (vs. 16, 23)

3. What was their favorite pastime? (v. 21)

TEAM 3

1. Who was the secret agent God sent? (v. 16)

2. What did the people call him? (v. 18)

3. How did people respond to his message? (vs. 19, 32, 34)

TEAM 2

1. What was the secret agent's message? (vs. 18, 32)

2. Where did he meet the people he was sent to find? (vs. 17, 19)

3. What did this agent do to carry out his assignment? (vs. 17, 18, 22, 23)

Read the situation. Write an ending to the sentence. Fold the paper down and pass it to the person on your right.

1. Your school classmates are standing around on the playground. Some of the boys decide to tease and chase the new boy who is very shy. "Let's surround him and grab his glasses!" one shouts. **You speak up and say . . .**

_____

2. You are walking up the street with some friends. One of them says, "Let's go over to my house and try some of the liquor in my dad's cupboard. It will be lots of fun." **You speak up and say . . .**

_____

3. You and a friend are in a store. "Come on, let's swipe some candy bars. Nobody will find out," your friend says. **You speak up and say . . .**

_____

4. Your family doesn't go with you to Bible class or church on Sunday morning. One day your older sister sees you reading your Bible. "Why do you read that book?" she asks. "It was written so long ago it doesn't even apply to today." **You speak up and say . . .**

_____

5. You and your best friend are playing a game. You mention that you became a follower of Jesus last summer at Bible camp. Your friend says to you, "I don't understand what that's all about. Why do you want to follow somebody who died a long time ago?" **You speak up and say . . .**

_____

6. You tell a friend you have been praying about your mom's serious illness. "How will praying help?" your friend asks. **You speak up and say . . .**

_____

PAUL'S JOURNEY TO ROME

AIM: That your students will trust the Lord to guide and be with them in all circumstances and will follow Him

SCRIPTURE: Acts 21:1-30; 27:20-25 (Paul trusts and courageously follows Christ no matter what obstacles stand in the way)

PREPARATION:
1. Photocopy activity sheets—one for each student.
2. List Bible passages establishing principles on handling obstacles as described in PERSONALIZE.

PRESESSION (5-10 minutes)

ACTIVITIES
* Read what people in authority said about Paul
* Paraphrase these opinions

MATERIALS
* Bibles
* "Jerusalem's Most Wanted" Activity Sheet
* Four sheets of 8 1/2" x 11" paper

PERSPECTIVE (10 minutes)

ACTIVITIES
* Take part in a skit revealing how Paul dealt with problems in his life

MATERIALS
* "Jerusalem's Most Wanted" Activity Sheet

PROBE (20 minutes)

ACTIVITIES
* Read a fictional letter about Paul's voyage to Rome

MATERIALS
* Bibles
* "The Unsinkable Apostle Paul" Activity Sheet

PERSONALIZE (15-20 minutes)

ACTIVITIES
* Learn some Biblical principles on how to handle the problems we face
* Choose the principle that is most helpful to you

MATERIALS
* Bibles
* Chalkboard and chalk or large sheet of paper and marker
* 3" x 5" cards—one for each student

PRESESSION

(5-10 minutes)

In today's lesson the PRESESSION and PERSPECTIVE sections will merge so they can be handled as one large segment of 15-20 minutes.

As the group gathers, hand out copies of "Jerusalem's Most Wanted" activity sheet to each person. Have students count off in fours to form small buzz groups. Each group will represent one person in the skit. Group one will be Claudius, two will be Joel, three is Festus and four is Agrippa. Also give one piece of blank paper to each group.

Ask each group to quickly choose a secretary. Then they will look up the verses belonging to their person in the skit and read them silently. For example: the group who is Festus should read Acts 25: 6, 7, 9-12. The group should decide what these people said and thought about Paul and have the secretary write it in the group's own words on the blank paper. Allow about 5-7 minutes for this part of the activity.

These groups should be able to converse quietly. You can permit them to move into the four corners of the room so they have more room and less distractions.

PERSPECTIVE

(10 minutes)

Ask one person from each group to read the group's paraphrase for the skit. Select one of your better readers to be the host, I. Will Catchem. Let the characters form a group around the host. Have them read the skit aloud while the rest of the class follow along on their activity sheets.

Optional: For extra realism let these characters use a disconnected microphone or a large spoon and hand it from one character to the other as they read. Adding some part of a costume or prop such as a robe (choir or bath), a piece of material for a belt or head covering, sandals, a toy sword, a crown (from a local fast-food restaurant), a scroll, *etc. makes this more enjoyable for your students.*

Have people regroup and debrief them using questions like these: What was the message that Paul kept repeating to his accusers? How did they react to his message? Why do you think they responded in this way?

In each situation the problem was a disguised opportunity that let Paul speak out and tell who Jesus is and why Paul trusted Him. As tough as some of these problems were, there were even more difficult ones ahead for Paul before he reached Rome and the court of Caesar.

PROBE

(20 minutes)

Pass out "The Unsinkable Apostle Paul" activity sheets. Have students take turns reading this aloud.

Paul was placed under the charge of a Roman officer named Julius. Luke went along with Paul to offer help and comfort.

They set sail for Italy together. The second ship they took was probably a grain ship which was one of a large fleet of freighters transporting wheat from Egypt to Rome on a regular basis. It had a group of prisoners and perhaps some other passengers, besides the freight it was carrying.

Travel during Paul's lifetime was difficult. There were no commercial passenger boats. Passengers had to bring their own food and go ashore to find sleeping places if there were night landings.

What was the trouble they had from the beginning of the trip? (Terrible windstorms.) **Sea travel was dangerous.** Windstorms often caused great delays in reaching the desired destinations.

Check out Acts 27:9. What was the reason Paul warned the captain not to continue the voyage? (Sailing was dangerous because it was after the Fast, i.e. late in the season.) Roman law banned voyages between November 10 through March 10. During this period the weather was bad and it was rainy. There were no navigation tools. Direction was based on the stars. If the skies were cloudy the stars couldn't be seen and navigation was questionable. Ships traveled as close to the shore lines as possible because of the dangers involved in open water.

How did the sailors feel about the storm? (They were afraid.) **What did they do to try and save the boat?** (Tied ropes around it to hold it together, dropped anchors, threw the cargo and equipment overboard.) **What was the attitude of almost everyone on the ship?** (They gave up hope of being saved.) Because they had reached the limit of their human resources, they despaired of life itself.

How did Paul react to the situation? (He was hopeful, believed the Lord would save them, encouraged everyone else.) **Why did he feel that way?** (God sent an angel to tell him it would be all right.) **Paul prayed about the problems they faced and trusted God to help them.** Paul knew about divine resources and turned to the only one who could help in this seemingly impossible circumstance.

Why do you think it is easier for people in a tough situation to react the way the crew did rather than the way Paul did? Point out that the crew was acting on what they could see— the wind, the waves, and being lost. Paul was acting on what he could <u>not</u> see—God's promise.

Check out Acts 27:31, 32. What did Paul tell the Roman officer to do when some of the sailors tried to escape? (Stop the men from getting into the lifeboat.) On board the ship the first in command was the Roman officer, then the ship captain, so Julius was in charge of giving the orders. This was important because later Julius stopped the soldiers from killing the prisoners, including Paul. God had planned everything perfectly. Everyone had to stay together or they wouldn't be saved.

What is the first thing people want to do in a tough situation? (Get out of it.) Point out that God didn't take Paul out of the storm, but He was with him in it and helped him get through it. Paul wasn't miraculously snatched from the ship and placed on shore. He had to try to reach shore the best he could like the others. But because he trusted Christ to help him, the Lord saved his life and those of everyone with him.

Read Acts 27:34, 35. What did Paul do just before the shipwreck? (Urged people to eat, ate some bread.) Notice that Paul was not only concerned about himself, but also the welfare of all those with him in the storm.

We are never in problems alone. Others are also involved. These are usually those who are closest to us—family and friends. **The Lord wants us to trust Him and bravely do what He commands. What happened when everyone followed Paul's example?** (All 276 of them were saved.) Our reactions to the obstacles can help or hinder others. If we trust God and follow Him they will be encouraged to do the same. If we doubt the Lord and disobey, that also affects them.

What happened to Paul when he put wood on the fire? (A snake bit him.) Again Paul trusted God and the Lord protected him. Later the islanders grew to respect and love Paul as he healed their sick and told them about Jesus. Paul saw every problem as an opportunity to tell others about Christ—even a shipwreck and a snake!

When Paul finally reached Rome he was allowed to rent a house. He lived there for two years. Even though a soldier guarded him at all times, Paul kept on telling everyone about Jesus.

PERSONALIZE

Before class, write the following references on the chalkboard: Psalm 91:14, 15; Proverbs 3:5, 6; John 14:1; John 16:33; Romans 8:35, 37-39; 1 Thessalonians 5:16-18. These are verses that will help your students identify Biblical principles in dealing with obstacles in their Christian walk. Assign these verses to different students and have them be prepared to read them aloud. **Let's see if we can find any clues from these verses on how to handle problems that we may have.**

As the verses are read, list the hints they give. Write these opposite the verses you listed. Examples are: Psalm 91:14, 15 (love God, call upon Him); Proverbs 3:5, 6 (trust God to direct you, acknowledge Him in everything); John 14:1 (don't be troubled but trust in Jesus as well as God); John 16:33 (be at peace because Jesus has overcome the world); Romans 8:35, 37-39 (nothing can separate us from God's love, through Him we are more than conquerors); 1 Thessalonians 5:16-18 (be joyful always, pray continually, give thanks in all circumstances).

Talk about these principles, using questions such as these: Are they always easy to follow? Why or why not? What do we need to be convinced of in order to trust God? What has the Lord promised for those who trust Him in every problem? How will following these tips help us? How will our obedience in doing them affect others?

Hand out a card to each person. **Every day we are called upon to show Christian courage and trust the Lord to help us conquer the obstacles that stand in our way. Choose the verse that is most helpful to you and copy it on the card. Keep it handy so it will help you to know what to do when you face obstacles in following Christ.**

PRAYER/PRAISE

Remember that the important thing is not escaping the problem, but trusting God to be with you in it. He will help you overcome it when you follow His guidance.

Encourage students to take their cards home and display them in a spot where they will be reminded of God's help.

Read the Bible verses. Tell what happened as if you are the witness on the show.

HOST: Welcome to the number one law enforcement show of the day, Jerusalem's Most Wanted. I'm your host, I. Will Catchem. This week we're profiling one of the top men on our criminal list, Paul of Tarsus. Let's allow our guest witnesses to tell us more about him. Claudius, the Roman officer in charge at Fort Antonio, will tell us about Paul's crime that caused his arrest.

CLAUDIUS: (Acts 21:31-34)

HOST: What happened then?

CLAUDIUS: (Acts 22:30)

HOST: Then he was guilty of . . . ?

CLAUDIUS: (Acts 23:29)

HOST: Hmm. I wonder if we have the right man? Perhaps a member of the Sanhedrin can help us. Joel, the Pharisee, what crime did you find Paul had committed?

JOEL: (Acts 23:6-9)

HOST: Uh, thank you, Joel. This is not what we expected. Later Paul was transferred from Jerusalem to Caesarea. Perhaps Festus, the Roman governor there, can clear things up.

FESTUS: (Acts 25:6, 7, 9-12)

HOST: I see. So far we haven't established this man's crime, but I'm sure there must be one. Right? King Agrippa, you have a Jewish background. What was your opinion of Paul?

AGRIPPA: (Acts 26:27-32)

HOST: This show is falling apart. Haven't we got anybody who can prove that Paul committed a crime? What? There isn't anybody left to interview? This program is a disaster. The only thing Paul seems to have done is to trust this Jesus no matter what obstacles stood in his way and tell others about Him. And that is not a crime. In fact if more people were like Paul we wouldn't need this program. What am I saying? I would be out of a job! Well, folks, if you can give us any more information on Paul, our phone lines are open and our operators are standing by. Until next week this is your host, I. Will Catchem, saying "Goodnight."

from the desk of . . .

Dr. Luke

THE UNSINKABLE APOSTLE PAUL

Dear Friends,

What a trip we've had with Paul! First we sailed north of the island of Cyprus to Myra. There we were moved to another ship for the rest of the voyage to Italy.

From the beginning we had terrible windstorms. It took a long time to reach a harbor on the island of Crete. Paul told the captain that if he went on he would lose the ship, its cargo, and maybe even our lives. But he kept on trying to reach a better harbor for the winter.

We set sail on a beautiful warm day with a gentle south breeze. But shortly after we got under way a hurricane wind swept down on us from the island. The sailors were hardly able to haul up the lifeboat. The crew tied ropes around the ship to hold it together. Because they were afraid of getting stuck on sandbars, they dropped anchor and let the ship be driven by the violent wind. Soon they threw all the cargo and equipment overboard. We stopped eating and even gave up hope of being saved.

Then Paul told us that God had sent an angel to tell him not to be afraid. The Lord told Paul he would safely reach Rome and tell people there about Jesus. God said He would protect all 276 of us and no one would die.

For fourteen horrible days we were driven wildly by the howling winds. Then one night the sailors discovered the water was getting shallow. They dropped four anchors and prayed for daylight. A few of them pretended to lower some anchors. But instead they were trying to escape in the lifeboat. Paul told Julius, the Roman officer in charge of the prisoners, that if they left the ship we could not be saved. So Julius ordered the ropes on the lifeboat to be cut and it fell away into the monster waves.

Just before dawn, Paul spoke to us. His trust in God's loving protection cheered all of us and we joined him in eating some bread. When daylight came, we saw land. The sailors hoped to be able to sail into harbor, but the ship got stuck on a sandbar. Soon the raging waves began to break the ship into pieces. The soldiers were going to kill the prisoners so none of them would escape. But Julius wanted to save Paul, so he ordered everyone who could swim to try to swim to shore. The rest of us floated on wooden boards and pieces of the ship. Paul was right, in spite of the smashing surf all of us made it safely to land!

The island was called Malta. The people were kind and made a fire on shore for us. Paul was putting a pile of wood on the fire when a poisonous snake came out of the sticks and bit him on the hand. We thought he would die, but Paul calmly shook the snake off into the fire. His hand never even swelled up! Paul surely trusts the Lord. I'm convinced we'll reach Rome safely. I just pray that I might follow Christ as bravely as Paul does!

Luke

PAUL'S LETTERS

AIM: That your students will realize that Paul's letters have meaning for them today

SCRIPTURE: Romans 1:1, 7; 2 Corinthians 1:1; Galatians 1:1, 2; Ephesians 1:1; 4:2-4; 6:1-22; 1 Thessalonians 1:1; 1 Timothy 1:1, 2; 2 Timothy 1:1, 2; Titus 1:1, 4; James 1:1; 2 Peter 1:1; 3 John 1:1; Jude 1:1

PREPARATION:
1. Photocopy activity sheets—one for each student.
2. Optional: Make a scroll from "old manuscript" paper as described in PRESESSION, Lesson 1, "My Bible Library."
3. Prepare balloons for the balloon bash as described in PERSPECTIVE.

PRESESSION (5-10 minutes)

ACTIVITIES
* Contrast letters in Bible times with those today

MATERIALS
* A letter
* A scroll: one sheet 8 1/2" x 13" paper, two 10" dowels
* *Optional: "old-manuscript" paper for scroll*

PERSPECTIVE (10 minutes)

ACTIVITIES
* Take part in a balloon bash to discover who wrote some of the letters in the New Testament and to whom they were written

MATERIALS
* Bibles
* Balloons, slips of paper—one for each student

PROBE (20 minutes)

ACTIVITIES
* Learn more about Paul's letter to the Ephesians by completing a book review column

MATERIALS
* Bibles
* "Question Mark" Activity Sheet
* *Optional: Map of Bible lands showing Ephesus*

PERSONALIZE (15-20 minutes)

ACTIVITIES
* Use a code to discover God's weapons you can use against Satan

MATERIALS
* Bibles
* "God's Armor" Activity Sheet
* *Optional: picture of a Roman soldier wearing armor*

PRESESSION

If desired, make your scroll look like an old manuscript by using the method suggested. Display your letter. **Probably all of you have a received a letter at some time or other. How do you know who sent it?** (By the name and return address on the envelope; the signature at the end of the letter.)

Letters that were written thousands of years ago looked much different from ours today. Display the scroll. **Letters then were written on the skin of a sheep or goat or made of papyrus, a paper made from a common water plant.** Unroll the scroll. If the letter was several feet long, it was difficult to completely unroll it to find out who sent it. So the name of the person who wrote the letter was placed right at the beginning, along with the name of the person or group to whom it was sent.

Why do people write letters? (Tell someone something; let others know how they are; ask a question; request a favor; get information about something; cheer people up; tell someone how much you love them.) **People in Bible times wrote letters for the very same reasons.**

What is your favorite kind of letter? Let students briefly share. Most people like to get letters from a friend or family member. **Why do you like to get letters?** (Makes me feel important; find out things; shows me somebody cares about me.)

There are twenty-one letters in the New Testament, written by at least five different men. Let's find out who wrote some of them, and to whom they sent the letters.

PERSPECTIVE

Before class, write several references from Bible letters on slips of paper for the balloon bash. You will need one reference for each student. Use some like these: Romans 1:1, 7; 2 Corinthians 1:1; Galatians 1:1, 2; Ephesians 1:1; 1 Thessalonians 1:1; 1 Timothy 1:1, 2; 2 Timothy 1:1, 2; Titus 1:1, 4; James 1:1; 2 Peter 1:1; 3 John 1:1*; Jude 1:1.

Insert the paper slips, blow up the balloons, and tie the balloons shut. Let students choose balloons and bash them any way they desire—sit on them, step on them, with their hands, etc. **Look up the reference and be ready to share the information as to who wrote the letter and to whom it was sent.**

Note: 1, 2, and 3 John reads, "the elder," which is a favorite term for John.

Most of the letters in the New Testament were written by Paul: Romans; 1 and 2 Corinthians; Galatians; Ephesians; Philippians; **Colossians; 1 and 2 Thessalonians; 1 and 2 Timothy; Titus; and Philemon.**

Two were written by Peter: 1 and 2 Peter. One was written by James, the brother of Jesus: James. Three were written by the apostle John: 1, 2, and 3 John. He also wrote the prophetic book of the Revelation. **One was written by Jude** (possibly also a brother of Jesus): **Jude.**

The writer of the letter to the Hebrews is not identified, but most scholars think it was Paul or someone close to Paul. He was a Jewish Christian befriended by Priscilla and Aquila.

Many of the places mentioned in the book of Acts are places to which Paul traveled. Later he sent letters to the people there. Paul wrote these letters to the churches and to individual Christians to help them live the way God wanted. Paul had been writing letters

as he traveled around establishing churches and visiting the family of God. As a prisoner in Rome, he continued to write letters to help Christians be faithful in their everyday lives. **One of the groups to which Paul wrote was the church at Ephesus.**

PROBE

If you have a map, point out Ephesus on it. Ephesus was the most important city in Asia Minor [Turkey]. It was located on the most direct sea and land routes to the eastern provinces of the Roman empire. **Paul had been in Ephesus more than once.** It was there that he took Priscilla and Aquila from Corinth to work for the Lord.

One outstanding event in Ephesus was the riot caused by the worshipers of Diana. Demetrius, the silversmith, stirred up trouble against Paul and his friends. The people were turning from the worship of Diana to the worship of the true God, and so they were no longer buying idols from the silversmiths. The riot finally was stopped by the town clerk and Paul and his companions were saved.

As Paul sat in his house in Rome, he thought about the Christians in Ephesus. He thought about the way the church had grown and he wanted to help them live lives pleasing to God. So he decided to write them a letter.

Pass out copies of "Question Mark" activity sheet. This is written as though a book reviewer was answering questions about this letter. Students will be filling in blanks to complete information about it. Most of the material is taken from the sixth chapter of this Bible book.

Depending on the size of your class, assign small groups or individuals to do each segment of this activity. **Look up the references and write the correct answers in the blanks. When you are finished, be prepared to share your information with the group.** Allow about half of this time period to complete the exercise.

Why did Paul write this letter? (Tell Christians to be humble and gentle, patient and loving; to keep the unity of the Spirit peacefully.) **Why do you think this is important?** (So they wouldn't fight among themselves; non-believers would see what following Christ really means; they could do the work God wanted them to do.) **Loving people who have differences and faults is sometimes hard to do.**

What did he remind them of that would be helpful in accomplishing this goal? (They were already unified into one body, called to one hope, and guided by one Spirit.) When we focus on the things that Christians have in common and let the Holy Spirit guide us, then we are truly unified.

What was Paul's advice to children? (To obey their parents and honor them.) We obey our parents while we are still children. When we become adults we are to continue to honor them—that is, to show them love and respect.

What was his caution to fathers and mothers? (To not make their children angry.) **What were they to do instead?** (Teach and train them to follow the Lord.) This means in a loving way like Jesus treated the children.

How did Paul tell Christian employees to live? (Employees should work hard and gladly as they would for Jesus, not just because their bosses were watching them.) **What about bosses?** (Treat the employees right because God is everyone's boss.) **What doesn't God show?** (Favoritism.) God treats everyone alike.

How should Christians live? (Be strong in the Lord's power; using God's armor to defeat Satan—that is truth, righteousness, peace, faith, salvation, and God's Word; praying for each other.) **What are some things we can pray about for each other?** (Health; guidance; family

problems; to love each other more; forgiveness; grow in Christ.)

Who brought the letter to the Ephesians? (Tychicus.) This man's home was in Asia Minor [Turkey]. He also brought a letter from Paul to the church in Colossae. He was one of Paul's trusted co-workers and did many errands for him.

Imagine how happy the Christians in Ephesus were when they opened and read this letter from their beloved teacher, Paul!

PERSONALIZE

(15-20 minutes)

When Paul wrote this letter he was a prisoner in Rome. A Roman soldier guarded him at all times. Perhaps he was looking at this soldier when he wrote the final words of his letter to the Ephesians. In those days soldiers fought in hand-to-hand combat with the enemy. They wore different uniforms and carried different weapons from those of today. Because Paul knew that being a Christian among unbelieving people is not easy, he used a word picture to explain how a Christian should live.

The same descriptive picture he used then can still help us today. Distribute copies of "God's Armor" activity sheet. Answers are: belt, truth, lies, truth; breastplate, righteousness, Jesus, time, obey; Gospel peace, others, Jesus; shield, faith, faith, Jesus, insults, setbacks, temptations; helmet, salvation, Heaven, doubts, God, Jesus, saving, sword, Spirit, Word, God, Satan, trust, Word. Go over this activity together. Have the group share their answers aloud.

Paul was very interested in one young Christian soldier, Timothy. When Paul knew that he would soon give his life for Christ, he wrote to Timothy telling him to endure hard-ship as a good soldier of Jesus Christ. **Check out 2 Timothy 4:7, 8 to see what he said would be the reward for _all_ Christian soldiers.** Have someone read this passage aloud. **What is the reward?** (Crown of righteousness.) In those days sports winners won a crown of laurel leaves. This was the most sought-after prize even though it soon turned brown and died. **The crown of God's approval waiting for us in Heaven will never decay.**

This letter to Timothy is believed to be the last letter Paul wrote. It is probable that Paul was beheaded during the time when Nero, emperor of Rome, persecuted Christians. **Paul died because of his faith, but rejoiced that a crown from Christ awaited him in Heaven!**

PRAYER/PRAISE

There is much evil in the world. Christians must be willing to fight for the right. We can only do that when we have on all of God's armor. Close in prayer asking God to help each person to remember and use all the weapons He has provided for them.

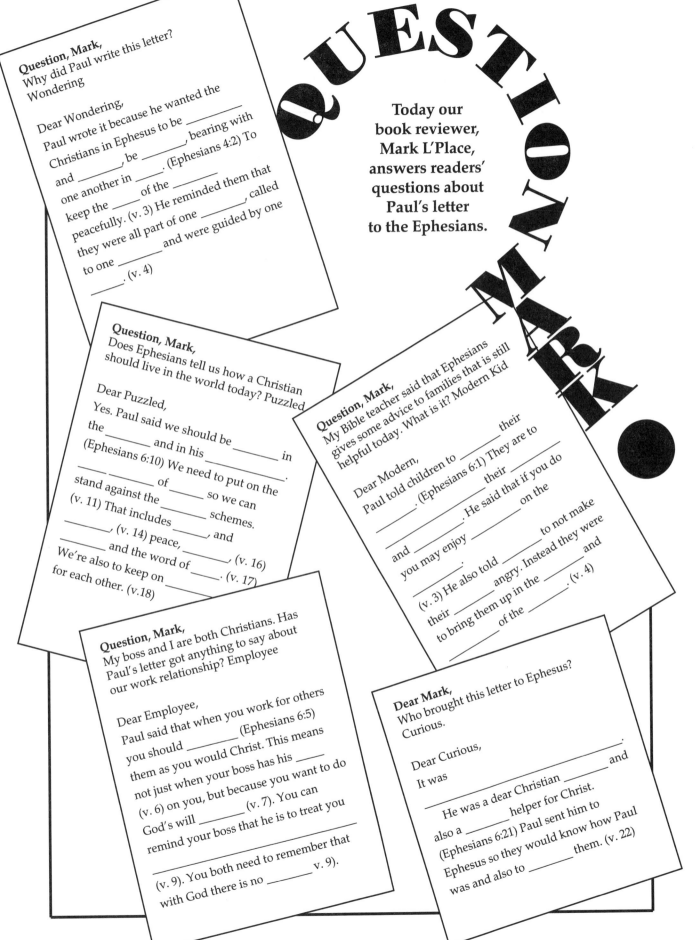

QUESTION MARK

Today our book reviewer, Mark L'Place, answers readers' questions about Paul's letter to the Ephesians.

Question, Mark,
Why did Paul write this letter? Wondering

Dear Wondering,
Paul wrote it because he wanted the Christians in Ephesus to be _____ and _____, be _____, bearing with one another in _____. (Ephesians 4:2) To keep the _____ of the _____ peacefully. (v. 3) He reminded them that they were all part of one _____, called to one _____ and were guided by one _____. (v. 4)

Question, Mark,
Does Ephesians tell us how a Christian should live in the world today? Puzzled

Dear Puzzled,
Yes. Paul said we should be _____ in the _____ and in his _____. (Ephesians 6:10) We need to put on the _____ of _____ so we can stand against the _____ schemes. (v. 11) That includes _____, (v. 14) peace, _____, and _____ and the word of _____. (v. 16) _____. (v. 17) We're also to keep on _____ for each other. (v.18)

Question, Mark,
My Bible teacher said that Ephesians gives some advice to families that is still helpful today. What is it? Modern Kid

Dear Modern,
Paul told children to _____ their _____. (Ephesians 6:1) They are to _____ their _____. He said that if you do _____ and _____ on the you may enjoy _____. (v. 3) He also told _____ to not make their _____ angry. Instead they were to bring them up in the _____ and _____ of the _____. (v. 4)

Question, Mark,
My boss and I are both Christians. Has Paul's letter got anything to say about our work relationship? Employee

Dear Employee,
Paul said that when you work for others you should _____ (Ephesians 6:5) them as you would Christ. This means not just when your boss has his _____ (v. 6) on you, but because you want to do God's will _____ (v. 7). You can remind your boss that he is to treat you _____ (v. 9). You both need to remember that with God there is no _____ v. 9).

Dear Mark,
Who brought this letter to Ephesus? Curious.

Dear Curious,
It was _____ and _____.
He was a dear Christian _____ also a _____ helper for Christ. (Ephesians 6:21) Paul sent him to Ephesus so they would know how Paul was and also to _____ them. (v. 22)

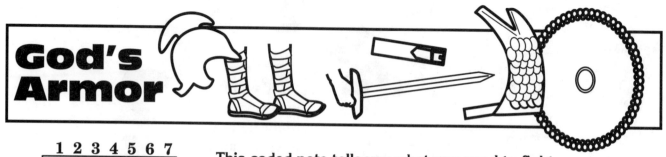

God's Armor

	1	2	3	4	5	6	7
W	A	E	I	M	Q	U	
X	B	F	J	N	R	V	
Y	C	G	K	O	S	W	Y
Z	D	H	L	P	T	X	Z

This coded note tells you what you need to fight the evil powers of darkness. Can you decode it so you can be strong in the Lord and His mighty power?

For example: W1= A

---

1. The __ __ __ __ of __ __ __ __ __ . Satan uses __ __ __ __
   X1 W2 Z3 Z5   Z5 X5 W6 Z5 Z2   Z3 W3 W2 Y5
   as weapons, but God's __ __ __ __ __ can defeat them.
   Z5 X5 W6 Z5 Z2

2. The __ __ __ __ __ __ __ __ __ __ __ of
   X1 X5 W2 W1 Y5 Z5 Z4 Z3 W1 Z5 W2
   __ __ __ __ __ __ __ __ __ __ __ __ __ . The only way you can be right with
   X5 W3 Y2 Z2 Z5 W2 Y4 W6 Y5 X4 W2 Y5 Y5
   God is to talk with __ __ __ __ __ , spend __ __ __ __ with Him, and __ __ __ __
   X3 W2 Y5 W6 Y5   Z5 W3 W4 W2   Y4 X1 W2 Y7
   Him.

3. Feet fitted with the readiness of the __ __ __ __ __ __ of __ __ __ __ __ . Part of your
   Y2 Y4 Y5 Z4 W2 Z3   Z4 W2 W1 Y1 W2
   job as a Christian is to tell __ __ __ __ __ __ about __ __ __ __ __ .
   Y4 Z5 Z2 W2 X5 Y5   X3 W2 Y5 W6 Y5

4. The __ __ __ __ __ __ of __ __ __ __ __ . Because of your __ __ __ __ __ in
   Y5 Z2 W3 W2 Z3 Z1   X2 W1 W3 Z5 Z2   X2 W1 W3 Z5 Z2
   __ __ __ __ __ you are able to see beyond Satan's arrows of __ __ __ __ __ __ __ ,
   X3 W2 Y5 W6 Y5   W3 X4 Y5 W6 Z3 Z5 Y5
   __ __ __ __ __ __ __ __ , and __ __ __ __ __ __ __ __ __ __ __ and know that
   Y5 W2 Z5 X1 W1 Y1 Y3 Y5   Z5 W2 W4 Z4 Z5 W1 Z5 W3 Y4 X4 Y5
   Christ has already defeated the devil.

5. The __ __ __ __ __ __ of __ __ __ __ __ __ __ __ __ . Knowing that you can look
   Z2 W2 Z3 W4 W2 Z5   Y5 W1 Z3 X6 W1 Z5 W3 Y4 X4
   forward to __ __ __ __ __ __ stops __ __ __ __ __ __ about __ __ __ ,
   Z2 W2 W1 X6 W2 X4   Z1 Y4 W6 X1 Z5 Y5   Y2 Y4 Z1
   __ __ __ __ __ and His __ __ __ __ __ __ work for you.
   X3 W2 Y5 W6 Y5   Y5 W1 X6 W3 X4 Y2

6. The __ __ __ __ __ of the __ __ __ __ __ __ which is the __ __ __ __ of
   Y5 Y6 Y4 X5 Z1   Y5 Z4 W3 X5 W3 Z5   Y6 Y4 X5 Z1
   __ __ __ . With this mighty weapon you can defeat __ __ __ __ __ as you
   Y2 Y4 Z1   Y5 W1 Z5 W1 X4
   __ __ __ __ __ in the truth of God's __ __ __ __ .
   Z5 X5 W6 Y5 Z5   Y6 Y4 X5 Z1

CREATION TO CHRIST

AIM: That your students will understand that when the time was right, God sent His only Son to bring salvation to all people

SCRIPTURE: Genesis 2:21-23; 7:6, 7; 12:3; Exodus 3:10, 14; Joshua 1:1, 5; Judges 2:16; 1 Samuel 10:1, 24; 2 Kings 17:13, 15; 2 Chronicles 36:15, 16, 20; Malachi 3:1; Luke 2:1-20 (When God is ready to complete His plan, He keeps His promise to send a Savior to the world)

PREPARATION:
1. Photocopy activity sheets—one for each student.

PRESESSION (5-10 minutes)

ACTIVITIES
* Write words that can be made from the letters in the phrase GOD'S PROMISE

MATERIALS
* 8 1/2" x 11" paper—one sheet for each student
* Optional: small award (sticker, pencil, bookmark, etc.)

PERSPECTIVE (10 minutes)

ACTIVITIES
* Compare God's promise of a Savior to the launching of a spacecraft

MATERIALS
* Bibles
* Optional: Picture of a rocket, spacecraft, or astronaut

PROBE (20 minutes)

ACTIVITIES
* Match Bible events with correct references
* Arrange events in "countdown" order

MATERIALS
* Bibles
* "History Mystery" Activity Sheet

PERSONALIZE (15-20 minutes)

ACTIVITIES
* Learn about some of the promises God has made to people
* Have an opportunity to accept Christ as your Savior

MATERIALS
* "Promises, Promises" Activity Sheet

PRESESSION

As students arrive today hand out sheets of paper. **Write the phrase "GOD'S PROMISES" at the top of the page. See how many words you can make out of the letters in that phrase.** Examples are: room; good; dog; prim; more; doom; etc.

When everyone has had an opportunity to make several words, have them share their lists with the group.

Optional: If desired, you may give a small award such as a sticker, pencil, or bookmark to the person who has the longest list.

Guide the conversation to focus on promises in general using questions like these: Do you ever make promises? What are they? Do you ever break promises? Why is a promise important? What do we mean when we say "I promise"?

The Bible is the story of a great promise from God. The Old Testament tells that God promised to send a Savior to His people, and the New Testament tells how He kept His promise.

PERSPECTIVE

Have you ever waited a long time for something you wanted very much? What was it? Allow students to briefly share. **While you are waiting for something, how does time pass for you?** (Slowly.) **Why do you think that is true?** (Want it so much; are so excited about it.) **How do you think an astronaut feels as he waits for the countdown before being launched into outer space?** (Like it takes forever.) Those last ten seconds must seem like ten years!

Display picture of spacecraft or astronaut if you have one. **When you see or hear about a rocket being launched in the space program, it is the result of many stages in a master plan.** The space administration sets specific times for these different phases. A certain amount of time is allowed to get everything ready. When the astronauts have completed their training and their spacecraft is ready, then the rocket is launched—weather conditions permitting.

Sometimes, however, plans have to be changed. Perhaps a defect in some mechanism is detected or the astronauts who were chosen for the mission are injured during the training program and other people have to be chosen to take their places. Plans of scientists, engineers, construction workers, and all the others involved often have to be changed.

It isn't possible for people to know everything, and sometimes their planning is wrong. Have you ever had a plan that went wrong? What happened? Let people briefly share their experiences. You can share something yourself such as rain on a day that you planned a picnic. **How do you feel when your plans have to be changed?** (Sad; angry; upset.) **How do you feel when everything goes just the way you plan it?** (Happy; relieved; excited.)

God had a plan and it was perfect. He sent His Son, Jesus, to be the Savior at exactly the right time in history!

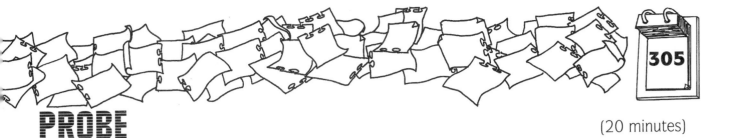

PROBE

(20 minutes)

Hand out copies of "History Mystery" activity sheet. Depending on the size of your class, divide the group into several small teams and assign each one several references. When they have matched the events to their references, they can share their findings with the class. Do only the first section of this exercise now. Answers are: a, j, h, b, c, f, d, i, k, g, e.

Now have students number these events in countdown order from ten to zero. Answers are: 5, 0, 1, 4, 9, 2, 8, 10, 3, 6, 7. Have students follow along on their activity sheets as you briefly review the events together.

10 God created a beautiful, perfect world and placed Adam and Eve in it. But when they gave in to Satan's temptation, sin entered the world. **What promise did God give Adam and Eve?** (Someday He would send someone who would overcome Satan.)

9 As the number of people increased so did sin, until only one man and his family were obedient to God. **What promise did God give Noah and his family?** (They would be saved in the ark from the great flood by which God destroyed the earth.) The population of the world started all over again with this family.

8 Many years later God began a special nation of people who would obey His Word and show the rest of the world that He is the true God. **What promise did God give Abraham?** (Someday all the nations of the world would be blessed by his family.)

7 Abraham's grandson, Jacob, and his family moved to Egypt because of a food shortage. When their number grew very large, a cruel king made them slaves. God chose Moses to lead His people to freedom. **What promise did God give Moses?** (He would guide them; give them a new homeland.)

6 God chose Joshua to lead the Israelites into Canaan, the promised land. **Joshua told the Israelites to choose whether they would worship idols or the one, true living God.**

What promise did the people give God? (Promised to serve Him and be faithful to Him.)

5 After the people were settled in the promised land, who did God give them to rule and lead them into battles? (Judges.) Some of these leaders were very faithful to God, and others were very disobedient. Later, the Israelites decided that they wanted a king like the nations around them. **Who was really their King?** (God.) Still they begged for an earthly ruler.

4 Finally God allowed His people to be ruled by kings. **Who were the first three Jewish kings?** (Saul, David, Solomon.) The kingdom of Israel became a great and powerful nation. God blessed them as long as they were obedient to Him.

3 The kingdom divided into two parts— (Israel—north and Judah—south.) Some of the kings were obedient to God but most were very wicked and led God's people away from worshiping Him. **What happened when the kings disobeyed God?** (They were punished.) **What happened when they worshiped Him?** (They were blessed.) They never seemed to learn their lesson.

2 Finally God allowed the Israelites to be taken captive by enemy armies. They dreamed of having a king, like David, who would set them free and build up a great kingdom again. God's spokesmen, the prophets, foretold that someday a King would come. More than 700 years before His birth, they foretold that He would be born in Bethlehem. He was not to be an earthly king. **What was His kingdom to be called?** (Kingdom of Heaven.)

1 For 400 years after the prophet Malachi gave God's message there was silence from Heaven. Finally, Rome ruled the world. God's people were under its control. They were unhappy and longed to be free. They wanted the promised Messiah to lead them in battles against the Romans.

The Bible says that in the "fullness of time" God sent His Son. Certain things had to be ready before the promised Savior could come. All these were brought about by the Romans: Peace—because Rome conquered all the surrounding nations; the freedom to worship God—different religions were permitted; a common language—nearly everyone in the Roman empire used Greek—the New Testament was written in Greek so nearly everyone could read it; good roads for traveling.

O Zero Hour! God kept His promise! At last His Son, Jesus Christ, was born to bring salvation to all people!

PERSONALIZE

(15-20 minutes)

The Bible is full of God's promises to people. Let's see what some of them are. Distribute copies of "Promises, Promises" activity sheet. Read the list of promises aloud while the group follows along on their papers. Briefly talk about the promises using questions like these: Which promises are for life now? Which ones are for the future? Are there any that are more important than the rest? Which ones? Is there any one that you want more than the others? Why?

Optional: Be alert to any words or terms your students might not understand such as "acceptance with God," "eternal life," or "crown of righteousness." Go over these with the group helping to explain them in terms they can understand.

Ask someone to read aloud the next instructions on the activity sheet. They will use the circled letters to write a sentence telling what they must do to claim all the promises listed above. Depending on your time schedule this can be done individually or as a group. The answer is "Accept Jesus as your Savior."

You can trust God to keep His promises. He has promised salvation and never-ending life to all who believe and obey His Son. Have you accepted Christ as your Savior so that you can enjoy these promises? If not, why not do it today?

Have you promised to be a faithful follower? Are you keeping that promise? If you are, thank God for the promised Savior, Jesus your Lord. If not, perhaps you want to ask His forgiveness and help to keep your promise to Him.

PRAYER/PRAISE

Have a time for silent prayer and thought. Encourage students to consider God's promised Savior, Jesus. This can be a time for a new commitment to Him or a renewal of that relationship.

Thank God for keeping His promises. Ask Jesus to help you keep your promises to Him. Be ready to talk and pray with needy students after class.

HISstory Mystery

Are you ready, Bible Investigators? Look up the references. Write the letter of the event in Column 2 by its match in Column 1.

Malachi 3:1 _____

Joshua 1:1, 5 _____

2 Chronicles 36:15,16, 20 _____

1 Samuel 10:1, 24 _____

Genesis 12:3 _____

Judges 2:16 _____

Luke 2:11-16 _____

Genesis 7:6, 7 _____

Exodus 3:10, 14 _____

2 Kings 17:13, 15 _____

Genesis 3:21-23 _____

a. prophet predicts coming of the Savior

b. Saul made first king over God's people

c. God promises worldwide blessing through Abraham

d. Jesus Christ, the son of God, is born!

e. beautiful garden no longer home for Adam and Eve

f. nation of Israel to be ruled by judges

g. both Israel and Judah disobey by worshiping idols

h. God's people taken as captives to enemy's land

i. God sends great flood; Noah and family saved

j. God picks Joshua to lead Israelites to promised land

k. God calls Moses to lead Israelites from slavery in Egypt

Now number them in "countdown" sequence from 10 to 0.

____ nation of Israel to be ruled by judges

____ Jesus Christ, the son of God, is born!

____ prophet predicts coming of the Savior

____ Saul made first king over God's people

____ God sends great flood; Noah and family saved

____ God's people taken as captives to enemy's land

____ God promises worldwide blessing through Abraham

____ beautiful garden no longer home for Adam and Eve

____ both Israel and Judah disobey by worshiping idols

____ God picks Joshua to lead Israelites into promised land

____ God calls Moses to lead Israelites from slavery in Egypt

50A

Promises, Promises

The Bible contains many promises for you. Here is a list of some of the things God wants to give you.

LOV[E]
CON[S]TANT [C]OMPANIONSHIP
FRIEND[S]HIP
FORGI[V]ENESS OF [S]INS
ACCEPTANCE FROM G[O]D
POWE[R] OVER TEMPTATION
PE[A]CE
HEAVENLY R[E]WARD
COMFO[R]T
[J]OY

PROTECTION FROM S[A]TAN
G[U]IDAN[C]E FOR LIFE
ETERNAL L[I]FE
HOME IN HE[A]VEN
NEW BOD[Y]
RELIEF FROM TEARS AND [P]AIN
FREED[O]M
CROWN OF RIGHTEO[U]SNESS
WI[S]DOM
LIGH[T]

You can have all these things. But there is one important thing you have to do first. Unscramble the boxed letters to discover what that is and write it on the lines below.

— — — — — — — —   — — — — — — —

— — — — — — .

Why not do it today?

JESUS CHRIST, SON OF GOD, SAVIOR

AIM: That your students will understand the importance of believing in Jesus as Son of God and Savior for all people

SCRIPTURE: Matthew 10:32; Mark 1:17; 16:15, 16; John 1:35-41, 43, 59; 3:1-7; 4:42; 6:47; 14:15; 15:17; 2 Corinthians 5:19; 6:2; Revelation 2:10 (Reviewing the purpose for Jesus' coming to the world)

PREPARATION:
1. Photocopy activity sheets—one for each student.
2. Prepare scrambled title cards as described in PRESESSION.
3. Make self-adhesive stickers as described in PERSONALIZE.

PRESESSION (5-10 minutes)

ACTIVITIES
* Work in teams to unscramble and identify titles given to Jesus

MATERIALS
* Bibles
* 3" x 5" cards for title cards

PERSPECTIVE (10 minutes)

ACTIVITIES
* Discuss the titles used in PRESESSION
* Become acquainted with the secret ICHTHUS sign used in the early church

MATERIALS
* Chalkboard and chalk or large sheet of paper and marker

PROBE (20 minutes)

ACTIVITIES
* Solve a puzzle about Jesus' purpose in coming to earth
* Make a coded message telling others about Jesus as the Christ, Son of God, the Savior of all people

MATERIALS
* Bibles
* "Mystery Messages" Activity Sheet

PERSONALIZE (15-20 minutes)

ACTIVITIES
* Create stickers to tell others about Jesus

MATERIALS
* Bibles
* "The Secret Sign" Activity Sheet
* Lepage's or Elmer's Mucilage, water, paint brush
* Scissors, markers or colored pencils

LESSON 51   **UNIT THEME: REVIEWING GOD'S PLAN FOR HIS PEOPLE**

PRESESSION

Before class write the following scrambled titles on 3" x 5" cards: MALB FO OGD; BARIB; SEMHIAS; THISRC; ROSVIA. Make one set of cards for every 3-4 students. As students arrive, have them form teams of no more than 3-4 people. Pass out one set of cards to each team. Explain that each of these scrambled phrases is a title that was given to Jesus.

Let teams work on unscrambling these terms for several minutes. Clap for the team members who unscramble the titles first. Allow them to read their titles. The answers are : Lamb of God; Rabbi; Messiah; Christ; Savior.

Let's all turn to John 1:35-41 and John 4:42 and take a closer look at these expressions.

PERSPECTIVE

Who called Jesus the Lamb of God? (John the Baptist.) Why do you think he used that term for Jesus? Scholars agree that this was a reference to the sacrificial lamb offered to atone for sin. John seems to be saying that sacrifice that would atone for the sin of the world. Be sure your students understand what "atone" means. A simple definition is to cleanse away or remove. In other words, Jesus would die to remove the sins of all people.

Who called Jesus "Rabbi"? (Andrew and John—two of John the Baptist's followers.) This was the Hebrew title of respect meaning "teacher."

What does Messiah mean? (The Christ.) Messiah is the Hebrew word for "anointed one" or "one chosen by God." **Christ is the Greek word that means the same thing.**

In John 4:42 some Samaritans called Jesus "Savior." What did they say about Him as Savior? (He is the Savior of the world.) Jesus is not only the one who saves, but his salvation is for all people everywhere.

There is a secret sign or name that early believers in the church used to identify themselves as followers of Jesus. During a time of persecution when believing in Jesus as the Son of God and accepting Him as Savior brought ridicule, punishment, and even death to many followers of Jesus, these Christians used a secret sign to let others know they, too, were followers.

When it was dangerous to openly proclaim the gospel, they continued to spread it by using this sign. Sometimes it was scrawled on public walls. Sometimes people would be standing talking and one person would use a walking stick or his foot to make the sign in the dust or sand. **What was it? A fish.** Make the fish symbol on the board.

Why did they use a fish? Throughout the Roman Empire the people spoke Greek. The first letters of the Greek words for "Jesus Christ, Son of God, Savior" spell the Greek word for "fish"—ICHTHUS. Write "Ichthus" on the board beside the fish symbol.

How do you think those first followers of Jesus felt, knowing that by telling others they put themselves in great danger? (Afraid; still wanted to tell others; trusted Jesus to take care of them.) **What about you? Is telling others about Jesus really important to you? Do you care what happens to them?**

Let's try an imagination situation. **Suppose you were one of those early followers of Jesus. Remember, the Romans were persecuting all Christians. Or perhaps you could be a present-day Christian in a nation that doesn't allow people to talk freely**

about Jesus, God's Son. It wouldn't be safe to admit you are a believer in Jesus because you could be thrown into jail or even lose your life! What kind of secret message might you receive from another follower of Jesus?

Optional: Really add to this imagination exercise by talking as if you are letting your students in on a secret. Talk low or whisper. Look around as if keeping watch for spies. This can be good role playing for some unknown future crisis situation. At any rate it will help your students to empathize with Christians in other lands who face this kind of persecution daily.

PROBE

(20 minutes)

Distribute copies of "Mystery Messages" activity sheet. Ask someone to read the directions at the top of the page. Allow students time to decode the first mystery message. The answer is: The Father has sent His Son to be the Savior of the world. If anyone acknowledges that Jesus is the Son of God, God lives in him and he in God. 1 John 4:14, 15. **Is that an important message to know and pass on? Why?** (Yes. It means that all people can have a loving relationship with God.)

Many of the people who followed Jesus wanted to crown Him as their king. They wanted Him to lead armies against their enemies, the Romans, and make their nation great once more. Jesus sent them away. When they came back, He said, "You do not follow me because you believe my message, but only because I provided food for you!"

Jesus did not come to be an army leader or an earthly king. Nor did He promise food for people's bodies, but food for their souls. Many turned away from Him and refused to follow Him anymore. Jesus asked His apostles if they were going to leave Him too. Peter answered, "Lord, to whom shall we go? You have the words of eternal life."

What would be different if Jesus had not come to be the Savior of the world? (Everyone would still be slaves to sin; no one would have never-ending life; couldn't be part of God's heavenly family; no one would have any hope of a better life.)

Many of the things that we take for granted because we live in a country with a Christian heritage would be omitted. Such things as hospitals and schools would be absent because they had their origins in the loving care that only Christians have for one another. People would still be living in fear, bound by superstition and the ever-present agony of death—both physical and spiritual.

The status of women would be very different as can readily be seen by comparing their status in Muslim countries with that in nations with a Christian background.

Does it make a difference if Jesus was a good man or the Son of God? Why or why not? (Yes, it makes a difference. No person can be good enough to take the punishment for the sins of all the people in the world. Only the perfect, sinless Son of God could do that.)

Like Peter, we must go to Jesus to learn about and receive eternal life. Only Jesus can save us from the punishment for our sins. Jesus once said, "No man comes to the Father but by me." **If we want to have our sins forgiven, be accepted by God, and live with Him forever in Heaven, we must believe that Jesus is the Christ, the Son of God, the Savior of the world.**

Suppose you were living under a government that persecuted Christians. You want to tell the good news about Jesus to all people. What would you say? Check out 2 Corinthians 5:19-6:2 for some ideas.

Have someone read aloud the second set of directions on the activity sheet. Maintain the feeling of using secrecy during this second part of the activity sheet. **Write what you want to say under the lines. Then put the coded words on the lines.** After students have completed this exercise, have them share their messages with the group.

Optional: An added dimension can be to have people exchange their messages and let classmates decode the messages.

Optional: If you have a longer time period, give recognition to all your students for their work. Congratulate them on becoming Fantastic Bible Investigators and encourage them to continue to check out God's Word on their own.

How important is your trust in God? Would you be willing to share it with others?

PERSONALIZE

(15-20 minutes)

Before class you will want to make the stickers in this section self-adhesive. Mix equal amounts of Elmer's or Lepage's Mucilage and water together in a small container. Apply this glue mixture to the back of each "The Secret Sign" activity page with a paintbrush. Let the pages dry completely with the glue side up.

Distribute copies of "The Secret Sign" activity sheet. Have someone read the directions aloud. Let students take turns looking up the references and reading them aloud.

Have students color the stickers with colored pencils or markers. If using the latter, wait until the pictures are dry. Students can then cut out the stickers and dampen the back side of them with a slightly wet sponge or brush.

Christians have had to give up friends, families, possessions, and sometimes even their lives for the cause of Christ. What are you willing to do to be known as a person who not only believes in Jesus Christ, Son of God, and Savior but also tells others about Him?

PRAYER/PRAISE

Allow a time for silent reflection on this question. Then have students indicate their willingness to follow Jesus regardless of the cost in exchange for the promise of never-ending life with God in *Heaven.*

Optional: Close by singing the chorus, "In My Life, Lord, Be Glorified."

Mystery Messages

You've been doing a great job, Bible Investigators. Decode the message to discover why Jesus came into the world.

CODE:

A	B	C	D	E	F	G	H	I	J	K	L	M	N	O	P	Q	R	S	T	U	V	W	X	Y	Z
S	A	V	I	O	R	B	C	D	E	F	G	H	J	K	L	M	N	P	Q	T	U	W	X	Y	Z

Example: H = M

Q C O   R S Q C O N   C S P   P O J Q   C D P

P K J   Q K   A O   Q C O   P S U E N   K R

Q C O   W K N G I   .   D R   S J Y K J O

S V F J K W G O I B O P   Q C S Q   E O P T P

D P   Q C O   P K J   K R   B K I , B K I

G D U O P   D J   C D H   S J I   C O   D J

B K I .   1   E K C J   4 : 1 4 , 1 5

Now here's your chance to become members of the super squad known as the F.B.I. (Fantastic Bible Investigators). Use the calendar code to write what you would want to tell someone about Jesus as the Christ, God's Son, your Savior. This assignment may be tough, but I know you can do it!

Sun	Mon	Tue	Wed	Thu	Fri	Sat
	1 A	2 C	3 E	4 G	5 I	6 K
7 B	8 D	9 F	10 H	11 J	12 L	13 N
14 M	15 P	16 R	17 T	18 V	19 X	20 Z
21 O	22 Q	23 S	24 U	25 W	26 Y	

_____

_____

_____

_____

THE SECRET SIGN

Since the days of the early church, Christians have used the sign of the fish as a secret symbol to show they were followers of Jesus. A list of references is given for you to use as ideas for designing your own stickers from the fish shapes. Use them to tell other people that Jesus is the Christ, Son of God, Savior.

Matthew 10:32
Mark 1:17
Mark 16:15, 16
John 1:41, 43, 49

John 6:47
John 14:15
John 15:17
Revelation 2:10

CHRIST IS COMING AGAIN!

AIM: That your students will be prepared for the second coming of Christ

SCRIPTURE: Matthew 28:19, 20; Acts 1:9-11; 2 Peter 1:5-8; 3:8-18 (Peter writes to remind Christians of the second coming of Christ)

PREPARATION:
1. Photocopy activity sheets—one for each student.
2. Prepare treats as described in PRESESSION.

PRESESSION (5-10 minutes)

ACTIVITIES
* Enjoy a treat
* Talk about time and waiting

MATERIALS
* Treats—one for each student

PERSPECTIVE (10 minutes)

ACTIVITIES
* Match Bible verses with reasons for rejoicing when Jesus comes again

MATERIALS
* Bibles
* "Happy Day!" Activity Sheet
* Scissors, transparent tape

PROBE (20 minutes)

ACTIVITIES
* Read a skit about the second coming

MATERIALS
* Bibles
* "Ready, Set, Grow!" Activity Sheet

PERSONALIZE (15-20 minutes)

ACTIVITIES
* Make a poster illustrating something about the second coming of Christ

MATERIALS
* Construction paper, crayons, colored pencils, or markers
* *Optional: Letter stencils*
* *Optional: Bible Investigator awards—one for each person completing this quarter's studies*

LESSON 52   **UNIT THEME: REVIEWING GOD'S PLAN FOR HIS PEOPLE**

PRESESSION

Before class today, prepare treats for a celebration. This doesn't need to be a big party. It can be fruit snacks with fruit juice or cupcakes and milk. Be sure to not only make one for each student but have extra in case of class visitors. Keep these treats out of sight when you get to class.

As the group gathers, whisper to early arrivals that the class is going to have a party today. Inform them that this is a secret and they are not to tell anyone else about the party but should get ready for it by laying their belongings aside to make room for the treats.

When everyone is present, bring out the treats and give them to only the students who are pre-pared for them. Don't let the students who get these treats eat them yet.

Talk about what happened using questions like these: How did it feel to be ready and receive the treats? How did you feel towards the people who were left out? What do you think you should have done? How did it feel to be left out? How did you feel towards the people who got treats? What do you think they should have done?

Pass out treats to the other members of the class. Tell everyone to enjoy their treats now. **Someday there will be a really wonderful time of celebration for those who love Jesus and follow Him in obedience. Let's find out what they will be celebrating then.**

PERSPECTIVE

Distribute copies of "Happy Day" activity sheet. Ask someone to read the directions aloud. Depending on your time schedule, this activity can be done individually or in pairs with each partner looking up three references. Allow time to complete this exercise. The answers are: no night or darkness; crowns of glory; joy and eternal pleasures; new bodies; no tears, death, sadness, pain; reunited with loved ones.

Time often seems different in different situations. Explain this by using some examples like these: How long does it seem when you are wait-ing for something good to happen? How long does it seem when you need to get a lot of things done? What makes the difference?

When Jesus went back to Heaven, His followers knew He would come again. Check out Acts 1:9-11 to see how they knew this. Have someone read these verses aloud. **Although they knew Christ would return, they did not know the exact time it would happen. How do you think they felt about waiting for that event?** (Impatient; excited.)

PROBE

Jesus didn't leave them to wait idly until that day. He gave them something to do until then. Let's check out Matthew 28:19, 20 to find out what it was. Ask a volunteer to read these verses. Point out that there were many things to do in order to be ready for Jesus to come again.

Peter spent his life preaching the gospel

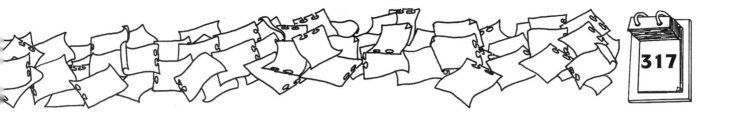

of Christ. He wrote two letters to encourage Christians who might face persecution for their faith. Let's find out more about part of Peter's second letter.

Hand out copies of "Ready, Set, Grow!" activity sheets. You will need three people to read the parts of Ben, Darcy, and the Reader. The rest of the class can follow along on their activity sheets and be prepared to discuss the skit.

There are many details we don't know about Christ's coming again. The important thing is that He is coming back and we need to be ready whenever that event takes place. This second coming will affect everyone.

In the skit, what did Ben say Christians should concentrate on? (Things that don't depend on this world; things that last forever.) **How does this compare with the things that most people think are important?** (It is just the opposite; most people place importance on material things that can be seen while Christians should be more concerned with eternal, unseen things.)

Check out 2 Peter 3:13. What are we going to have when this world is gone? (A new heaven and earth; home of righteousness—where there is only goodness.) **What did Darcy say that Jesus' followers should be doing to help that wonderful day arrive?** (Tell others about Jesus.)

In our treat time today, only part of the group were first to get their treats. How is that experience like waiting for Jesus to return? (Some of the people were left out because they didn't know about a celebration or being prepared.) Briefly review the differences in feelings between those who received treats and those who did not. Being prepared for Christ to come again is far more important than being left out of a celebration. It can mean the difference between a never-ending time of joy and fellowship with God and a never-ending time of anguish and despair without Him.

What other things should Jesus' followers be doing so they will be prepared for His return? Have someone read aloud verse 14. **In the skit Ben said that we should live each day as if we expected Jesus to come that day. What differences would that make for Christians?** Point out that as Christ's followers we should take every opportunity to be about His business. That includes telling others about Him, doing things that would please Him, and getting to know Him better.

Ask students to help you list some things Christians should and should not be focused on. Encourage them to be specific about this and relate it to kids their own age. Stress that failing to do good things is just as bad as doing bad ones. Use questions like these: What do you spend your time doing each day? Is most of your time spent on yourself? On things that won't last? Are there things that you could spend more time on that would help to share the gospel? How can you get to know Christ better? Are you making wise choices that will please God? Would you change your behavior if Jesus were with you in person? What would you do differently?

In chapter one of this same letter, Peter gives us some ideas on how Christians can grow. Let's turn to chapter 1:5-8 and see what he says. As they mention each step, write it on the chalkboard. You should write the first item, faith, on the bottom. Write goodness above faith. Continue in this manner until they are all listed: knowledge; self-control; perseverance [the ability of holding on] ; godliness [service for God]; brotherly kindness; love. **When we put our efforts into these things we will grow to know Christ more and be better prepared for His return. Christians should be ready for that great day.**

PERSONALIZE

(15-20 minutes)

Hand out construction paper and crayons or markers to students. If you have them, lay the letter stencils where they can easily be reached. **Today let's make posters that will remind us and other followers of Christ about being prepared for His return.**

Allow time for students to work on this activity. They can use verses that were mentioned in this lesson or create their own texts and decorate them as desired. Display these posters around the church to remind others that Christ is coming again.

PRAYER/PRAISE

Every Christian should be watching for the coming of Jesus and be ready to meet Him whenever He comes. Have students form a circle and join hands. Read aloud Revelation 22:20, 21. Close in prayer, asking God's help in being watchful and prepared for Christ's coming again.

Optional: Make copies of the following award and hand them out to students who have completed at least one quarter's studies.

ALL THE CLUES SAY

_____

has done a great job
learning more about God's Word.

You're a Fantastic Bible Investigator.

Keep up the good work!

_____
Chief Investigator

HAPPY DAY!

There will be much for Christians to celebrate when Jesus comes again. Look up the references. Cut out the matching phrase and tape it on the correct balloon.

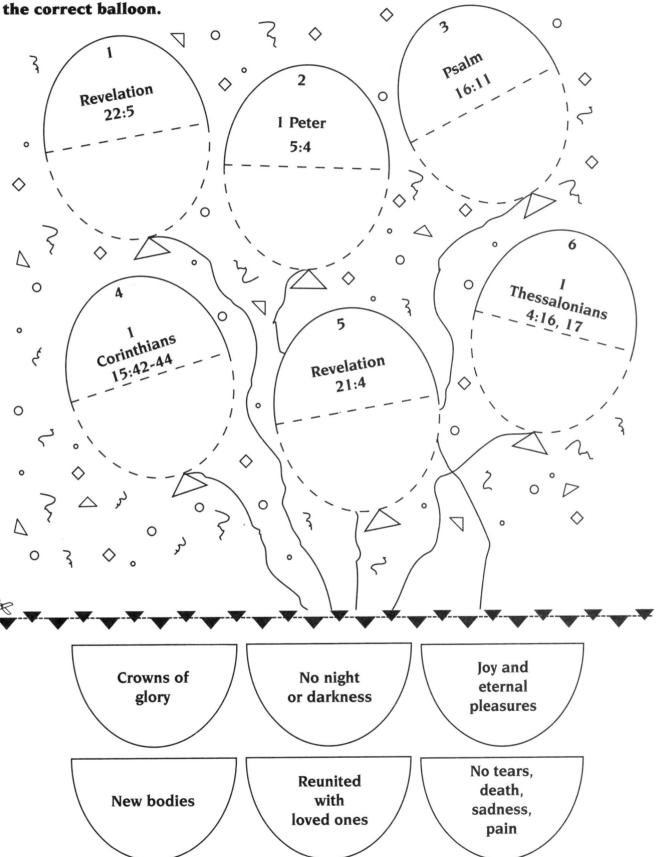

1 — Revelation 22:5

2 — 1 Peter 5:4

3 — Psalm 16:11

4 — 1 Corinthians 15:42-44

5 — Revelation 21:4

6 — 1 Thessalonians 4:16, 17

Crowns of glory

No night or darkness

Joy and eternal pleasures

New bodies

Reunited with loved ones

No tears, death, sadness, pain

BEN: Wow! That's really something to think about.

DARCY: What are you talking about, Ben? And what's that you're reading?

BEN: I'm talking about when Jesus comes again. It's right here in 2 Peter 3. Listen to this . . .

READER: "Since everything will be destroyed in this way, what kind of people should you be? You ought to live holy and godly lives as you look forward to the day of God and speed its coming."

DARCY: What does it mean that everything will be destroyed?

BEN: Well, Darcy, it means that all the material things we value here like money, looks, fame, and possessions will be gone some day. So we ought to concentrate on the things that don't depend on this world.

DARCY: You mean things like loving and caring for one another?

BEN: That's right. Things that last forever. Listen to what it says next . . .

READER: "But in keeping with his promise we are looking forward to a new heaven and a new earth, the home of righteousness."

DARCY: That's great—a place where there will be only goodness. You mean we should be ready for Jesus to come again. But how can we hurry Christ's return?

BEN: Listen to what the apostle Peter says about it . . .

READER: "Bear in mind that our Lord's patience means salvation."

DARCY: I see. Since Christ is waiting for more people to become His followers, we should work hard to tell others about Him.

BEN: That's not all we should do . . .

READER: "Make every effort to be found spotless, blameless, and at peace with him."

DARCY: I'm not sure what that means.

BEN: It means we should live each day as if we expected Jesus to come that day. So we should be sure that we live as He wants us to all the time, not just on Sundays. That includes being peacemakers.

DARCY: That would really make a difference, wouldn't it? I mean, there are some things that I wouldn't want to be doing when Christ comes. You know, things like watching bad TV shows, quarreling with you, or just being careless and neglecting my Bible reading.

BEN: Or thinking only of myself and not praying for others or helping them when they need it. I want to be ready when Jesus comes, not just wasting my time with things that won't last.

DARCY: You know, Ben, it sounds like the best way to be prepared is to learn more about Christ.

BEN: Right you are. Listen to Peter again . . .

READER: "Be on your guard so that you may not be carried away by the error of lawless men."

BEN: The more we know about God and His Word, the less chance there is to follow false teachers. Peter gives us the secret to being ready for Jesus.

READER: "Grow in the grace and knowledge of our Lord and Savior Jesus Christ."

DARCY: So the key to being ready when Jesus comes again is to keep on getting to know Christ and God's Word better?

BEN: Everybody should keep on growing in Christ, no matter how old they are physically or how long ago they decided to be His follower.

DARCY: I'm going to try to find ways to be closer to Jesus every day. Then I'll be ready for Him to come and take me to Heaven.

BEN: If we're ready, and living right, Jesus will be pleased and praise us.